Creating Jobs

Brookings Institution
STUDIES IN SOCIAL ECONOMICS

Institute for Research on Poverty
MONOGRAPH SERIES

John L. Palmer, Editor

Creating Jobs: Public Employment Programs and Wage Subsidies

A study sponsored jointly by the Institute for Research on Poverty and the Brookings Institution

THE BROOKINGS INSTITUTION
Washington, D.C.

Library of Congress Cataloging in Publication Data:

Main entry under title:

Creating jobs.

   (Studies in social economics; 18)
   Includes bibliographical references and index.
   1. Public service employment—United States—Ad-
dresses, essays, lectures.   I. Palmer, John Logan.
II. Series.
HD5724.C78   331.1′377′0973   78-12241
ISBN 0-8157-6892-3
ISBN 0-8157-6891-5 pbk.

9 8 7 6 5 4 3 2 1

THE BROOKINGS INSTITUTION is an independent organization devoted to nonpartisan research, education, and publication in economics, government, foreign policy, and the social sciences generally. Its principal purposes are to aid in the development of sound public policies and to promote public understanding of issues of national importance.

The Institution was founded on December 8, 1927, to merge the activities of the Institute for Government Research, founded in 1916, the Institute of Economics, founded in 1922, and the Robert Brookings Graduate School of Economics and Government, founded in 1924.

The Board of Trustees is responsible for the general administration of the Institution, while the immediate direction of the policies, program, and staff is vested in the President, assisted by an advisory committee of the officers and staff. The by-laws of the Institution state: "It is the function of the Trustees to make possible the conduct of scientific research, and publication, under the most favorable conditions, and to safeguard the independence of the research staff in the pursuit of their studies and in the publication of the results of such studies. It is not a part of their function to determine, control, or influence the conduct of particular investigations or the conclusions reached."

The President bears final responsibility for the decision to publish a manuscript as a Brookings book. In reaching his judgment on the competence, accuracy, and objectivity of each study, the President is advised by the director of the appropriate research program and weighs the views of a panel of expert outside readers who report to him in confidence on the quality of the work. Publication of a work signifies that it is deemed a competent treatment worthy of public consideration but does not imply endorsement of conclusions or recommendations.

The Institution maintains its position of neutrality on issues of public policy in order to safeguard the intellectual freedom of the staff. Hence interpretations or conclusions in Brookings publications should be understood to be solely those of the authors and should not be attributed to the Institution, to its trustees, officers, or other staff members, or to the organizations that support its research.

Foreword

Over the past few years, public employment programs have grown dramatically in the United States. The federal government obligated nearly $7 billion in 1978 to provide jobs for both the structurally and the cyclically unemployed, primarily through grants to state and local governments under the Comprehensive Employment and Training Act. Moreover, recent welfare reform and employment proposals have called for further expansion of federally subsidized public service employment. Many of these efforts to lower unemployment without increasing inflation and to aid disadvantaged workers and their families also call for subsidies to private firms conditioned on their performance as job creators. Similar policies have been proposed or implemented in other industrialized countries.

As interest in and use of job creation policies have increased, so has the controversy surrounding them. This is due in part to a dearth of analytic information on such basic issues as: How many net jobs can be created, over what time period, and at what cost? What are the consequences for inflation and for income distribution? How much additional output is produced, and of what value is it? How effective are these programs in increasing employment among particular groups? How do their costs and benefits compare with alternative policy approaches to the same objectives? How will general economic conditions and the specific design of the policies affect the results of the programs?

In order to examine these issues and their policy implications, the Brookings Institution and the Institute for Research on Poverty sponsored a conference on April 7 and 8, 1977, attended by the participants listed on pages 369–70. The conference papers and the formal discussion that appear in this volume deal with a wide range of concerns. They address both countercyclical and structural objectives, including macroeconomic and microeconomic perspectives, and take both theoretical and applied approaches. The first chapter, developed from the conference papers and discussion as well as other research, provides a broad assessment of job creation policies.

John L. Palmer, a senior fellow in the Brookings Economic Studies program, edited the conference proceedings. In commissioning the papers and organizing the conference, he was aided by Irwin Garfinkel, Director of the Institute for Research on Poverty, and Ernst W. Stromsdorfer, then Deputy Assistant Secretary for Research and Evaluation, U.S. Department of Labor. James Altman provided research assistance. The manuscript was edited for publication by Alice M. Carroll; it was checked for factual accuracy by Evelyn P. Fisher, assisted by Cynthia E. Nethercut and Ellen W. Smith; the index was prepared by Florence Robinson.

Financial support was provided by the Ford Foundation, the Institute for Research on Poverty, and the U.S. Department of Labor.

The views expressed here are those of the authors and discussants and should not be ascribed to the funding organizations or to the trustees, officers, or other staff members of the Brookings Institution.

BRUCE K. MAC LAURY
President

September 1978
Washington, D.C.

Contents

Tables

Figures

Martin Neil Baily and James Tobin

Daniel S. Hamermesh

Irwin Garfinkel and John L. Palmer

Issues, Evidence, and Implications

During the mid-1970s both unemployment and inflation in the United States set post-World War II record highs. Even after several years of vigorous recovery from the 1974–75 recession both are well in excess of comfortable rates. And many economists maintain that the persistence of high levels of structural unemployment may make it difficult to lower unemployment much below 6 percent through conventional macroeconomic policies without reaccelerating inflation.[1] (Although unemployment rates are generally lower in Western Europe, a similar problem exists there.) For these reasons, selective federal policies to promote directly the creation of jobs are increasingly seen as desirable means of promoting two related objectives—reaching and sustaining low levels of unemployment without excessive inflationary pressure and insuring minimally adequate incomes for families with workers. These approaches have two distinctive characteristics: federal funds are granted to public or private employers conditioned on their performance in pro-

The authors are indebted to the conference participants for much of the material on which this paper is based. They also wish to acknowledge the helpful comments on a draft of Robert H. Haveman, Charles C. Holt, Jonathan R. Kesselman, Stanley H. Masters, Arnold H. Packer, Isabel V. Sawhill, and Ernst W. Stromsdorfer.

1. In the 1960s structural unemployment was viewed primarily as resulting from a mismatch (in education, skill, work experience, or geographical location) in employers' job requirements and the characteristics of the unemployed. More recently the focus has been on subgroups of the labor force, such as nonwhites, youth, and the long-term unemployed, whose unemployment rates are persistently far in excess of the average. (For example, teenagers' unemployment rates are generally about three times the average, nonwhites' twice; even when overall unemployment is as low as 5 percent, 10–15 percent of the unemployed are out of work for three months or longer.) Although the higher-than-average unemployment rates are due in part to mismatching, they can also be traced to discrimination and the particular labor market behavior of some of the groups involved, such as the high rates of labor force entry and exit by teenagers and women.

1

viding employment; and restrictions are placed on eligibility and, possibly, other aspects of employment.[2]

Such job creation programs can take many forms. Until recently they had been used intensively in the United States only during the Great Depression. At that time, a large portion of the labor force was at one time or another in federally subsidized and administered public employment programs, generally in outdoor work performing tasks ranging from construction to sanitary maintenance. On the other hand, many Western European countries have made use of public employment programs or employment-related subsidies to private employers for structural purposes since the 1950s.[3] With the high unemployment rates of the 1970s, job creation programs once again have been heavily used in the United States. The two predominant types are state and locally administered public service employment programs and employment tax credits for private employers.[4]

Public service employment in the United States has evolved from very limited use in the late 1960s for particular groups of disadvantaged workers into several major programs with a mix of countercyclical and structural objectives. The federal budget for 1978 provides for 725,000 public service jobs for previously unemployed workers under titles 2 and 6 of the Comprehensive Employment and Training Act (CETA) at a cost of about $6 billion. The programs are administered by designated agents (local prime sponsors) of state and local governments. Almost $1 billion more is being spent on public employment projects for unemployed youth, and smaller amounts on other special groups.[5] Other large expenditures

2. These features differentiate direct creation of jobs both from ordinary government expenditure activities and from government actions such as income tax cuts that affect the job market only indirectly.

3. Examples of European programs can be found in the papers by Haveman and Hamermesh in this volume.

4. The term *public employment* is intended in this paper to be broader than public service employment. It also can include specially created, subsidized jobs in the public sector that involve labor-intensive activities other than the delivery of public services. This use of the term is approximately consistent with Kesselman's use of the term *work relief*. Public works, on the other hand, are generally considered skill- and capital-intensive construction projects that are contracted out to the private sector; such policies are not considered in this volume. However, public works that involve direct hiring onto public payrolls for relatively labor-intensive construction (as was done in the Great Depression) fall under our use of the term *public employment*.

5. For more detail on these programs and proposals for CETA, see John L. Palmer, "Employment and Training Assistance," and "Employment and Income

on public employment are being considered by Congress in conjunction with welfare reform, and passage of the Humphrey-Hawkins full employment and balanced growth bill would increase the likelihood of large-scale, long-term use of public employment for broader purposes.[6]

Employment tax credits have only recently come into use in the United States. They are simply employer wage subsidies administered through the federal income tax system. The work incentive (WIN) tax credit, first passed in 1971 and then expanded in 1975, reimburses private employers for a flat percentage of the first year's wages they pay to any recipient of aid to families with dependent children (AFDC). It has operated only on a very small scale. A second, temporary measure, passed as part of the economic stimulus package in 1977 and estimated to cost $2.5 billion in 1978, provides a tax credit to private employers for wages paid in excess of a base related to their prior year's wage bill. The credit applies only to wages that are less than half the median annual level; thus it favors low-wage workers. Many other forms of employer wage subsidies have been proposed recently that could cost several billions of dollars per year. In many instances they are targeted on specific groups of workers—such as youth and the long-term unemployed—with particularly difficult employment problems.[7]

Despite the recent expansion of the use of and interest in federal programs to create jobs, their efficacy is in considerable dispute. This is in

---

Security," in, respectively, Joseph A. Pechman, ed., *Setting National Priorities: The 1978 Budget* (Brookings Institution, 1977), pp. 143–75, and *The 1979 Budget* (1978), pp. 61–90.

6. The Carter administration in 1977 proposed providing over a million jobs in public service employment for welfare recipients at an annual cost of about $11.5 billion by 1982; congressional proposals also provided for large numbers of public service jobs. Under the Humphrey-Hawkins bill, public employment would be one of many tools prescribed but not mandated to facilitate increased employment. Any program that approached government-as-employer-of-last-resort for all members of society would cost several times as much as the jobs component of Carter's welfare proposal, which is limited to principal earners in families with children. Precise estimates are very sensitive to the state of the economy, assumed wage rate, and other crucial program parameters.

7. See Palmer, "Employment and Training Assistance," for more details on both the WIN and temporary tax credits. Among other proposals is a part of the President's March 1978 urban policy initiative that would provide a tax credit of $2,000 for the first year of employment and $1,500 for the second for all disadvantaged youth (between eighteen and twenty-four years old) hired into full-time employment by private employers and retained for at least three months. It would cost an estimated $1.5 billion annually.

part due to a dearth of contemporary analysis on this subject. (The voluminous literature concerned with the Great Depression experience has not been well integrated into current thought.) Not surprisingly, views differ widely on the degree of reliance that should be placed on jobs programs of various types. For each of the policies of interest the following questions need to be answered. How many jobs can be created for a given expenditure or budgetary impact? How fast will employment be increased and with what degree of inflationary pressure? Who will get the jobs and what effect will this have on the overall composition of employment and unemployment? What net additional output will be provided and what will be its value to society? What will be the effect on the employment and earnings of target groups? How do answers to these questions vary between the short term and long term and with specific aspects of the program design?

The conference reported on in this volume was an attempt to shed light on several of these questions and the issues underlying them. Both wage subsidies to private employers and public employment programs were considered, although the emphasis was on the latter.[8] This paper draws on the conference papers, formal and informal discussion at the conference, and other analyses to present an overview of the current state of knowledge of direct job creating policies. The first two sections address questions relevant to the objective of achieving and sustaining higher levels of employment without excessive inflationary pressure. In particular they discuss whether direct job creation policies are superior to more conventional alternatives for reducing cyclical unemployment and how capable they are of reducing structural unemployment. The third section focuses on the microeconomic efficiency of public employment programs and compares their efficacy with that of income maintenance programs. Policy implications are discussed in the final section.

Countercyclical Approaches

Jobs programs in the United States have been used primarily for countercyclical purposes during recessionary periods. They are thus competi-

8. In fact, public employment programs can be viewed as a special case of employer wage subsidies—one that approaches 100 percent and is limited to the nonprofit sector. (Under CETA, local prime sponsors may contract with private nonprofit organizations to provide public service jobs. Also, the federal subsidy may be supplemented by other monies to achieve higher wage rates.) Several of the conference papers take this approach in their analysis.

tors of such fiscal measures as general tax cuts and expenditure increases, and their consequences should be compared against those of the other policy alternatives. Five areas of concern for both public employment programs and employer wage subsidies are discussed here; they are the employment impact for each dollar of increase in expenditures or in the federal deficit, the timing of stimulative effects, the value of the additional output, distributional consequences, and inflationary consequences.

Bang for the Buck

As Baily and Tobin note in this volume, there is considerable policy interest in the relative strength of the "bang for the buck" achieved by various countercyclical fiscal policy measures—where the bang is the increase in employment or in the gross national product and the buck is the increase in federal outlays or in the deficit. Increases in government expenditure are usually presumed to have a greater stimulative effect than equivalent decreases in taxes because the initial injection of monies into the economy purchases goods and services, whereas a portion of a tax cut may be saved rather than spent. Increases in expenditures for public employment and in other forms of federal spending are more difficult to compare, however.

The effect of public employment expenditures on total employment may differ from that of general expenditures because public employment expenditures are more highly concentrated on labor, program participants may have a different, presumably higher, marginal propensity to consume out of disposable income, and they may face marginal tax rates that deviate substantially from those the general population faces, taking into account reductions in government transfers as well as increased taxes. (If public employment expenditures cause a reduction in unemployment insurance or welfare payments, GNP and employment multipliers will be less.)

Baily and Tobin present a rigorous formulation of these relationships and illustrate some possible outcomes by assuming numerical values for the relevant parameters. They demonstrate that the question of whether public employment programs are a better bargain than other countercyclical fiscal policies cannot be determined a priori, but is at bottom an empirical issue. Although they do not pursue this issue at length, their rough empirical estimates indicate that the gross national product and employment effects generally will be larger for expenditure increases than broad tax cuts, and the employment effects larger for public employment than other government expenditure increases, unless the public employment is carefully targeted on recipients of transfer programs. In this latter case the employment per dollar increase in the deficit is still likely to be larger for public employment, but the dollar increase in the deficit will be less than the increase in public employment expenditures because of the decline in transfer payments.

But, as Baily and Tobin note, the effect of public employment expenditures on employment may not be as advantageous as it appears, because a sizable portion of the new jobs generated are the specially created public jobs, which may be less socially useful than jobs outside the program. Also, despite federal restrictions, public employment expenditures in the form of federal categorical grants to state and local governments may increase net employment by far less than the number of subsidized jobs, since these governments have every incentive to use the grants to underwrite employment that they would have undertaken otherwise and either direct their own revenues to other state and local priorities or reduce their taxes.

In his paper in this volume, Johnson reports that his earlier research suggests that, for public service employment programs like those of the early 1970s, this fiscal substitution increases with time, perhaps becoming as high as 60 percent within a year after the grants have been made and still growing after that. Although the precise degree of substitution remains a matter of controversy, there is little doubt that it is sizable.[9] (Congressional concern over this issue led to changes in 1976 in the public service employment programs under CETA titles 2 and 6. A requirement was imposed that most of the employment be in special projects of short duration, where there presumably would be less potential for fiscal substitution than with more permanent jobs identical to those regularly performed by state and local employees.[10])

9. Michael Wiseman, "Public Employment as Fiscal Policy," *Brookings Papers on Economic Activity, 1:1976,* pp. 67–104, summarizes the econometric literature on this issue. More recently, Michael E. Borus and Daniel S. Hamermesh, "Study of the Net Employment Effects of Public Service Employment—Econometric Analyses," briefing paper, NCMP 6-3-78 (National Commission for Manpower Policy, February 1978; processed), in assessing this literature suggest that specific estimates of the fiscal substitution effect are quite sensitive to the specification of the models. A preliminary report of a study for the National Commission for Manpower Policy based on field surveys of state and local government spending suggests a lower estimate of fiscal substitution than the econometric studies.

10. Johnson suggests in his paper that the federal government administer the

While fiscal substitution may hamper the effectiveness of a counter-cyclical public employment program, it is important to keep it in perspective. If the program is not to be in effect very long, the degree of substitution may be modest. And the result of even full fiscal substitution is not the loss of all fiscal or employment stimulus. In such a case the potential effect of the public employment program is diluted to the strength of revenue sharing—to whatever would be yielded by the mixture of increased expenditures, larger surpluses, debt retirement, and tax reduction that would result from larger unrestricted revenue sharing grants.[11]

Because employer wage subsidies or employment tax credits provide a direct inducement to employers to expand their labor force, they should have a greater employment impact (per dollar of reduced revenue) than most other forms of tax cuts, particularly income tax cuts. Their effectiveness depends primarily on the form of the subsidy, and the responsiveness (elasticity) of employers' demand for labor to a change in the cost of labor.

Hamermesh argues that the most effective wage subsidy for counter-cyclical purposes is one that is noncategorical—not restricted to workers with particular demographic characteristics—and marginal—applied only to employment in excess of some predetermined base related to each firm's previous employment level. A noncategorical subsidy will encourage greater utilization of all labor. Applied marginally, it will minimize the subsidization of employment that employers otherwise would have funded entirely on their own—a consequence of a wage subsidy analogous to fiscal substitution in public employment programs.[12] Although this substitution can be controlled to some extent, it cannot be avoided entirely.

---

program and determine the job mix to restrict such fiscal substitution. While this has some advantages, it has the overwhelming liability for countercyclical purposes of requiring the creation of a new administrative mechanism.

11. There is some evidence that, at least in recent years, state and local governments used growing federal grants to accumulate surpluses. Such behavior would greatly reduce the stimulative effects of any public service employment programs that involve considerable fiscal substitution. See Edward M. Gramlich, "State and Local Budgets the Day after It Rained: Why Is the Surplus So High?" *BPEA, 1:1978,* pp. 191–214.

12. Hamermesh uses the term *windfall* to describe that portion of subsidy costs that employers would have supplied in the absence of the subsidy. Nevertheless, that part of the expenditure should still have indirect stimulative effects and, in fact, to the extent that the economy is competitive, the windfall should eventually be passed on to consumers in the form of lower prices. However, it may still be a serious liability to the political attractiveness of an employer wage subsidy.

In order to quantify the likely consequences of a noncategorical, marginal wage subsidy, Hamermesh applies a simulation model to the private, nonfarm sector of the economy. Because there is considerable uncertainty over the appropriate value of the elasticity of demand for labor, he employs a wide range of estimates in his simulations, along with different assumptions about the employment base that defines the marginal nature of the subsidy.[13] His results suggest that the cost-per-job-created of a temporary wage subsidy can compare quite favorably with current public service employment programs. When the base is the firm's previous year's employment, the portion of the subsidy going for workers who otherwise would have been employed is about half the total, which also is competitive with the consequences of public employment programs; for lower bases this proportion is substantially larger.[14]

From a purely economic point of view, there is no reason to apply the stimulative effect of countercyclical policies as a primary criterion for deciding among alternatives with equivalent deficit impacts. The appropriate goal is the highest growth path of GNP and employment (or some other appropriate measure of social welfare) compatible with acceptable rates of inflation. If other forms of stimulus better promote this objective than public employment programs, they should be preferred even though they might require temporarily larger deficits. As several conference participants noted, however, political constraints on the size of the budget deficit are often more binding than economic ones, and there is strong competition among alternative uses of potential federal revenues. This may necessitate placing considerable importance on spending economies.

Timing of Stimulative Effects

Policies intended to meet countercyclical needs must be able to expand and contract rather quickly over the business cycle, if they are to have the desired effect. Once congressional approval is obtained, tax cuts

13. Hamermesh adjusts empirical estimates of elasticity downward since they are based on permanent subsidies, and he assumes that employer responses will be weaker to a temporary reduction in the costs of labor. Also, he argues that the elasticity is likely to be at its highest in the recovery phase of a moderate recession in contrast to a deep recession or periods of relatively full employment.

14. Under certain reasonable assumptions, the higher the base is set, the lower will be the windfall as a percentage of total subsidy costs. But the lower also will be the net employment effect and the more unpredictable the costs. Such uncertainty about the ultimate cost of the subsidy makes it less attractive as a countercyclical policy.

clearly can be implemented quickly, as can increases in government expenditures for such programs likely to be singled out for countercyclical purposes as general revenue sharing or one-time payments to social security or welfare recipients. It also has been demonstrated that public employment programs can be implemented fairly rapidly[15]—although haste may compromise other desired objectives. Phasing down economic stimuli in a timely fashion, however, is often more problematic. It is generally not a difficult issue with tax cuts—in large part because the built-in progressivity of the federal income tax automatically increases revenues as a percentage of gross national product as the economy grows. But political pressures make it difficult to phase down governmental expenditures—particularly when they are directly subsidizing jobs and state and local governments, as in the case of public service employment.

How quickly the stimulus of an employer wage subsidy is felt depends on the extent to which it is subsidizing labor that would have been employed in any event, how rapidly employers are induced to expand their employment, and how businesses alter their practices with regard to investment, payment of dividends, and so forth. All of these are matters of some uncertainty. In general, however, the timing of the effects of a wage subsidy can be expected to be on a par with that of other forms of general business tax cuts, perhaps somewhat quicker if a large portion of the total subsidy induces additional employment. There is no experience to suggest how politically difficult it would be to phase out a wage subsidy once the need for it had passed.

Value of Output

The choice among a roughly equal expansion of the private sector, the regular public sector, and public employment programs should depend in part on the value of the additional output each produces, including future increases resulting from any higher productivity of target groups. One part of Kesselman's paper in this volume focuses on this issue. After

15. An expansion of nearly 400,000 jobs under CETA titles 2 and 6 was accomplished in less than one year after the passage of the economic stimulus package in early 1977. Emergency public works programs, on the other hand, are notorious for the slowness with which actual expenditures are made. Studies of their experience in the 1960s and early 1970s indicate their effect is at best neutral and may even be procyclical on balance. In the expansion of emergency public works included in the 1977 economic stimulus package, steps that were taken to facilitate faster expenditure of funds appear to be having some success.

examining the vast literature on the public employment programs of the Great Depression, Kesselman concludes that those programs contained little training of relevance to regular jobs or other efforts to move people up job ladders and into regular employment. Moreover, he claims that the value of the goods and services produced by those programs was substantially less than would have been produced by an equally stimulative fiscal policy—such as a tax cut or wage subsidy—that emphasized expansion of the private sector.

Kesselman argues that the public employment programs' output was produced inefficiently. The programs unduly favored directly hired as opposed to contracted workers, labor versus the use of materials and equipment, and less productive versus more productive workers. Because they did not have to meet the private market test (that is, consumers' willingness to purchase the goods or services produced), public employment programs' output was often of low priority to society. Presumably, the public would have preferred more consumption goods, such as food and clothing, to most of the public works produced at the time, however useful some of the latter became for subsequent, far wealthier generations.

These criticisms appear to be valid, though not with the same force, for the countercyclical public service employment programs of the 1970s.[16] This should not be surprising since many of the 1930s pressures that Kesselman observed are also present today. Indeed, current federal restrictions preventing fiscal substitution probably further reduce the value of the program output since they encourage the expansion of public output for which voters have not been willing to raise taxes. (On the other hand, special public employment programs may encourage valuable innovation in the provision of goods and services by stimulating creativity in public officials.) Those restrictions, combined with the need for a countercyclical program that can be rapidly expanded and subsequently contracted, make it difficult to provide jobs that have high social value, training content, and links to regular employment. Assuming that

16. See, for example, Sar A. Levitan and Robert Taggart, eds., *Emergency Employment Act: The PEP Generation* (Olympus, 1974), pp. 20–25 and 32–40; and Michael Wiseman, "On Giving A Job: The Implementation and Allocation of Public Service Employment," paper 1 in *Achieving the Goals of the Employment Act of 1946—Thirtieth Anniversary Review,* vol. 1, prepared for the Subcommittee on Economic Growth of the Joint Economic Committee, 94:1 (GPO, 1975), pp. 11–14. Of course, given the prolonged and widespread unemployment of the Great Depression, simple maintenance of job skills and work habits was a notable achievement. More is expected of today's programs because they are operating in a much more favorable economic climate.

employer wage subsidies are successful in stimulating additional employment and output, they are more likely to produce economically efficient
outcomes. In addition to insuring that the added output meets the market
test, they have the advantage of creating jobs directly in regular employment, so workers are not dependent on making a transition from special
temporary programs.[17]

At the conference, some discussants took issue with Kesselman's assertion that the public employment programs' bias toward labor intensity
necessarily signified a socially inefficient outcome. In the midst of considerable unemployment, they argued, prevailing wage rates might far
exceed the value of alternative uses of labor. In such instances, a strong
case can be made for a countercyclical government policy that lowers
the relative price of labor to employers. This, however, argues more
strongly for some fractional across-the-board employer wage subsidy for
all regular employment, public as well as private, than for full subsidization of specially created jobs in the public sector.

Finally, if it is believed—as John Kenneth Galbraith has argued—that
the U.S. economy is systematically biased toward a smaller public sector
than is necessary to optimize social welfare, then favoring creating jobs
in the public sector could help to right an imbalance between public and
private production and consumption. Again, however, there is no reason
on these grounds to prefer specially created public employment programs
to a general subsidy for regular public employment.

Distributional Consequences

One distinguishing feature of both employer wage subsidies and public
employment programs is their presumed usefulness for geographic and
demographic targeting of job opportunities created by the stimulus. Although there is political pressure during a recession for all localities to
receive some such assistance, criteria can be developed for providing
greater shares (per capita) to areas that have relatively high unemployment or are otherwise distressed. Such formulas have been used in distributing public service employment grants under CETA, but their fair-

17. A large portion of private sector workers who become unemployed over
the business cycle are only temporarily laid off from jobs to which they expect to
return. An employment wage subsidy might operate largely by reducing the numbers of such layoffs in the downswing and increasing the speed of rehiring in the
upswing.

ness has been attacked. Their shortcomings are due in part to the high degree of unreliability in the measurement of area unemployment rates.[18] (Regionally targeted employer wage subsidies have not been employed in the United States; however, as Hamermesh notes, they have been used both in Japan and in the United Kingdom.[19]) Other forms of increases in federal expenditures for countercyclical purposes, of course, also can be targeted geographically, whereas tax cuts do not generally lend themselves to this.

The demographic targeting of job creating programs results primarily from their ability to prescribe which workers benefit from the direct effect of the program. For example, public service employment programs in the United States have focused on such broad target groups as the long-term unemployed and members of low-income families and on even narrower categories, such as welfare recipients or disabled veterans. Similar types of targeting are often proposed for employer wage subsidies. Such targeting is clearly a crucial consideration for programs motivated primarily by structural concerns but is of less relevance to countercyclically motivated policies.

If the major objective of the government action is to insure that lower income groups generally benefit from the stimulus, those groups could be made the focus of tax cuts or of transfer program increases. However, even if the distribution of the additional jobs is important, it is difficult to insure that countercyclical programs focus on disadvantaged target groups. This is particularly true for public employment programs when state and local governments are the administering agents. As Johnson notes, despite strong priorities in the regulations, representation of disadvantaged target groups in the public service employment programs of the early 1970s did not differ significantly from their representation in the entire labor force. This should not be surprising. Employers generally select the workers they view as most qualified from the pool of those eligible.[20] Since the skill and education requirements for state and local employment are well above the average for the labor force, and the pool of unemployed is far more representative of the general labor force during

18. Martin Ziegler, "Efforts to Improve Estimates of State and Local Unemployment," *Monthly Labor Review,* vol. 100 (November 1977), pp. 12–18.

19. Additional discussion of the use of such subsidies in Western Europe can be found in James L. Sundquist, *Dispersing Population: What America Can Learn from Europe* (Brookings Institution, 1975).

20. Kesselman notes this tendency in the public employment programs of the Great Depression.

a recession, the "creaming" of the labor pool would leave disadvantaged workers in their usual position. Analogous problems of reaching the desired target group exist for wage subsidy programs if the eligible population is broadly defined.

Although eligibility criteria could be more tightly drawn in favor of disadvantaged target groups, the consequence of a rigid policy may be a less effective countercyclical tool.[21] This is partially because drawing from a much smaller pool of eligible workers will slow the speed of implementation of public employment programs or the additional hiring caused by wage subsidies. The employment of more marginal workers requires greater training and ingenuity in production and, in the case of public employment, in output selection. These present very difficult challenges even under structurally oriented policies that can have a long lead time and continuity of operation. The rapid phasing in and out of countercyclical job creation programs exacerbates the difficulties.

Hamermesh assumes that a marginal employer wage subsidy or tax credit that subsidizes a fixed percentage of all wages would provide additional job opportunities to a population with demographic characteristics similar to those of workers who typically become unemployed in the downswing or employed in the upswing of a cycle. Though the program would favor low-wage workers because they are more likely to become unemployed than others, it would not favor those with the lowest wages nor those who might be thought of as particularly hard to employ or disadvantaged. Thus, it is unlikely that such a subsidy would have any distributional advantage over conventional macroeconomic policy tools.

Hamermesh suggests that a fixed dollar (per hour of work) subsidy would be superior in this regard, since it would underwrite a higher percentage of low relative to high wages. Although he does not simulate the distributional effects of such a subsidy, he believes that it would have a strong bias in favor of the lowest wage workers. Even so, employer subsidies need not be superior on distributional grounds to such conventional countercyclical tools as tax cuts and expenditure increases—which can

21. Congressional concern over the characteristics of participants in the public service employment program under CETA titles 2 and 6 in the 1974–75 recession led to legislation in 1976 that required a high percentage of all slots to go to those from low-income families who were unemployed fifteen weeks or longer, or to welfare recipients. Johnson is pessimistic about the ability of even such measures as these to alter substantially the distributional mix of total additional state and local employment.

also be targeted—unless it is the distribution of jobs, per se, that is at issue.

Finally, whereas the benefits of a countercyclical public employment program would be confined to employees in the public sector, a general employment subsidy that is available to public as well as private employers would help to stabilize the employment of all workers. In fact, employment typically is more cyclically unstable in the private than in the public sector.

Effect on Inflation

Direct job creation programs, it is often argued, should result in less inflationary pressure than alternative fiscal stimuli of comparable magnitude because of their differential effects on labor markets. For example, Baily and Tobin maintain that this is likely to be true of policies directed at groups of workers or geographical areas whose unemployment rates are much higher than the average. The inflationary effects of programs motivated by pure countercyclical concerns are less relevant, since such programs should be implemented only during periods of high unemployment and phased out before labor market factors become a major inflationary factor. (Also, as noted above, there are arguments against narrow targeting of programs countercyclically motivated.) However, inflationary consequences clearly should be a crucial consideration at fuller levels of employment when tightness in labor markets can exert considerable inflationary pressure.

One characteristic of employer wage subsidies gives them a major advantage over most other forms of fiscal stimulus during periods of substantial cyclical unemployment combined with inflation. Over time, increases in the hourly compensation costs of labor are reflected in commensurate increases in the general price level, adjusted for productivity advances. Since employer wage subsidies directly reduce labor costs, they can be expected to be less inflationary than alternative policies for achieving equivalent increases in employment and output, other things being equal. This should allow the federal government to take a more expansionary stance, since concern over inflation is one of the most crucial constraints on macroeconomic policy.[22]

22. Cuts in payroll taxes are advocated for a similar reason. See Arthur M. Okun, "The Great Stagflation Swamp," *Challenge*, vol. 20 (November–December 1977), pp. 6–13, for a discussion of the value of policies that reduce inflation from the supply side.

Macroeconomic Effects of Structural Actions

Structurally oriented policies aimed at creating jobs are even more difficult than countercyclical ones to analyze. They are the policies intended to aid particular groups of workers or potential workers whose employment opportunities are severely limited, or policies designed to reduce aggregate unemployment with less inflationary consequences than conventional macroeconomic policies. Their objectives are to improve both equity and the macroeconomic performance of the economy. The former, needless to say, includes the distribution of employment among workers as well as the distribution of income.[23]

Not only are the consequences of structurally oriented programs difficult to assess, but there is a wide set of policy alternatives to which such job creation policies ought to be compared in determining what role they best can play. For example, affirmative action, regional development, worker mobility, industry relocation, and institutional training programs are but a few of many approaches that might be helpful in upgrading employment opportunities for common target groups. The ideal degree of emphasis to be put on job creation policies as a means of combating structural problems should depend on their consequences relative to alternative policies as well as relative to doing nothing. Similarly, with respect to a more narrow income-maintenance objective, the consequences of job creation policies, including the value of work per se, should be compared to those of various forms of direct cash transfers.

None of the conference papers undertook such an ambitious task. Nevertheless, a number of them did come to grips with many of the concerns that are relevant to such an assessment. The Johnson and Baily-Tobin papers treat structurally oriented policies to create jobs from a macroeconomic perspective. The principal question addressed here is under what conditions these policies can improve the relation between inflation and unemployment.

23. For the most part, the targeting requirements of the two objectives are similar. The papers and discussion at the conference focused on the efficacy of job creating policies as a method of reducing high unemployment rates among the unskilled. Structural programs, of course, may be targeted on skilled workers who are temporarily in excess supply—such as engineers in Seattle when Boeing cut back its employment—in which case the targeting requirements of the two objectives would not be the same.

Improving the Relation between Inflation and Unemployment

Conventional measures for stimulating the economy can make major short-term inroads into structural (and even high frictional) unemployment while yielding an expanding real GNP and favorable consequences for all workers. It does not appear, however, that under those measures desirably low levels of unemployment can be maintained without generating unacceptably high, perhaps even accelerating, rates of inflation— which are likely to lead to deflationary policies that may leave most workers worse off than if somewhat higher levels of unemployment had been tolerated. An important reason for this is that rapidly rising wage rates in particular occupations or regions that are short of labor contribute to excessive inflationary pressure well before unemployment decreases to desirable levels among many broad target groups of workers.

Because of their potential for concentrating a higher proportion of any expansion of jobs on particular target groups, direct job creation policies have been advocated as a means of partially circumventing the problem of inflation. This is accomplished by favorably altering the terms of trade between increases in employment and inflationary pressures vis-à-vis the pursuit of conventional expansionary macroeconomic policies. Superficially it might appear that simply targeting jobs programs on workers with low wages and skills and high unemployment would insure more favorable inflationary consequences; this is not sufficient, however. The outcome depends critically on how labor markets actually work, in particular on the causes of the relatively high unemployment rates of the target groups and the process of adjustment of relative wage rates to shifts in labor supply and demand.

Both the Baily-Tobin and the Johnson papers develop models for exploring the additional necessary conditions for targeted job creation to have the desired inflationary effects.[24] Between them they identify three that involve wage rates and a fourth concerned with job search.[25]

24. Baily and Tobin pose the issue as whether or not direct job creation policies can shift the Phillips curve inward or reduce the rate of unemployment below which the rate of inflation tends to accelerate (often called the natural rate). Johnson focuses on the efficacy of public service employment as an antipoverty policy and, as an aid to addressing this subject, constructs a model quite similar to the one that Baily and Tobin employ. Baily and Tobin's analysis is in terms of teenagers and adults, but their conclusions are unaffected by changing these to unskilled and skilled workers, consistent with Johnson's terminology.

25. Baily and Tobin also note that, if structural unemployment is due to tempo-

THE PRESSURE OF MINIMUM WAGES. Minimum wages—whether socially or legislatively based—may prevent low-wage labor markets from clearing, therefore resulting in excessive involuntary unemployment of low-skill workers. Public jobs programs can reduce such unemployment by hiring particular workers at a wage that private employers are unable or unwilling to pay, while employer wage subsidies reduce the cost to employers of paying the minimum wage and increase their willingness or ability to hire the same workers. In both instances, little or no upward pressure is exerted on wage rates as a consequence of the increased labor demand for and employment of target group workers. In this event, as George Johnson puts it, the result approaches "an unmitigated free lunch." Employment and output are increased with insignificant inflationary costs, both in the short and long run, and no one is made worse off.[26] Baily and Tobin note that for public employment the result is favorable only if the program wage rates are at or below the minimum. To the extent they are tied to prevailing union wages, the ability to alter the relation between inflation and unemployment is lost.

Of course, the extent to which the minimum wage is a cause of the relatively high unemployment of unskilled workers is a controversial issue. Recent evidence suggests that, while it may not be the primary factor, it is a significant contributor, particularly for teenagers.[27] On the other hand, the relatively high unemployment of low-skill workers may be largely voluntary, reflecting their tendency to engage in long job searches or move in and out of the labor force because other options are more attractive to them than work. To the extent this is the case, any favorable inflationary consequences of job programs would have to depend on other assumed characteristics of the operation of the labor market.

RIGIDITY OF RELATIVE WAGES. In fact, the minimum wage is a special case of the long-run unresponsiveness of the relative wages of unskilled laborers to relative changes in the supply of and demand for their

---

rary bottlenecks in capital capacity, and job creation policies lead to more labor-intensive production, then those policies could help to reduce unemployment with less inflationary pressure than conventional expansionary means.

26. The same objective could be pursued by reducing the minimum wage for target group workers. Thus, costs associated with the imposition of the minimum wage and the diversion of resources to the jobs programs would be avoided. However, reductions in the minimum wage may be undesirable for other reasons or politically infeasible, in which case jobs programs are an attractive alternative.

27. Edward M. Gramlich, "Impact of Minimum Wages on Other Wages, Employment, and Family Incomes," BPEA, 2:1976, pp. 409–51.

labor. Just as the existence of a widespread minimum wage can mean that no upward pressure will be exerted on low wage rates in the face of a major increase in demand for low-skill workers, so can it prevent the downward adjustment of low wages that conventional economic theory predicts would occur when there is widespread unemployment among low-skill workers. According to some other views of the labor market, however—including queue, job competition, and dual labor market theories—relative wages in many parts of the economy are similarly unresponsive because other factors, such as tradition, are the crucial determinants of the relative wage structure.[28] In such cases, carefully targeted public employment programs and employment tax credits can alter favorably the relationship between unemployment and inflation.

Again, though, the critical question is to what extent labor markets are actually characterized by rigidity in relative wage rates. Neither Baily and Tobin nor Johnson believe this to be of great significance in the long run, a view that is consistent with the weak evidence in the literature on the subject.[29] But Johnson notes that in the case of a sharp increase in the relative demand for low-skill workers, the long run could be five to ten years (depending on the slope of the wage adjustment function for low-skill labor). And, although under such circumstances his model predicts no lasting increase in unskilled employment, output (as measured by GNP), or inflation, there are temporary gains in unskilled employment and output and a permanent redistribution of income from skilled to unskilled workers—purchased at the expense of temporarily higher rates of inflation.

EFFECT OF RELATIVE WAGES ON WAGE RATES. Even if relative wage rates are quite responsive to relative changes in supply and demand, however, job creation policies might still reduce structural unemployment with more favorable inflationary consequences than conventional expansionary policies if a third condition is met. It is that wage rate increases of workers at various skill levels depend on their relative wage rates, as well as on their unemployment rate. Baily and Tobin assume this to be the case; Johnson implicitly assumes the increases depend only on unemployment rates.

28. For a description of these theories and their implications for the operation of labor markets, see Glenn G. Cain, "The Challenge of Segmented Labor Market Theories to Orthodox Theory: A Survey," *Journal of Economic Literature,* vol. 14 (December 1976), pp. 1215–57.
29. See ibid.

Unemployment restrains wage rate increases in a competitive economy. When there is an excess supply of a certain class of workers, the bargaining position of employers vis-à-vis such workers is improved. Baily and Tobin argue that a high relative wage has the same effect. For example, the higher the wage rate of skilled workers relative to that of unskilled workers, the more moderate are likely to be skilled workers' demands and actual increases. Similarly, unskilled workers, such as teenagers, are more likely to be satisfied with their jobs and less apt to leave them the closer their wage rates and working conditions are to those of skilled workers. Thus, the higher the relative wage rate of unskilled workers at any given level of unemployment, the less upward pressure there will be on their wage rates.

Given this assumption, public jobs programs and employment tax credits targeted on unskilled workers can permanently reduce the unemployment rate of unskilled workers even after wages have adjusted fully. But the increase in employment among the unskilled comes at the expense of less employment among skilled workers (through displacement). And, if the employment of additional unskilled workers exerts less upward pressure on economy-wide wage rates than the employment of an equivalent number of skilled workers, it should be possible to reduce unemployment among the unskilled by a greater amount than the increase in unemployment among the skilled without increasing the inflation rate.

Baily and Tobin roughly estimate that, if it is not to increase the rate of inflation, a jobs program that adds a hundred unskilled workers to the ranks of the employed will reduce the number of unemployed workers in the economy in the long run by fifty—reflecting a reduction of seventy-five unemployed unskilled workers and an increase of twenty-five unemployed skilled workers. Although under certain assumptions these results hold for both public employment programs and employer wage subsidies, Baily and Tobin suggest that they may be diluted somewhat in the latter case.[30] They also conclude that while the redistributive and employment effects are sizable and in the correct direction, it is unclear whether the value of output actually will be expanded. This depends on the productivity of the additionally employed unskilled workers relative to that of

30. This would be the case if there is little possibility of substitution in regular employment in favor of low-wage, low-skill groups; if wage-rate increases are a function of relative wage costs to employers (taking into account the subsidy) rather than the relative wage received by workers; or if in response to the subsidy skilled workers insist on higher relative wages for the unskilled in order to prevent substitution by employers of unskilled for skilled workers.

the skilled workers not employed because of the policy and on the nature of the shift in composition of output. This latter is particularly relevant in the case of public employment programs since their output is gained partially at the expense of that of regular employment.

JOB SEARCH. The fourth way in which jobs programs could reduce unemployment with less inflationary pressure than conventional macroeconomic policies pertains only to public employment programs. If the public jobs are short term, low-skill workers who take them may search for regular employment as effectively as if they were unemployed, and more so than if they were employed in regular jobs. In such a case, they could exert relatively more downward pressure on wage rates than if they were regularly employed. Baily and Tobin show that if this mechanism is to work, job vacancy rates must have an independent effect in addition to that of unemployment rates on the inflation rate. Although their empirical tests provide evidence of such an independent relationship, they devote less attention to this case than to the relative wages of workers.

Targeting on Unskilled Workers

At the conference several issues arose that were relevant to various conditions under which the terms of trade between employment and inflation could be altered by jobs programs. First, can the targeting requirements be met—or, put differently, to what extent can job creating policies, particularly employer wage subsidies, actually add to the net employment of unskilled target groups even in the short run? Second, is it true that hiring an unemployed, unskilled worker exerts less immediate inflationary pressure than hiring an unemployed skilled one? Third, even if it is possible to reduce the overall unemployment with less inflationary pressure by decreasing unemployment rates among the unskilled at the expense of the skilled, is it a desirable public policy to do so?

In his paper, Hamermesh raised objections to the use of categorical employer wage subsidies for structural purposes. He argued that employers would shy away from hiring the target group workers even though their wages would be subsidized—that, precisely because of the subsidy attached to them, such workers might be stigmatized in employers' minds and considered unproductive. This phenomenon, he believes, explains employers' low interest in subsidy schemes.

In his paper focusing on public service employment programs administered by state and local governments Johnson does not argue that hiring under the program will not occur; however, he suggests that there probably will be a far less than commensurate net increase in total employment and little or no change in the overall skill mix of state and local government employees (both regular and subsidized). The former will result from fiscal substitution and the latter from either program managers' labeling as unskilled those unemployed skilled workers they hire or state and local governments' hiring fewer unskilled workers outside of the program to compensate for the program's targeting. According to Johnson these results should be expected because they are in the self-interest of the administering agencies and difficult to prevent.

Issue was taken in discussion at the conference with Johnson's and particularly Hamermesh's pessimism. In the case of categorical wage subsidies, it was pointed out that little or no additional information would be imparted about the eligible workers beyond that already available by virtue of their low skill levels and high unemployment rates. The lack of private employers' interest in such programs was believed to be due to the extreme narrowness of the eligibility criteria and the amount of federal red tape involved. Presumably both problems would be of less consequence in a broad-based wage subsidy. In the case of public service employment programs, it was argued that, if the federal government would underwrite only jobs paying unskilled wage rates, only unskilled laborers generally would take them. While this suggests that Johnson may be overly concerned about labeling, it does not address the problem of fiscal substitution. The potential for such substitution clearly will be far greater for a structurally oriented program than for a countercyclical one, since the former presumably would have a long life.

Unskilled Workers and Inflation

In their paper Baily and Tobin report on empirical tests that confirm their belief that unskilled or secondary workers have less effect on inflation than skilled workers. They find that, although unemployment rates of primary workers have a statistically significant effect on the inflation rate, the unemployment rates of secondary workers do not. But, as one of their discussants points out, the absence of as strong an empirical relationship between inflation and unemployment among secondary workers may be due to the fact that the measurement of unemployment is much less accurate for secondary than for primary workers. (Official data on unemployment among secondary workers is a less reliable measure of tightness of labor markets because of the greater movement into and out of the labor force among secondary workers.) Thus, while there is some empirical support for the proposition that secondary workers have less effect on inflation, the evidence is far from conclusive.

Is the Outcome Desirable?

If unskilled unemployment is due largely to rigidity in relative wage rates and can be decreased by jobs programs with minimal inflationary consequences, such programs clearly have strong appeal. But what if relative wage rates are flexible in the long run, and reductions in unskilled unemployment can come only at some expense to skilled employment? Baily and Tobin, Johnson, and many other conference participants viewed these as appropriate assumptions except in times of significant cyclical unemployment.[31] Are jobs programs still a desirable policy under such conditions? The answer to this question depends on both factual issues and value judgments.

The extent to which jobs programs are targeted by age or income class could make an important difference. Supposing large differences attributable to income class, jobs programs with structural objectives would redistribute income and opportunity toward the lower end of the income distribution. But if age were the important factor, such policies could redistribute income and opportunity toward an earlier part of the life cycle. To paraphrase one conference participant, "Do we really want to put a husband with a wife and kids out of work in order to give two or three teenagers more steady employment?"

The effect on program participants also must be considered. Will the productivity of the unskilled workers increase as a result of the reduction in their unemployment? Although both Baily and Tobin and Johnson acknowledge this possibility, their models are not designed to incorporate it. In addition, several discussants noted that a likely effect of lower unemployment rates and higher relative wages among unskilled workers might be to lower their turnover and equilibrium rate of unemployment. This would yield still further favorable consequences for inflation.

Just how would a public jobs program that reduced unemployment

---

31. Certainly not all, if even a majority, of the conference participants agreed with this view, which is a topic of considerable dispute within the economics profession.

among unskilled workers, increased it by less among skilled workers, and expanded the public sector partially at the expense of the private sector affect the value of the current output of goods and services? As Baily and Tobin note, even though conventionally measured GNP would rise, the value of aggregate output to society still might be reduced because of a shift from higher valued regular employment output to lower valued public employment program output. Would the redistribution of income and opportunity achieved by such a program be worth such a reduction? Clearly, difficult value judgments are involved here.

Finally, if as in the Johnson model, relative wages are free to adjust and increases in wage rates depend only on unemployment rates, targeted job creation policies will not lead to a long-run reduction in the overall unemployment rate with less inflationary pressure than conventional expansionary policies. They still would redistribute income from skilled to unskilled workers, however. Moreover, Johnson shows that there are temporary employment and output gains whose magnitude varies inversely with the speed of the wage adjustment process. Whether the temporary short-run gains outweigh the eventual costs of higher inflation depends on how big the former are relative to the latter and the relative value society places on present versus future income gains.

Microeconomic Effects of Structural Actions

Whether public jobs are intended to insure minimally adequate incomes to workers and their families or simply to reduce structural unemployment, or both, their effect on microeconomic efficiency should be a crucial part of any assessment of their desirability. This is the primary concern of the Haveman and Kemper-Moss papers. Although both deal with particular program structures, the issues they discuss are applicable to any subsidized public employment activity focused on the hard-to-employ.

Haveman applies benefit-cost analysis to the Dutch Social Employment program, which provides subsidized employment to handicapped and other disadvantaged workers who are unable to find regular employment. The program is funded largely by the national government and administered by municipalities under national guidelines. Emphasis is placed on producing valued goods—some of which are marketed at competitive prices—and services, as well as on preparing participants for regular employment.[32] Though rather small initially, the program has grown rapidly and now accounts for about 1.5 percent of total Dutch employment. Kemper and Moss draw on the early experience of "Supported Work" demonstration projects in the United States, which are somewhat similar to the Dutch program, to discuss the elements of a cost-benefit analysis and selected problems and issues of program design and operation.

In this section the cost-benefit framework adopted by Haveman and Kemper and Moss is sketched and then related to the prior macroeconomic perspective. Then two key elements of the benefit-cost ratio are analyzed: the opportunity cost of program participants' time and the value of the output they produce. After a summary of the results of Haveman's benefit-cost analysis of the Dutch Social Employment program, the effects of public job creation and cash income maintenance programs are briefly compared.

A Cost-Benefit Framework

Both Haveman and Kemper and Moss in their analyses consider benefits and costs from a societal point of view; the distribution among various members of society, whether beneficiaries or taxpayers, is not considered. From the societal perspective, pure income transfers are neither a cost nor a benefit since they do not add to or subtract from total economic output but merely redistribute purchasing power over existing economic resources. (This latter point has to be qualified to the extent there are administrative costs and disincentive effects such as those concerning work effort.) The redistributive consequences may be an important concern, of course, but they are treated as an independent issue.[33] This is a particularly appropriate framework to apply to public employment pro-

32. There are two components—open-air and administrative activities, which provide conventional low-skill public services and required funding of $7,600 per worker in 1975, and industrial centers, which manufacture goods for sale and required funding of $10,400 per worker in 1975 (net of the revenue from the sale of goods).

33. As is pointed out in Stromsdorfer's comments following the Kemper-Moss paper, a cost-benefit analysis could be performed from a number of other perspectives—those of the program participants, taxpayers, or the public sector balance sheet. Each of these mirrors the net economic consequences of the program to different significant groups in society but not to the whole. However, they may illuminate some of the distributive consequences of the program, contributing to a richer view of the overall societal impact.

grams for hard-to-employ populations, since the relevant alternative in such cases is often income maintenance of some sort, whether through disability programs, unemployment insurance, or welfare programs. Thus, benefit-cost analysis can illuminate the extent to which there are likely to be economic gains or losses to society as a result of subsidizing target populations through employment programs rather than pure transfer programs, and what some of the important determinants of these gains or losses might be.

Among the key elements of social costs identified is the forgone output that would have been produced in regular employment in the absence of the program. While much of public employment program participants' time otherwise may have been spent unemployed or out of the labor market, it is unlikely that all of it would have been. This "opportunity cost" of their participation in the program will reflect a social cost to the extent that the regular employment opportunities they vacate are not filled by other workers who otherwise would have been unemployed. A second element of social costs is the program operating costs other than the salaries of the subsidized workers—the expense of supervisors, materials, buildings, and other resources necessary to the programs that otherwise could have been employed in some alternative use. Finally, if the output of the public employment programs displaces any regular public or private output, and the resources that would have produced the latter are not reemployed, this forgone output is also a social cost.

On the other side of the ledger are the benefits of the value of the output produced by the program and the additional future output that program participants will be able to provide because of any increases in their productivity fostered by the subsidized work experience. Haveman also points to three additional "social-psychological" benefits which he makes no attempt to estimate: (1) any improved well-being of participants that is not reflected in increased economic productivity; (2) any reduction in social costs or increases in output that might occur as a result of the first benefit—such as lower medical expenses or improved productivity of a spouse; and (3) any improved satisfaction among the community at large because of the program's results.

The net social benefits and costs of the program, except for those related to participants' well-being and the community's sense of satisfaction, indicate whether it will move the economy over the long run to a higher or lower valued GNP growth path (setting aside the possibility that an improved employment-inflation relationship permits a more aggressive expansionary policy). An important determinant of the magnitude of the program's costs is the state of the economy. If the economy is far short of full employment, the regular employment output forgone due to the labor supplied to the program should be at, or close to, zero. Similarly, the operating costs of the program are likely to be an overstatement of the value of the alternative uses of those resources. Finally, it should be easier to produce output that is of obvious social value without displacing what otherwise would have been produced. On the other hand, if the program does displace other output, the displaced resources of production are unlikely to be reemployed.

The context of a relatively full employment economy, however, is of more relevance and interest to the discussion of a structurally oriented public employment program.[34] Assuming, at one extreme, that such a program could not reduce structural unemployment with less inflationary pressure than conventional macroeconomic policies, the program would not result in a net increase in employed resources in the economy. From society's point of view, the opportunity cost of employing a program participant is the lack of employment of someone else who otherwise would have been employed. Moreover, unless the program's job training were superior to what participants would have received elsewhere, the economic benefits of the program can only exceed its costs if the program's output is more valuable than the output that would have been produced in the absence of the program in the regular public or private sectors. For this to occur, the program would have to be correcting some existing micro inefficiency in the economy.

At the opposite extreme, a structurally oriented public jobs program could reduce the number of unemployed in the economy by one person for each person employed in the program without any adverse effects on inflation. In this case, the opportunity cost of labor employed by the program is zero. Although this does not insure that the program's social benefits will exceed its social costs, it makes this outcome much more likely.

Neither extreme case is likely to hold, however. But there are reasons to believe that at least modest-sized, carefully targeted public employment programs can contribute to a reduction in structural unemployment with minimal inflationary consequences. Two very important questions,

34. It is assumed here that the program would be successfully targeted on low-employment, low-skill groups.

then, are how program design affects the opportunity cost of the program participants' labor and the value of program output.

Opportunity Cost of Program Participants

Both the Kesselman and the Greenberg papers deal with the extent to which public employment programs are likely to attract or retain workers who otherwise would be employed. In Kesselman's model the displacement of labor from regular employment is assumed to increase with the net advantages or rent that a public employment program provides to the worker. This rent, in turn, is a positive function of several characteristics of the program—the wage rate, hours of employment offered, the pleasantness and usefulness of the work experience, the advancement and income supplementation possibilities provided, and the ease of initial entry into the program.

On the basis of his review of the WPA program and the experience of its participants, Kesselman is able to conclude that there was little, if any, displacement caused by supply-side effects during the Depression.[35] In his view this was due in large part to the extraordinary underutilization of labor. Despite the sizable percentage of all workers participating in public employment programs, there were enough unemployed workers to fill many times over any regular jobs that became available. However, in a more fully employed economy, if such programs were sizable relative to the total amount of unemployment, more substantial displacement might be expected.

Greenberg employs a more limited version of this same model to simulate participation in variously designed public employment programs had they been in place in 1973—a year of relatively full employment. Worker choices are based on maximization of their future earnings stream. The primary program parameters that Greenberg varies are the wage rate, necessary time unemployed in order to become eligible for entry to the program (the waiting period), and the hours of work per

35. Kesselman notes that displacement can occur through induced reductions of other demands on the economy, particularly in the private sector, as well as induced reductions in labor supplied elsewhere than to the public employment programs. Fiscal substitution is but one of many means by which the former can occur. A comprehensive analysis of displacement from all demand-side effects would be so complex, and probably ambiguous in its results, that Kesselman does not undertake it. He therefore gives no judgment on the extent of such displacement in the 1930s.

week offered by the program.[36] His data base covers only husband-wife households.

Several interesting findings emerge from Greenberg's simulations. As would be expected, the size of the population that desires to participate in a public employment program is positively related to the wage rate and hours of work offered and inversely related to the length of the waiting period. It is much less sensitive to hours of work than to the other two variables, however. The absolute size of this population is, perhaps, surprisingly large. Even for the lowest wage rate he simulates, $2.00 per hour—roughly the minimum wage in 1973—well over half a million job slots annually would be necessary with a thirteen-week waiting period and a million with a waiting period of five weeks. Later work with the model reported in his paper has resulted in much higher participation estimates.[37] For example, if eligibility were restricted to primary earners of families with children, over one million job slots would be required with a waiting period of five weeks and a wage between the minimum and 10 percent above the minimum.[38] And, if eligibility were extended to all primary earners of households (including unrelated individuals), participation would be over five times as high.[39] In all cases as the wage rate is increased, the number of people choosing to participate increases at a proportionately faster rate.[40]

36. He also considers the length of stay permitted in the program, but concludes that as long as it is sufficient to compensate adequately for the waiting period for entry, it is not a critical variable.

37. This later version, known as the KGB model, uses observed wage rates rather than imputed wage rates for potential participants' regular employment. See David Betson, David H. Greenberg, and Richard Kasten, "A Microsimulation Model for Analyzing Alternative Welfare Reform Proposals: An Application to the Program for Better Jobs and Income," in Robert H. Haveman and Kevin Hollenbeck, eds., *Microeconomic Simulation Models for Public Policy Analysis* (Academic Press, forthcoming).

38. These are the characteristics of the public service job component of the welfare reform proposal put forth by the Carter administration in 1977. It is estimated that 1.1 million full-time slots would be necessary under that program.

39. See Robert Haveman and Eugene Smolensky, *The Program for Better Jobs and Income: An Analysis of Costs and Distributional Effects,* prepared for the Joint Economic Committee, 95:2 (GPO, 1978), p. 10. Their estimate is derived from the KGB model.

40. As Greenberg demonstrates, at higher wage rates, the size of the population desiring to participate is quite sensitive to the response of regular employers to this increase in the effective minimum wage (since he assumes they would have to pay at least the program wage rate to retain workers eligible for the program). The greater the reduction in their demand for low-wage workers, the more such work-

Greenberg's estimates broken down by how workers who wish to participate in the program would otherwise be occupied suggest what the displacement of labor in the regular sector might be. The proportion of hours of labor supplied to the program that otherwise would have been spent in regular employment rises dramatically with the wage rate. At $2.00 per hour it is fairly small, around 10 percent, but at $3.50 it might easily be 50 percent or higher.[41] These estimates are greatly increased in Greenberg's later work: under a program with a five-week waiting period that pays no more than 10 percent above the minimum wage and is restricted to primary earners in families with children, as much as half of the participants' hours of work otherwise would have been spent in regular employment. This estimate would be much larger for broader populations or higher wage rates. The potential of structurally oriented public employment programs to displace regular employment and output through the labor supply side thus appears to be considerable if program wage rates are not kept quite low, and the opportunity cost of the program participants could be quite high.

Value of Output

Kemper and Moss focus on the value of the output of subsidized public employment programs. They believe this is important, both because it is likely to be the dominant benefit and because it is typically the most criticized and least analyzed aspect of such programs. They make the conceptual distinction between the issues of how effectively the output is produced—*productive efficiency*—and how useful the output is—*allocative efficiency*. Essentially the former refers to the productivity (re-

---

ers will want to shift from regular employment to the public employment program. Greenberg assumes this employer response will be sensitive to the number of workers eligible for the program (that is, whether the potentially eligible categories of workers represent a small or large proportion of all low-wage workers, and whether the funding is open-ended or limited to a specific number of slots). For adults in husband-wife families, he estimates that, as the wage moves from $2.00 to $3.00, a low employer response might only double the number of desired participants, whereas a high employer response could raise it about sixfold.

41. These percentages are from estimates based on a five-week waiting period and a forty-hour week with no limit on length of stay. Surprisingly, this proportion is not very sensitive to the length of the waiting period. Although a longer waiting period discourages workers from attempting to become eligible if they could have regular employment, it also discourages people from leaving the program to seek regular employment because reentry to the program is more costly to them.

source cost per unit of output) of a public employment program as compared to alternative suppliers of the same output, and the latter to the value of the program output relative to other outputs that could have been produced with the same resources. This distinction, they argue, facilitates measurement of the value of output, clarifies where subjective judgments enter more strongly into such measurement (in particular in determining the usefulness of the output), and provides a more disaggregated look at program operations which can better inform judgments on how to improve them.[42]

The basic message of the Kemper-Moss paper is threefold: achieving high levels of productive and allocative efficiency would be difficult in a world in which there were no external constraints on program managers and they had every incentive to maximize both; the incentives and constraints likely to be faced by program managers are not likely to encourage productive and allocative efficiency; and there is likely to be some conflict between the goals of productive and allocative efficiency and increasing the postprogram earnings and productivity of program participants.

In the case of productive efficiency, Kemper and Moss point out that the skills of the workers on whom the program is targeted may poorly match the skills required to produce the output—at least as the production process is conventionally organized. The very existence of chronic low wages and unemployment among the target populations suggests that existing producers have some difficulty utilizing this type of labor. Simply imitating their methods of organizing production and supervising workers is unlikely to improve the productivity of the program participants. Considerable experimentation may be necessary to discover efficient techniques.

To maximize allocative efficiency the challenge is to identify and rectify market failures that cause output to fall short of the intrinsic demand for it. The failure could be due to a monopolized private market, or a political process that does not appropriately register its constituents' wishes. Correcting such market failures is no easy matter either, especially in the absence of traditional market signals for output demand.

Thus, according to Kemper and Moss, under the best of circumstances,

42. At the most general level this distinction illuminates whether there are greater gains to be realized from experimenting with the method of production or even the participant characteristics, or from altering the choice of what is produced and how it is marketed.

innovative and creative management techniques, as well as time, probably are necessary to overcome these difficulties and promote efficient choices of output and methods of production. But, they argue, program survival and expansion may not depend on maximizing efficiency so much as on avoiding opposition from influential groups and ensuring a stable source of funding. And these latter objectives are unlikely to provide incentives consistent with achieving the former.[43] If the credentials required of workers are in excess of the job needs in certain areas of the public sector (as is frequently alleged), regular state and local employees are unlikely to stand by while services similar to those they provide are supplied by subsidized workers at lower wages. If an industry or union in the private sector has gained a monopoly position, it will adamantly oppose a lower priced expansion under public auspices of the type of output it provides. In general, very few signals and feedback mechanisms are likely to exist in public employment programs, and those that do may not encourage movement in the direction favored by society.

Lessons from a Dutch Program

The cautionary note struck by Kemper and Moss regarding the efficiency of public programs targeted on workers whose productivity is low is strongly reinforced by Haveman. Using data gathered for this purpose, and supplementing them with assumptions that bracket the likely value of variables that cannot be directly measured, Haveman performs a cost-benefit analysis of the Dutch Social Employment program. His calculations yield only a partial net social benefit (or cost) because his analysis excludes the variables related to improved social-psychological well-being.

Aggregating over all 155 projects of the program, Haveman's analysis shows a partial net social cost for 1973 ranging from about $1,000 to $4,000 per worker. His medium estimate is $2,000 to $2,400, which he indicates would translate into $3,200 to $4,400 for 1977.[44] The cost is the estimated value of the excess of the lost economic output over the economic gains due to the program output and the postprogram productivity increases of participants. It does not include wages paid to participants, which are viewed as simple transfers.

43. Kesselman's paper contains extensive evidence of such conflicts in objectives during the Depression.
44. The higher figure reflects increases in program costs since 1973, net of increased revenue in projects whose output is sold.

These rather sizable estimates of partial net social cost are not surprising in light of Haveman's appraisal—which parallels some of the concerns raised by Kemper and Moss to a remarkable degree—of the program's structure and performance. The program provides only weak incentives either to increase revenues from the sale of output or to minimize costs. Since the vast bulk of the final bill is paid by the national government, local program managers and municipal officials perceive neither rewards for reducing costs or increasing worker productivity, nor penalties for higher costs or reduced sales revenues. The open-ended and undefined nature of the tasks that may be performed under many components of the program and the lack of effective control in the growth of these components have led to considerable fiscal substitution by municipalities. In effect much of the cost of local activities has been shifted to the national government. Finally, because the level of income provided to program participants compares favorably with what they can earn in unsubsidized employment, the flow of workers out of the program is discouraged.

Haveman cautions that the Dutch Social Employment program contains many warnings about the use of structurally oriented public employment programs in the United States. In particular he echoes Kemper and Moss's view that serious difficulties in the design and operation of such programs place inherent limitations on their efficiency. On the other hand, Haveman's disaggregated cost-benefit results show that some projects can do reasonably well on efficiency grounds, just as early experience suggests some Supported Work projects can succeed.[45] This means that there is likely to be considerable room for improvement among those projects that are faring less well, which reinforces the importance of understanding what factors relate most strongly to high efficiency so that programs can be designed most appropriately. Thus, along with Kemper and Moss, Haveman emphasizes the crucial importance of concentrating on the financing arrangements and general incentive structure faced by local program managers to insure they encourage the maximization of net social benefits.

45. See Stan Masters and others, "Analysis of Nine-Month Interviews for Supported Work: Results of an Early Sample" (New York: Manpower Demonstration Research Corp., 1977; processed); and Rebecca Maynard and others, "Analysis of Nine-Month Interviews for Supported Work: Results of an Early AFDC Sample" (MDRC, 1977; processed).

In addition, he advocates careful targeting and design of programs to insure that participants are those with low forgone earnings opportunities (opportunity cost). And if society wishes to encourage in those participants greater and more productive work, it is essential that income from subsidized public employment be significantly above what workers can receive through income maintenance programs and significantly below what they would receive in regular employment after participating in the program. The first condition is met by the Dutch Social Employment program, but not the second.

Public Employment Programs versus Cash Transfers

Lest the messages of the Haveman and Kemper-Moss papers appear too discouraging about the micro efficiency of public employment programs, it is important to recall the terms of these studies. The negative partial net social benefit measured by Haveman in no way indicates the programs are not good social policy. The unmeasurable, primarily non-economic, benefits not included in his calculation may well be substantial enough to more than offset the negative net efficiency. In addition, income redistribution objectives, if met, confer benefits on society.

There are many indications that societies would prefer to provide jobs rather than direct income support for those portions of the population who are able to work. Programs that create special public jobs can be viewed as a special form of in-kind redistribution. Providing jobs rather than cash, like any in-kind transfer, restricts beneficiaries' choices, and particularly circumscribes the possibility of their using transfer income to purchase leisure. Public preference for jobs programs is motivated at least in part by a desire to prevent work reductions. If this preference is sufficiently strong, society may, in fact, be willing to pay some premium in terms of forgone economic output to satisfy it.

Furthermore, many of the intended beneficiaries also might prefer a job to straight cash assistance if the attendant attitude of society toward them is considerably improved, or if the job is one that allows them to derive greater self-esteem. Generally, beneficiaries are assumed to prefer cash to in-kind transfers because the cash gives them the freedom to choose how to spend their money. But do cash transfers enable beneficiaries to buy a job? Perhaps they do, because the alternative source of income increases their ability to afford to work for lower wage rates. But to the extent that beneficiaries measure the worth of a job in part in terms of dignity and pride and in part by the wage rate, this is not very helpful. It may be preferable from the beneficiaries' point of view to merge the cash transfer and wage payment. Thus, if the preferences of either taxpayers or beneficiaries, or both, for transfers through jobs rather than cash are strong enough, jobs programs may be more efficient than cash even if the former entail greater social costs.

Finally, in cases where society is committed to providing income assistance of some type to certain target groups, the alternative of cash transfers has its own net social costs. The disincentive to work fosters net reductions in regular employment that may not be large for most of the target groups of structurally oriented public employment programs (since the presumption is that their alternative opportunities for work were quite limited); however, in combination with administrative costs, their contribution to social costs may well be 10 percent to 15 percent of the monetary costs of the transfer program.[46] Thus, the appropriate comparison in such cases for public employment programs is not with a policy of doing nothing, but with an alternative that is also likely to have significant effects on economic output.[47]

Policy Implications

What uses ought to be made of policies for creating jobs in the future and how should they be designed? Clearly the conference papers reviewed here have only made a beginning in presenting fundamental information and analytical detail on which to base policy. Since value judgments often are crucial in determining the desirability of job creating relative to alternative policies, conclusions ought to be approached cautiously. Nevertheless, the already extensive use of public employment and wage subsidies, and the strong and immediate interest among policymakers in

46. This estimate is based on the assumption that administrative costs of cash transfer programs are 5–10 percent of total transfers, and the work disincentive effect 10–15 percent applied to a base of regular employment earnings equivalent to one-third of full-time minimum wage employment.

47. This does not in any way imply that public employment programs are necessarily *the* preferred alternative to straight cash assistance. Other policy measures to promote regular employment opportunities may be more efficient and therefore preferred.

improving and possibly expanding their use, make it imperative that these questions be addressed. The papers in this volume are quite helpful for so doing.[48]

Countercyclical Policy

During periods of high unemployment, any expansionary fiscal policy is likely to yield strong economic benefits on balance. However, although they have some merits, the case for the use of public employment programs or wage subsidies for countercyclical purposes in preference to other macroeconomic policies is not strong.

The primary advantage of public employment programs is the potential for targeting the jobs directly created by the additional stimulus. This, in turn, could help disadvantaged workers or regions to participate more fully in the economic recovery and may exert less inflationary pressure than alternative fiscal stimuli of comparable magnitude. Public employment programs may also have a greater employment impact per temporary dollar increase in the federal deficit. But both effects are likely to be quite modest if state and local governments are the administering agents because there are strong incentives for such governments to choose the most qualified applicants from among the eligible population and to use the federal funds to underwrite activities they otherwise would have undertaken with unrestricted funds.[49]

On the negative side, the timing and efficiency of public employment programs intended for countercyclical purposes appear to be less favorable than alternative fiscal stimuli that emphasize expansion of the private and regular public sectors. Rapid implementation is possible, but may come at some expense to targeting on the disadvantaged and avoiding fiscal substitution. (It is more difficult to design and implement special projects than to expand employment already being performed.) And the

48. No attempt was made at the conference to arrive at majority or consensus judgments; thus, while the policy conclusions set forth here are informed by the conference discussion and (generally) supported by the conference papers, they are the authors' and are not necessarily attributable to conference participants at large.

49. There are indications that the restrictive targeting criteria for the expansion of CETA title 6 during the latter part of 1977 increased somewhat the participation of disadvantaged workers in the program. Representation of AFDC recipients, blacks, and members of low-income families increased. The average level of education of participants, however, remained above that of all those unemployed.

timely phasing down of countercyclical public employment programs is politically difficult. Similarly, such programs appear unlikely to provide additional output that would be valued as highly by society as the output that would result from an expansion of the regular public and private sectors of the economy, since the former is subjected to neither regular market or political tests. And while in theory public employment might have a training effect that could raise the postprogram productivity of the working population beyond what an equivalent expansion of the regular sectors of the economy would, there is no evidence that this would happen—nor should it be expected of temporary programs that must be rapidly implemented and subsequently phased out.

It has been argued that the very large public service employment grants made in the mid-1970s have been a critical source of revenue and employment support for many cities during the recent economic recession and recovery. However, given the relative size, cyclical stability, and skill distribution of public-sector employment, it is not clear that it should receive a higher priority than the expansion of employment in the private sector during a recession. And to the extent that it is desired to provide a federal subsidy for state and local activities, general revenue sharing grants or employer wage subsidies may have more desirable characteristics than public service employment programs.

It is also difficult to make a strong a priori case for preferring employer wage subsidies for countercyclical purposes to more conventional macroeconomic policies. However, such subsidies do have some appealing characteristics that suggest they should be given greater consideration, particularly as an alternative to public employment programs if direct job creating policies are to be favored over more indirect stimulative measures. This applies to their use for regular public as well as private-sector employment.

The evidence suggests that wage subsidies or tax credits could have as large an employment effect as public employment programs per dollar increase in the deficit. They also can be structured to favor low-skilled workers. They may be more economically efficient than public employment programs because the jobs directly created are in regular sectors of the economy, and the output therefore subject to conventional tests of consumer demand. And, since the jobs are regular ones, the problem of transition from specially created public jobs is avoided. Finally, general wage subsidies have the advantages of directly lowering labor costs to private employers, which should lead to lower product prices and inflation, of offering flexibility in the degree of the subsidy, and (perhaps) of being easier to phase out.

Structural Policy

The usefulness of direct job creating policies for structural rather than countercyclical purposes appears more promising. This is largely due to the lack of sufficiently effective alternative structural policies, whereas other countercyclical macroeconomic policies than jobs programs have proven quite effective. However, considerable modesty about both the current state of knowledge and expertise regarding their use and their likely ultimate potential is in order.

If certain conditions are met, direct job creating policies can permit continued expansion of employment at relatively full employment levels with less long-run inflationary pressure than conventional fiscal policies. Appropriate targeting is necessary but not sufficient. In addition, the disproportionately high unemployment rates among certain groups of workers must be due to particular kinds of rigidities in wage determination and wage adjustment processes. Since these are currently issues of considerable uncertainty and dispute, the extent to which the inflationary consequences of direct job creating policies are superior to those of other expansionary policies is a speculative matter. However, their potential is clearly greatest if they are narrowly targeted and carefully designed. The more they are restricted to workers with the poorest regular employment opportunities, and the lower the wage paid in public employment programs, the better their prospects for minimizing inflationary pressures. Even so, higher employment among workers in the target group may be partially at the expense of higher unemployment among other workers.

Public employment and employer subsidy programs also can help to insure minimally adequate incomes to families with workers. The targeting requirements for this purpose are likely to overlap considerably with those for the objective of increasing employment with minimal inflationary pressure. When the primary objective is distributional, a jobs program that has the disadvantage of reducing gross national product over the long run may nevertheless be desirable, if its economic efficiency compares favorably with direct cash assistance programs or if a high premium is placed on providing assistance through jobs rather than cash. In fact, if taxpayers are willing to pay more to provide aid to those expected to work through subsidized jobs rather than direct cash assistance, and the former is more costly, it is almost certain that some combination of cash and jobs is optimal.[50]

Although structurally oriented job creating programs do not have to promote economic efficiency to be desirable, the degree to which they do should influence the extent of their use, and the maximization of their economic efficiency should be a principal policy objective. Little is known about the economic efficiency of narrowly targeted public employment and wage subsidy programs, largely because the experience with them has been extremely limited and not subject to rigorous scrutiny. What is known suggests that they have potential, but that it is difficult for them to be efficient.

In the case of wage subsidies the main problem is to induce employers to hire and train workers with characteristics other than those of their usual employees. Once this is successfully accomplished, one can be reasonably hopeful about the outcome since the output will be meeting the market test and the workers will have learned a salable skill while in the regular labor market. In the case of public employment programs, it should be easier to provide jobs for the desired target groups. However, deciding what to produce and how to produce and market the output is difficult, as is helping workers make the transition to regular employment. Furthermore, the incentive structure faced by managers of public employment programs is unlikely to lead them to place much weight on achieving economic efficiency.

For these reasons, policymakers should proceed cautiously. The inherent limitations of job creating programs probably will preclude their ever becoming a panacea for structural unemployment, but they may be able to play a sizable constructive role for particular groups of workers. (Given the severity of structural unemployment among many groups in the population, considerable experimentation with policies with any promise is worthwhile.) Wage subsidies might be more advantageously focused on the more employable members of disadvantaged target groups, with public employment programs reserved for those who are most difficult to employ. In the latter case, though, considerable thought has to

---

50. Beginning with a pure cash program, taxpayers would be willing to spend a bit more to provide additional aid through jobs and less through cash. With greater funds available it should be possible to design a combination income and jobs program that would improve the well-being of beneficiaries. For further development of this argument see Irwin Garfinkel, "Is In-kind Redistribution Efficient?" *Quarterly Journal of Economics*, vol. 87 (May 1973), pp. 320–30.

be given to the design of regulations and funding procedures to provide an appropriate incentive structure for program operators.[51]

Program Design

The design and operational requirements of countercyclically and structurally oriented job creating policies are quite different and, ideally, ought to be pursued through different program structures. Trying to accomplish both types of objectives within a common framework will compromise both.

Table 1 lists the desirable design features of public employment programs. If such programs are going to be administered through state and local governments for countercyclical purposes, their eligibility criteria ought to be fairly broad, and state and local governments should not be restricted to special projects.[52] Even though these conditions encourage fiscal substitution, they are important to facilitate rapid implementation and the provision of highly valued output. (Since the program is to be temporary, the degree of fiscal substitution will be limited.) The wage rate is not crucial from the point of view of displacing regular employment because of the assumed widespread cyclical unemployment.

In contrast, for structural programs, quite restrictive eligibility criteria are appropriate, as are low wage rates, in order to insure participation of workers with lower opportunity costs. These also may be favored on distributional grounds since they reserve the jobs for the most needy and, within a fixed appropriation level, reach the greatest number of workers. Emphasis on special projects will be necessary since the nature of the work generally will have to be tailored to meet the characteristics and needs of particular target groups and because the relatively permanent funding and assumed high employment rate make fiscal substitution and other forms of displacement more severe problems.

Although wages at or very near the minimum are desirable on some

51. Although the Kemper-Moss and Haveman papers highlighted this problem, they offered no policy prescriptions. This ought to be a priority area for future analysis.

52. This does not mean there should be no attempt to restrict eligibility to the program, only that the restrictions should not interfere with the desired implementation schedule or jeopardize the ability of state and local governments to provide highly valued additional services. In fact it would be desirable for state and local governments to have a set of well-designed projects that can be rapidly implemented sitting on the shelf awaiting the next recession.

Table 1. Major Desirable Design Features of Public Employment Programs with Countercyclical and Structural Objectives

Countercyclical criteria	Structural criteria
Temporary funding with level varying inversely and rapidly with aggregate unemployment rate	Permanent funding[a]
Funds allocated primarily to those local areas suffering from higher unemployment	Funds allocated to all local areas[b]
Broad targeting on the unemployed	Narrow targeting on those with poor employment prospects even in a high employment economy
Emphasis on highly valued output	Emphasis on relevance of work experience to regular employment opportunities and transitional assistance
Employment of a type that can be promptly and effectively phased in and out	Employment in carefully designed, long-term projects[c]
Wage rates that can be as high as prevailing rates	Wage rates close to minimum wage

a. Structural unemployment will be a problem even at relatively low rates of aggregate unemployment. The amount of money expended for this purpose might vary somewhat with the overall rate of unemployment.

b. Even in relatively low-unemployment areas there is likely to be some structural unemployment. The allocation formula could be weighted in favor of areas with high unemployment rates (adjusted for size of labor force).

c. Although length of tenure of participants in programs should be restricted, considerable time will be needed to design and implement projects; they should not be forced to terminate if they prove effective.

grounds in structural public employment programs, they can present difficulties. In many locales such wages are well below those of the lowest paid jobs in the regular public sector. Consequently, the program jobs could either become dead-end with no relevance to regular employment or undermine standards in the public sector. In any event, the creation of a very large number of public employment jobs at a subsidized minimum wage raises the spectre of a stigmatized second-class work force being permanently "warehoused" in the public sector. Thus, the setting of the wage rate structure for public employment programs presents a severe dilemma. It can be sidestepped partially if structural programs are not very large, even though they pay prevailing wage rates. Eligibility criteria could be relied on heavily to insure narrow targeting on those with the lowest opportunity costs and tenure in the program could be limited to force participants to search for regular employment.[53]

53. This resolution obviously would not be available if public employment programs were ever used to establish a job guarantee as envisioned under early versions of the Humphrey-Hawkins bill. In such a case either minimum (or even

The distinction between countercyclical and structural policies also has implications for the design of employer wage subsidies or of employment tax credits. In both cases it is important to minimize (consistent with other objectives) the reporting requirements and other red tape associated with the subsidy. A subsidy with countercyclical objectives should be temporary, also varying in size inversely with the aggregate unemployment rate. Its precise structure should depend on estimates of employers' demand response; however, given the desire to maximize the net employment effect per dollar increase in the deficit, the subsidy should be marginal. It is probably desirable to apply it to a base of significantly less than 100 percent of employers' prior-year employment. This will provide greater certainty to the aggregate amount of the subsidy and insure that all marginal employment of declining as well as growing employers is eligible.[54] Finally, within these constraints, eligibility should be extended to all jobs; but if low-wage workers are to be favored, the subsidy should be either a fixed dollar per hour of work or a percentage of wages.

On the other hand, eligibility for structurally oriented employer subsidies should be restricted to workers being hired from appropriate target groups. The availability of the subsidy to employers should be relatively permanent, but its applicability to given employees should be gradually phased out. It is also tempting to apply such a categorical subsidy to only marginal employment—defined either in terms of an employer's total work force or as only those members of a target group. Both limitations have drawbacks, however. The administrative requirements of defining the base relative to a target group can easily become prohibitive. And in addition to complicating program administration, defining the base relative to the employer's total labor force unduly restricts the opportunities for substituting subsidized for nonsubsidized workers. While the potential for such substitution presents a political obstacle to categorical wage subsidies, it is a desired outcome from the point of view of structural objectives.[55]

---

subminimum) wages would have to be paid in the program or the long-run effects on inflation would be no different than if conventional macroeconomic policies were used to push the unemployment rate down.

54. Upper limits on the amount of subsidy a firm can receive, such as the $100,000 limit on the 1977 employment tax credit, can severely restrict its effectiveness as a countercyclical tool. They should be set very high or be omitted.

55. Provisions should be included that preclude the firing or laying off of nonsubsidized workers so that they can be replaced by subsidized workers, of course. But with natural attrition, it is desirable to affect employers' inframarginal hiring

Conclusion

More research is needed on most of the issues raised in this paper. However, a great deal of the necessary understanding of the consequences of job creating policies—particularly ones with structural objectives— can best be obtained through a learning-by-doing process with careful monitoring and analysis of a host of planned and natural variations. Several useful experimental public employment efforts are under way but there is little relating to employer subsidies.[56]

Both public employment programs and wage subsidies have significant advantages and disadvantages for dealing with structural unemployment. Until more is learned about them, the scale on which they eventually might operate effectively is highly uncertain. There appears to be no general reason to greatly prefer one approach over the other (although one may have more potential effectiveness than the other for particular target groups). Current policies in the United States heavily favor public employment programs.[57] A more balanced approach, with wage subsidies applicable to regular public as well as private employment, is likely to be more fruitful.

---

decisions as well as their extramarginal decisions. If the policy is effective in shifting the Phillips curve, nonsubsidized workers would suffer little or no overall reduction in employment since more expansionary macroeconomic policies could be pursued.

56. Experimental public employment activities in the United States include the Supported Work demonstrations that are the topic of the Kemper-Moss paper and several demonstrations instituted under the Youth Employment and Demonstration Projects Act of 1977. The Department of Labor is designing a number of welfare reform demonstrations.

57. This heavy emphasis on public employment programs may reflect their political attractiveness more than the belief that they are actually more effective than wage subsidies. The visibility of the jobs created works in favor of such a program, as does the pressure from state and local government for more federal assistance, as well as the concern that wage subsidies will add to the profits of private firms.

Martin Neil Baily and James Tobin

Inflation-Unemployment Consequences of Job Creation Policies

The central problem of political economy of our times is the incompatibility of widely held social goals for unemployment and inflation. This cruel dilemma has plagued the United States and the whole noncommunist world ever since 1946 and has been especially severe in the last decade. Diagnosis and resolution of the conflict have divided the economics profession, dominated the concerns and disputes of economic policymakers in Washington and other capitals, and confused and moved politicians and voters. The world awaits, not very hopefully, revelation of the way out.

The traditional tools of monetary and fiscal policy, it is painfully evident, cannot resolve the conflict. How successful they have been or can be in stabilizing global spending for goods and services is itself controversial. In any event, they clearly cannot achieve simultaneously as low unemployment as the society would like and a path of prices the society finds acceptable. Varying the mixture of government spending, taxes, and monetary measures may make the conflicting objectives slightly more or less compatible. But there is not much in it, for the simple reason that all these measures affect principally the dollar volume of spending and not the division of the economy's response between output and prices, or employment and wages.

For a long time economists, policymakers, and politicians have sought additional tools. Direct government intervention in wage and price decisions is the most obvious tool, and it has been frequently used in this country and elsewhere. The euphemism *incomes policies* covers the spec-

We thank the participants in the conference and Ronald Bodkin for their comments. Richard Kolsky, Hiroshi Yoshikawa, and David Coppock provided excellent research assistance. Part of the funding for the study was provided by the National Science Foundation.

43

trum from universal detailed compulsory price and wage control to advisory and hortatory guideposts to ad hoc jawboning. The popularity of incomes policies varies directly with the time elapsed since their last trial, and in the United States today they are strongly opposed by both business and organized labor.

Another supplementary approach is *labor market policy,* a term that encompasses a host of measures designed to reduce unemployment by improving the match between available or potentially available jobs and job seekers. Specific measures include improving information and its exchange, training and relocating workers, and developing the economies of particular regions and urban districts. The principal macroeconomic purpose is to diminish the deadweight inefficiency implicit in the simultaneous existence of job vacancies and unemployed workers, permitting the conventional instruments of demand management to achieve lower unemployment without unacceptable inflationary pressure. Indeed this is precisely how President Kennedy's Council of Economic Advisers expressed the matter in 1962; its target of 4 percent unemployment was an "interim" goal for fiscal and monetary policy, to be lowered as labor market policies ameliorated the trade-off. The model for this strategy was Sweden, where the vigorous use of labor market policies advocated by Gösta Rehn and others was given credit for the absence of significant unemployment. For whatever reasons, the labor market policies undertaken in the United States in the 1960s were not similarly successful.

Direct job creation (DJC) may be viewed, in this perspective, as another supplementary macroeconomic policy, designed to mitigate the conflict between society's goals for unemployment and inflation. The purpose of this paper is to examine theoretically and conceptually the role of DJC in macroeconomic strategy and to describe the possible mechanisms, if any, by which public employment programs might diminish the inflationary consequences of higher rates of employment. This has been one major motivation of the proponents of DJC; the Humphrey-Hawkins bill (the proposed Full Employment and Balanced Growth Act), for example, acknowledges the inflationary limits to job creation by demand management alone and emphasizes DJC as a vehicle for moving the rest of the distance to the 4 percent unemployment goal.

This macroeconomic role is, of course, not the only purpose or possible justification of DJC. Even if DJC would not relax the inflation-unemployment dilemma, it might still be desirable on other grounds: distributing unemployment more fairly among individuals and groups; increasing long-run productivity by improving the skills, experience, and work habits of particular unemployed persons; accomplishing tasks of high social value that would otherwise not be done; and defending the work ethic by substituting jobs for handouts. The design of public employment programs probably depends on the weights given to these objectives relative to the macroeconomic goal. If the main priority is, put loosely, "to cheat the Phillips curve," then it is important to ask whether and to what extent this is possible and how the answer depends on the features of DJC programs.

Direct job creation, in this discussion, involves two essential features: (1) federal funds are granted to public, private nonprofit, and conceivably other private employers conditioned on performance in providing employment; and (2) eligibility for employment with these funds is restricted to persons who meet certain criteria like low income, welfare dependency, previous unemployment, youth, or residence in areas of labor surplus. These features differentiate DJC from ordinary government expenditures for goods and services, such as public works, where the purpose is to serve particular government functions, employment performance is a by-product rather than a condition, and the pool of eligible employees is not restricted. This is not to say that employment considerations may not motivate the size and allocation of such expenditures, or that it may not be possible to mix DJC considerations with public works grants.

Much of our analysis focuses on public service employment and not on subsidies for private employment.[1] However, we do compare DJC and wage subsidies as means of obtaining permanent improvement in the relation of unemployment and inflation. The paper does not treat open-ended "employer of last resort" programs that would employ anyone on demand regardless of need, performance, prior unemployment, prior employment, and other criteria. Selectivity of the target labor force is an essential element of a DJC strategy that serves macroeconomic goals.

Direct Job Creation as Fiscal Stimulus

"Bang for a buck" is a traditional concern of students and practitioners of fiscal policy in comparing alternative fiscal measures. The "bang" is the outcome in employment, production, or income; the "buck" is the

---

1. With minor variation and one exception—the discussion of reducing frictional unemployment in the next section—analogous arguments to the ones made about DJC hold for wage subsidies.

increase in federal outlay or deficit. This concern has been evident recently in discussions of fiscal stimuli for 1977 and 1978. An extreme manifestation is the instinctive contrast many members of Congress and other officials and commentators draw between "jobs programs" and other stimuli. From a macroeconomist's viewpoint, increases in ordinary federal spending for goods and services, additional transfers to individuals or state and local governments, and reductions in taxes or universal "rebates" are all job-creating programs. They doubtless differ from each other and from DJC in the sizes and time paths of their output and employment consequences. But as fiscal stimuli to economic activity they all rely on the presumption that additional spending, direct or induced, will generate additional production and employment. Their success does not depend on legislative requirements linking dollars expended directly to jobs.

Significant aggregate effects of fiscal stimuli depend on widely diffused secondary spending, not just on the first round of government outlay. The indirect effects are not under legislative control, and those of DJC outlays probably differ little from other fiscal stimuli. As Arthur Okun has picturesquely said, "Penicillin doesn't have to be injected into the Adam's apple to cure a strep throat." Perhaps the concern of congressmen to see and count the employees supported by their appropriations is not really macroeconomic. They want to be sure the target population is benefited, or they want to get credit in their districts for tangible, identifiable results.

Crowding Out of Private Expenditure

At the opposite macroeconomic pole is the view that neither DJC nor any other fiscal measure can result in net job creation. Milton Friedman has stated this view emphatically in *Newsweek* and elsewhere.[2] The argument is that additional government expenditure will crowd out an equal amount of private expenditure. Direct job creation may redistribute jobs from regular workers to the programs' beneficiaries, but it will not add to total employment.

Advocates of this position appeal to two different mechanisms. One is that deficit-financed fiscal stimulus cannot succeed without permissive monetary policy. With unchanged paths of monetary aggregates, fiscal ex-

2. "But where does the government get the money? Ultimately, from you and me. . . . If it spends, we don't. If it employs people, we don't." Milton Friedman, "Humphrey-Hawkins," *Newsweek*, Aug. 2, 1976, p. 55.

pansion will raise interest rates and deter private spending. Monetary economists differ on whether this "crowding out" is partial or complete; but in any case there is general agreement that the central bank could make it complete if it wished to do so, by tightening its policies as necessary. The opposite side of this coin is that, in a slack economy with high unemployment and excess capacity, the monetary authorities could avoid all crowding out by accommodative policy, allowing sufficient monetary growth to avoid increases in interest rates. Friedman and some other monetarists deny this possibility, asserting that faster monetary growth will trigger heightened expectations of inflation. Inflationary expectations might seem favorable to investment expenditure rather than the reverse, but the assertion is that they also breed anticipations of subsequent recession.

The second mechanism is that of "ex ante" crowding out. The public, it is argued, responds to bond-financed government spending the same way as to tax-financed spending. Consumption is adjusted downward, no less to provide saving to pay future taxes than to pay current taxes. An increase in GNP equal to the government expenditure—the "balanced budget multiplier" of unity—remains nonetheless. And would not monetary financing relieve the public of worry about future taxes? The monetarist answer is that expectations of future inflation have the same effect as expectations of future taxes.

This paper is not the place for an analysis of crowding out. Briefly stated, our view is that proponents of these arguments either mistakenly apply them to an economy with underemployed resources[3] or, equally mistakenly, argue that recessions never persist long enough to permit an effective countercyclical policy to operate. The expectational responses on which the crowding-out impasses rely are not rational when underemployed resources are available. The public can expect higher real incomes from the reemployment of these resources, not just higher taxes and higher prices. Of course businessmen and consumers may be skeptical of the longevity of a recovery if they think that any fiscal and monetary package that promotes it will be followed by severe monetary contraction and business recession. This is not our conception of accommodative or permissive monetary policy.

We will assume, therefore, that fiscal stimulus can work, at least when accompanied by appropriate monetary policy. We will also assume that

3. This should not be taken as acceptance of the correctness of all the arguments, even applied to a full-employment economy.

price and wage inflation, actual and expected, depend on the tightness of goods and labor markets, and that fiscal and monetary policies affect prices and wages not directly but by their consequences for the pressure of aggregate demand on supplies in those markets.

GNP and Employment Effects of DJC and Other Fiscal Stimuli

The GNP multiplier for DJC expenditures may differ from the multiplier for other fiscal stimuli for two primary reasons: (1) DJC recipients may have a different, presumably higher, marginal propensity to spend from disposable income; and (2) DJC recipients may face above- or below-average marginal tax rates, taking into account not only regular taxes but possible reductions in government transfers. In addition the answer will depend on (3) whether wage payments to DJC employees are regarded as GNP purchases or as transfers or as some mixture of the two.

The employment multiplier for DJC expenditure will differ from the general employment multiplier for the first two of the above reasons. An important additional reason is the relative labor-intensiveness of DJC projects. One of the appeals of DJC is the provision of more jobs per dollar.

With respect to the ultimate deficit resulting from a dollar outlay, points (1) and (2) above are the main factors. The possibility that DJC outlays will save the government money otherwise spent on welfare, food stamps, and unemployment compensation may appeal to deficit-conscious legislators. But the same offset holds down the GNP and employment multipliers of DJC. Thus, whether concentrating DJC on transfer program beneficiaries increases or decreases the "bang" per deficit "buck" is not obvious a priori.

Displacement of regular expenditures by state and local governments and nonprofit institutions is a consequence of DJC that has attracted much study and comment.[4] Estimates of substitution for programs under the Comprehensive Employment and Training Act are as high as 60 percent within the first year and 90–100 percent after two or more years.[5] Federal finance is substituted for local taxes or other sources of funds, and regular employees are often retained or reemployed after meeting

4. Michael Wiseman, "Public Employment as Fiscal Policy," *Brookings Papers on Economic Activity, 1:1976,* pp. 67–104.
5. Congressional Budget Office, *Public Employment and Training Assistance: Alternative Federal Approaches, Budget Issue Paper* (GPO, 1977), p. xiii.

CETA eligibility requirements. Displacement defeats important purposes of the program. But from a macroeconomic viewpoint, not all fiscal stimulus is lost. The stimulus of DJC is diluted to the more normal stimulus of fungible federal transfers to state and local governments, that is, to some mixture of GNP purchases, tax reduction, and debt reduction. In the illustrative analysis that follows the differentiated multipliers for DJC assume that no displacement occurs. Allowance for displacement can be made by giving fractional weight to the specific DJC multiplier and the remainder to the normal multiplier.

Derivation of Normal and DJC Multipliers

In the appendix a general framework for comparative analysis of the GNP, deficit, and employment effects of different types of government expenditure is presented algebraically. The following discussion in the text is based on that framework.

The normal multiplier for the economy, m, applicable to autonomous private expenditure and to a comparable mix of federal purchases, is equal to $1/(1 - a + at)$, where a is the marginal propensity to consume (mpc) from disposable income (income after taxes and transfers) and t is the marginal tax rate (the sum of the increase in taxes and reduction in transfers accompanying a dollar increase in regular pretax income).[6] Two amendments to the multiplier formula are needed in order to analyze the differential multiplier effects of a particular type of government expenditure like DJC. The first affects the mpc a; the second affects the marginal tax rate t.

As for the first, the target population of a particular type of government expenditure may differ from the general population in its marginal propensity to spend earnings. In the case of DJC the mpc may be expected to be well above average, for two reasons. The labor-intensive nature of the expenditures will give them a high wage component. While it is true that the resulting higher consumption propensity might be offset by lower induced investment, this offset is unlikely to be large in the slack economic climate for which the introduction of DJC is usually proposed. The second reason is that the DJC wage earners, given a needs criterion of eligibility, are likely to be liquidity-constrained consumers who will

6. In the appendix formulas for the derivation of multipliers are developed and a number of complications are allowed for. One is the possibility that the marginal propensity to spend is not the same for taxes and transfers as for pretax incomes.

spend all extra cash within a short time, irrespective of their view of the permanence of their employment. Let a' be the mpc from income generated by DJC expenditure G'. This specific mpc, a', will be close to unity, compared to a general mpc of the order of 0.7 or 0.8.

The second amendment takes account of the possibility that income from DJC is subject to special marginal tax and transfer rates. The obvious reason would be the selective eligibility criteria. Let t' be the marginal rate of tax or transfer reduction for income received by beneficiaries of DJC. Then the total mpc with respect to income G' is $a' - a't'$.

The multiplier m' applicable to G' can now be written:[7]

(1) $$m' = m + m[(a' - a) - (a't' - at)].$$

The difference $m' - m$ can be interpreted as the GNP effect of diverting to DJC a dollar of government expenditure that has the same multiplier m as autonomous private spending. Public works expenditure is a possible example. Of course some specific expenditure programs carry multipliers lower than m, and diversion from them to DJC would raise further the GNP bang per buck.

It may be useful to indicate orders of magnitude by numerical example, using formula 1. Suppose that a is 0.8 and t is 0.3, so that m is $1/0.44$ or 2.27. At one extreme, a' is 1.0 and t' is 0, so that m' is $1.44m$ or 3.27. A dollar of DJC would increase GNP by a dollar more than a dollar of normal expenditure. On the other hand, if DJC participants are drawn from the rolls of income-conditioned transfer programs with high implicit tax rates (consider 0.67 for aid to families with dependent children and 0.33 for food stamps), the differential bang is diminished or eliminated. Suppose that a' remains 1.0 but t' is 0.5. Then m' is only $0.94m$ or 2.14, and a dollar shifted to DJC loses 13 cents of GNP.[8]

The multiplier for generalized tax reduction or transfer would be ma which, under the above numerical assumptions, would be 1.82. Clearly DJC would compare more favorably to such stimulus than to other government purchases.

---

7. This is easily derived from the aggregate expenditure-output identity: $Y = A + G + G' + (a' - a't')G' + (a - at)(Y - G')$, where A is autonomous nongovernmental expenditure for goods and services, G is federal services, and the last two terms are induced private expenditures.

8. In mid-1976 only 14 percent of CETA public service employees had been on unemployment insurance, and only 15 percent on welfare. But these percentages were expected to increase. Congressional Budget Office, *Public Employment and Training Assistance,* pp. 23 and 26–28.

The foregoing analysis and illustrative calculation assume that DJC expenditures are 100 percent purchases of GNP. If they were regarded wholly as transfers, then the DJC multiplier m' would be $ma'\gamma'$, where $1 - \gamma'$ is the fraction of DJC outlays that directly replace other transfers. In the more favorable of the two cases above, a' is 1, γ' is 1, m' is just equal to m and exceeds the tax cut or transfer multiplier ma. In the less favorable example, γ' is 0.5 and m' is only half of m.

No doubt the official national income accountants will include DJC in GNP. The larger issue is one of economic welfare and social priorities. The product of DJC, critics might argue, has met neither market nor political test. It is being purchased not for its own sake but to give employment. The employment may, it is true, build human capital; but this by-product is generally ignored in other cases.

The normal employment multiplier—jobs per dollar of private investment or public expenditure—is equal to mn, where n is the number of jobs per dollar of GNP. The employment multiplier for DJC expenditure is $m'n + n' - n = n(m' - 1) + n'$ where n' is jobs per dollar of DJC. The Congressional Budget Office estimates that n' is 0.14 (million jobs per billion dollars),[9] while n is about 0.05. With the illustrative figures above, the normal employment multiplier is 0.11, while that of DJC is 0.25 (first case) or 0.20 (second case).

The increase in deficit per dollar of DJC expenditure is $1 - m't - (t' - t)$. To extend the calculations above, if t' is 0, then the deficit per dollar of DJC is $1 - 3.27 \times 0.3 + 0.3 = 0.32$. But if t' is 0.5, the deficit is $1 - 2.13 \times 0.3 - 0.2 = 0.16$. The GNP bang per dollar of deficit is in the one case 10.2, and in the other 13.3. For increases in general expenditures it is 7.1.

Cheating the Phillips Curve

"Bang for a buck" questions are of some intellectual interest and considerable political relevance. But from a theoretical macroeconomic viewpoint, there is no good intrinsic reason to limit the number of bucks, either of budget outlay or of deficit. The economic target is the highest path of real GNP and employment compatible with acceptable rates of inflation. Monetary and fiscal stimuli, small or large, are welcome when they move the economy toward the target.

9. Ibid., p. xiii.

The central question, then, is whether DJC makes it possible to lift the GNP target, to lower the unemployment rate at which monetary and fiscal policy can aim without continuously raising the rate of inflation. For the long run, does DJC lower this "natural rate" of unemployment, or to use a less normative term, the nonaccelerating-inflation rate of unemployment (NAIRU)? For the short run, when the economy is operating with unemployment higher than the NAIRU, does DJC reduce the inflationary content of any given real growth of GNP?

There are several ways in which DJC might be used to cheat the Phillips curve or lower the NAIRU: reducing frictional unemployment, hiring "end of queue" workers, hiring minimum wage workers, bypassing capacity bottlenecks, and changing the structural pattern of unemployment. These will be discussed in order. The last one is the subject of detailed analysis.

Reducing Frictional Unemployment

Excess demand in any labor market is measured conceptually by the algebraic excess of jobs over labor force, or of job vacancies over unemployed. For given excess demand, both vacancies and unemployment may be high, or they may be low. Unemployment matched by simultaneous vacancies is frictional unemployment. It is a reasonable assumption that inflationary pressure on wages is proportional to excess demand, or depends separately on its components, vacancies and unemployment. If so, both the trade-off and the NAIRU can be improved by reductions of frictional unemployment. Some labor market policies—more efficient exchanges of information, retraining and relocating workers—are specifically designed to place the unemployed in existing vacancies, or to facilitate job searches and shifts without intervening spells of unemployment. These are not central features of DJC. Nevertheless such programs may indirectly diminish frictional unemployment.

First, DJC may improve the vacancy-unemployment relation. Vacancies are not associated with DJC in the same way as with private employment. A new employer has been created who need have no tendency to raise his relative wage because of unfilled openings. Direct job creation can thus effect a structural shift in the usual relation between vacancies and unemployment. Compared to a normal, unselective increase in labor demand, a DJC reduction in unemployment is associated with a smaller increase in vacancies. The NAIRU will be reduced if vacancies have an independent inflationary effect on wages.[10]

This idea is illustrated in figure 1, in which the number of jobs J is measured horizontally, the labor force L and employment N vertically. The curve $L(J)$ indicates the dependence of labor force on job availability; its positive slope represents the well-known fact that labor force participation is responsive to job opportunities. The curve $N(J)$ represents the transformation of jobs into actual employment. Because of "friction," the transformation is imperfect. The vertical shortfall of $N(J)$ from the 45° reference line J indicates the number of vacancies. Unemployment is of course the vertical distance $L - N$. In the lower panel the vacancy rate, relative to jobs, and the unemployment rate, relative to labor force, are shown. One pair of these rates is consistent with stable wage inflation, and this determines the NAIRU and corresponding jobs, vacancies, employment, and labor force.

The dashed lines represent some favorable shifts due to policy actions, perhaps DJC. As indicated, these permit increases in the NAIRU levels of jobs and employment, and a reduction in the unemployment rate. Given the assumption that vacancies have an independent inflationary effect, a policy that will reduce the vacancy slippage in $N(J)$ will diminish the NAIRU. The key point is the control of the rate of change of wages paid in the program. For the picture in figure 1 to work, vacancies in public employment either must be rare or must not have the normal effect on wage inflation.

Figure 1 shows DJC shifting $L(J)$ as well as $N(J)$. This will occur on the reasonable assumption that labor force participation responds to the number of jobs, not just to the number of jobs filled. Here the key feature of DJC is limited eligibility. If vacancies in public employment jobs are not open to persons not previously in the labor force, then such jobs would not draw new workers into the labor force to the same extent that vacancies in the private sector do. Such a shift in $L(J)$ will lower the NAIRU.

Second, DJC may change the relation between unemployment and the amount of job search activity. Direct job creation could reduce actual unemployment without reducing (or only slightly reducing) "effective"

10. In Martin Neil Baily and James Tobin, "Macroeconomic Effects of Selective Public Employment and Wage Subsidies," *BPEA, 2:1977,* pp. 511–41, a simple formal model of the interrelationships described here is developed.

Figure 1. Effects of Labor Market Policy in Reducing Frictional Unemployment

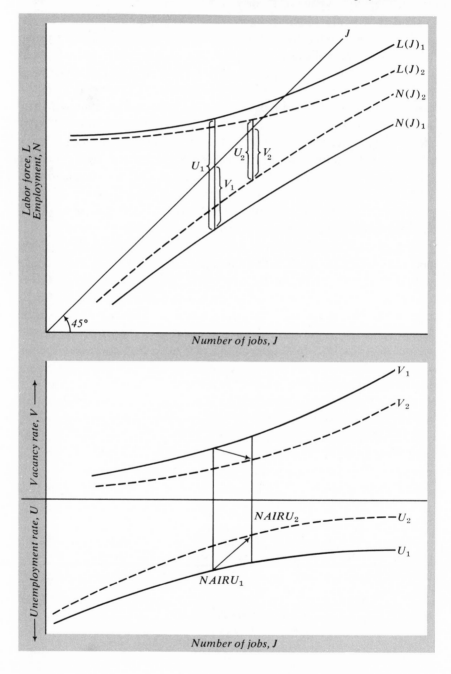

unemployment, that is, the excess supply pressure exerted by the unemployed in restraining wage bargains and in seeking and filling vacancies. In order to achieve this goal, DJC would have to set wages below union or prevailing market rates, and possibly limit the length of job tenure. If it were really true, as some search models say, that seeking information about jobs is the full-time activity of unemployed workers, then there would be few takers for public jobs below market wage rates, and those who did take the jobs would no longer be able to search elsewhere. But, in fact, an employed worker can easily look for a new job. The real advantage, if any, of staying unemployed is not to gain information. It is to remain uncommitted on the chance that a better job, perhaps a job previously held, will open up.[11]

The above argument does not imply that providing public jobs would leave search behavior unchanged. If public jobs were made available to unemployed workers who would otherwise have no source of income while unemployed, such workers might reduce the intensity of their search effort and raise somewhat their standards for accepting a regular job. In practice, however, a large fraction of the unemployed already have access to unemployment insurance or welfare. Hence DJC could transfer workers from the category "unemployed receiving transfers" to the category "employed in temporary public jobs" and lower the unemployment rate without reducing overall excess supply pressure in labor markets. This could be achieved by offering jobs that are only somewhat more attractive than remaining on unemployment insurance, or by reducing or withdrawing transfer benefits for workers who decline the jobs.[12]

A NAIRU-reducing change is not necessarily socially desirable. Whether it is depends on the value of the output produced and the value of intangible results like support of the work ethic. One thing DJC might do much better than transfer payments is to screen out those who really are not unemployed.[13]

---

11. An analogy is search for an apartment or a house while in temporary lodging. It is not very hard to find out what is available at any instant within a chosen area, but the searcher often waits weeks or months for turnover to open up better options.

12. The Carter administration's welfare reform proposals of 1977 included provisions of this type.

13. Several of the issues raised in this section of the paper are discussed in Robert J. Gordon, "The Welfare Cost of Higher Unemployment," *BPEA, 1:1973,* pp. 133–95; J. Peter Mattila, "Job Quitting and Frictional Unemployment," *American Economic Review,* vol. 64 (March 1974), pp. 235–39; Martin S. Feldstein,

The above discussion has been framed in terms of lowering the NAIRU. Both the arguments made about changing the relationship between vacancies and unemployment and those about unemployment and search apply equally in the short run. Direct job creation as part of a fiscal stimulus could flatten the short-run Phillips curve.

Hiring End-of-Queue Workers

According to some models of labor markets, the unemployed are standing in lines at hiring gates, ranked according to their desirability to employers. At the front of the line are employees on temporary layoff with seniority claims to rehiring. After them come other workers with characteristics attractive to employers. Important dimensions are skill and experience, reliability of attendance and performance, probable length of commitment to the labor force and to a particular job, motivation for learning and advancement. In the absence of discriminating tests of individuals on these counts, employers rely on general correlates: education, age, marital and family status, race, sex.

The queue model is consistent with the observation that unemployment rates are much higher for demographic groups with low average scores on these criteria than for prime workers—experienced, well educated, prime age, married white males. Unemployment rates for the secondary groups are especially sensitive to aggregate demand. For wage inflation, the model implies that unemployed workers far back in the queues make very little difference. This is confirmed by econometric Phillips curves, where the unemployment rate for prime workers explains more of the variance of wage movements than unemployment rates for broader categories.

The policy implication is that direct employment of secondary workers can reduce total unemployment with little, if any, effect on wage inflation. This would be true not only in the short run but also in the long run. Although the NAIRU for prime workers would be unchanged, it would

"The Importance of Temporary Layoffs: An Empirical Analysis," *BPEA, 3:1975,* pp. 725–44, and "Temporary Layoffs in the Theory of Unemployment," *Journal of Political Economy,* vol. 84 (October 1976), pp. 937–57; Thomas F. Bradshaw and Janet L. Scholl, "The Extent of Job Search during Layoff" (and the discussion), *BPEA, 2:1976,* pp. 515–26; Martin Neil Baily, "On the Theory of Layoffs and Unemployment," *Econometrica,* vol. 45 (July 1977), pp. 1043–63, and "Some Aspects of Optimal Unemployment Insurance," *Journal of Public Economics,* forthcoming.

correspond to a lower rate of overall unemployment as long as DJC continued. However, the queue model also predicts a nonlinear dependence of secondary unemployment on prime unemployment; the effect should be stronger when prime unemployment is low. The data do not support this implication.[14]

The dual labor market hypothesis differs from the queue model in postulating segmented markets. In the primary market, workers obtain fairly permanent jobs, with fringe benefits, advancement opportunities, seniority rights, and other perquisites. The typical employers are large organizations with technology that puts a premium on specific individual and group experience, low turnover, and common working hours. These characteristics induce employers to offer terms that encourage continuity of employment. The organizations are always vulnerable to demands by their experienced workers for improved benefits. Because of these costs, employers are careful and selective in recruiting. In the secondary market, jobs are temporary, demand less skill, experience, teamwork, and regularity, offer less opportunity for learning and advancement, and provide fewer fringe benefits, seniority protection, and other rights. On the assumption that there is chronic excess supply in the secondary market, the dual market theory has much the same implications as the queue model. Wage trends are dominated by the degree of tightness of the primary market, and direct employment of secondary workers would reduce the overall NAIRU and improve the short-run trade-off.

A puzzle of both the queue and dual models is that they imply persistent failure of labor markets to adapt job specifications and wage rates to the actual distribution of workers of various characteristics and productivities. Are there not jobs for which teenagers, willing to accept temporary employment at low wage rates, are the prime candidates, at the head of the queue? If secondary worker unemployment rates nevertheless remain high, this could be attributed to a number of factors: high mobility between jobs and between gainful employment and other activities gives secondary workers high rates of voluntary unemployment. Minimum wages and significant costs of hiring and separation (for example, employer's unemployment insurance contributions as affected by experience

14. Martin Feldstein and Brian Wright, "High Unemployment Groups in Tight Labor Markets," discussion paper 488 (Harvard Institute of Economic Research, 1976; processed). Additional tests for nonlinearity found no evidence that secondary unemployment is more responsive to changes in primary unemployment in tight markets than in slack markets.

ratings) are imposed by law or union contract and restrict employers' demands for these workers.

Hiring Minimum Wage Workers

To the extent that the minimum wage is the reason for chronic excess supply of teenagers and other secondary workers, DJC would improve the trade-off and lower the overall NAIRU.[15] One way to describe the opportunity is to say that these workers are on a flat segment of their Phillips curve, where excess supply at the minimum wage keeps the rate of wage increase zero over a wide interval of specific unemployment rates. Of course DJC will achieve this result only if the wages of the new jobs are at or below the minimum. Tying wages in public service jobs to union or market wages in primary labor markets would sacrifice the opportunity to cheat the Phillips curve.

This rationalization of DJC strategy does, of course, open the door to the counterproposal of reducing or suspending the minimum wage, at least for those workers who would be eligible for DJC. We would support such a policy, although without the confidence of its enthusiasts that it would solve the whole problem. Anyway, if for other economic, social, and political reasons the minimum wage continues intact, the case for DJC is stronger.

Bypassing Capacity Bottlenecks

Capital capacity may limit the expansion of demand, production, and employment attainable without temporarily high inflation. Indeed capacity limitations may raise the NAIRU, saddling even advanced economies with a species of structural unemployment. Direct job creation, concentrating on labor-intensive production, raises both employment and output without intensifying capacity utilization.

15. Making this assumption requires one to blame the minimum wage for all or most of the problem. The careful study by Edward M. Gramlich, "Impact of Minimum Wages on Other Wages, Employment, and Family Incomes," *BPEA, 2:1976*, pp. 409–51, finds that the 25 percent increase in the minimum wage in 1974 resulted in a 2 percentage point or 13 percent increase in the unemployment rate of workers sixteen to nineteen years old. This is not trivial, but clearly is not the whole story either. Gramlich finds that 22 percent of teenagers earn less than the minimum. Such widespread noncompliance may explain why the law does not have as much impact as some have suggested. Thus, overall, it should not be denied that the minimum wage is a factor, but it may well have been overemphasized.

Changing the Structural Pattern of Unemployment

This section describes the findings of a formal model of labor markets and wage determination within which DJC, wage subsidies, and other policies can be analyzed.[16] Labor markets are segmented but related to each other. While the model does not embody either the queue or dual theory, the basic ideas of both are retained. Wage inflation, for the economy as a whole and for specific industries, is related to several unemployment rates, those for prime workers and for other demographic categories. These unemployment rates may differ in their effects on wage inflation.[17] Thus public employment, concentrated on groups whose unemployment has only a small impact on wage inflation, offers a possible way of reducing the long-run NAIRU and improving the short-run Phillips curve trade-off. But exploiting the possibility presents a more subtle problem than appears at first sight. In the long run, selective employment policies will reduce the unemployment of the target group, but increase the unemployment of prime workers. The net outcome of the trade-off seems quite likely to be a reduction in the number of persons unemployed. There may also be an increase in GNP. Because of the greater productivity of prime workers, though, the conditions for a GNP gain are more stringent than those for an employment gain.

In analysis of DJC and other selective employment policies, it is natural to think of labor markets segmented along demographic lines. In the illustrative model described below, the labor force is divided into two groups, prime-age adults and youth, and policies designed to provide jobs for young people are considered. The choice is not accidental. Jobs for youth surely deserve high priority, given the frightful unemployment rates for teenagers and young adults, particularly nonwhites. But the same principles apply to finer classifications and to criteria other than age. The eligible target population also could be defined by employment experience, skill, occupation, education, wealth, race, or location. For example,

16. The formal model is presented in Baily and Tobin, "Macroeconomic Effects of Selective Public Employment and Wage Subsidies."

17. Perry found that women, young people, blacks, and unskilled workers who are unemployed have a smaller impact per person on the general rate of wage inflation than unemployed adult males. George L. Perry, "Changing Labor Markets and Inflation," *BPEA, 3:1970,* pp. 411–41.

if unemployed workers in inner cities or in depressed regions of the country have a small impact on wage inflation, the analysis would apply to policies creating jobs for them.

The Short Run

In the short run, it is easy to see how concentrating labor demand on sectors of the labor market where the wage response is lower than average can improve the inflation-unemployment trade-off. For a given overall unemployment rate, the average rate of wage inflation will be smaller. But it is not so obvious that this conclusion carries over to the long run. A likely short-run by-product of DJC is to raise the wage of the target group —for example, teenagers—relative to that of prime workers. Relative wages will continue to change as long as the two unemployment rates generate different rates of wage inflation. But wage movements cannot diverge indefinitely; for one thing, persistent changes in relative wages will induce employers to substitute one kind of labor for the other.[18] In the long run, relative wages must settle down, and the two unemployment rates will gravitate to levels consistent with comparable rates of increase of the two wage rates. Moreover, the NAIRU condition—stable rates of inflation—must also be satisfied; that is, aggregate demand and employment will be adjusted to the maximum levels that do not accelerate inflation rates. When these long-run conditions are taken into account, it is not so clear that the short-run gains from public employment programs are permanent.

The Long Run

How is long-run relative wage stability to be reconciled to short-run Phillips curves for the two labor markets? One possible specification for wage adjustment is that the proportional rate of change of wages of each group depends only on the two rates of unemployment and on "feedbacks" from past rates of wage or price inflation. This is the usual "augmented" Phillips curve applied to each labor market separately. If such a formulation is combined with the long-run condition that the relative wage be stable, the implication is that the economy is "locked in" to two

18. It is assumed that there are some technical substitution possibilities. Certainly adults can be substituted for teenagers, and on the margin there are some tasks in which teenagers can take the place of older workers. The condition that the relative wage must be constant in the long run abstracts from secular trends in technology or in the sizes of the two populations.

unique unemployment rates and thus to a unique aggregate NAIRU.[19] There are not enough degrees of freedom to allow DJC, or any other policy, to change the NAIRU. The program is defeated because hiring teenagers into public jobs, lowering their unemployment rate in the short run, drives up their relative wage and leads to the substitution of adults for teenagers in private employment. This process, plus the necessary adjustment of private output to avoid wage acceleration, will eventually stop when a number of teenagers equal to the number employed in public jobs has been displaced from private employment. We do not subscribe to this impossibility theorem. As will be explained, the formulation that leads to it ignores a significant degree of freedom. But qualitatively, the displacement effect *is* important. It is quite distinct both from overall "crowding out" and from "displacement" due to direct substitution of DJC for regular public services, points discussed earlier.

The missing degree of freedom is the effect of the relative wage itself on wage inflation in the two markets. There are several reasons to expect the wage in a labor market to rise faster when it is low relative to other wages. First, employers pay attention to relative wages in setting wage offers to the two types of labor. Second, and perhaps more compelling, the job search and turnover behavior of teenagers or other secondary workers will be affected by their relative wage. Much teenage unemployment, it is often observed, comes from dissatisfaction with the available job options, a gap between expectations or aspirations and the realities of low wages and poor working conditions. One consequence is high turnover. Even when jobs are available, therefore, unemployment is high; in the interval between two unattractive jobs, an individual teenager does not provide much excess supply pressure on the market. If the relative position of teenagers were improved—in both wages and working conditions—turnover would be less and the availability of unemployed teenagers would be a more effective brake on wages. Third, when adult workers are bargaining for wage increases, they consider the risk of losing jobs to cheaper and younger competitors. When their relative wage is high, adult workers may moderate their own wage demands or even bargain for higher teenage wages.[20]

19. This is the formulation focused on by George Johnson in his paper in this volume.

20. Some analysis of behavior of this kind is in Martin Neil Baily, "Contract Theory and the Moderation of Inflation by Recession and by Controls," *BPEA, 3:1976,* pp. 585–622.

Introducing the relative wage into sectoral wage equations provides the missing degree of freedom. With this addendum to conventional Phillips curves, DJC can lower the NAIRU. Figure 2 is illustrative. The horizontal length of the box is the adult labor force. Employment of adults is measured horizontally from the left-hand corners, their unemployment from the right. Similarly the height of the box is the teenage labor force, with employment measured upward, unemployment downward. The curve *CBA* is the NAIRU locus, the combinations of the two numbers of unemployed consistent with nonaccelerating inflation. Each point on this locus corresponds to a different relative wage; moving up the locus to the left, the adult wage falls relative to that of teenagers. Lines of 45° slope, such as the ones through *A* and tangent at *B,* indicate constant total employment and unemployment. Thus, *B* gives the minimum number of persons unemployed consistent with nonaccelerating inflation.

The initial mix of government jobs is reflected in the position of point *E*. Private employers hire the two types of workers in amounts indicated by path *EA* for a particular relative wage, namely the one that supports point *A* on the locus. The NAIRU corresponding to point *A* is attainable by suitable aggregate demand policy. A jobs-for-youth program is shown as a shift in government employment for young people from *E* to *D*.[21] If there were no change in the relative wage, the point *C* on the locus would be reached. *DC* is shown as a parallel displacement of *EA*. Because the relative wage does change in favor of teenagers, however, there is some displacement of young workers from private employment.

In the new equilibrium, *DB* is the employment path, corresponding to a relative wage consistent with point *B* on the locus. In this new equilibrium, adult unemployment is higher than at *A*. The increase in adult unemployment is necessary to offset the pressure for faster wage increases generated by the relative decline in the adult wage. Thus increased government employment displaces some workers of both kinds from private employment. Since by assumption the DJC was introduced into an economy already at full employment (point *A*), it is not surprising that, in order to avoid accelerating inflation, the government must manage aggregate demand so as to diminish private output and employment.

An increase in overall employment is not necessarily an increase in GNP. That requires an increase in wage-weighted employment—assum-

21. For illustrative purposes the shift is made very large—big enough to reach point *B,* the minimum overall NAIRU. Actual programs would presumably be much smaller.

Figure 2. Impact of a Program of Direct Job Creation for Teenagers

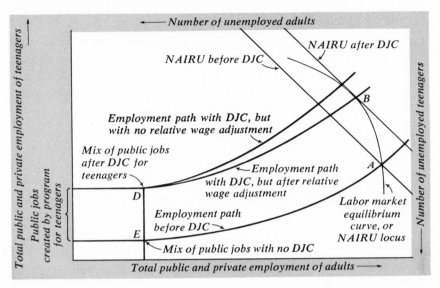

ing that the relative wages of the two groups approximate their relative productivities per worker. In figure 2 a line through A (not shown) with a slope equal to the ratio of adult wage to teenage wage would be steeper than the 45° line shown. Only if such a line is less steep than the NAIRU locus at point A would it be possible for policy to engineer a gain in wage-weighted employment and GNP.

Some Empirical Estimates

It is important to know not only whether DJC can conceivably reduce unemployment in the long run, but also how effectively, and to know whether it can raise GNP, and, if so, by how much. According to our analysis, the key parameters are those of the wage adjustment relation or Phillips curves for the two groups of workers—adults and teenagers in this example. To get an idea of the possible effectiveness of DJC, some educated guesses about the values of these parameters can be made.

The greater the response of adult wages to a given absolute change in adult unemployment than the response of teenage wages to the same change in teenage unemployment, the greater the reduction in unemployment in the long run. Estimates of aggregate wage equations suggest a ratio of the two slopes as a little more than three to one.[22] But this is probably rather a conservative figure. For example, in 1974 the adult and teenage unemployment rates were 4.5 percent and 16 percent, respectively. This was when the aggregate unemployment rate was 5.5 percent, close to many people's estimated NAIRU. If one disaggregates to separate sectoral Phillips curves for adults and teenagers, and these curves depend on the reciprocals of the adult and teenage unemployment rates, respectively, then a larger ratio of slopes (six to one is estimated here) is quite feasible.[23]

Other parameters are, first, the elasticity of substitution between adults and teenagers. A Cobb-Douglas production function implies an elasticity of unity. This value plus the smaller value of one-half to span the reasonable range is used. Second, it is necessary to know roughly what increase in the adult unemployment rate would be necessary in order to maintain equilibrium in the adult labor market if the adult relative wage fell by 10 percent. Two alternative answers are considered, a 10 percent increase (say, from 4.5 percent to 4.95 percent) and a 5 percent increase (from 4.5 percent to 4.73 percent).

Given a pair of alternative values for each parameter, it is not surprising that there is a fairly wide range of estimated outcomes of a DJC program. Suppose one hundred teenagers are hired into a jobs program. The central estimates are that this will reduce the number of teenaged unemployed by about seventy-five and reduce the total number of unemployed by about fifty (adult unemployment increases by about twenty-five). The confidence intervals around these values are wide, however.[24] The impact on GNP depends crucially on which of the two NAIRU locus slope values is chosen. If the value of three to one is chosen, the impact of the program on GNP is zero. If the value of six to one is chosen, then about one-half of the budgetary cost of hiring the teenagers shows up as a gain in GNP.

In one important way the above unemployment numbers are too optimistic, because variations in labor force participation were ignored. Tak-

22. Perry's aggregate curve in "Changing Labor Markets and Inflation" suggests this ratio. But it is not a parameter whose magnitude he freely estimates.

23. See Baily and Tobin, "Macroeconomic Effects of Selective Public Employment and Wage Subsidies," for further details.

24. The reduction in teenage unemployment could be as little as forty-three or as much as eighty-five. The reduction in total unemployment could be as little as twenty-nine or as much as seventy-one.

ing this into account would certainly weaken the impact of DJC on the NAIRU. However, to the extent that young persons drawn into the labor market are from the ranks of the discouraged idle or from actual or potential delinquents, the desirability of such programs is not changed. In addition, an increase in the size of the teenage labor force would mean that the above estimates of the GNP impact of a jobs program are too pessimistic.

Wage Subsidies as an Alternative to DJC

The previous discussion has focused primarily on the consequences of public employment programs. With some amendment, it is also relevant to a broad class of wage subsidies.

The idea of paying a wage subsidy to increase employment has been around for a long time. Recently, temporary but general wage subsidies have been proposed as a remedy for high unemployment, possibly confined to incremental hiring.[25] A second type, the one considered here, is a selective wage subsidy limited to particular categories of workers. For example, Feldstein has suggested giving to all teenagers vouchers that could be used either for schooling or for subsidizing employers who hire them.[26] The Orcutts have recently proposed a wage subsidy for all workers who, during the preceding twelve months, had been unemployed for more than some stated amount of time.[27]

Feldstein's classification fits with the analysis here, since his proposal is intended to improve the position of a particular demographic group. The Orcutts' segmentation of the labor market differs from the classifications used in this paper. However, their proposal too would presumably give the most assistance to those groups with the highest unemployment rates. Within groups there is almost certainly a wide dispersion of unemployment experience, and the Orcutts propose to help the relatively disadvantaged, whatever their demographic group. In Phillips curve terms the argument must be that the disadvantaged—defined by high incidence of unemployment in the preceding period—exert less restraining pressure

25. This is the type of subsidy focused upon by Daniel S. Hamermesh in his paper in this volume.

26. Martin S. Feldstein, *Lowering the Permanent Rate of Unemployment,* A Study for the Joint Economic Committee of Congress, 1:93 (GPO, 1973), chap. 3.

27. Guy Orcutt and Geil Orcutt, "A Proposal to Increase Employment" (Yale University, February 1977; processed).

on wages. This is probably true, although a counterargument is that persons who have been unemployed a long time are more anxious to find new jobs and are more willing to accept a given wage.[28]

SIMILARITY OF DJC AND WAGE SUBSIDY. Certainly a wage subsidy scheme can be devised as an alternative to DJC, to apply to the same group of workers. The same analytical apparatus can be used to analyze the impact of a wage subsidy on the NAIRU. The basic mechanism is an induced shift in the employment mix (as depicted, for example, by the expansion path EA in figure 2) in favor of subsidized workers. In an extreme case, the relative wage rates received by both groups would remain the same as before the subsidy. Employers would then substitute subsidized workers for the now relatively more expensive unsubsidized workers. At the other extreme, the entire subsidy is passed through to low-wage workers in the form of higher wages; postsubsidy relative wage rates paid by employers remain unchanged, there is no substitution in employment, and the subsidy benefits only those low-wage workers already employed. So the question is: what happens to wage rates received and paid? A similar question was, of course, crucial to the analysis of DJC.

Three cases may be distinguished. First, relative wage rates received by workers could be rigid, possibly as a result of the minimum wage law. If so, a subsidy would encourage employers to hire minimum-wage workers and allow a reduction in the NAIRU. Feldstein explicitly assumes such a model, placing the blame for high teenage unemployment on the minimum wage. The second possibility is that sectoral Phillips curves determine uniquely two equilibrium unemployment rates and a unique overall NAIRU. In this case, as we saw above, DJC could not lower the NAIRU and neither can a wage subsidy. A subsidy on teenage wage rates would lower teenage unemployment for a while, but over time the wage received by teenagers would rise by the amount of the subsidy, leaving unemployment where it was before.

---

28. There is even evidence to support this—at least the acceptance wage part. See Hirschel Kasper, "The Asking Price of Labor and the Duration of Unemployment," *Review of Economics and Statistics,* vol. 49 (May 1967), pp. 165–72. Another potential difficulty with the Orcutt proposal is "moral hazard." It is difficult and costly to determine whether or not someone is really looking for work or is out of the labor force. In addition, firms would have an incentive to concentrate temporary layoffs on a small group of workers (even more than they already do) rather than spreading the burden more evenly (by short-term plant closings, for example). By this means some workers would build up eligibility for the subsidy.

The third, and most interesting and realistic case, is intermediate: the sectoral Phillips curve relations are influenced by the relative wages received by the different groups of workers. It was shown above that in this case DJC can increase employment of the beneficiary group, partly at the expense of other workers, and lower the NAIRU. The wage subsidy has much the same effect. Employers substitute subsidized for unsubsidized workers. The reduction in unemployment of the subsidized group speeds up their wage inflation, while the increase in unemployment of other workers slows down their wage inflation. But the process stops before it erases the substitution incentive provided by the subsidy. This can be seen by imagining the contrary, that unemployment rates revert to their presubsidy levels, with relative wage costs to employers the same as before. The wage received by subsidized workers would then have risen relative to other wages, and this would slow down the inflation of subsidized workers' wages compared to other wages.[29] The NAIRU equilibrium is at an intermediate point: the relative wage received by subsidized workers is higher, but by less than the subsidy; substitution in favor of subsidized workers has occurred.

The similarity of DJC and wage subsidies is more than qualitative. It can be shown that under the simplifying assumption that the elasticity of substitution between two groups of workers is unity, there is a budgetary equivalence between the two approaches. If the money used to employ one hundred teenagers in public jobs were used to provide a wage subsidy to all teenagers, then there would be the exact same long-run reduction in unemployment (about fifty workers in our numerical example). If the two types of workers are not very substitutable, then public jobs give a greater reduction in unemployment per budget dollar; the opposite is true if the two types are highly substitutable.

DEPICTING THE WAGE SUBSIDY. The working of the wage subsidy is illustrated in figure 3, which is analogous to figure 2. As before, the locus *CBA* gives the combinations of adult and teenage unemployment rates

29. This account assumes that the relative wage effect on sectoral wage change reflects worker behavior, search, and bargaining. Thus relative wages received and perceived by workers are what matter. An alternative interpretation would be that the Phillips relations, including the relative wage terms, describe firm behavior, with relative wage costs to the employer the relevant calculation. If so, the wage subsidy could not alter NAIRU, although in the same circumstances DJC could. But, even if the Phillips relations describe, in important degree, employers' wage-setting behavior, the wages they are setting are those to which they perceive their existing workers and possible recruits are responding.

that equilibrate both labor markets. To each point corresponds a relative wage, the wage received by an adult worker relative to the wage received by a young worker. This relative wage rises as the point moves southwest along the locus, for example, from C to B to A. At point A adult unemployment is lower than at C; this evokes greater pressure for wage increases, and it takes a higher adult wage level to contain it. At point A teenage unemployment is higher than at C; the deflationary effect on teenage wages is offset by the low level of the teenage wage compared to the adult wage.

Point E represents government employment, and the path EA the mix of private employment of the two kinds of workers. The path depends on the relative wage from the employers' perspective. A high adult wage makes the path steeper, diminishing the adult component of employment along the path. In the absence of a wage subsidy or jobs program, point A is the full equilibrium. This means that the relative wage associated with point A of the NAIRU locus is the same as that associated with path EA. Now suppose a subsidy is introduced while the wages received by adults and teenagers are temporarily unchanged. The relative wage confronting employers is changed favorably to employment of teenagers.

Figure 3. Impact of a Wage Subsidy for Teenagers

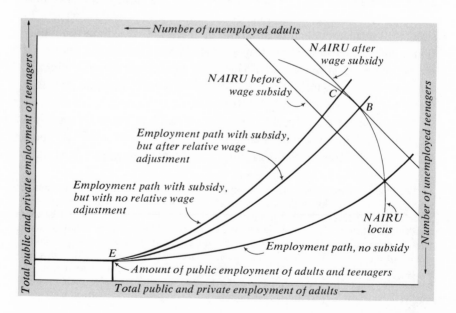

Graphically, the employment path shifts from *EA* to *EC*. But on the NAIRU locus point *C* is no longer consistent with stability of relative wages received by workers; the adult wage must fall relative to the teenage wage. As this happens, the employment path rotates clockwise. The new equilibrium is at point *B*. Thanks to the subsidy, the employment expansion path *EB* is more favorable to teenagers than the original one *EA*. Thanks to the resulting increase in teenage wages, which partially offsets the employment incentive of the subsidy, NAIRU point *B* is consistent with lower teenage unemployment, higher adult unemployment, lower overall unemployment.

THE CHOICE BETWEEN DJC AND WAGE SUBSIDIES. The above discussion has, of course, oversimplified the comparison between the programs in several respects. First, choice between the two programs would involve evaluation of DJC output relative to that of increased private employment. Second, DJC would require additional budgetary outlays for administration and materials. Third, political resistance to a wage subsidy is likely to be stronger than to DJC. Workers are most aware of and most concerned about events they can perceive and understand in their immediate environment. If there were a wage subsidy program for youths, adult workers would perceive rather quickly the incentive for firms to substitute youth employment for adult employment. One consequence is that workers will start to insist on higher wages paid to young workers in order to resist the substitution.

This adverse reaction to selective wage subsidies may be minimized by limiting voucher redemption to employers who can show that their total employment of unsubsidized workers has not decreased, or has increased by a specified amount. But such constraints, if binding, would limit the attractiveness of the subsidy to individual employers and its effectiveness in reducing NAIRU. There is no getting round the implication of this analysis that the policy, if it works at all in the long run, does increase the NAIRU of prime workers.

As for the political acceptability of DJC, adult workers do not perceive incremental public jobs, especially of a "make-work" type, as competing with their own private employment. However, if the jobs program tries to do some of the most socially productive things, like rehabilitating neighborhood buildings and improving city services, then specific unions will resist what they see as displacement of their jobs.

Fourth, the comparison of effectiveness of the two approaches depends on the assumption that there would be a general wage subsidy to all teenagers. A more closely targeted subsidy, or one subsidizing incremental hiring, might be more effective.

DJC and Wage Inflation in the Short Run

In the previous two sections the emphasis has been on the long-run equilibrium effects of DJC, and whether and how it is possible to reduce the minimal unemployment rate associated with nonaccelerating inflation. A related but somewhat different question has been referred to in passing: Does DJC improve the short-run inflation-unemployment trade-off? This is important in current discussions of jobs programs as an instrument of short-run fiscal policy, part of a package to stimulate economic recovery.

In the discussion of the possibility that DJC could reduce frictional unemployment, it was argued that it could reduce the NAIRU by: (a) reducing the slippage between job creation and employment—the vacancy rate; (b) diminishing the response of labor force participation to the availability of jobs; and (c) reducing the wage pressure associated with a given reduction of unemployment. (The first two effects depend on the assumption that the vacancy rate, independently of the unemployment rate, affects the rate of wage inflation.) The features of DJC that could lead to these three effects are: the selective eligibility of workers, the administrative control of the wage rate, and the special incentive DJC employees have to search for normal jobs. These conclusions all apply to the short-run trade-off as well. Anything that reduces frictional unemployment at the NAIRU will also make the short-run Phillips curve for the economy flatter.

The strategy discussed in the previous section is to use DJC to lower the NAIRU by changing the employment mix in favor of groups of workers whose unemployment has below-average effect on aggregate wage inflation. Clearly the same strategy will work in the short run too. Indeed there is more scope for the strategy in the short run, because the long-run constraint that all wage rates must be moving in step, preserving the relative wage structure, does not apply.

There are two circumstances in which this short-run strategy can "cheat the Phillips curve." The obvious one, and the more important, is that DJC workers are on flatter portions of their Phillips curves than other workers. But even if this is not so, the policy may work. Suppose eligible workers have a smaller share of the aggregate wage bill than of the labor force. This is likely because they are low-wage and high-unemployment types of workers. It means they have less weight in the overall wage index than in the overall unemployment rate. Shifting jobs to them will, just because of the weighting difference, yield an improvement of the trade-off. However, much of this gain would vanish if a wage-weighted unemployment measure were substituted for a count of persons. In other words, DJC and other labor market interventions might improve the unemployment-inflation trade-off without improving, and conceivably even worsening, the GNP-inflation trade-off.

Summary of Additional Empirical Findings

The possibilities of "cheating the Phillips curve" by DJC—or by other labor market policies—depend importantly, according to the arguments presented above, on four hypotheses: (a) vacancies are, independently of unemployment rates, significant for wage inflation; (b) primary unemployment, for example of adults, is more determinative of aggregate wage behavior than unemployment of other workers; (c) relative wage levels affect wage adjustments in specific markets or industries; (d) some workers are on flat Phillips curves because of the minimum wage. For such workers, changes in the minimum wage will be a significant determinant of their wage rates.

Some econometric calculations bearing on the four important hypotheses just listed have been attempted. The findings have been reported in some detail elsewhere.[30] Confidence in them should be limited; anyone who tries to estimate Phillips curves from time series must admit that the data do not speak loudly and clearly.

Wage inflation regressions were estimated for the economy as a whole (quarterly 1958–76) and for seven industrial sectors[31] (quarterly for varying sample periods). The explanatory variables included: (a) unemployment rates for three age groups, adjusted for the labor force shares of the groups; (b) as a proxy for the vacancy rate, the Conference Board help-wanted index relative to total employment (HWI); (c) various

30. Baily and Tobin, "Macroeconomic Effects of Selective Public Employment and Wage Subsidies."
31. Manufacturing; wholesale and retail trade; services; mining; transportation; construction; finance, insurance, and real estate.

lagged wage and price indexes, including the minimum wage, to represent inflation patterns and expectations; (d) in the disaggregated equations, the ratio of the sector wage to the overall average.

The vacancy proxy, HWI, proved to be significant and important in the aggregate regressions, indeed stronger than unemployment rates. Three of the sectoral equations, including manufacturing, confirmed this finding. Of the unemployment rates, that for workers over twenty-five was generally the only one that appeared to matter for wage inflation. Changes in the minimum wage performed well in both the aggregate and disaggregated equations.

The central theoretical proposition in this paper was the influence of relative wage *levels* on the rates of increase of sectoral wages. This hypothesis received quite impressive support from the sectoral regressions. Of the twenty-one equations estimated (three specifications for each sector), sixteen coefficients of the relative wage variable had the expected sign and many of them were significant. The only consistently perverse signs were in the equations for construction, an industry known for bizarre wage behavior during the sample period.

The findings encourage the belief that the theoretical analysis has some relevance. But the evidence is qualitative, not quantitative. It is not now possible to estimate reliably the reduction in the NAIRU or in the short-run wage inflation to be expected from direct employment policies.

Conclusion

This paper has investigated the possibility that direct job creation can mitigate the painful conflict of objectives in macroeconomic policy. The hopes are that DJC can diminish the inflationary by-products of unemployment reductions in the short run and can in the long run permit monetary and fiscal policies to aim at lower unemployment rates without so tightening labor markets that inflation persistently accelerates.

The analysis lends some credence to these hopes, but justifies only restrained optimism. The simplistic negative view that every public job displaces a private job is rejected. The "crowding out" propositions advanced to support such sweeping generalizations do not apply to an underemployed economy. Even when the economy is at full employment—that is, the natural rate or nonaccelerating-inflation rate of unemployment—direct policy to change the mix of employment can reduce overall unemployment. On the other hand, the naive view of some DJC enthusiasts that every new public job reduces unemployment without any inflationary consequence or any displacement of other jobs must also be rejected. Public employment programs will, if only indirectly, tighten some labor markets and increase wage pressures. In the long run, containment of these pressures will require some reduction in private employment. The displacement is likely to be fractional rather than job-for-job, so that unemployment is reduced in aggregate, not simply redistributed. Moreover, the conditions for a GNP-increasing reduction of unemployment are more stringent than for a reduction in the unemployment count. After all, the high-wage workers who become unemployed are the more productive. GNP may be increased, and, even if it is not, the redistribution of employment may be socially and economically desirable. But proponents of DJC should not expect or claim too much.

The macroeconomic success of jobs programs will depend on certain specific features. The labor market tightening impact of DJC can be minimized in several ways. Eligibility for the jobs should be strictly controlled and priority given to workers who are not strongly competitive in normal labor markets; the wage paid should be fixed, independently of the numbers of vacancies and applicants, and held below prevailing market wages, preferably at or below the legal minimum; employees should be encouraged to seek normal jobs, and their tenure in a DJC program should be limited; emphasis should be placed on experience, training, and work habits suitable for normal jobs.

Even with these features, one must suspect that DJC and related employment policies are far from the whole answer to the unemployment-inflation dilemma. While these measures can make some contribution, it is doubtful that society will succeed in achieving tolerably low rates of unemployment and inflation simultaneously without some kind of incomes policy, directly affecting the setting of wages and prices in both public and private sectors.

The motivations for DJC are not solely macroeconomic; the policies may be justified on considerations other than their modest amelioration of the unemployment-inflation trade-off. One should, in any case, beware of purely statistical and cosmetic changes in price indexes and unemployment counts. Shifting a person from recorded unemployment to employment in a job empty of product and training is useless or worse. Employing productively a discouraged or demoralized person previously "not in labor force" is worthwhile even though the unemployment statistic shows no reduction. The outputs of public jobs—in socially useful tasks accomplished and in human capital preserved and improved—are in the end the principal criteria for evaluating the programs.

Appendix: Algebraic Model for Differential Multipliers

This appendix presents a formal algebraic model for comparing the multipliers for DJC expenditure with those of other fiscal stimuli.

The model is as follows:

$$(1) \qquad\qquad Y = A + E + G.$$

This is the conventional GNP (Y) identity, where A is autonomous private (really nonfederal) expenditure, E is induced nonfederal spending, G is federal purchases. G is equal to $\sum_i G_i$ where each G_i is spending of type i. DJC would be one such type.

$$(2) \qquad\qquad E = aA + aE + \sum_i a_i G_i - \sum_j C_j(T_j).$$

Induced spending E is linearly related to various kinds of income. The marginal propensity to spend from income generated by nonfederal purchases of GNP is a. For other purposes it would be possible to distinguish among such purchases and associate a specific marginal propensity with each type. Here this is done only for government purchases G_i. The T_js represent various federal taxes ($+$) and transfers ($-$). The spending associated with T_j is given by the function $C_j(T_j)$, to be described below in 5. The a_i may differ from a and $C_j(T_j)$ from aT_j because the government programs reach special population subsets, or because they evoke different expectations from other sources of income.

$$(3) \qquad\qquad T_j = \bar{T}_j + t_j(A + E) + \sum_i t_{ji} G_i - \sum_{k, k \neq j} t_{jk} T_k.$$

A tax or transfer program is described as a linear function of GNP Y, government purchases of various types G_i, and other government tax and transfer programs. $\bar{T}_j$ is the intercept, t_j the usual aggregative marginal tax rate, t_{ji} the specific marginal rate for income generated by government purchases of type i, t_{jk} the marginal tax rate on receipts from other transfer programs or the marginal allowance in program j for taxes paid on account k. Equation 3 is a linear equation system for the T_j in terms of $\bar{T}_j$, Y, G_i. It may be solved to give

$$(4) \qquad T_j = \bar{T}'_j + t'_j(A + E) + \sum_i t'_{ji} G_i,$$

where the $\bar{T}'_j$, t'_j, and t'_{ji} depend on the parameters of 3, including the interaction coefficients t_{jk}. The linear tax and transfer system 4, therefore, should be interpreted to include tax deductions for taxes, taxes on transfers, and similar interrelationships.

$$(5) \qquad C_j(T_j) = c_j \bar{T}'_j + c_j t'_j(A + E) + \sum_i c_{ji} t'_{ji} G_i.$$

Here the general marginal propensity to spend from transfers is c_j, which might be equal to a. However, allowance is made for differential propensity from taxes and transfers for recipients of income from the various G_i, the c_{ji}. These might be equal to a_i.

$$(6) \qquad E = a(A + E + G) + \sum_i (a_i - a)G_i - \sum_j c_j \bar{T}'_j$$
$$- \left(\sum_j c_j t'_j \right)(Y - G) - \sum_i \left(\sum_j c_{ji} t'_{ji} \right) G_i.$$

Let $c = \sum_j c_j t'_j$, and use 1:

$$(7) \qquad Y(1 - a + c) = A + G + \sum_i (a_i - a)G_i$$
$$- \sum_i \left(\sum_j c_{ji} t'_{ji} - c \right) G_i - \sum_j c_j \bar{T}'_j.$$

Thus the standard multiplier m (for A), is $1/(1 - a + c)$.

Under the conventional assumption that disposable income is what matters, regardless of source, $c_j = a$ and $c = a \sum_j t'_j$. Likewise $c_{ji} = a_i$. Let $\sum_j t'_j$ be t', $\sum_j \bar{T}'_j$ be $\bar{T}'$, and $\sum_j t'_{ji}$ be t'_i. Then

$$(8) \quad Y(1 - a + at') = A + G + \sum_i (a_i - a)G_i - \sum (a_i t'_i - at')G_i - a\bar{T}'.$$

The GNP multiplier for G_i is, from 7:

$$(9) \qquad m_i = \frac{1 + (a_i - a) - \left(\sum_i c_{ji}t'_{ji} - c\right)}{1 - a + c}$$

or from 8:

$$(10) \qquad m_i = \frac{1 + (a_i - a) - (a_i t'_i - at')}{1 - a + at'}.$$

The *budget deficit* D is $G - \sum_j T_j$:

$$(11) \qquad D = G - \sum_j \bar{T}'_j - \left(\sum_j t'_j\right) Y - \sum_j \sum_i (t'_{ji} - t'_j)G_i$$

$$(12) \qquad \frac{\partial D}{\partial G_i} = 1 - \left(\sum_j t'_j\right) m_i - \sum_j (t_{ji} - t'_j).$$

Total employment N is given by:

$$(13) \qquad N = n(A + E) + \sum_i n_i G_i = nY + \sum_i (n_i - n)G_i$$

$$(14) \qquad \frac{\partial N}{\partial G_i} = nm_i + (n_i - n) = n(m_i - 1) + n_i,$$

a formula that says simply that the specific jobs coefficient n_i applies to the "first round" and the generalized jobs coefficient n to the remainder of the multiplier m_i.

Comments by Charles C. Holt

Baily and Tobin have precisely defined their target which is one of the critical issues of this conference. They are concerned with measures to shift the Phillips curve in order to allow further reductions in unemployment without excessive inflation once aggregate demand policy has accomplished all that it can. There are two broad manpower policy approaches for shifting the Phillips curve: traditional manpower programs such as training, mobility, and so on that improve the efficiency of labor markets; and manipulation of the structure of demand so that it is concentrated in the slack areas of the labor market where it will give more stimulus to employment and a minimal stimulus to inflation. The paper by Baily and Tobin is most welcome because it focuses on the latter approach, which has received relatively little attention in the public debates and policy analysis.

Within the broad framework of the inflation-unemployment problem, Baily and Tobin consider the following issues: (1) crowding out (will there be a net effect on unemployment?); (2) bang for the buck (how much stimulus to GNP does one get from public service employment compared to alternative public expenditures?); and (3) the effect on the Phillips curve (how effective is the public service employment approach to lowering unemployment without contributing to inflation?). They present formal models for analyzing these issues and apply one of the models to the wage subsidy approach to shifting demand toward slack sectors.

Their treatment of the crowding-out issue is essentially a tipping of their hats to Milton Friedman, who argues you cannot accomplish anything with fiscal policy and, if you could, you should not. I think that what Baily and Tobin say in this regard is precisely right. Their discussion might have been reduced to a footnote, but it is probably just as well to indicate that one is aware of some likely counterarguments. A lot depends on the relative impact of monetary policy compared to fiscal policy, but they do not devote a great deal of attention to this, and I believe that is appropriate.

The bang for the buck is analyzed with a conventional multiplier model. Only at the end of the analysis do they mention why this is an important question to consider. To most economists at least, the risk of inflation usually limits how much the economy can be stimulated. Other than this it is not obvious why the government should have any particular concern for limiting the total of public and private expenditures.

However, there are three reasons why bang for the buck is an important issue. One is the size of the deficit, which appears to be very important to the public. Another is the budget allocation process. There is tremendous competition among government agencies for spending money, so any program is under pressure to indicate relative beneficial results for each dollar spent in competition with other programs. If public service employment legislation is to pass, it is necessary to deal with both the political and budget issues that are involved. To the amazement and chagrin of most economists, the balanced budget and the concern with the deficit still have tremendous clout in the political arena. The third reason concerns monetary policy, under the control of the Federal Reserve System, which traditionally puts great stress on the threat of inflation. When monetary policy tends to be excessively conservative, fiscal stimulus must be doubly effective.

An advantage of public service employment programs then is their high first-order impact on GNP. If public service employment channels money to low-income people who have high marginal propensities to consume, this will strongly stimulate the economy. The stimulus to the economy will be even greater if this group's income is taxed at relatively low rates. Offsetting these substantial gains to the economy is the likelihood that the total flow to low-income people is not great because they are already beneficiaries of governmental transfer programs. These are, I think, straightforward and well understood issues.

The principal thrust of the paper is concerned with shifting the Phillips curve by manipulating demand in the direction of the slack sectors of the economy.[32] Baily and Tobin illustrate this by contrasting unemployment among youth and adults. However, their discussion could apply to slack employment sectors defined along regional, occupational, industrial, or other lines. Slack could occur in all at the same time with corresponding implications for employment policy. Baily and Tobin suggest that, in a supply and demand market structure that is segmented in various ways—regionally, occupationally, and demographically—and in which there is not a complete, frictionless transfer of resources back and forth, channeling demand into those areas where demand is low will have a relatively large impact on employment with a relatively small impact on inflation. Note that such a program would constitute a type of structural change.

In order for the strategy of channeling demand toward slack sectors to be effective in a private economy whose composition of demand (industrially and regionally) is constantly changing, the targets of jobs programs have to be equally dynamic. The authors do not discuss this issue, but it should be considered when designing public service employment programs.

While economists will find a plausible appeal in this approach to reducing unemployment and inflation, there is not an adequately developed body of theory for dealing with the inflation process on a structural basis.

32. Baily and Tobin use the expression "cheating the Phillips curve," which is undesirably loaded. I think that "shifting the Phillips curve" is not only neutral but more accurate. I suppose everyone is against cheating, but I hope that all are *for* shifting the Phillips curve.

This paper advances in rather general terms a theoretical model for coping with segmented labor markets. The authors estimate some key parameters, but the paucity of empirical work that they can draw on reflects the fact that structural research relating to inflation and unemployment has been largely neglected. Most of the policy concern and analysis of inflation and unemployment has been at the macro level. This paper makes an important contribution by crystallizing some key structural problems and proposing a framework for analysis of the problems.

At one point Baily and Tobin, having examined correlation evidence, point out that the inflation rate is more highly correlated with prime-age unemployment than with more broadly defined unemployment, and they conclude that the inflation process is more directly related to what goes on in the prime markets. This is followed by a good deal of discussion about primary and secondary labor markets. They are really using the notion of a "dual labor market" as a proxy for *all* the different ways that the labor market is segmented; this ought to be clarified. There clearly is occupational, regional, sexual, and racial segmentation, with important real phenomena connected with each. Reality is much more complex than is suggested by the term *secondary* labor markets.

I have two additional problems with this conclusion. First, no correlation necessarily shows causality. Second, *changes* in rates of participation in the labor force are much less important in primary than in secondary labor markets. For that reason alone, even if secondary labor markets were just as much involved in the inflation process as the primary ones, using an unemployment measure that does not adequately reflect this participation phenomenon would cause primary unemployment to correlate better with inflation.

The authors face very tough statistical problems in trying to infer the impact of structural measures. *All* of the wage changes and unemployment rates tend to be highly correlated; they move together. The empirical evidence available has been generated in an economy that has not had many significant structural interventions.

Even though there may be scant empirical support for the position that the primary labor markets are more correlated with the inflation process than the slack sectors, there is no question that fluctuation in the unemployment rate for given changes in the inflation rate is much larger for secondary labor markets than for primary markets. What is relevant for predicting inflation changes are percentage changes in unemployment rather than incremental changes in its level.

Thus, for a given change in inflation impact, the unemployment rate in a primary sector might change by 0.5 percent while the unemployment rate in a secondary labor market changes by 2 percent. For a given inflationary impact fewer people could be employed in the primary sectors of the labor market than in the secondary. This provides empirical support for the employment strategy that Baily and Tobin are proposing. A job created in a secondary labor market will have less inflationary impact than one in a primary market.

But the real difficulty in assessing this policy approach arises from the fact that all of these labor markets are tied together through a structure of relative wages. Much more needs to be known about the equilibrating processes that the policy is working against. The authors' formula for dealing with this issue relates percentage changes in money wages in a particular sector of the economy to both the unemployment rate in that sector and the wages in that sector relative to the rest of the economy. If wages in that sector already are relatively high, that will restrain further increases, because demand will tend to be diverted to other sectors. Consequently, the inflation process can be restrained by increasing unemployment or by increasing relative wages. That provides the opening for intervention in the slack sector to reduce both inflation and unemployment, by changing both the composition of unemployment and the structure of relative wages.

For example, if an employment policy is used to increase demand for teenagers and thereby lower unemployment among youth, the relative wage for teenagers must rise in order for the inflation rate to be unaffected. This lowers the relative wage for adults, thereby lessening the restraint on adult wages. If their wage inflation rate is not to be increased, the adult unemployment rate must rise. The net effect is to bring the wage and unemployment rates of adults and teenagers closer together, but because teenagers gain more than adults lose, there presumably is a net social gain in efficiency and equity. Since the net gains in efficiency depend on combining positive and negative effects on employment, output, and earnings, the exact magnitudes are critically important.

Baily and Tobin apply the same model to a wage subsidy and come out with virtually identical results: a wage subsidy to teenagers would lower the noninflationary unemployment rate. In both cases, while the theory is clear, the empirical base is weak.

The key to their model is using relative wage effects as well as unemployment for restraining inflation. I think that this is a sound approach to the problem. The paper makes substantial progress in dealing with the basic theoretical issues involved in predicting the impact of structural labor market programs, but the theory needs to be extended to a multi-sector labor market.

One final point which is implicit in the Baily-Tobin paper deserves emphasis. In the traditional neoclassical model, wage change occurs when excess supply is not equal to zero. But Baily and Tobin interpret unemployment as excess supply only when it exceeds vacancies—they consider any unemployment below that level to be structural in nature. They find that even the crude help-wanted index of job vacancies is a better predictor of wage inflation than unemployment.

In their model, pressure for wage change depends not only on imbalances arising from wage-guided decisions on quantity supplied and quantity demanded, but also on the frictions in the labor market. This is equivalent to saying that the decisions by employers and workers that allocate resources in the labor market are guided not only by price considerations but also by "availability" as it is experienced in complex search and turnover processes. Where there is an availability allocator as well as a price allocator operating in the market, there will not necessarily be a unique equilibrium price. For example, high wages can be offset by low job availability in influencing workers' decisions.

Thus, you can visualize an equilibrium in which, say, one city has a high wage rate and an offsetting high unemployment rate while another city has a low wage rate and a low unemployment rate. There can be a whole set of equilibrium points in this two-dimensional space. This paper moves in the direction of this area of analysis. Clearly much more needs to be done in developing sectoral allocation theories within such a framework.

The imbalances of unemployment and wage rates that targeted jobs programs are designed to correct undoubtedly can be traced to differentials in information, access, and the employment experience of various groups of workers. Policies directed at creating jobs should be accompanied by complementary approaches aimed at reducing market frictions.

Comments by Michael L. Wachter

The Baily-Tobin paper provides an excellent and comprehensive evaluation of the conceptual workings of the genre of government efforts labeled "public service employment" or "direct job creation" programs. The authors organize their points around two basic themes: the relative multiplier effect of public service employment compared with other fiscal measures to deal with unemployment and the ability of direct job creation to cheat the Phillips curve by lowering the nonaccelerating-inflation rate of unemployment (NAIRU).

Because Baily and Tobin have not previously been involved in the debate about jobs programs, they are able to take a fresh look at this popular instrument of policy. The result is a concentration on topics and issues that have often been ignored. Although one may disagree with some aspects of their model and some of their empirical assertions, this paper is must reading for all policymakers and economists who are interested in employment policy.

In previous evaluation studies, public service employment has often been lauded as the program with the highest or one of the highest demand multipliers in the fiscal policy arsenal. That is, it is presumed that the government can create more jobs faster through an employment program than by cutting taxes, by building mass transit, or by straight revenue sharing. Baily and Tobin provide general support for this favorable assertion and indicate what factors need to hold for the employment multipliers to, in fact, be the largest.

On the other hand, the authors indicate two important reservations. First, do small differences among multipliers really matter? Their answer is no. I would criticize Baily and Tobin only for not going further in debunking policymakers' emphasis on evaluating policy options largely on the basis of relative multipliers. Other factors also matter: alternative policy options may differ greatly in their inflationary implications, the output and employment mix that they create (between private and public sector goods, for example), and their ability to solve, over the longer run, some of the structural problems facing the labor market. When these other factors are taken into account, there is evidence that direct job creation may lose the high ranking it receives from the isolated multiplier analysis.

Secondly, past public service employment programs have exhibited very large displacement effects. That is, state and local governments have increased employment, beyond what they otherwise would do, in the first year of the program, but thereafter the funds have seemed to slowly make their way into supporting employees who would be on the payroll in any case. In this case, the jobs program "degenerates"—to use the language of its supporters—into straight revenue sharing for state and local governments. As one who believes that revenue sharing is a valuable program, especially if it is part of a systematic urban policy, I am not alarmed by this development. Indeed, for those who are concerned with the growth of the government sector as a percentage of GNP, the tendency of public service employment to degenerate into state and local tax relief is the saving feature of the program.

To an important extent, the multiplier debate concerns whether we should reach full employment (however defined) relatively quickly by using programs with high multipliers, but few other redeeming features, or whether we should adopt better programs with a greater structural payoff even if they reach the unemployment target at a slightly later date. But even this story is too favorable for the multiplier story. The estimated discrepancies among multipliers is sufficiently small that, taking account of the standard errors in the underlying parameter estimates in the multiplier calculations, the differences among most standard stimulus programs do not arise in the first instance.

Public service employment may be valuable, but its *presumably* sizable multiplier effect should not be one of its selling points. What, then, of its ability to lower the NAIRU of society?

I do not believe it is capable of doing that. To cheat the Phillips curve and to lower NAIRU require certain conditions that, empirically, have not been satisfied. Baily and Tobin place considerable weight on the notion that public service employment programs must focus on the lowest skilled workers. In this way, several (unskilled) workers on a flat Phillips curve can be hired in place of one (skilled) worker on a steeper Phillips curve.

The Baily-Tobin model as applied to our actual recent experiences with public service employment programs suggests no change or even a slight increase in NAIRU. The reason, which is well documented in the literature, is that CETA and earlier public service employment programs have hired workers who, on average, have relatively high skill levels. Furthermore, there is little evidence that this has occurred by accident. For example, a not insignificant amount of CETA money has been used to maintain or rehire municipal employees who might otherwise have been laid off in the "urban crisis" of the past few years. That is, Congress focuses on numerous objectives which, on average, have not favored the least skilled workers whom the Baily-Tobin plan is centered on.

There is little evidence that this state of affairs is about to change. The 1977 Carter proposals for reforming welfare would shift public service slots toward lower skilled workers. On the other hand, they would significantly increase this group's participation in the labor force. As Baily and Tobin make clear, if public service employment is to lower the

NAIRU, it must focus on the lowest skilled workers without increasing their participation rate.

To summarize, one of the significant improvements in the literature made by the Baily-Tobin paper is the outline of the necessary conditions for an employment program to lower the NAIRU. If one believes the Baily-Tobin model and looks at the actual practice of public service employment programs, it is clear that the Phillips curve has not been cheated and the NAIRU has not been reduced.

Another important result of the Baily-Tobin work is that it clarifies an issue that has been thoroughly obscured in the policy debate over direct job creation. It indicates that once the economy is at its sustainable unemployment rate, further reductions in overall unemployment can only be made by shifting the burden from lower to higher skilled workers. The Humphrey-Hawkins full-employment bill (any version), for example, gives the impression that the economy can reach 4–4.5 percent unemployment by reducing the unemployed rate of the low skilled—but at no cost to the unionized manufacturing, construction, and mining sectors. This paper makes it clear that, at unusually low rates of unemployment, the economy is trading off employment of low-wage workers for higher skilled unionized employment. My guess is that this central conclusion of the Baily-Tobin paper could generate some heavy normative debate among different groups in our society.

I detect a few conceptual problems in the Baily-Tobin model. In particular, the modeling of the labor force participation and unemployment processes is not altogether clear. For example, it is not obvious that, after adjusting for the NAIRUs of the various age-sex-race groups, the slopes of the Phillips curves should be different for the various groups. Second, if low-skilled workers are unemployed because their reservation wage (given government transfer payments) exceeds their potential market wage, even a program focused on disadvantaged workers would not work. Low-wage jobs, a desideratum of the Baily-Tobin package, would not encourage these people to leave the ranks of the unemployed.

My final comments concern two issues that Baily and Tobin have omitted.[33] First, job creation programs have largely prospered at the

---

33. These issues are discussed in a different context in Michael L. Wachter and Susan M. Wachter, "The Fiscal Policy Dilemma: Cyclical Swings Dominated By Supply Side Constraints," in Thomas J. Espenshade and William J. Serow, eds., *The Economic Consequences of Slowing Population Growth* (Academic Press, forthcoming).

expense of manpower training programs. Unfortunately, this is not the place to debate the relative merits of the two types of program. I would suggest, however, that training programs have the potential of lowering the sustainable unemployment rate without shifting the burden among groups. That is, whereas training can shift out the supply constraints facing society, employment programs can only stimulate aggregate demand. Although one can always entertain the hope that public service jobs will enhance the skill of jobholders, such an effect would be fortuitous. These programs are most often geared to providing the maximum number of jobs at the expense of even rudimentary training or provision of capital equipment.

My last concern involves the dynamics of the demographic factor in the labor force. The Baily-Tobin model assumes that the labor force is essentially static. For modeling purposes this is reasonable. Evaluations of actual or prospective jobs programs, however, should take account of the very specific problems caused by the entry of the baby-boom generation into the labor force. I believe that the imbalance in the labor force, beginning in the late 1960s, has not only caused the rise in NAIRU from approximately 4.5 percent in 1966 to 5.6 percent in 1977, but the rise in popularity of public employment programs. These programs provide a mechanism for sheltering older workers from the competition of the oversized baby-boom cohort.

This baby-boom group has relatively low wages, low school enrollment, and, as a result, high unemployment. As this group ages, its unemployment rate will decrease, but it will continue to bear the burden of being an unusually large cohort with relatively low education (general and specific training) credentials. It is unclear in the Baily-Tobin framework that jobs programs with little training input can deal with these cohort-specific problems. Are the "structurally unemployed" supposed to stay under the protection of a public employment program throughout their lives or is there some notion of transferability to unsheltered employment? How can a transfer be successful if the employment program does not provide training?

Daniel S. Hamermesh

Subsidies for Jobs in the Private Sector

In recent years there has been an increasing interest in the use of subsidies to wages in the private sector as a means of inducing employers to expand their work forces. One senator is "very impressed by the potential of using an employment tax credit," while another feels "we have not utilized the private sector's position in our labor market."[1] President Carter in 1977 proposed a permanent credit against social security payroll taxes which Congress changed to a temporary but very much larger credit.[2] At least one state legislator proposed a similar employment subsidy at the state level.[3] This sudden surge of concern may be due in part to disenchantment with the rapidly expanding component of the Comprehensive Employment and Training Act (CETA) of 1973 that creates subsidized jobs in the public sector. It undoubtedly stems also from some people's inherent preference for expansion of the private rather than the public sector in the face of considerable cyclical as well as structural unemployment.

While most of the recent attention has focused on broad-based wage subsidies, the United States has at various times in the past ten years experimented with categorical wage subsidies. The WIN tax credit, a subsidy on wages of those welfare recipients registered in the work-incentive program, is one such experiment. A similar, temporary program for all welfare recipients, created in 1975, was later extended to January 1,

Edward M. Gramlich, Robert H. Haveman, and Jonathan R. Kesselman provided comments on drafts of this paper.

1. Statements by Senators Lloyd M. Bentsen and Jacob K. Javits, quoted in *Daily Labor Report* (Bureau of National Affairs), July 22, 1976, p. A-1, and Mar. 19, 1976, p. A-11.

2. The President's proposal was part of his economic stimulus package.

3. Senator Norman J. Levy introduced a bill in the New York legislature offering tax credits to firms for expanding their employment. *New York Times,* Mar. 21, 1976.

1980.[4] The contract component of Job Opportunities in the Business Sector (JOBS), a late 1960s effort to hire and train disadvantaged workers, is analytically equivalent to a wage subsidy on new employees, for it offset part of the wage costs during the initial part of employees' tenure with a firm.

This study analyzes many of the administrative and economic aspects of both categorical and general wage subsidies paid to employers. In the first section, various kinds of subsidies are described and both foreign and domestic examples of them are given. Various types of subsidies are often confused in popular discussions and erroneous conclusions are drawn about their likely impacts. The description is a useful way of organizing the analysis of some of the economic effects of wage subsidies designed to create jobs in the private sector. The second section discusses categorical programs of wage subsidy tried in the United States in the last few years, including an experiment that was never broadened to a full-scale program. The third section provides a detailed analysis of a number of economic factors essential to evaluating the impact of wage subsidies, and the next section simulates the likely impact of one such subsidy on both the amount and the distribution of employment. Finally, the overall desirability of wage subsidies is considered, and ways of increasing their likely success are recommended.

Types of Wage Subsidies

The terms *employment subsidy, wage subsidy,* and *hiring subsidy* have been used interchangeably to refer to programs that subsidize efforts to create jobs in the private sector. For example, a recent OECD report stated that "employment subsidies . . . lessen the pressure for a decrease in employment. . . . They may be intended to offset higher running-in [training and hiring] costs."[5] These are in fact *hiring subsidies,* for they

---

4. The WIN tax credit was included in the Revenue Act of 1971. The welfare recipient employment incentive credit was section 401 of the Tax Reduction Act of 1975 and was to remain in existence from Mar. 29, 1975, through June 30, 1976. It required only that the eligible employee be a recipient of aid for families with dependent children. It was extended by the Tax Reform Act of 1976 to Jan. 1, 1980.

5. Organisation for Economic Co-operation and Development, Working Party on Employment, *Inventory of Short-Term Measures Taken in the Light of the Employment Situations: Note by the Secretariat,* MO/WP5(75)5 (Paris: OECD, 1975).

offset wage costs in the initial part of an employee's period of employment with a particular firm. In this paper an *employment subsidy* is defined as one that applies during the entire time a worker is employed in a particular firm; it is a subsidy designed to increase the stock of employees rather than the flow of labor. Both types subsidize wages, but they differ in whose wages are being subsidized.

The first criterion for distinguishing among subsidy programs is their application—either nationwide or regional. The latter programs, for selected jurisdictions, are usually intended to stimulate employment growth in chronically depressed areas or to retard migration from these areas. Implicitly they are another (perhaps more politically palatable) means of providing transfers to people in areas with severe unemployment problems. Insofar as part of the problem in depressed areas is lack of demand for their products, a regional subsidy can increase demand by enabling firms to produce more cheaply and thus sell more goods. Expansion of demand for output can have an additional beneficial effect on inflation since it puts less initial pressure on wages and material prices than would a nationwide expansion of aggregate demand.

The major economic impediment to success in reducing unemployment through regional programs is the possible reversal of migration from the subsidized areas. The young are especially sensitive to information about income and job availability.[6] A subsidy's potential impact on area unemployment may therefore be limited;[7] it may nonetheless be positive in the short run, before information about the program begins to affect migration.

A wage subsidy can be general or categorical. The categorical subsidy, applying to selected groups of individuals, occupations, or industries, appears superficially to be a useful way of aiming a program toward individuals whose employment opportunities need to be increased. However, the very categorization of a demographic group as qualifying for the subsidy may reduce its members' chance of employment, or at least fail to raise their probability of employment by as much as estimated elasticities of labor demand would project. Depending on the targeting

6. See Aba Schwartz, "Interpreting the Effect of Distance on Migration," *Journal of Political Economy,* vol. 81 (September-October 1973), pp. 1153–69; and Larry A. Sjaastad, "The Costs and Returns of Human Migration," ibid., vol. 70 supplement (October 1962), pp. 80–93.

7. See Michael P. Todaro, "A Model of Labor Migration and Urban Unemployment in Less Developed Countries," *American Economic Review,* vol. 59 (March 1969), pp. 138–48.

of the subsidy, a worker's eligibility for it could signal potential employers that he has certain labor market deficiencies. (The same problem appears to arise in employers' attitudes toward those whose search for new jobs is subsidized by state employment services.)

The subsidization of wages in certain occupations or industries to increase their demand for labor can be a useful short-run palliative. In the long run, however, the competition among employers for workers in the subsidized occupations or industries will produce higher wages and new workers will enter the occupation or industry. Only if labor demand were perceived to be below equilibrium would such a subsidy succeed in maintaining employment and wages of current members of the occupation without attracting new entrants.

A wage subsidy can be applied to all employment, to net changes in employment, or to gross flows into employment reflecting increased hiring or reduced layoffs. Subsidies based on total employment create windfalls for employers on that part of employment that would exist in the absence of the subsidy. (These are analogous to the windfalls that would arise from a tax credit on the entire capital stock rather than on gross investment.) Clearly, this problem would not arise when subsidies are granted to new firms or firms that are relocating, and subsidies on total employment are thus recommended in such cases. Even the net employment and hiring subsidies will produce windfalls, but at least these can be limited to a much smaller fraction of a firm's work force.

A serious problem is engendered by hiring subsidies (or by their equivalent, subsidies that pay part of the expenses of training new employees). Unless there is a stringent requirement on retaining newly hired workers (which ipso facto converts the hiring subsidy into a net employment subsidy), the hiring subsidy provides an incentive to churn workers through the firm. The net result of this churning is unclear: it gives more people than otherwise a taste of employment, but it can also produce workers whose subsequent job search is colored by the failure to be retained at their initial, subsidized employment. The return on investment in on-the-job training depends on the nature of the production function for the training. Returns may be constant with respect to time spent on the job, or they may be first increasing and then decreasing. If, as seems plausible, there are increasing returns in the early phases of job tenure, churning could lower the average amount of training of the labor force. In short, the induced increase in turnover can be beneficial or detrimental depending on the nature of production of on-the-job training.

Increased turnover need not imply an improvement in the functioning of the labor market; a hiring subsidy can lower average tenure and reduce labor-market efficiency.

A wage subsidy can be a fixed percentage of each eligible worker's wage or earnings, a flat dollar amount per worker, or a fixed percentage of earnings up to a specific dollar figure. The dollar-amount subsidy causes a greater shift in employment away from high-wage and toward low-wage labor in the short run than the percentage subsidy does. But once all supply adjustments have had time to work themselves out, more workers will have moved into low-wage occupations with a dollar-amount subsidy than with the percentage subsidy. This is true partly because the dollar-amount subsidy induces participation in the labor force among people with few skills and partly because those who would be part of the labor force under any circumstances do not accumulate as much training as they otherwise would. In the long run a dollar-amount subsidy does not obviously have a beneficial effect on the ability of labor-force participants to earn high wages.

The dollar-amount subsidy is less difficult to administer than the percentage subsidy, for it is based on the number of full-time employees, while the percentage subsidy is based on the total wage bill. The percentage subsidy on earnings up to a fixed amount is administratively far more expensive, requiring knowledge of the earnings of each employee in the firm (presumably obtainable from social security records). The administrative costs of percentage subsidies are large enough, and extra short-run benefits to low-wage workers provided by a dollar-amount subsidy likely enough, to militate in favor of using the latter approach.

The diversity of wage subsidies that have been attempted or are now in operation in various countries is illustrated in table 1. The WIN credit, a nationwide categorical subsidy, applied to workers eligible for the work-incentive program and required that they be retained for two years. It provided a 20 percent tax credit up to a limit of $1,000 on each employee's annual wages, with the rate falling to 10 percent after a firm's credits for the year reached $25,000. The 1975 welfare credit also provides a 20 percent credit but has a retention period of only ninety days and a 10 percent rate after the firm's credits reach $50,000.

This contrasts sharply with the British regional employment premium designed to stimulate manufacturing production in depressed regions. Rebates on the selective employment tax were available only in development areas and only to industry. They applied to all employment and

Table 1. Characteristics of Wage Subsidy Programs

Program, by year and country	Coverage	Application	Employment base	Subsidy as related to earnings
1. WIN and welfare tax credits, 1972 and 1975; United States	national	categorical	new	percentage of a limited amount
2. Regional employment premium, 1967; United Kingdom	regional	categorical	total	percentage
3. Regional employment promotion premium, 1974; Japan	regional	categorical	new	fixed amount
4. Proposed tax credit on social security payroll taxes, 1977; United States	national	general	total	percentage of a limited amount
5. Employment tax credit, 1977; United States	national	general	net change	percentage of a limited amount
6. Employment promotion measures of 1974; Netherlands	national	general	new	percentage of a limited amount
7. Job creation bonus, 1975; France	national	categorical	new	fixed amount
8. JOBS, 1968; United States	national	categorical	new	fixed amount
9. Employment adjustment grant scheme, 1975; Japan	national	general and categorical	new	percentage
10. Employment protection bill, redundancies procedure, 1965; United Kingdom	national	general	new	percentage of a limited amount

amounted to a percentage subsidy on wages. The Japanese, in their regional employment promotion premium adopted in 1974, offered wage subsidies only to selected industries (mainly manufacturing) for certain categories of employers (small and medium employers); the Japanese program paid a fixed amount (9,000 yen per month) per worker for up to one year.[8]

8. These and the other foreign programs included in table 1 are described in OECD, *Inventory of Short-Term Measures,* addenda 3, 5, 6, and 7, July 9 and 31 and Aug. 8 and 13, 1975.

In several countries wage subsidies have been used as antirecessionary measures. In January 1977 President Carter proposed a credit on corporate income taxes of 4 percent of employer-paid social security payroll taxes; Congress rejected this but passed a temporary marginal employment credit applied to a fixed percentage of earnings up to a specified dollar limit.[9] The Netherlands' program, adopted in response to the dislocations induced by increases in the price of oil, offers a subsidy for up to twenty-six weeks of 30 percent of the wages of workers less than forty-five years old up to a limit of 5,000 guilders in any year, and double that limit for older workers. A similar French program paid a flat subsidy of 500 francs per month for six months on each new worker retained for at least one year; workers had to be among the long-term unemployed or new labor-market entrants less than twenty-five years old. The United States' JOBS program, whose purpose was entirely different, was analytically similar to the antirecession wage subsidies used in the Netherlands and France.

The last two measures in table 1 are slightly different forms of subsidy designed to preserve employment. In Japan, subsidies encourage firms to lay off workers rather than discharge them. If both employers and unions agree to the layoff, subsidies amounting to two-thirds of layoff pay (one-half for large firms) or at least 35 percent of wages may be paid for up to seventy-five days. The British redundancy act reimburses employers for lump-sum payments to laid-off workers, provided the employers give advance notification of layoffs to the government. Both programs are essentially the obverse of hiring subsidies since their legislated intent is to reduce gross flows out of employment rather than increase gross flows into employment.

Wage subsidies applied on a large scale are not a new device; indeed, the United States has been relatively backward in its use of this technique for stimulating employment. The wage subsidies that have been adopted around the world have usually applied to specific categories of recipients or to specific occupations or industries. There appears to have been a reluctance to subsidize net changes in employment, and in most cases the subsidies have been either a flat amount or a percentage of wages with an upper limit.

---

9. The credit is 50 percent of the first $4,200 of each employee's annual wages for all such wages in excess of 102 percent of the prior year's level and up to a maximum of $100,000 per firm.

U.S. Experience with Subsidies

The JOBS program started in 1968 as a voluntary effort by the National Alliance of Businessmen (NAB) to hire disadvantaged, unemployed workers. While the definition of a disadvantaged worker changed over the program's life, the workers hired were always among the youngest, poorest, and least educated of the recipients of manpower services in the late 1960s and early 1970s.[10] To qualify for the program in 1972, for example, a person had to be either a high school dropout, less than twenty-two or more than forty-five years old, handicapped, or in a family with income below the poverty level. To assist the NAB in finding jobs for those people, the federal government offered to issue contracts that would reimburse business for part of the employment costs of workers. The rationale was that this would offset the search costs, discrimination, or whatever barriers there were to hiring disadvantaged workers and would integrate them into firms' promotion ladders.

While highly touted initially, the JOBS program never lived up to its first rave reviews. Even the number of contract placements grew only from 51,000 in fiscal 1969 to 93,000 in fiscal 1971, declining thereafter until the program was eliminated with the passage of the Comprehensive Employment and Training Act in 1973. The 51,000 contract placements in 1969 cost the federal treasury $161 million—$3,200 per placement—and they only accounted for about a third of all JOBS placements. The $3,200 figure of course understates the cost per job actually created by the program, for many workers presumably would have been hired without the subsidy. Despite the availability of this fairly large hiring subsidy and the publicity provided for it by the NAB, surprisingly few of the employers who cooperated with the NAB and accepted placements took advantage of it.

Because of the small number of contract placements relative to the pool of the unemployed, it is extremely difficult to evaluate the program's net impact. One study that used longitudinal data to evaluate the program found small gains in annual earnings for males covered by contracts (compared to a control group) but fairly large ones for fe-

10. For a detailed discussion of the operations of the JOBS program and of evaluations of it, see Charles R. Perry and others, *The Impact of Government Manpower Programs: In General, and on Minorities and Women* (University of Pennsylvania, Wharton School, Industrial Research Unit, 1975).

males.[11] The well-known decline in earnings during the year before enrollment in any manpower program suggests these estimates are biased upward and that, at least for men, the net gains are probably very small.[12] Further, any such evaluation of net impact ignores the likelihood that some of the jobs would have been available without the JOBS contract. Finally, and most important, the fact that employers of only about one-third of the JOBS enrollees saw fit to enter into a contractual arrangement (be paid for what they were supposed to be doing anyway) suggests either a strong aversion to real or imagined red tape or a stigma against job applicants who were deemed eligible for the subsidy.[13]

The tax credit that was designed to induce firms to hire welfare recipients who were WIN enrollees was paid on only 88,000 workers in fiscal 1973–75. Yet 515,000 WIN enrollees entered the labor market in this period, and there were 952,000 new enrollees during these three years. Further, the amount credited against taxes was about $9 million in fiscal 1973, suggesting that the average wage subsidy in that year, based on 25,000 certifications, was about $360.[14] Both the size of the

11. David J. Farber, "Highlights: Some Findings from a Follow-Up Study of Pre- and Post-Training Earnings Histories of 215,000 Trainees Participating in Two 1964 and Four 1968 Training Programs" (U.S. Department of Labor, Office of Policy, Evaluation, and Research, 1971; processed).

12. Using income in the year prior to training as a base for comparison leads to artificially large estimated increases in trainees' earnings since their unemployment rate has been much higher than that of the control group. For a discussion of this problem see Orley Ashenfelter, "The Effect of Manpower Training on Earnings," in Farrell Bloch, ed., *Evaluating Manpower Training Programs* (JAI Press, 1978).

13. In the context of models of statistical discrimination, employer's knowledge that a worker qualifies for the subsidy could lower the mean and decrease the variance of the employer's prior probability distribution on the worker's productivity. See Dennis J. Aigner and Glen G. Cain, "Statistical Theories of Discrimination in Labor Markets," *Industrial and Labor Relations Review*, vol. 30 (January 1977), pp. 175–87.

14. Data on WIN workers and enrollees are from *The Work Incentive Program—Fourth Annual Report to the Congress on Training and Employment Under Title IV of the Social Security Act, July 1, 1972—June 30, 1973*, developed by the U.S. Departments of Labor and Health, Education, and Welfare for the House Committee on Ways and Means, 93:2 (GPO, 1974), pp. 15, 19, and 20; and *WIN at Work: The Work Incentive Program—Sixth Annual Report to the Congress on Employment and Training Under Title IV of the Social Security Act, July 1, 1974—June 30, 1975*, U.S. Departments of Labor and Health, Education, and Welfare (The Departments, 1976), pp. 3 and 35. The information on the amount credited has been supplied by the Internal Revenue Service. In fact, part of the credit was for jobs that were later decertified because the employees were not retained for the required two years.

incentive and the number of employees covered by the credit indicate clearly that this part of the program was not a smashing success. Two surveys of employers who used the credit found that less than 10 percent attributed their hiring of the WIN enrollee to the credit.[15] Given the well-known difficulties in making inferences about the causes of labor market behavior from surveys about what employers (or workers) think they do, and the likelihood that much of the employment that was eligible for the credit would exist anyway, this result is unsurprising. Much more disturbing is the recurrence of the difficulty noted in the JOBS program—employers' unwillingness to hire under a subsidy that requires paperwork not normally included in the hiring process in the private sector, or an unwillingness to hire workers possibly stigmatized by eligibility for the subsidy.

The tax credit that in 1975 extended coverage to all welfare recipients and shortened the period during which the new worker must be retained should increase employers' use of the credit, because it reduces the cost of labor for more potential employers.[16] Whether a 20 percent credit is sufficient inducement to hire this class of workers, who must be paid the minimum wage, and whether the possibility of churning employees more rapidly will lead to shorter job tenure for former welfare recipients are not yet clear. Experience under WIN suggests there will not be a great expansion in the use of the credits.

An interesting experimental subsidy, TIPP (training incentive payments program), was funded by the Department of Labor during the years 1969 to 1975. Based on an idea suggested by Thurow, it subsidized increases in the wages that workers received from their employer.[17] This upgrading subsidy was given to a total of 231 workers in nineteen firms. Unfortunately, there was no evaluation of the net effect on employment and training so the results cannot be compared to what would have occurred in the absence of the subsidy.[18] It appears, however, that the pro-

15. Institute for Manpower Program Analysis, "An Assessment of WIN and Welfare Tax Credits" (Minneapolis: IMPACT, March 1977; processed), p. 53.

16. Eligible employees must have received financial assistance for ninety days prior to hiring and must have been employed full time for more than thirty consecutive days. They remain eligible for the first twelve months of employment.

17. See Lester C. Thurow, *Poverty and Discrimination* (Brookings Institution, 1969), pp. 191–96.

18. Institute of Public Administration, "Training Incentive Payments Program (TIPP), Final Report to the U.S. Department of Labor" (New York: IPA, 1975; processed).

gram helped a number of workers to advance in their firms, and that the experimental program could be worth reviving.

The common thread in these few, limited wage subsidies is the failure of employers to respond to programs whose magnitude and expected effect on labor demand (discussed below) would seem to make them attractive. Experience suggests that there is a severe problem, either of resistance to paperwork or reaction to the implications of a worker's eligibility for the wage subsidy, that must be overcome if such subsidies are to have a strong impact.

Economic Effect of Subsidies

Any wage subsidy stimulates employment in two ways. First, by lowering the price of labor relative to other inputs in the production process, it encourages *substitution* of labor for these other inputs. Even without any change in the level of output, the wage subsidy should induce firms to use relatively more labor. It may also affect the *scale* of production, by inducing firms to produce more goods. Part or all of the lowered labor cost gets passed on to the consumer in the form of lower prices. These in turn stimulate demand for the product, causing increases in output as the extra spending spreads through the economy.

The net effect of the wage subsidy depends on the employers' response to the reduction in cost—their demand for the type of labor being subsidized. (The problem of employers' failure to participate in the programs is ignored here.) The many empirical studies of labor demand, which cover different groups of industries and extend over different time periods, are in surprising agreement about the effect of subsidies.[19] Including both the substitution and the scale effects of a drop in wage costs, the demand for labor four quarters after a 1 percent drop appears to increase around 0.30 percent. In the longer run, after all adjustment costs have been overcome, the response to the drop in wage costs appears to be between a 0.75 percent and 1 percent increase in labor demand.

These estimated elasticities (the percentage change in demand in response to a percentage change in wage costs) are based on the demand for all labor in the industries covered as it responds to a permanent change

19. See Daniel S. Hamermesh, "Econometric Studies of Labor Demand and Their Application to Policy Analysis," *Journal of Human Resources,* vol. 11 (Fall 1976), pp. 507–25.

in wages, with the response implicitly estimated at the average degree of labor market tightness and capacity utilization that prevail during the period covered in each study. To the extent that a wage subsidy is limited to low-wage workers and implemented temporarily as an antirecession device, the estimates may be incorrect.

Low-wage workers are the most likely targets of a categorical wage subsidy. Most of the estimates of elasticity of demand for these workers have been designed to evaluate the impact of the minimum wage on the demand for teenage labor.[20] Those that apply to low-wage workers generally find elasticities at least as large as those for all workers.[21] It is thus likely that the percentage increase in low-wage employment for a given percentage subsidy applied only to low-wage workers is at least as high as the effects of the same subsidy applied to all employment.

The apparently large impact of a categorical subsidy on the low-wage employees it is aimed at must be weighed against its negative effect on the demand for other types of labor. There is good empirical evidence that labor markets for workers of different ages or education are not segmented, and that a change in the wage of one group of workers will affect employers' demand for other groups.[22] In particular, if the cost of em-

20. These studies imply a very low elasticity of employment of teenagers with respect to wages. However, as Gramlich points out, this result is not surprising, since a large majority of teenage employees earn a sufficient amount to leave them unaffected by legislated changes in the minimum wage. Also, because the so-called demand equations are not properly identified, and because there is a fairly elastic supply of teenage labor, the demand estimates become biased toward zero. See Robert S. Goldfarb, "The Policy Content of Quantitative Minimum Wage Research," in James L. Stern and Barbara D. Dennis, *Proceedings of the Twenty-Seventh Annual Winter Meeting, 1974* (Industrial Relations Research Association, 1975), pp. 261–68; and Edward M. Gramlich, "Impact of Minimum Wages on Other Wages, Employment, and Family Incomes," *Brookings Papers on Economic Activity, 2:1976*, pp. 409–51.

21. Robert W. Crandall, C. Duncan MacRae, and Lorene Y. L. Yap, "An Econometric Model of the Low-Skill Labor Market," *Journal of Human Resources*, vol. 10 (Winter 1975), pp. 3–24, find a long-run substitution effect of 0.90 using private household workers, service workers, and nonfarm laborers in 1970. Reed Hansen, Ben Klotz, and Rey Madoo, "The Structure of Demand for Low-Wage Labor in U.S. Manufacturing, 1967" (Urban Institute, 1975; processed), pp. 42–45, estimate an average elasticity of 1.5 based on the lowest quartile of plants ranked by payroll per employee in 195 industries. Philip Cotterill, "The Elasticity of Demand for Low-Wage Labor," *Southern Economic Journal*, vol. 41 (January 1975), pp. 520–25, estimates an elasticity of about 0.75 using cross-section data on retail industries.

22. See Joseph M. Anderson, "An Economic-Demographic Model of the United States Labor Market" (Ph.D. dissertation, Harvard University, 1977), chap. 2;

ploying low-wage and younger workers is subsidized, they are to some extent substituted for more skilled and older workers. Thus the impact on total employment of a categorical subsidy for low-wage workers may be considerably less than is implied by the elasticity of demand for those workers' services.

All available estimates of elasticity of demand for labor are based on average experience over some fairly long period of time. It is very likely, though, that employers' response differs as the state of the labor market changes, and that the elasticity of demand is smaller when unemployment is high. In fact, in the model of labor demand for the private nonfarm sector of the United States reported in appendix A, the substitution of employment for other inputs to production varies after nine quarters of adjustment from 0.25, when the prime-age male unemployment rate is 1.5 percent, to 0.12, when that rate is at 5.5 percent (roughly its highest value since 1946). The scale effect does not appear to vary over the business cycle. These results suggest that a wage subsidy will be less effective in a very deep than in a moderate recession.

These considerations apply only when there is some slack in the economy. If labor markets are sufficiently tight, employers will not be able to hire more workers even though a wage subsidy is available. The subsidy will increase employment indirectly, however, as employers bid for scarce labor, if the rising real wages induce more people to enter the labor force. Whether a wage subsidy merely bids up wages or induces increases in labor supply is unclear. Evidence related to the effect on wages deals only with payroll taxes, not subsidies, and is quite mixed.[23] Evidence on the

---

Zvi Griliches, "Capital-Skill Complementarity," *Review of Economics and Statistics,* vol. 51 (November 1969), pp. 465–68; George E. Johnson, "The Demand for Labor by Educational Category," *Southern Economic Journal,* vol. 37 (October 1970), pp. 190–204; Randall Weiss, "Sources of Change in the Occupational Structures of American Manufacturing Industries, 1950–1960: An Application of Production Function Analysis" (Ph.D. dissertation, Harvard University, 1974); F. Welch, "Education in Production," *Journal of Political Economy,* vol. 78 (January-February 1970), pp. 35–59; and Daniel S. Hamermesh and James Grant, "Econometric Studies of Labor–Labor Substitution and Their Implications for Policy" (Michigan State University, June 1978; processed).

23. John A. Brittain, *The Payroll Tax for Social Security* (Brookings Institution, 1972), chap. 3, provides estimates that the payroll tax for social security is shifted backward entirely. Ray C. Fair, *A Model of Macroeconomic Activity,* vol. 2, *The Empirical Model* (Ballinger, 1976), p. 129; and Wayne Vroman, "Employer Payroll Taxes and Money Wage Behaviour," *Applied Economics,* vol. 6 (September 1974), pp. 189–204, use time-series evidence to suggest that this is not the case.

effect on labor supply shows that, except for all teenagers, housewives (decreasingly so) and husbands at or approaching retirement age, little extra labor is likely to be forthcoming at higher wages.[24] This implies that much of the effect of a wage subsidy will show up as higher wage rates rather than employment increases, and that this is more the case the lower the aggregate rate of unemployment.

A general wage subsidy thus would seem to be most effective as a stimulus to the economy during the recovery phase of a moderate recession. As a device to lower the noninflationary rate of unemployment it is unlikely to succeed, for it will instead mainly bid up wages.

This is less true of categorical subsidies aimed at low-wage workers. Since the evidence suggests that their labor supply is more elastic, their employment is more readily stimulated (indirectly) by these subsidies, even if the economy as a whole is operating fairly near to the capacity of its industrial plant. This employment increase need not result in a reduction of unemployment for the subsidized group, though, and thus the categorical subsidy may not lower the unacceptably high unemployment rates observed among low-wage workers even near cyclical peaks.

The reliability of estimates of the elasticity of demand for labor also depends on the permanence of any wage subsidy. If there are costs of adjusting employment, and if employers believe a subsidy to be temporary, then they are unlikely to respond as fully as if they thought the subsidy were permanent. Any substitution of labor for capital must be motivated by cost savings, and if the subsidy is only temporary there may not be a sufficiently long payout period to justify a response to lower wages. The effects of a wage subsidy triggered by the aggregate unemployment rate, such as that proposed by Fethke and Williamson, are even more complex, because of the uncertainty over the duration of the subsidy.[25]

In sum, existing estimates of labor demand elasticities are a poor guide to the likely responses of employers to a wage subsidy. While demand for low-wage labor may be somewhat more elastic than that for all labor, a subsidy applied only to low-wage workers will produce a decline in demand for other workers. A temporary subsidy will not produce the same

24. See the various econometric studies of labor supply in Glen G. Cain and Harold Watts, eds., *Income Maintenance and Labor Supply: Econometric Studies* (Rand McNally, 1973), p. 179.

25. Gary C. Fethke and Samuel H. Williamson, "Employment Tax Credits as a Fiscal Policy Tool," prepared for the Subcommittee on Economic Growth of the Joint Economic Committee of Congress, 94:2 (GPO, 1976), pp. 3–4.

response in labor demand as a permanent one, and a permanent subsidy is more likely to be shifted to workers in the form of a higher supply price of labor rather than greater employment. Further, subsidies designed to stimulate labor demand in a recession can do so chiefly by inducing increases in demand for output, for little substitution of labor for capital is likely at such a time. Even if the difficulties arising from employers' lack of interest in wage subsidies are circumvented, economic considerations suggest that the labor demand elasticity appropriate for simulating the effects of this type of subsidy is quite low.

Simulating the Effects of a Wage Subsidy

In this section the effects of some wage subsidies on total employment and its distribution across workers are simulated. The subsidy considered is a marginal employment tax credit similar to the temporary one adopted in the United States in 1977, but without an upper limit on the applicable wage base. This credit would allow employers to offset some fraction of their wage bill against their federal corporate income tax liability, the amount dependent on the net growth in employment over a specified period and on the fraction of wages subsidized. The tax credit can be classified as a nationwide subsidy applying to all industries and occupations and based on net change in employment. Subsidies based on both a percentage of the wage bill and a dollar amount for each additional job created are considered.

Unlike the WIN and JOBS programs, this tax credit is explicitly intended as a *countercyclical* device.[26] (It is analogous in intent, though not in design, to items 4–7 in table 1, other antirecession subsidies for

26. Use of a general wage subsidy as a device to stimulate employment in a depression was first suggested by Nicholas Kaldor, "Wage Subsidies as a Remedy for Unemployment," *Journal of Political Economy,* vol. 44 (December 1936), pp. 721–42. He argued that it would be superior to a pay cut, recognized that it could lower budget costs of income maintenance programs, was aware of the shifting problem, and felt it would be efficient because he believed the labor demand elasticity to be at least 2. Ragnar Frisch, *Price-Wage-Tax-Subsidy Policies as Instruments in Maintaining Optimal Employment,* E/CN.1/Sub. 2/13 (United Nations Economic and Social Council, 1949), recommended a similar subsidy scheme. Howard M. Wachtel, "Employment Incentive Programs: Who Are They For and What Is Their Purpose?" (paper delivered at the 1976 meeting of the American Economic Association—Association for the Study of Grants Economy; processed), offers a radical critique of this type of wage subsidy.

creating employment in the private sector.) Its effects should be compared to those of other countercyclical measures such as income tax cuts, public service employment, and general expenditure increases. The simulations say nothing about the efficacy of a wage-subsidy program aimed at *structural* unemployment problems. The permanent nature of a categorical subsidy means that the simulations would have to allow for the eventual shifting of its costs. (Supply considerations would also need to be included in the simulations.)[27]

The financing of this credit is assumed to leave the mix of fiscal and monetary policy undisturbed. Thus its employment-generating effects are directly comparable to those that would be produced by any general expansionary policy. Because the analysis focuses on microeconomic effects of the credit,[28] it is assumed that establishment of the credit is the only change that occurs in the economy.

The supply of labor to the firm is assumed to be perfectly elastic (that is, unlimited at the going wage rate) and the rate of unemployment higher than average. The simulation results are thus more appropriate to the short-run effects of the credit, for the full employment that is likely to be established in the long run is ruled out. Those conditions that govern elasticity estimates in a recession are assumed to apply; those more appropriate to the long run and to low unemployment (that would shift the effects of the subsidy from primarily increasing employment to primarily increasing wages) are ignored. Only the induced change in employment occurring four quarters after the subsidy is instituted is examined. (Presumably, the results over a longer period would be clouded by the effects of shifting, and over a shorter period by employers' lack of knowledge of the program's existence.) Four-quarter elasticities of 0.1 and 0.3, which appear to be reasonable, are used in the simulations to take into account the likely lessening of the wage elasticity of labor demand when there is excess industrial capacity (the value of the elasticity will depend, of course, on the state of the labor market when the subsidy is instituted). Estimates for an elasticity of 0.5 are also included to illustrate the effect of assuming labor market behavior that is somewhat more elastic than empirical evidence indicates it would be.

In the simulations, actual employment in 1975 is compared to what it would have been had an employment tax credit been put into operation

27. See George Johnson's paper in this volume.
28. See Fethke and Williamson, "Employment Tax Credits as a Fiscal Policy Tool," discussed on page 107 below.

at mid-year 1974.[29] The credit is assumed to apply to net changes in employment over the base period of 1974, in some simulations to employment above that in the base period, and in others to employment above 85, 90, or 95 percent of that in the base period. The latter specifications allow firms to qualify for the subsidy even if their employment has declined. There is no specified limit on the amount of the subsidy a firm can receive; thus, a firm that grew naturally during the recession would be subsidized for both natural and induced growth.

The subsidy is applied to all private nonfarm industry—64 million employees in 1974—since this is the part of the private sector for which the necessary data are available. In order to investigate more carefully the credit's link to net changes in employment, each of the 171 two-, three-, and four-digit industries of the standard industrial classification that constitute the private nonfarm sector is treated as if it were a firm; disaggregating this way allows for the likelihood that many firms do not qualify for the subsidy because their employment in 1975 was below the triggering point that would qualify them to receive the credit. (The biases induced by this aggregation from firms, the actual recipients of the credit, to industries are discussed in appendix B.) Finally, it is assumed that the subsidy equals 10 percent of the relevant wage base.

The percentage change in employment is derived by combining the percentage wage subsidy (multiplied by wages' share in total compensation) with the substitution and scale elasticities. Because the credit is on marginal employment, the substitution effect is much larger than the scale effect: with the subsidy applying to employment above 90 percent of base-period employment, only about 1 percent of the *entire* wage bill is subsidized under a 10 percent marginal subsidy, even though the cost of an *additional* worker to eligible employers is 10 percent lower.

Costs and Changes in Aggregate Employment

Table 2 presents the results of the simulations for the four-quarter impact of the 10 percent marginal employment tax credit.[30] Not surprisingly, given the sharp drop in employment between 1974 and 1975, a

29. Employment data used in the simulations are annual averages for 1974 and 1975, from U.S. Bureau of Labor Statistics, *Employment and Earnings,* vol. 21 (March 1975) and vol. 22 (March 1976).

30. Tax credits of 5, 15, and 20 percent of the wage bill for marginal changes in employment result in numbers of jobs created and costs and windfalls that are nearly multiples of those in table 2, while the costs per job are essentially unchanged.

Daniel S. Hamermesh

Table 2. Simulations of Impact of a 10 Percent Wage Subsidy

Percentage of base-year employment above which subsidy is applied	Elasticity of labor demand	Jobs created (thousands)	Cost (billions of dollars)	Windfall (billions of dollars)[a]	Cost per job (dollars)
85	0.1	288	6.461	6.213	22,461
90	0.1	250	3.958	3.752	15,816
95	0.1	189	1.993	1.843	10,537
100	0.1	110	0.651	0.580	5,867
85	0.3	866	6.958	6.213	8,039
90	0.3	766	4.383	3.752	5,725
95	0.3	592	2.305	1.843	3,893
100	0.3	369	0.816	0.580	2,210
85	0.5	1,468	7.465	6.213	5,083
90	0.5	1,291	4.817	3.752	3,731
95	0.5	1,056	2.633	1.843	2,492
100	0.5	744	1.021	0.580	1,373

a. Payment on jobs that would exist even were there no subsidy.

subsidy that is limited to the net creation of jobs produces relatively few jobs; in many industries even the extra employment that could be generated by the subsidy is insufficient to raise 1975 employment above 1974's level. Only by triggering the subsidy at employment of 85 or 90 percent of the base year can a marginal employment tax credit create a substantial number of jobs at a time when employment is decreasing.

Most of the cost of the program is a windfall to employers, in that it is paid on jobs that were not induced by the subsidy.[31] While the windfall can be reduced by raising the qualifying employment base, this comes at the expense of job creation, as table 2 shows. As an alternative, a period of normal (as opposed to recessionary) employment could be used as the base period, but this would exclude from the program the firms whose employment had fallen most in a recession and whose stock of trained employees available to be rehired would be largest.

Like most of the calculations of the effects of other job-creation programs, these estimates of costs exclude the reduction in expenditures related to unemployment and the increased tax revenues occasioned by

31. Recall, however, that much of this windfall is shifted forward to consumers in the form of lower than otherwise product prices. This type of windfall is endemic to all subsidies. Its relative importance in this case depends on the elasticity assumption and the employment base above which the subsidy applies.

the net jobs created. Ignoring these effects implies a substantial upward bias in the estimated cost per job of the employment tax credit. (Some unpublished work by Gösta Rehn suggests that, under reasonable assumptions, these secondary effects may be large enough to make the net budget cost of the employment tax credit nearly zero in the short run.)

Despite the large windfall under all the subsidy plans, the cost per job created is not particularly high. Even with a four-quarter employment elasticity of 0.1, a subsidy applied to net job creation above 90 percent of base-period employment costs only $15,816 per job. If the elasticity is 0.3, the cost per job is only $5,725. (With the improbably high elasticity of 0.5, the cost per job is $3,731.) Johnson and Tomola have calculated that the cost of creating a job through generalized government purchases is $18,600 after four quarters; through a tax cut, $212,800 (but $19,700 after eight quarters); and through a public service employment program in which 54 percent of jobs funded represent net job creation, $14,500.[32] Cost of creating a job through a tax credit program depends critically on the assumed value of the demand elasticity for labor. The simulation results suggest, however, that even with a very low elasticity of 0.1 and a 10 percent subsidy to all growth above 90 percent of base-period employment, the budget costs per job created are no more than with other measures that have been used.

Without a larger model containing two classes of labor it is not possible to capture all the employment effects of a dollar-amount wage subsidy or a subsidy aimed at a particular group of workers. It is possible, however, to estimate the aggregate effects of a subsidy of, say, $3 per employee per day, paid on all employment in excess of some fraction of base-period (1974) employment. The results of such a subsidy, presented in table 3,[33] are generally comparable to those for percentage subsidies of roughly equal cost, but the dollar-amount subsidy appears to operate at a slightly lower cost per job created. This may result from relatively smaller windfall payments to firms in those industries paying below-average wages (and thus receiving a greater percentage subsidy under the dollar-amount subsidy scheme).

One way to limit the amount of windfall payments to employers and thereby lower program costs is to place an upper limit on the amount

32. See George E. Johnson and James D. Tomola, "The Efficacy of Public Service Employment Programs" (University of Michigan, 1975; processed).
33. Here, too, different dollar-amount subsidies were simulated, and the results on cost per job did not differ greatly from the results listed in table 3.

Table 3. Simulations of Impact of a Wage Subsidy of $3 per Day

Percentage of base-year employment above which subsidy is applied	Elasticity of labor demand	Jobs created (thousands) (1)	Cost (billions of dollars) (2)	Windfall (billions of dollars)[a] (3)	Cost per job (dollars) (4)
85	0.1	297	5.346	5.148	18,000
90	0.1	264	3.415	3.240	12,926
95	0.1	207	1.817	1.679	8,794
100	0.1	137	0.671	0.582	4,889
85	0.3	893	5.746	5.148	6,434
90	0.3	802	3.773	3.240	4,706
95	0.3	686	2.101	1.679	3,062
100	0.3	446	0.861	0.582	1,931
85	0.5	1,492	6.147	5.148	4,121
90	0.5	1,353	4.136	3.240	3,055
95	0.5	1,156	2.411	1.679	2,085
100	0.5	788	1.067	0.582	1,354

a. Payment on jobs that would exist even were there no subsidy.

of employment subsidized. (However, this would also limit the number of jobs created.) For example, the subsidy could apply only up to some multiple of base-period employment (perhaps 1.1 when the subsidy is calculated on net employment change above 90 percent of base-period employment). In a recession such a limit makes little sense, for without the subsidy few firms would have sufficiently large increases in employment to be constrained by this regulation. Between 1974 and 1975 employment increased by more than 10 percent in industries representing only 1 percent of private nonfarm employment, and by 5–10 percent in industries representing only 9 percent. Even between June 1975 and June 1976, when private nonfarm employment grew by 4 percent, industries representing only 7 percent of employment experienced employment increases above 10 percent.

Clearly, placing an upper limit on the subsidy will not reduce the windfall during a recession unless the limit is quite severe. And a ceiling would at all times add one more complication to the administrative regulations governing this wage subsidy program; though it would not necessitate collecting more information from participating employers, its existence might deter some employers from participating. The demonstrably small gains and the possibly large losses from such a limit make it appear inadvisable.

Results of Other Studies

Two other studies of employment tax credits have concentrated on particular aspects that are ignored here. Fethke and Williamson propose a variable credit applying to workers employed (they use the word *hired*, but net changes in employment are clearly implied) in excess of a changing base period of employment.[34] They propose that the credit be offered as a percentage of the hourly wage, rather than as a percentage of the wage bill. Their main contribution is to embed the labor-demand decision in a complete macroeconomic model. This allows them to simulate the effects of the credit under various government expenditure and tax policies. Their simulations indicate that such a credit will not cause prices to rise but will increase employment; it produces this felicitous result because of the assumption that labor supply is fairly elastic. This assumption is contradictory to observed fact during times of low unemployment and seems even less likely to hold when few job vacancies exist. It, and the assumption that the demand elasticity for labor is 1.0—a very large response in light of the discussion above—make the Fethke-Williamson results highly suspect.

Kesselman, Williamson, and Berndt ask what the path of the economy from 1962 to 1971 would have been had an employment tax credit been adopted instead of the investment tax credit that was instituted.[35] Dividing productive inputs into white-collar labor, blue-collar labor, and capital, they find that total employment would have been higher, but white-collar employment and the capital stock would have been lower. The study is useful in focusing on substitution among different types of labor. However, it is based on a very crude form of marginal credit, one far simpler than that discussed here. Further, it implicitly assumes there is no shifting, so that the entire credit acts as a wage reduction to employers. This ignores competition in the labor market among employers and the likely change in investment in training that would occur in the long run in response to a general wage subsidy. The main value of the study is to point out that if simply creating more jobs was the goal of the investment tax credit, that goal could have been better met by an employment tax credit.

34. "Employment Tax Credits as a Fiscal Policy Tool."
35. Jonathan R. Kesselman, Samuel H. Williamson, and Ernst R. Berndt, "Tax Credits for Employment Rather Than Investment," *American Economic Review*, vol. 67 (June 1977), pp. 339–49.

The simulations in this paper add to the earlier studies in two important ways: they use a demand elasticity that accords with the empirical literature *and* accounts for modifications necessitated by the type and timing of the subsidy; and they are based on a fine disaggregation of employment, which is essential in evaluating a subsidy that is linked to employment changes above a base. Taken together, the results of the three studies imply that an administratively simple subsidy that is generally applicable to all new employees will increase employment in the private sector in the short run at a cost not greater than the estimated cost of public service employment programs.

Changes in the Distribution of Employment

The distributional effects of a tax credit applied to the wage bill can be estimated by using past experience as a guide to the likely demographic characteristics of the marginal employee hired at different points in the business cycle.[36] Table 4 illustrates the demographic composition of marginal employment changes at different degrees of labor market tightness. A 6 percent unemployment rate among prime-age males was near the peak for the sample period, while 3.2 percent was the average. If a percentage wage subsidy is assumed to lead to an expansion of employment having the same demographic mix as has been observed in recent expansions due to increases in labor demand, a strict percentage employment tax credit in a recession would be biased slightly toward the hiring of prime-age workers and slightly against hiring younger, particularly black, workers. A dollar-amount subsidy would presumably lead to more favorable results, insofar as it provides a greater percentage subsidy for hiring low-wage workers. Although employment changes and budget costs per job differ little between the percentage and dollar-amount subsidies shown in tables 2 and 3, the distributional effects of marginal employment tax credits suggest that the dollar-amount subsidy is preferable.

36. The equation is: $E_i/E = a_0 + a_1 U + a_2 t + a_3 tU$, where E_i/E is the share in employment of the ith demographic group; U is the prime-age male unemployment rate, and t is a time trend. The employment data, from the Current Population Survey, are taken from Bureau of Labor Statistics, *Handbook of Labor Statistics, 1975 —Reference Edition*. The variable U is constructed from employment and labor force data from the same source. The equation is estimated using annual data, 1954– 75, for whites and nonwhites, males and females, for eight age groups.

Table 4. Simulated Demographic Composition of Net Change in Employment under a Percentage Employment Tax Credit
Percentage of total labor force

Workers, by age group	Prime-age male unemployment rate	
	6 percent	3.2 percent
White males		
16–19	4.00	4.40
20–24	7.40	7.00
55 and over	9.40	9.20
White females		
16–19	3.30	3.60
20–24	5.60	5.80
55 and over	6.10	6.00
Nonwhite males		
16–19	0.28	0.41
20–24	0.82	0.87
55 and over	0.90	0.91
Nonwhite females		
16–19	0.18	0.31
20–24	0.68	0.76
55 and over	0.64	0.64
All workers, 25–54	60.70	60.10

The demographic composition of the employment induced by a percentage marginal employment tax credit is likely to differ somewhat from the composition of public service employment under the Comprehensive Employment and Training Act (CETA) presented by Johnson and Tomola.[37] Their data show that 24 percent of enrollees in CETA were below twenty-two years of age and that nonwhites accounted for 34 percent of the enrollment. In table 4, youths sixteen to twenty-four years old constitute 22.3 percent of net employment changes at high unemployment; however, although it is not calculable from table 4, all nonwhites constitute only 9 percent of the changes. Recent changes restricting the targeting under CETA should orient the program even more toward low-income and minority workers.

These comparisons suggest that if a subsidy program of the same cost as a public employment program is to have the same demographic results, it will have to be based on a high dollar-amount subsidy per day. Only

37. George E. Johnson and James D. Tomola, "The Fiscal Substitution Effect of Alternative Approaches to Public Service Employment Policy," *Journal of Human Resources,* vol. 12 (Winter 1977), pp. 3–26.

then would the subsidy induce employment gains chiefly for the younger, low-income, and minority workers whose wages are likely to be below those of the average employee hired during a recession.

Policy Conclusions

The clear lack of employer enthusiasm for the categorical wage subsidies contained in the WIN and JOBS programs points to a different conclusion than does the low budgetary cost of an employment tax credit implied in the simulations here. Which is the more indicative of the likely experience if more widespread subsidies are given to expanding employment in the private sector? The best answer is that both provide information that is important for constructing successful wage subsidy policies. Experience with categorical subsidies suggests the importance of making the subsidy simple administratively and visible to people actually doing the hiring. Burying the credit on the back page of a tax return does not bring home the advantage of the subsidy to personnel offices. (In that regard, the smaller employer interest in WIN than in JOBS contracts indicates that it pays to involve personnel workers, as was done directly in JOBS, but not under the WIN credit.) Experience also suggests that any categorical subsidy or employment voucher scheme that offers subsidies that employers correlate with low productivity may be self-defeating. Singling out individuals or groups for a subsidy can imply that the subsidy is necessary in order for them to be worthwhile employees, which might be detrimental to their likelihood of becoming employed.

A preferable approach might be to offer a general wage subsidy that pays a high amount (say, $5) for each worker day of net increase in employment. Workers would not be stigmatized, but the subsidy would be biased in favor of low-wage workers. Such a subsidy should be relatively easy to administer, and personnel directors can easily understand it. However, as a long-term or permanent program, it induces less accumulation of physical capital and less investment in training than would otherwise occur. (Accepting the lower average output per worker that this implies may be a reasonable price to pay to increase and redistribute employment opportunities.) Thus it is as a short-term antirecession device that this subsidy, applied to employment changes above some fraction of base-period employment, is more appealing. Even when qualified by those conditions that govern estimates of the elasticity of labor demand in a recession, the dollar-amount marginal employment tax credit should have a relatively low budget cost per job created.

The controversy over public versus private job creation is obviously heavily ideological. The evidence here shows that private-sector job programs are not the panacea that some proponents claim them to be. Neither, though, is public service employment the boon that its proponents claim. Rather, each has its special economic and administrative problems that must be taken into account if the program is to be effective. Under CETA, especially in the 1973–75 recession and with the rapid expansion of title 6 since 1976, direct efforts to create jobs have been tilted sharply toward the public sector. A dollar-amount credit for marginal employment on corporate tax liability, with appropriate carry-forward provisions, simple to administer and temporary in nature, can be a worthwhile addition to the arsenal of job-creating weapons during recovery. It can redress the imbalance in subsidized job-creation efforts and do so at a cost per job roughly comparable to that of subsidized public service employment.

Appendix A: Elasticities of Labor Demand over the Business Cycle

The following equations were estimated for the private nonfarm sector, for the first quarter of 1955 through the fourth quarter of 1973:

(1)
$$\log N = 1.05 - 0.0059t + \sum_{i=0}^{7} \log W_{t-i-1}[\beta_{0i} + \beta_{1i}U]$$
$$(3.29) \quad (6.14)$$

$$+ \sum_{i=0}^{3} \log Q_{t-i-1}[\gamma_{0i} + \gamma_{1i}U];$$

$$R^2 = 0.992$$

and

(2)
$$\log (E/H) - \log (\overline{E/H}) = -0.030 + 0.0005t$$
$$(6.14) \quad (6.66)$$

$$+ \sum_{i=0}^{3} \log (N/\overline{N})_{t-i}[\delta_{0i} + \delta_{1i}U],$$

$$R^2 = 0.661$$

where

t = a time trend;

i = lag in quarters;

N = man-hours worked (by employees, proprietors, and unpaid family workers), in billions;

W = real compensation per man-hour, in dollars (the consumer price index was used to deflate the series; compensation consists of wages and salaries, employer contributions to social security, and employer-paid benefits);

Q = output (gross national product including government and farm production), in billions of constant dollars;

E = employment (including employees, proprietors, and unpaid family workers), in millions;

H = man-hours per employee (N/E);

$\overline{N}$ = full-employment man-hours, interpolated in a linear trend of log N between the fourth quarter of 1948, third quarters of 1953 and 1957, second quarter of 1960, and fourth quarters of 1969 and 1973;

$(\overline{E/H})$ = full-employment employment-hours ratio, interpolated in a linear trend between values of log E/H for one quarter after the peaks used for $\overline{N}$; and

U = unemployment rate of males between the ages of twenty-five and fifty-four, in percent.

The absolute values of the t statistics are in parentheses below the coefficient estimates. The first four variables defined are from unpublished data provided by the U.S. Bureau of Labor Statistics; U is calculated from BLS, *Handbook of Labor Statistics, 1974*. The model implied in the equations is an extended version of the demand equations in the model of Black and Kelejian.[38]

In table 5 the coefficient estimates and t statistics for the parameters β, γ, and δ are listed. As can be seen, the net effects of the interaction terms on log W are far greater than those on log Q.[39] A test of the interaction

38. S. W. Black and H. H. Kelejian, "A Macro Model of the U.S. Labor Market," *Econometrica*, vol. 38 (September 1970), pp. 712–41.

39. If the world is characterized by putty-clay technology, this result is precisely what one expects to observe. The output elasticity should be constant over the cycle (if technical change is either unbiased or proceeds slowly), for labor must be used in the fixed coefficients of clay technology if output is to expand regardless of the level of capacity utilization. The lower wage elasticity when unemployment is high

Table 5. Parameter Estimates of Labor Demand Equations[a]

Lag (in quarters)	β_0	β_1	γ_0	γ_1	δ_0	δ_1
0	−0.014	0.012	0.209	−0.005	0.312	−0.006
	(0.70)	(1.57)	(2.13)	(2.53)	(1.32)	(0.13)
1	−0.030	0.008	0.337	−0.001	0.365	−0.032
	(2.27)	(1.50)	(11.38)	(0.65)	(4.32)	(1.75)
2	−0.041	0.005	0.345	0.001	0.331	−0.039
	(4.70)	(1.38)	(5.61)	(1.62)	(2.44)	(1.44)
3	−0.047	0.002	0.233	0.002	0.209	−0.029
	(6.76)	(1.10)	(4.15)	(3.27)	(1.72)	(1.19)
4	−0.048	0.001	...	...	...	...
	(6.88)	(0.28)				
5	−0.044	−0.001	...	...	...	...
	(6.26)	(1.73)				
6	−0.034	−0.001	...	...	...	...
	(5.69)	(2.19)				
7	−0.020	−0.001	...	...	...	...
	(5.27)	(2.11)				

a. Numbers in parentheses are t statistics.

terms involving Q in equation 1 against the alternative equation with no interaction terms yields a value $F(2,68) = 2.70$. Since the 90 percent significance level with these degrees of freedom is 2.38, the hypothesis that the interaction terms on Q are all zero is rejected, although at a higher significance level it would not have been. The test on including the interaction terms in W in equation 1, given inclusion of those on Q, yields $F(2,66) = 13.47$, significantly different from zero even at the 99.9 percent level. Thus one can strongly reject the hypothesis that the interactions on W do not belong in equation 1. Finally, a test of the hypothesis that the interactions in equation 2 do not belong yields $F(2,70) = 1.65$; the hypothesis cannot be rejected.

Appendix B: Aggregation Biases in the Simulations

The simulations of the impact on employment of a marginal employment tax credit use data on 171 industries at the two-, three-, and four-digit

is consistent with the observation that little investment takes place then, and thus there is little opportunity for labor-capital subsitution. See Leif Johansen, "Substitution versus Fixed Production Coefficients in the Theory of Economic Growth: A Synthesis," *Econometrica,* vol. 27 (April 1959), pp. 157–76.

level of the standard industrial classification, but the credit will actually go to firms. What biases does this induce in the estimates of number of jobs created, program cost, and cost per job?

Aggregating data reduces the estimated variance of the observed ratios of employment in year t to that in year $t - 1$, denoted by y, in the absence of the tax credit. Using a symmetric distribution as an example, the true distribution of y for firms, $g(y)$, and the distribution for industries, $f(y)$, are shown in figure 1.

Let B denote the employment in year t relative to year $t - 1$ which must be reached before the firm qualifies for the credit. Consider three cases:

Case 1. $B = B_1 = 1$. Only firms whose employment does not decline qualify for the credit. Since, by construction, $g(y)$ and $f(y)$ are symmetric around B_1, the same number of firms (one-half) actually qualify as estimated in the simulations. Actual thus equals simulated job creation. However, $E[y \mid y > 1; g(y)] > E[y \mid y \geq 1; f(y)]$, where E is the expectations operator, so true program cost exceeds simulated cost, as does the cost per job.

Case 2. $B = B_2$. Then $F(\infty) \mid y \geq B_2$ exceeds $G(\infty) \mid y \geq B_2$ by the maximum amount possible, where F and G are truncated cumulative distributions. When the lower limit subsidized equals B_2, simulated job creation

Figure 1. Distribution of Firms and Industries in Private Nonfarm Sector

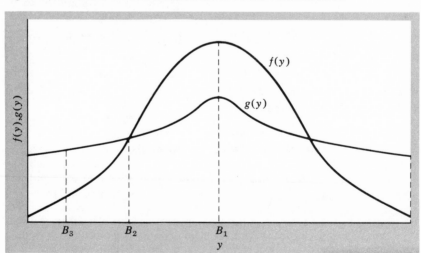

exceeds actual by the greatest margin. Further $E[y|y \geq B_2; g(y)] > E[y|y \geq B_2; f(y)]$, as in case 1, but now by an even larger amount. Program cost is underestimated, as is the cost per job.

Case 3. $B = B_3$. Although $F(\infty)|y \geq B_3$ exceeds $G(\infty)|y \geq B_3$, the difference is less than in case 2, and thus the overestimate of the number of jobs created is smaller. Similarly, although the actual expected value of y truncated at B_3 exceeds the simulated expected value, the difference is smaller than in case 2, as is the downward bias in the cost per job.

Clearly, for symmetric distributions f and g, for which the demand elasticities are identical, or at least distributed identically for all firms, the simulations usually overstate the number of jobs created and understate costs. The extent of these biases cannot be determined, but two considerations suggest they are small. First, it is likely even in a recession year that only a very small fraction of firms (weighted by employment) find their employment below 85 percent of the previous year's. If so, the differences between simulated and actual number of jobs created and program costs are small. Second, with disaggregation as fine as it is in these simulations, the differences between the distributions f and g are probably small. Indeed, the variance among industries can exceed that among firms to the extent that conglomerate firms account for a large fraction of employment.

Comments by Edward M. Gramlich

Daniel Hamermesh has given a useful review of wage subsidy programs that operates on both the factual and the simulation level. He describes various wage subsidies offered in various countries, reviews the pros and cons of each, and discusses the likely effects of wage subsidies based both on the experience of small-scale programs and on standard econometric estimates of labor demand elasticities.

The paper forced me to think about the general issue of how best to stimulate employment. In these comments I would like to add to Hamermesh's thoughts, focusing on two important issues: whether a wage subsidy program to create jobs should be basically cyclical or basically structural; and what kind of subsidy deal the federal government should make with a prospective employer.

Although Hamermesh does discuss the difference between the cyclical and structural variants of employer wage subsidies, most of his work and all of his simulation evidence refer to cyclical programs. In the simulations he assumes a subsidy for all workers regardless of their wage rate and he observes the four-quarter impact of the subsidy, coming out with a fairly positive verdict on the cost-effectiveness of that approach. While I make no claims of expertise, the cyclical programs seem less appealing politically than the structural type. There are now alternatives to wage subsidies as countercyclical policy—the country can lower taxes and beef up automatic stabilizers such as unemployment insurance—but the same may not be true for structural policy. Underemployment of certain types of workers is a problem that persists in good years and bad, and it may be that wage subsidies offer a good way to attack the problem. I would have liked more discussion and simulation treatment of structural policy in the paper.

In addition, I do not believe that two problems with wage subsidies that Hamermesh identifies are difficulties for the structural variant. Hamermesh points out that any attempt to augment demand only works insofar as supply is reasonably elastic—otherwise it will just result in higher wages with little effect on employment. If one adheres to the traditional view that employment is low because legal or social minimum wages are high, Hamermesh's criticism is not relevant because demand would be expanded over an elastic portion of the supply curve. Once this excess supply was eliminated, Hamermesh's criticism would be right, but that is no more a drawback of wage subsidies than saying aspirin is no good because you no longer have a headache. If, on the other hand, you believe that statistical unemployment is high among low-skill groups because low wages lead to high turnover, then an employer wage subsidy will indeed cause low wages to be bid up. But that would give a healthy boost to earned income and would even serve to reduce unemployment. Either way, therefore, I think proponents of wage subsidies should not be embarrassed by this argument.

A second argument, new in the Hamermesh paper, is that identifying the least employable workers puts a stigma on them. Hamermesh speculates that targeting wage subsidies on them, as a structural program would, will be self-defeating because it signals to employers that these workers are of low productivity. But if the program is targeted according to low wage rates (a reasonable measure), then surely this criticism becomes a red herring. What bad information can such a government program give out that the market is not already giving out?

The second extension I would like to make on the Hamermesh paper involves an important difference between private wage subsidies, as they are usually understood, and public employment as it is usually understood. The federal government is assumed to be making a different deal with employers in each case—on private wage subsidies paying a certain proportion of the cost of employing either all workers (in the cyclical program) or disadvantaged workers (in the structural variant), and for public service employment making a fixed grant to local governments for the wages (and possibly overhead) of certain workers, some of whom the local government may already be employing. If for simplicity's sake both types of employers or their consumers (taxpayers, in the case of public employment) are assumed to be consuming the services of employees, the wage subsidy program is tantamount to an open-end categorical price reduction grant, while public service employment is tantamount to a closed-end categorical grant.

The two cases are illustrated in figure 2. If standard reasoning is followed, the open-end subsidy will stimulate employers to move along the price-consumption line; the closed-end subsidy, even if it pays all of the costs of employment over a limited range, will have no marginal effect on relative wages and will just encourage employers to move along the income-consumption line. Consumers' or taxpayers' utility is higher per dollar of federal grant in the first case because it is not necessary to alter

Figure 2. Effect on Employment of Closed-end and Open-end Subsidies

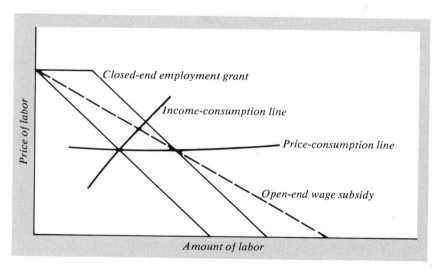

consumption to get the federal money, but the employment increase per dollar is larger in the second case, because the relative wage substitution effect is added to the income effect. These conclusions hinge, of course, on the public employment grant being limited to employment levels that are small relative to normal employment by local governments. However, fear of displacement has provoked vehement arguments against a public-service-employment approach, and in a world of limited federal budgetary dollars and large state and local employment this fear must be viewed as a valid problem. The difference between the two approaches, then, depends on the elasticity of employment demand. Hamermesh evaluates the two in terms of their relative price effects—the terms that usually distinguish economists' approach to a problem. It has always seemed to me that empirical researchers both work hard to find relative price effects and in summarizing the work of others tend to magnify them. In the paper that Hamermesh draws on for his estimate of the long-run elasticity of demand, the median he cited was 0.75.[40] According to my reading of table 1 in that paper, ten of the thirteen studies he summarized had estimates below that. I would not conclude that there is a lot of "agreement" on this point among past examinations of labor demand.

Many readers may be surprised at Hamermesh's assertion that an even higher demand elasticity may be appropriate for low-wage workers (as opposed to all workers) because most of the work on minimum wages has found rather low elasticities. As Hamermesh notes, I believe that the apparent anomaly is partly due to a dilution effect.[41] Minimum-wage equations usually explain teenage employment or unemployment, but less than half of all teenagers are getting wages close to the minimum; therefore the elasticity of demand for them in response to changes in the minimum shows up as zero. Another explanation, again focusing on teenagers, is due to measurement. A major effect on the relative availability of full-time versus part-time jobs in response to changes in the minimum wage is masked by a much smaller total employment effect.

While these factors can reduce the disparity between the econometric evidence for labor as a whole and for low-wage workers, I do not believe the elasticities for the latter should be very high. On the basis of both the overall labor-force work and the low-wage work, a reasonable median for low-wage workers alone would be somewhere between 0.5 and 0.75.

Let me give a hand-calculator computation of the relative employ-

40. Hamermesh, "Econometric Studies of Labor Demand."
41. See Gramlich, "Impact of Minimum Wages."

ment increases from both types of approaches—an open-end wage subsidy for employers and a closed-end public service employment grant. In both cases I assume that only low-wage employment is being subsidized, and prevailing wages are in the elastic portion of the aggregate supply curve for these workers (blame it on the minimum wage if you wish). The final figure is the federal budget cost of creating a low-wage job. I am focusing on the bang for the buck since federal taxpayers should want to get the greatest reduction in structural unemployment per tax dollar.

I compare the budget costs for a 25 percent wage subsidy for private firms and a $10 billion public employment program. In each case the target population is the 9.3 million workers who made less than $2.25 per hour in 1975. This group worked an average of about thirty-five hours per week, at a mean wage of about $2.00 per hour, earning total wages of $33.9 billion. A private wage subsidy is assumed to pay one-quarter of the $33.9 billion that firms now spend on low-wage labor plus one-quarter of the cost of any employment increases—the subsidy is not confined to increases in employment. The employment increases obviously depend on estimates of the elasticity of demand for low-wage labor; I have used long-run estimates of 0.5 and 0.75.

On the public employment side, I assume that the federal government grants an additional $10 billion to states and localities and that their marginal spending propensity is either 0.4 (as in most estimates of revenue sharing) or 0.6 (the estimate of Johnson and Tomola and Wiseman, that is based on less displacement).[42] In either case, two-thirds of this money is actually spent on wages, with the remainder going to overhead (approximately the proportions in the state-local nonconstruction budget in 1975). Jobs are created that are assumed to pay $2.25 an hour for thirty-five hours a week, or $4,095 per year.

Under these assumptions, which should bracket most of the possibilities, private wage subsidies would create more low-wage jobs per dollar than public employment. The cost of a wage subsidy is only $5,795 per job using Hamermesh's long-run elasticity of demand of 0.75 and $8,136 under my less optimistic version of 0.5. Public employment, on the other hand, costs between $9,709 and $14,706 per job, depending on the degree of displacement. A full benefit-cost calculation that included gains to taxpayers and consumers would show public employment to have somewhat

42. See Johnson and Tomola, "Efficacy of Public Service Employment Programs"; and Michael Wiseman, "Public Employment as Fiscal Policy," *BPEA, 1:1976,* pp. 67–104.

lower costs than the above numbers, but open-end subsidies would continue to be more cost-effective from the standpoint of low-wage workers than their closed-end counterparts.

There are many differences between programs of wage subsidies paid to private employers and public employment grants made to local governments. The skill mix is different in the two sectors, the degree of potential displacement is different, the output produced by the workers will be subjected to a different "market" test, and the subsidy rates will probably be different. I have ignored these differences and focused instead on the nature of the bribe the federal government is making to low-wage employers. If public employment is to be used to attain structural objectives, I would argue first for focusing the subsidy on low-wage disadvantaged workers, and second for making it an open-end price reduction for employers. If the policy mandate is aimed at stimulating employment more broadly, I also would argue for including private employers in the program. Indeed, if its aim is very broad, the potential price sensitivity of demand for low-wage employment might be another important consideration guiding the choice of precisely which employers are, and which are not, eligible for the subsidy.

Comments by Robert I. Lerman

Too frequently in analyses of problems of unemployment and low income, the dichotomies of the two problems are overemphasized. One consequence is a tendency to design entirely separate policies to deal with each problem. To solve the low-income problem, we focus exclusively on designing transfers efficiently; to solve the unemployment problem, we emphasize jobs, training, and transfers for the unemployed. Until recently, little attention has been paid to the interaction between the two kinds of policies. We have just begun to look carefully at the overlap between income maintenance for the unemployed (unemployment insurance) and income maintenance for the poor (aid to families with dependent children). Even less attention has been given to labor subsidies as a means of income maintenance. Here, policymakers are ahead of economists, as indicated both by the demonstration projects in which state officials propose to use unemployment insurance and other income maintenance money to create jobs and by the emphasis on creating jobs in recent welfare reform proposals.

Analyses of wage subsidies and public employment should consider not only their employment effects but their effectiveness in achieving income-transfer objectives. A jobs or wage-subsidy program might involve lost output yet still be a less costly manner of transferring income than a straight transfer program. With this standard of comparison, the design of subsidies and our judgments of their value might be different from what they otherwise would be.

Some of my comments on the Hamermesh paper are from this perspective. He downgrades categorical wage subsidies on the grounds that they will not do much to reduce unemployment rates even though they will raise earnings somewhat. What is wrong with that result? Even if wage subsidies do not have much effect on overall unemployment they may be preferable to other policies as a means of increasing the income of low-wage workers.

I do not fully understand Hamermesh's point that categorical wage subsidies may not help the unemployment rate of unskilled workers in periods of high employment. He seems to say that additional unskilled workers must enter the labor force if employment among that group is to increase, and, thus, that their unemployment rate may not fall.

I have two objections. First, if unemployment rates are high among unskilled groups even near cyclical peaks, why is an increase in their participation in the labor force necessary in order to raise their employment when their wages are subsidized for employers? Even if their rate of participation does increase and measured unemployment rates do not fall much, their net increase in employment should be welcomed. Surely we are more interested in this than their measured unemployment rate.

In general, I do not think Hamermesh deals sufficiently with the possibility that by targeting subsidies and jobs programs on low-skilled groups, the tightening of labor markets can be made selective enough to limit the contribution to inflation as demand expands.

Hamermesh separates the effects of a hiring subsidy (or equivalently, of a training subsidy for new employees) on turnover and on-the-job training. He postulates that a hiring subsidy will increase turnover and have a churning effect. Then he goes on to say the long-run effect of high turnover on training is going to depend on whether the training occurs mostly in the initial stages of job tenure or more uniformly over the whole period. He concludes that the induced churning is likely to lead to a lower accumulation of human capital, because it will lower the average tenure of new employees and push them into the range where there are still increasing returns. However, if workers accumulate sufficient training along any training curve shortly after being hired, then the hiring subsidy need not have the postulated turnover effects and adverse effects on training. Turnover and on-the-job training must be considered simultaneously, not sequentially.

In his simulation results, Hamermesh focuses on the breakdown by age, sex, and race of induced employment. It is their distribution effects he considers, and not the income distribution effects. But if a major concern is targeting, unskilled primary workers—even white males between the ages of twenty-five and fifty who head families—may be of as much interest as teenagers. Note, however, that if a program is targeted on the most disadvantaged of males twenty-five to fifty years old, then using regressions based on age, sex, race, and unemployment rates would not be too instructive for determining the effects of wage subsidies on unemployment and inflation.

Hamermesh asserts that a major problem of categorical subsidies is that they may be counterproductive, since they may tell employers something about people who the government thinks need a subsidy that would lead employers to shy away from them. I could find no direct evidence to demonstrate that this really happens, and it seems to me that it is not nearly as plausible as Hamermesh would want us to believe. Two conditions have to be satisfied for Hamermesh's assertion to be valid. First, the information about the subsidized worker that is being transmitted by the subsidy must not be easily obtainable by the employer any other way. If it is easy to discover a person's welfare status (in the case of the WIN tax credit), then the subsidy should have no added adverse effects. Second, the subsidy must not apply to a broad group, one that employers believe has members with a wide variation in skills. If it does, the subsidy's information value is too general to have much relevance to the hiring decision.

Finally, let me point out that the wage rate subsidies with the best potential for achieving a combination of employment and income support goals are those paid to workers, rather than employers. Hamermesh does not discuss these, perhaps because simple wage rate subsidies would not be highly targeted on the poor. Unfortunately, it is less well known that certain categorical wage rate subsidies, such as those paid only to primary earners in families with children, compare well in targeting with income transfer programs. Since these wage rate subsidies also have work incentive features superior to those of direct transfer programs, they deserve serious consideration as part of a mix of employment and income-support policies.

George E. Johnson

Structural Unemployment Consequences of Job Creation Policies

The predominant approach to public service employment programs in the United States, as carried out under the Comprehensive Employment and Training Act, has been the transfer of federal funds to local governments to help them expand employment. Programs of this sort can have short-term countercyclical objectives of preventing contraction of state and local employment during recessions, or longer term antipoverty goals of providing jobs for individuals subject to low income and high unemployment; or they may be a disguised form of general revenue sharing (generally resulting in property tax relief in the guise of more jobs). This paper concentrates on selected issues associated with programs aimed at improving the labor market position of the disadvantaged.

Historically, employment in the state and local government sector has been much less cyclically sensitive than has private sector employment, so used as a countercyclical instrument, employment programs probably should not focus on the public sector.[1] In any event, there is little reason to prefer them over general revenue sharing grants for countercyclical purposes. Programs that are designed to accomplish other objectives, such as property tax relief, should be described in their proper terms rather than as programs to create jobs for the unemployed. The most important objective of public service employment programs is to improve the earnings position of the disadvantaged.

I am grateful to Orley C. Ashenfelter, Harvey E. Brazer, Edward M. Gramlich, Frank P. Stafford, and Ernst W. Stromsdorfer for comments on an earlier version of this paper.

1. See George E. Johnson and James D. Tomola, "The Fiscal Substitution Effect of Alternative Approaches to Public Service Employment Policy," *Journal of Human Resources,* vol. 12 (Winter 1977), pp. 3–26.

A public employment program that is successful in providing jobs for the poor is formally equivalent to an economy-wide subsidy on unskilled (or low-wage) labor. The first section of the paper investigates the probable impact of such a subsidy on output, employment, and the distribution of net income. From a normative point of view, the answer to the question of whether such a program is desirable depends on how labor markets work—in particular, how rapidly unskilled wages adjust in the face of abnormally high or low unemployment, the degree to which different skills are substitutable for each other in the production process, and the elasticity of occupational choice with respect to relative net incomes. The answer depends also on how benefits and costs are measured—by the discounted value of future gross national product, the net real income of the poor or the upper middle class, and the unemployment rate at a nonaccelerating rate of inflation. This paper does not attempt to specify how such benefits and costs should be measured—that is essentially a political question. Rather it points out how a generalized subsidy would affect these measures. A somewhat disturbing factor is the high degree of uncertainty the professional economics literature reflects about the way labor markets work. It is possible to predict a very wide range of outcomes of a generalized wage subsidy on the basis of the received wisdom of modern labor economics.

The second section of the paper examines problems associated with the use of the public sector as the exclusive vehicle for subsidizing low-wage labor. The best known of these is the fiscal substitution effect, the tendency for local governments to use employment grants as a substitute for local tax revenues or general revenue sharing grants meant to meet other needs. It can be argued, however, that this problem is of much less consequence than the fact that the state and local government sector is extremely skill intensive—more so than any other major industry classification. Thus, a general expansion of the state and local sector is equivalent to a subsidy on skilled labor rather than on low-wage labor, and it has perverse effects on output, employment, and income distribution. This might be overcome by changing the nature of jobs programs, but the conditions for overcoming it are rather stringent.

The Impact of a General Wage Subsidy

A public service employment program that is intended as a permanent antipoverty program provides a certain number of jobs in the public sector to members of the low-wage or unskilled labor force. That number of unskilled persons is thus removed from the unskilled labor force of the private sector. From the point of view of the aggregate labor market, this is equivalent to imposing a subsidy on low-wage employment such that the additional public workers would be hired at the going unskilled wage. It is thus useful to examine the impact of such a subsidy on output, employment, and the distribution of income, for this helps clarify (depending on what is considered important) whether or not public employment programs are desirable.

Model of the Labor Market's Adjustment to a Wage Change

To keep matters straightforward, assume that each person in the labor force is readily classifiable as either skilled (high wage) or unskilled (low wage). Except in times of severe recession, skilled labor is close to fully employed (that is, its equilibrium unemployment rate is 2.5–3 percent); but the same cannot be said of unskilled labor. Even when the aggregate unemployment rate is around 5 percent, given the current composition of the labor force, the unskilled unemployment rate is usually between 12 percent and 20 percent, depending on how *skill* is defined. And this rate is much higher if the potential rather than the measured labor force is used in calculating the unemployment rate.

Why is there such a disparity in the labor market situation facing the two types of workers? Consider the demand conditions they each face. Each employer hires a combination of skilled and unskilled workers, and the ratio in which they are hired depends on the ratio of their wage rates. If the unskilled wage rises relative to the skilled wage, each employer will attempt to substitute skilled for unskilled workers,[2] and the level of employment of unskilled labor relative to the employment of skilled labor will fall. Thus, in the aggregate, the ratio of unskilled to skilled employment varies inversely with R, the wage of unskilled relative to that of skilled workers.

2. The elasticity of substitution between the two classes of labor is defined as the negative of the percentage change in the relative demand for the two types of labor with respect to a percentage change in the relative wage. Estimates of its value vary widely, but it probably ranges from 1.0 to 1.5. See Philip Cotterill, "The Elasticity of Demand for Low-Wage Labor," *Southern Economic Journal*, vol. 41 (January 1975), pp. 520–25; and Albert Zucker, "Minimum Wages and the Long-Run Elasticity of Demand for Low-Wage Labor," *Quarterly Journal of Economics*, vol. 87 (May 1973), pp. 267–77.

The geometric depiction of the equilibrium of the aggregate market is given in figure 1. The ratio of unskilled to skilled workers is downward-sloping with respect to the relative wage, and the ratio of the unskilled potential labor force to the skilled labor force is assumed to be exogenously determined. (The number of hours of work is also assumed to be both exogenous and the same for all employed workers.) At the initial relative wage R_0, the distance ab reflects the fact that the unskilled unemployment rate is greater than the skilled unemployment rate.

This diagram does not explain why the unskilled unemployment rate is so high, but it points to the polar explanations of the phenomenon. It is possible that the relative wage is institutionally fixed at too high a level, so that the number of job opportunities for unskilled workers is rationed by unemployment. The institutional mechanism by which this takes place could be legal minimum wages. The legal minimum has historically been set at roughly half the average manufacturing wage, and minimum wages do appear to have an effect on those above the minimum.[3] Whatever the mechanism by which the relative wage has been set at R_0, however, the *minimum wage* is assumed in figure 1 to be the reason for the disparity in unemployment rates. If it were possible to lower the relative wage to R', unemployment rates of the two types of labor would be equal.

An alternative explanation focuses on the possibility that, due to the enormous turnover of labor in unskilled jobs, the unskilled labor market *is* in equilibrium at a high unemployment rate and relative wage of R_0.[4] In this quasi-full-employment model there has to be a certain very high unemployment rate in the unskilled market because an enormous amount of turnover and job search is required for the market to be in equilibrium. Thus, if for some reason the relative wage got down to R', severe vacancies would exist in jobs for the unskilled until the relative wage was driven back to R_0 (and the unskilled unemployment rate up to its normal value).

The minimum wage and quasi-full-employment models have very sim-

3. See Finis Welch, "Minimum Wage Legislation in the United States," *Economic Inquiry*, vol. 12 (September 1974), pp. 285–318. Also see Edward M. Gramlich, "Impact of Minimum Wages on Other Wages, Employment, and Family Incomes," *Brookings Papers on Economic Activity*, 2:1976, pp. 409–51. Among other explanations for the high relative wage is the "key worker" hypothesis advanced by Sara Behman in "Labor Mobility, Increasing Labor Demand, and Money Wage-Rate Increases in United States Manufacturing," *Review of Economic Studies*, vol. 31 (October 1964), pp. 267–86.

4. See Robert E. Hall, "Turnover in the Labor Force," *BPEA, 3:1972*, pp. 709–56; and Stephen T. Marston, "Employment Instability and High Unemployment Rates," *BPEA, 1:1976*, pp. 169–203.

Figure 1. Equilibrium of the Labor Market

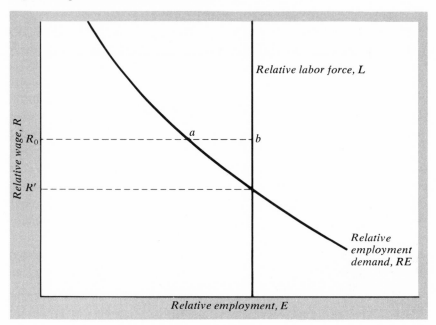

ilar implications for the effect of monetary and fiscal policy on the employment of low-wage labor. An increase in, say, federal government spending unaccompanied by an increase in taxes will increase the demand for both skilled and unskilled labor. This will cause abnormally high vacancies in the skilled labor market, and the skilled wage will be bid up until the skilled unemployment rate is back to its equilibrium value of 2.5–3 percent.[5] If, on the other hand, the wage rate for unskilled labor remains fixed (or rises much less than the rate for skilled labor), this fiscal policy will cause an increase in unskilled employment; in terms of figure 1 the relative wage will fall on a more or less permanent basis, and the two unemployment rates will be driven closer to equality.

According to the minimum wage model, however, the wage rate for unskilled workers will not remain constant. If a rise in the skilled wage causes an increase in the legislated minimum wage, the wage of unskilled

5. Edmund S. Phelps, "Money-Wage Dynamics and Labor-Market Equilibrium," *Journal of Political Economy*, vol. 76, pt. 2 (July-August 1968), pp. 678–711, describes the type of mechanism by which this might occur. Empirical estimates along the lines of his model have been carried out.

relative to skilled workers will return to R_0, thus choking off the expansion of unskilled employment. The same thing will happen if wages change for some other reason—for example, if for reasons of equity, employers give percentage increases to all employees, skilled and unskilled. Thus, in the face of a stimulative fiscal policy, as skilled labor goes so goes unskilled labor. Similarly, in the quasi-full-employment model, since the unskilled labor market is assumed to be in equilibrium before the increase in the demand, the increase will simply cause the unskilled wage to be bid up by exactly the same process as the skilled wage is bid up; so monetary and fiscal policy cannot have a long-term effect on unskilled employment.

The minimum wage and quasi-full-employment models, however, do have very different implications for the impact of a wage subsidy on unskilled labor. Suppose that the federal government offers a tax rebate to employers in proportion to the number of unskilled workers they employ such that, at the original relative wage R_0, the relative employment demand function shifts from RE' to RE'' (see figure 2). In the minimum wage model, this causes an increase in the relative employment of un-

Figure 2. Adjustment of Labor Market to Abnormal Unemployment of Low-skilled Labor

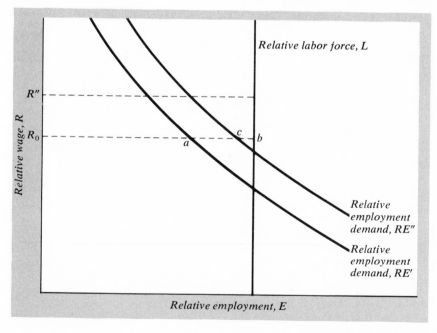

skilled labor from *a* to *c* and, of course, a narrowing of the unemployment disparity between unskilled and skilled labor. In the quasi-full-employment model, on the other hand, the long-run impact of the wage subsidy is solely an increase in the relative wage to R'', for the unemployment rates of both types of labor must return to their equilibrium values.

The minimum wage and quasi-full-employment models are in fact polar cases of the adjustment of the relative wage in the face of abnormally high or low unemployment of unskilled labor. The crucial parameter is the slope of the short-run Phillips curve for unskilled labor—the relationship between that group's unemployment rate and the rate of change of its wage rate. In the minimum wage model its value is assumed to be zero and in the quasi-full-employment model it is assumed to be positive. Surprisingly little is known about the wage flexibility of the unskilled labor market. Recent estimates of aggregate Phillips curves have been based on unemployment rates that assign a fixed weight to less skilled workers in the aggregate labor force.[6] This is consistent with the conclusion of the minimum wage model that unskilled unemployment does not matter. There is substantial evidence, however, that at least some unskilled labor markets do adjust in the face of abnormal unemployment, as the quasi-full-employment model implies they will in the long run.[7] The rate of adjustment for unskilled labor markets is probably much lower than that for skilled labor markets. The evidence for this is fragmentary, however, and reasonable estimates of the adjustment parameter could encompass quite a wide range.

Effect of a Subsidy on Low-skilled Labor

To determine the likely impact of a jobs program on employment and the size and distribution of output, the general model can be written algebraically and solved for the relevant variables in terms of time and the values of the parameters.[8] For numerical purposes assume that 30 percent of the aggregate potential labor force of 100 million persons falls into the

6. See, for example, Robert E. Hall, "The Process of Inflation in the Labor Market," *BPEA, 2:1974,* pp. 343–93; and Michael L. Wachter, "The Changing Cyclical Responsiveness of Wage Inflation," *BPEA, 1:1976,* pp. 115–59.

7. See, for example, Robert W. Crandall, C. Duncan MacRae, and Lorene Y. L. Yap, "An Econometric Model of the Low-Skill Labor Market," *Journal of Human Resources,* vol. 10 (Winter 1975), pp. 3–24.

8. See George E. Johnson, "The Potential Efficacy of Labor Market Policy" (January 1977; processed).

unskilled category and that the equilibrium unemployment rate of unskilled workers is 20 percent. Further, assume that the skilled unemployment rate is always zero (a rate of 3 percent would cause only a trivial change in income distribution). The annual wages of skilled and unskilled workers are assumed to be $8,000 and $6,000, respectively.[9]

Given these assumptions, the impact of a $1 billion wage subsidy for unskilled labor on aggregate employment is shown in table 1. The instantaneous impact is 208,000 jobs, which by the minimum wage model lasts indefinitely. If, however, the relative wage is free to adjust, the impact of the program on employment eventually goes to zero. How rapidly the impact diminishes depends on the slope of the wage adjustment function for unskilled labor. If the unskilled wage is as flexible as the skilled wage, a slope of about 0.7, the impact is essentially zero after a few years. If there is some, but very little wage flexibility (a slope of 0.1), the impact on employment persists for some time.[10] Thus, the effect of a wage subsidy scheme on unemployment is greater the more slowly wages of the unskilled adjust.

The impact of a wage subsidy on the level and distribution of output is more interesting. First, in the minimum wage model the program is an unmitigated free lunch—a $1 billion subsidy increases GNP by $1.25 billion immediately and for all time.[11] Assuming that government spending, not including transfers, is fixed at 20 percent of the original value of GNP and that income taxes are proportional, the distribution of this increase between skilled and unskilled workers depends on the replacement ratio, the fraction of potential income of the unskilled that is replaced by transfers such as unemployment insurance. If there is no replacement, $1.05 billion goes to the unskilled and $0.20 billion to the skilled (the latter gain because some previously unemployed unskilled persons now pay taxes); for a replacement ratio of 30 percent, $0.81 billion goes to the unskilled and $0.44 billion to the skilled; and for a

9. A value of 1.25 is assumed for the elasticity of substitution of skilled for unskilled workers. This is the midpoint of the range mentioned in note 2, above.

10. It can be shown algebraically that the total cumulative impact of the wage subsidy on unskilled employment is given by the reciprocal of the product of the slope of the Phillips curve for unskilled labor and the elasticity of substitution between skilled and unskilled labor. This is true even if, as has not been assumed in the above numerical example, actual unskilled employment adjusts to desired skilled employment with a lag or the skilled wage rate adjusts less than instantaneously to deviations in the equilibrium unemployment rate for skilled workers.

11. Since the wage subsidy is simply a transfer program and only a minor part of it (administrative costs) reflects the use of productive resources, any increase in GNP represents a net gain to society.

Table 1. Effect of $1 Billion Subsidy for Unskilled Labor, by Rate of Wage Adjustment
Thousands of jobs

Rate of wage adjustment	Years				
	1	2	5	10	15
0	208	208	208	208	208
0.1	184	162	112	60	32
0.2	162	126	60	17	5
0.4	126	77	17	1	0
0.7	87	36	3	0	0

replacement ratio of 70 percent, which is much more liberal than the present system, unskilled net income increases by $0.51 billion and skilled net income by $0.74 billion. Thus, the size of the replacement ratio is critical in assessing the distributional consequences of the wage subsidy scheme.[12]

If there is a tendency for relative wages to adjust, the long-run effect of the program on GNP and its distribution is different. In the long run—which is from five to ten years, depending on how quickly wages adjust—the program only transfers net income from the skilled to the unskilled and does not add to overall GNP. The time paths of these impacts are shown for a replacement ratio of 30 percent in table 2. It is clear, then, that the wage subsidy scheme is an effective method of transferring income from skilled to unskilled labor. Also, along the way to complete adjustment of the labor market, the policy has *net* positive effects on GNP. On grounds of strict self-interest, of course, skilled persons will never buy the program (unless they have such high discount rates that the initial saving in taxes outweighs the subsequent reduction in their net income). But such a program would make their less fortunate cousins better off.

The preceding results are based on the assumption that the wage subsidy on unskilled income has no effect on training decisions of future cohorts entering the labor force. This is, in fact, unrealistic, for it is well known that particular labor supply curves are very elastic with respect to returns.[13] If it is assumed instead that future cohorts base their decisions

12. For estimates of the replacement ratios faced by different demographic groups, see Edward M. Gramlich, "The Distributional Effects of Higher Unemployment," *BPEA, 2:1974*, pp. 293–336.

13. See, for example, Richard B. Freeman, "Overinvestment in College Training?" *Journal of Human Resources*, vol. 10 (Summer 1975), pp. 287–311; and George E. Johnson, "The Demand for Labor by Educational Category," *Southern Economic Journal*, vol. 37 (October 1970), pp. 190–204.

Table 2. Impact of $1 Billion Subsidy on Income of Skilled and Unskilled Labor, by Rate of Wage Adjustment
Billions of constant dollars

Rate of wage adjustment and effect on GNP	Years			
	1	5	10	Long run
Moderate rate (0.2)				
Change in GNP	0.97	0.36	0.10	0
Unskilled labor's share	0.78	0.71	0.68	0.67
Skilled labor's share	0.19	−0.35	−0.58	−0.67
High rate (0.7)				
Change in GNP	0.52	0.02	0	0
Unskilled labor's share	0.73	0.67	0.67	0.67
Skilled labor's share	−0.21	−0.65	−0.67	−0.67

in part on the relative net incomes of skilled and unskilled labor, the implications of a wage subsidy program may be very different. An improvement in the relative position of unskilled labor due to the subsidy—because of lower unemployment, higher relative wages, or both—may cause some young persons to decide against completing a community college program and thus may increase the future ratio of unskilled to skilled labor force. This will in turn dampen the favorable impact of the wage subsidy on unskilled labor.

The implications of this disincentive can be explored by considering the impact of a $1 billion subsidy on skilled and unskilled employment at different values of the elasticity (with respect to relative wages) of the relative supply of labor.[14] The variation in the supply of labor is assumed to be affected only by new entrants into the labor force, whose mean potential attachment to the labor force is assumed to be forty years.

As table 3 shows, if there is no adjustment in relative wages the program still yields a positive increase in employment at all times. There will, however, be a reduction in the skilled labor force, and since unskilled employment is a constant proportion of skilled employment, the increase in unskilled employment will be lower than the 208,000 initial impact

14. Not very much is known about the actual value of the educational parameter (it is roughly akin to the elasticity of high school completion with respect to the expected earnings of those who graduate relative to those who do not among individuals who would not be expected to go on to postsecondary schooling). It is generally assumed that it is fairly high because the wage elasticity of the supply of college graduates is high (over 2.0). (Freeman, "Overinvestment?" and Johnson, "Demand for Labor.")

(table 1). For any degree of labor market adjustment, however, the long-run effect of the wage subsidy scheme on total employment is negative simply because the equilibrium unemployment rate of unskilled workers exceeds that of skilled workers; hence any program that raises the relative size of the unskilled labor force raises the long-run level of unemployment. Notice in table 3, however, that no matter how the relative supply of labor varies, the subsidy results in an increase in employment in the short run.

These results suggest a method of determining from a conventional benefit-cost point of view whether or not a program of wage subsidies should be undertaken. The change in GNP due to the program is roughly equal to the skilled wage times the change in skilled employment, plus the unskilled wage times the change in unskilled employment. If there is any adjustment in relative wages, the change in aggregate GNP is initially positive (208,000 times the unskilled wage rate), but it subsequently falls until it reaches a negative value, as is shown in figure 3. The net present value of the program (ignoring administrative costs) is the discounted

Table 3. Effect of $1 Billion Subsidy on Skilled and Unskilled Employment, by Supply Elasticity and Rate of Wage Adjustment

Thousands of jobs

Elasticity of labor supply and rate of wage adjustment	Years					
	1	2	5	10	15	Long run
Moderate elasticity (1.75)						
No adjustment						
Skilled labor	−5	−10	−23	−40	−54	−97
Unskilled labor	207	205	201	195	190	175
Moderate adjustment (0.2)						
Skilled labor	−5	−10	−25	−46	−62	−106
Unskilled labor	161	125	64	36	39	85
High adjustment (0.7)						
Skilled labor	−5	−11	−27	−47	−63	−106
Unskilled labor	87	39	17	33	47	85
Low elasticity (1.0)						
Moderate adjustment (0.2)						
Skilled labor	−3	−6	−15	−28	−39	−81
Unskilled labor	162	126	62	28	26	65
High elasticity (2.5)						
Moderate adjustment (0.2)						
Skilled labor	−7	−15	−35	−61	−81	−121
Unskilled labor	161	125	65	43	51	97

value of the area under the curve; for a subsidy on unskilled employment, this is more likely to be positive the higher is the social discount rate.[15] If, for example, both the rate of wage adjustment and supply elasticity were moderate, the wage subsidy scheme would be considered desirable if the social discount rate were greater than 4.6 percent (or if the relevant time horizon were short—say, four years).

The impact of a subsidy on skilled employment is in all respects the opposite of that on unskilled employment, as figure 3 indicates. Based solely on the conventional criterion, a wage subsidy on skilled labor is considered desirable if the social discount rate is less than the critical value described above for unskilled labor. For the moderate values of the parameters, if the social discount rate were equal to the real yield on Aaa bonds, which is generally about 2 percent, a subsidy on skilled employment would by the conventional criterion be preferable to a subsidy on unskilled employment (that is, it would be a good investment from a social point of view to make conditions worse for the unskilled so that more people would have the incentive to acquire skills and there would be fewer unskilled in the future). No one would seriously propose, however, that wage subsidies on skilled labor be considered as a component of labor market policy; there are more direct and less pernicious ways of increasing the number of skilled workers in the economy (for example, training programs). Rather, the comparative costs and benefits of the two subsidy schemes raise obvious questions concerning the desirability of a subsidy on unskilled employment.

Modifications of the Model

Focusing on some aspects of behavior that were suppressed in the model described here could alter the implications drawn about the effects of a wage subsidy scheme.[16] For instance, it might be assumed that holding a job augments human capital of unskilled workers. In terms of the model it should be assumed that there is either a probability that an unemployed unskilled worker will leave the labor force altogether because

15. The discount rate that makes the net present value of the program zero can be calculated for the numerical values of the parameters used to derive the results in table 3. For the moderate rate of wage adjustment the critical discount rate is 0, 2.3, 4.6, and 6.2 percent as the elasticity of supply is zero, low, moderate, or high.

16. The modifications considered in this section were added to the paper because their importance was stressed by the discussants at the conference.

Figure 3. Impact on GNP of a Subsidy on Skilled and Unskilled Labor

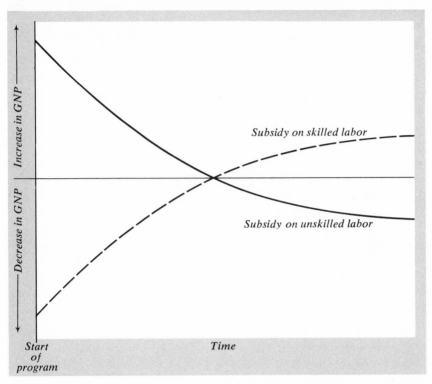

his stock of human capital has fallen below some minimum value, or that an employed unskilled worker will become skilled after gaining a certain amount of work experience. In both cases the returns to a wage subsidy are higher than would be implied if augmentation of human capital were ignored. If there is, however, any adjustment of relative wages, the steady state effects of the wage subsidy will be unaffected. Instead, the path of benefits accruing to a subsidy on unskilled labor given in figure 3 would in the long run be shifted up at all points (and the path of benefits accruing to a subsidy on skilled labor would be shifted down). Thus, including an augmentation of human capital in the model would increase the attractiveness of a wage subsidy scheme.

The results presented in the numerical examples are based on the assumption that actual employment adjusts instantaneously to desired employment. Not very much is known about the econometrics of the determination of employment, but it is known that the adjustment is not instantaneous.[17] Altering the assumption, however, does not change the nature of the basic results very much. For any degree of wage adjustment, the benefits in adjustment of employment come slowly because of lags in the employment response. The (undiscounted) sum of the benefits is unaffected by the speed at which employment adjusts to its desired level. Given a positive discount rate, however, a wage subsidy on unskilled labor is the less desirable the lower is the adjustment parameter.

Another possible modification is based on the assumption that the equilibrium unskilled unemployment rate depends negatively on the wage differential of unskilled and skilled workers.[18] The long-run effect of a wage subsidy on unskilled labor then would be to lower the equilibrium unemployment rate of unskilled labor, and it would obviously have more favorable redistributive implications. Whether the policy increases or decreases GNP depends on the relative sizes of the relative wage elasticities for unskilled workers and the relative supplies of the two types of labor.[19]

The Impact of Federal Funding for State and Local Employment

Under the public service employment format governed by the Comprehensive Employment and Training Act, funds are made available to state and local governments to expand their employment levels. The jobs generally are restricted to the long-term unemployed, have a wage ceiling, and are not intended to be permanent; in other words, the intent of the program is to create net new jobs for unskilled persons. If the program works, it is analytically equivalent to the wage subsidy scheme discussed above.

17. See, for example, the paper by Daniel S. Hamermesh in this volume.

18. See the paper by Martin Baily and James Tobin in this volume. Their model is more general than this one. There are, however, both theoretical and empirical grounds for skepticism that the rate of acceleration of skilled wages depends directly on the wage of unskilled labor relative to that of skilled labor. Resolution of this question—as well as that of the extent to which unskilled wages are responsive to unskilled unemployment—awaits the development of much better data than are currently available.

19. My estimates of the parameter describing the effect of the relative wage on the equilibrium unemployment rate for unskilled labor, using data on occupation wages and unemployment rates rather than the interindustry data used by Baily-Tobin, are quite large. Indeed, they are most likely consistent with a positive long-run effect of a wage subsidy scheme on aggregate GNP—even for fairly large supply elasticities. Both my results and my conclusion, though, are still tentative.

Does Public Service Employment Work?

Elementary economic analysis would suggest that, despite regulations requiring "maintenance of effort" by recipients of employment grants, governmental units would attempt to use them as they would a general revenue sharing grant and address the highest priorities as locally perceived. Since the wage bill of local governments is usually less than 10 percent of total community income, however, the employment grant would have a relatively small effect on total employment. The rational local manager would probably, despite provisions that employment slots be targeted to specific groups, attempt to hire those he would hire in the absence of the restrictions. For example, if told that all public employment participants must be unskilled workers, local government would have every incentive to use the federal grants to pay all new employees who meet the appropriate qualifications and to cut back on its hiring of workers who do not meet the qualifications. Of course, the flexibility that local managers have in using public employment funds depends on whether the regulations are rigorously enforced. To date they apparently have not been (in part because of the courts).

The empirical evidence that there is fiscal substitution of employment funds is not overwhelming and many of the analyses of substitution are indirect. Ashenfelter and Ehrenberg, for instance, failed to refute the null hypothesis that grant income influences employment the same way regular community income does. This leads to a predicted marginal expenditure on the wage bill of between zero, if the program is financed by a tax increase, and about 0.11, if it is financed by deficit spending or by cutting other programs.[20] The weight of evidence on the impact of other revenue sharing programs, however, forces one to be agnostic on this issue. Other approaches to local government behavior imply lower (but still fairly high) rates of fiscal substitution.[21]

20. This is based on the Ashenfelter-Ehrenberg estimated income elasticity of employment with respect to community income of 1.2. See Orley C. Ashenfelter and Ronald G. Ehrenberg, "The Demand for Labor in the Public Sector," in Daniel S. Hamermesh, ed., *Labor in the Public and Nonprofit Sectors* (Princeton University Press, 1975), pp. 55–78.

21. See Edward M. Gramlich, "Intergovernmental Grants: A Review of the Empirical Literature," in Wallace E. Oates, ed., *The Political Economy of Fiscal Federalism* (Heath, 1977), pp. 219–39; Edward M. Gramlich and Harvey Galper, "State and Local Fiscal Behavior and Federal Grant Policy," *BPEA, 1:1973*, pp. 15–58; and Alan Fechter, *Public Employment Programs* (Washington: American Enterprise Institute for Public Policy Research, 1975).

There are only two direct studies of the impact of these programs on employment. One estimates the impact of 100 public service jobs on total state and local employment for six quarters after introduction of the public employment program (PEP) and its successor, public service employment under the Comprehensive Employment and Training Act. The impact is large at first: 104 and 91 jobs created in the first two quarters. The numbers decrease to 69 and 42 jobs created in the third and fourth quarters and then move toward zero—in the fifth and sixth quarters 18 and 3 jobs are created.[22] In other words, the programs work reasonably well for a few quarters, but thereafter they are subject to a high rate of fiscal substitution. Wiseman estimates the effect of 100 additional public service slots on total employment is to create 60 jobs in the third quarter, which is obviously very close to the other estimate.[23]

The evidence on the impact of employment grants on the composition of labor demand is fairly straightforward. Table 4 shows the age, education, sex, and race characteristics of public service participants, the aggregate labor force, and state and local government employees. To put appropriate weights on these various characteristics, a regression of the unemployment rate of the ith demographic group (in the 1970 census period) was run on these characteristics. From the coefficients of this regression an estimated equilibrium unemployment rate was calculated for each of the groups in table 4.[24] The results suggest that, on balance, CETA participants were drawn from approximately the middle of the skill distribution.

The problem with using state and local government for jobs programs is that, as the last two columns of table 4 suggest, it is an extremely skill intensive sector. Even a significant relaxation in hiring standards would not make a jobs program based on grants to state and local governments equivalent to a subsidy on low-wage labor. The incentive of the local

22. Johnson and Tomola, "The Fiscal Substitution Effect." Standard errors for the six quarters, beginning with the first quarter, are 18, 28, 33, 40, 49, and 56.

23. See Michael Wiseman, "Public Employment as Fiscal Policy," *BPEA*, *1:1976*, pp. 67–104.

24. See Johnson and Tomola, "The Fiscal Substitution Effect," for details. There are (at least) three sources of bias in this procedure. The proper form of the regression may not be (and, in this case, is not) linear. When an adjustment for this possibility was made for CETA participants, their estimated equilibrium rate of unemployment fell from 5.2 to 5.0. Other biases may arise from the fact that jobs program participants may be either more or less employable than implied by their observable characteristics, and that these statistics refer only to those who were labeled participants.

Table 4. Percentage Distribution of Selected Skill Characteristics for Selected Groups in U.S. Labor Force

| Characteristics | Public service employment | | CETA training | Experienced civilian labor force | State and local government employment | |
	PEP	CETA			All	Excluding teachers
Age						
Under 22	31	24	27	13	11	11
22–44	57	63	62	51	50	46
Over 44	12	13	10	36	39	43
Education						
Less than 12 years	30	24	39	39	18	24
Exactly 12 years	41	44	42	35	28	39
More than 12 years	29	32	19	26	54	37
Sex						
Male	72	71	54	63	50	55
Female	28	29	46	37	50	45
Race						
White	60	66	53	84	85	84
Black	22	23	32	11	11	12
Spanish	14	8	12	4	3	3
Other	4	3	3	1	1	1
Estimated equilibrium unemployment rate (percent)	5.8	5.2	6.2	5.0	3.6	3.8

Source: George E. Johnson and James D. Tomola, "The Fiscal Substitution Effect of Alternative Approaches to Public Service Employment Policy," *Journal of Human Resources*, vol. 12 (Winter 1977), p. 20.

government manager is to use the grants to hire persons he believes will be the most productive given his needs (and probably whom he would have hired anyway). Notice that CETA participants in public service employment programs are much more skilled than persons in CETA training programs. This underscores the basic point: the "good" workers were given public service jobs; the "bad" ones were not.

Experience with public service employment programs thus far indicates that they are not very easy to run as antipoverty programs.[25] At first glance they appear to be a subsidy on fairly highly skilled workers, but

25. Interestingly, the problems with the proportionately much larger program in the Netherlands reported in the Haveman paper in this volume are very similar to the problems with public service employment in the United States.

this conclusion is softened by the possibility that, because of the fiscal substitution effect, they are merely a device for shuffling money between different levels of government.

Other Designs for Public Programs

Three major options are available for improving public service employment programs: tightening up the program restrictions; replacing the grant with a wage subsidy tied to hiring low-wage labor; or abandoning the local grants for a federal program. Already, under the expanded title 6 of CETA,[26] program regulations are being strengthened and more rigidly enforced. A great deal should be learned about the feasibility of running a strong employment program through the state and local sector from the experience accumulated in 1977–78. The success of the title 6 program depends on the available funds being utilized fully by local governments, and on participants being taken from the low end of the skill distribution (that is, being similar to participants in training programs). Adherence to the skill requirement would indicate that despite political, legal, and administrative hurdles the federal government can get state and local governments to follow its regulations. And using all the funds available would show that, if pressed, state and local governments can actually utilize low-wage workers.[27] If either condition is not satisfied, however, the present approach to public service employment will be very difficult to defend in the future.

Setting up a wage subsidy scheme on state and local government employment would be more likely to have a positive effect on the demand for unskilled labor. If, however, the subsidy were based on the total wage bill of state and local government, it would be likely to have a negative effect on the labor market since (as demonstrated in table 4) that sector is much more skill intensive than the average industry in the economy.

26. Restrictions passed in 1976 limit most hiring under CETA title 6 programs to low-income workers who either are recipients of aid to families with dependent children or have been unemployed for fifteen weeks or longer. In addition, in order to reduce the potential for fiscal substitution, these workers must be placed in projects that are to last one year or less. Emergency Jobs Programs Extension Act of 1976.

27. Though there remains a possibility of fiscal substitution, a program that succeeded in replacing skilled local government workers with disadvantaged persons would be a successful antipoverty program even if total employment did not immediately rise.

Instead, the subsidy would have to be targeted to unskilled labor in some way. A lump-sum subsidy on all employees, which would favor low-wage workers if applied to the private sector, would not necessarily favor the less skilled if applied only to state and local government (again, because that sector is so skill intensive). Therefore the subsidy would have to be provided primarily only to unskilled public sector workers.

Obviously there is a strong incentive for managers in local government to get as many employees as possible labeled unskilled so as to increase their revenues. To the extent that they are successful in collecting a subsidy on actually skilled workers, the policy degenerates to being a lump sum subsidy and therefore is of little help. Confining the subsidy to persons with poor work histories might cause them to be labeled as problems and avoided.[28]

Thus, although a subsidy scheme might appear on first reflection to be an efficient way to increase unskilled employment in local governments, it is not clear that it would be any more successful than the revenue sharing programs have been. Further, it would probably be very difficult to evaluate the impact of such a program; at least under CETA it is possible to tell who the participants are.

The option of running a jobs program on the federal level rather than relying on the state and local sector as middle person affords close control and poses formidable problems. Such a program would, of course, have to be set up so that participants would not displace incumbent federal workers (or replace regular workers who have quit) and marginal participants would be taken from the low end of the skill distribution of the labor force. Presumably, the incentives to meet these two conditions could be built into a federal program more easily than into one involving state and local governments.

Participants in a successful federal program could not perform tasks that compete with functions of state and local workers. If, for example, the program provided ten firemen to Akron, the local government would respond accordingly and fail to fill ten vacancies in the Akron fire department. On the other hand, if participants were used to improve the railbed of the Erie-Lackawanna branch line between Akron and Fernwood (which was abandoned in 1957), it is unlikely that there would be any displacement. In the former case the federal program degenerates to pure revenue sharing; in the latter it has a 100 percent impact on employment.

28. Hamermesh discusses this possibility for wage subsidies in the private sector in his paper in this volume. Gramlich, in his comments, takes issue with him.

This points to the most vexing question associated with a federally operated program: What should the participants do? The projects must produce some useful output; otherwise the program will be labeled a boondoggle and probably abandoned. They must not compete with regular government functions at any level; otherwise they will have little impact on the labor market. They must depend less on skilled labor than does the private sector of the economy; otherwise they will have no overall effect on the labor market or, what is more likely, a negative effect. The conditions that planners of a federal project must satisfy are stringent, but perhaps American ingenuity will find a way around the obstacles to such a program.

Public Jobs as an Instrument of Employment Policy

This paper has set out a framework for assessing the impact of various forms of employment programs on the labor market. The approach is admittedly eclectic, and a number of behavioral aspects that many economists might feel are important (for example, short-run labor supply responses, the augmentation of human capital through work experience, and the division of skill into at least three categories) have been forthrightly ignored. The paper concentrates on two important behavioral aspects of the labor market: the apparently slow rate at which unskilled labor markets adjust to excess supply, and the effect of incentives on occupational choice. The former makes a wage subsidy or public service employment potentially more potent; the latter has the opposite effect.

The desirability of raising the relative demand curve for low-wage labor in the first place depends on a number of factors. However, given some tendency for unskilled wages to adjust to relative supply and demand conditions and for occupational choice to respond to relative net incomes, a large wage subsidy on the unskilled or a public service employment program that concentrates on the unskilled will have these effects: employment and output will increase in the short run and decrease slightly after seven to nine years (because there is less skilled labor); the net incomes of skilled workers will increase in the short run, but decline substantially after a few years; and the net incomes of the unskilled will rise by the decline in the net income of the skilled less the size of the fall in aggregate output. Whether society wants this to happen is a political question. By traditional benefit-cost analysis (focusing on the discounted value of future GNP) the program is more desirable the higher the discount rate. If one cares primarily about reducing the gap between the net incomes of the better and worse off segments of society, it is a good program.

There are conditions under which such a program would be deemed unambiguously good. Within the model discussed in this paper, if there is no tendency for the unskilled wage to adjust to an increase in unskilled employment (because, say, it is legally fixed at a certain fraction of the skilled wage), then the program yields net benefits for everyone in society. Further, there may be other sets of conditions that yield similarly favorable results (though inserting various plausible modifications in the model has yet to prove productive).

The major implication of the modification examined in this paper is that, in order to have beneficial effects on the short-run level of employment and on income distribution, a public service employment program must focus on members of the labor force who are more disadvantaged than typical members in the private sector. Otherwise, a jobs program is, effectively, no program at all or, worse, a subsidy on skilled labor. This result (which is, of course, obvious) would hold for any modification (within reason) of the basic model. However, the standard data for programs operated in the early 1970s strongly suggest that participants have been taken from the middle to the upper middle of the skill distribution. Because state and local governments are an extremely skill intensive industry, even a stringent reduction might not bring standards low enough to reach the unskilled. In addition, there is some evidence that federal grants for jobs programs are absorbed into the general income of local communities, but given the effect of the programs on the composition of labor demand, this fiscal substitution is not a major drawback.

If public service employment is to be a feasible instrument of labor market policy, therefore, it is necessary to change its format. The three ways of doing this considered here are an increase in (and *enforcement* of) eligibility restrictions, a wage subsidy on all state and local government employees, and a federally run program. The wage subsidy plan is difficult because it requires differentiating between skilled and unskilled employees. Because the state and local sector is so skill intensive, a general subsidy on the wage bill would have a negative effect, and a lump sum tax would have at most a very small effect on the relative demand for unskilled employment. Attempts to restrict the subsidy to certain groups, however, would probably be frustrated, for it is always in the interest of local managers to define *unskilled* as broadly as possible. A federally operated program can overcome most of the difficulties with state and locally run programs, but raises other problems—most prominently, what do the participants do?[29]

Comments by Michael Wiseman

George Johnson is an expert at telling people what he thinks they want to hear and then making them feel guilty about it. In this case what the public wants to hear is that a wage subsidy (read "public employment program") for unskilled labor will have the effect of increasing both the relative and absolute incomes of those at the lower end of the income distribution. But if one reads the story carefully, one finds that to be pleased with this conclusion, as reached by Johnson, one has to be myopic and unconcerned about a long-run loss (using the Johnson "moderate" estimates) of thirty-four cents in real national product for every dollar spent on subsidized employment in the public sector. The reason for this long-run result is easy to identify: hiring more low-skilled workers causes some people to forgo training. Over time this reduction in human capital investment increases the ratio of unskilled to skilled labor. Since the former group will be unemployed more frequently than the latter, and is by definition less productive, national output declines.

This conclusion is derived from simulation of the effects of wage subsidies for unskilled labor in a simple model in which skilled and unskilled labor are combined in varying proportions to produce an undifferentiated output. In the model, relative wages for the two labor classes affect both the combination of factors selected by entrepreneurs and the training decisions of persons about to enter the labor force. While the results are affected by many parameters, among them the elasticity of substitution between labor types and the responsiveness of wages to unemployment rates, Johnson discusses only a few.

Johnson's simulations are based on the assumption that the equilibrium unemployment rates for unskilled and skilled workers are exogenously determined. As he mentions, in the long run the negative conclusions of the paper might be reversed if "tightening" of low-skill labor markets reduces the equilibrium unemployment rates of the unskilled. The paper

29. Policymakers have opted for tightening up the existing program under CETA. The consequences of this have yet to be determined.

does not include a model of the labor market, so we do not know how this comes about. Despite the importance of this possibility, most of the information provided on it is relegated to a footnote.[30]

Johnson reports that "it is well known that particular labor supply curves are very elastic with respect to returns." In other words, if wage rates for unskilled laborers are bid up by a subsidy placed on their employment, a substantial increase in the supply of such labor will occur as people forgo training to remain "unskilled." The two papers on this subject—that presumably make this conclusion "well known"—relate only to the supply of college-educated workers. Johnson's model presupposes that if they avoid college, those people who are making the choice between college and work will experience the same wages and unemployment in their voluntary status as low-skilled workers as do people currently in that labor market. Put differently, he is assuming that such factors are determined by demand; they are intrinsic characteristics of jobs that require little skill.

However, alternative models of the market for low-skilled labor emphasize the substantial contribution to aggregate unemployment and the size of the poverty population made by people who do not seem to experience the "to be or not to be" skill question. High unemployment and frequent turnover in this picture are in part supply phenomena: for a variety of reasons some people simply seem unable to hold steady jobs. In a supply model a subsidized public employment policy might be used to remedy problems of such workers while policies such as training are used to assure that the size of the high-turnover, low-wage population does not grow. Of course the fact that a supply model might be articulated and justified with data on characteristics of the unemployed or underemployed poor does not mean that public employment programs as currently constituted are correctly dealing with the problem. But whether or not public employment programs as now operated can be treated as analytically equivalent to a wage subsidy on unskilled labor may not be the critical empirical question in evaluating their usefulness as an antipoverty strategy.

In discussing the consequences of a wage subsidy on the training decisions of workers, Johnson seems to forget that policymakers have more than one instrument to achieve the ends he seeks. Surely if public employment programs can be shown on the basis of a completely articulated

30. Irwin Garfinkel discusses this problem further in his comments.

model of labor markets to be likely to reduce the unemployment rates of low-skilled workers, any adverse consequences for training choices made by older teenagers that occur as a result of tightening of low-skill labor markets could be offset by training subsidies. Other studies have emphasized the salutary effect of such subsidies; not only do they raise the wages of low-skilled workers by retracking labor out of these markets, but they also serve to hold down prices for the skill-intensive goods the poor buy.[31]

For analytical purposes a public employment program can be treated as an increase in the demand for unskilled labor for unskilled jobs, a variety of on-the-job training that enhances the skills and employability of workers, or a backup program for a work-conditioned system of income transfers. The first option is emphasized by Johnson. If public employment programs simply increase the demand for unskilled workers, they are likely to have the same impact on the economy as subsidies of wages paid for such labor, although it is conceivable that more efficient procedures could be found for operating such a program than are implicit in funneling all such money through local governments. On-the-job training has a different effect; as Johnson admits, if subsidized public employment with this quality is incorporated into the model as it now stands, many of his conclusions would be changed. Presumably such training would raise the supply of skilled workers and have consequences similar to those of a general training subsidy. Here also adverse consequences of the wage effects of such a program on training decisions made by young people would have to be offset with training subsidies.

Subsidized public employment as a backup for a work requirement in an income transfer system is a prominent part of the Carter administration's thinking about welfare reform. It is possible that such a program would push wages down in low-skilled labor markets as the requirements of the transfer system pushed participation in the labor force up. Not only would this increase GNP (and therefore be desirable using the Johnson criteria), it would also increase incentives for voluntary accumulation of skill. I suspect Johnson chose the wage subsidy alternative because existing public employment seems to include little training and, in any event, welfare does not now include a work requirement backed up by a public jobs program.

31. See John H. Bishop, "The General Equilibrium Impact of Alternative Antipoverty Strategies: Income Maintenance, Training, and Job Creation," discussion paper 386–77 (University of Wisconsin, Institute for Research on Poverty, 1977; processed).

Given the decision to model the program as a wage subsidy and his (at least superficially) positive conclusions about the effects of such programs, Johnson turns to the issue of congruence of existing programs with his notion of what public employment programs targeted at the unskilled should be. He makes four points. First, CETA jobholders do not appear to be very unskilled, at least when education levels are considered. This is not surprising, for most of the stock of CETA employees he examines was acquired during 1975 in response to demands for rapid counter-cyclical employment expansion. Those people tended to look like the people whose unemployment rates were substantially increased by the 1974–75 recession.[32] The fact that employment in state and local governments is not particularly cyclically sensitive does not mean, as Johnson implies, that such employment should not be manipulated countercyclically (as it was) to offset declines elsewhere. I think what Johnson means to say is that, if the conclusion of this conference is that we need an anti-poverty public employment program, we cannot necessarily assume we have one.

A consumer protection note is in order here. One must be very cautious about drawing inferences from the data on CETA participants that Johnson reprints. Even if state and local governments were conscientiously to utilize only unskilled persons, I am not sure the effect would show up in these data. How much skill does a high school diploma granted by an inner city school impart? Employees under existing public employment programs tend to be younger than the civilian labor force as a whole. The fact that they are on the average better educated may simply reflect the fact that all young people are, in terms of years of school completed, better educated than preceding generations. The relevant comparison would be between program participants and people of the same age within the same labor market areas. In Alameda County, California (which includes Oakland), over half of mothers receiving aid for families with dependent children have a high school education or better. That proportion rose from 0.34 in 1967 to 0.51 in 1972.[33] If Johnson saw these people in the CETA statistics, he would claim that the program was not being targeted correctly. Yet these are the poor.

Second, state and local employment, according to Johnson, is very skill

---

32. See Wiseman, "Public Employment as Fiscal Policy."

33. Cynthia Rence and Michael Wiseman, "The California Welfare Reform Act and Participation in AFDC," *Journal of Human Resources,* vol. 13 (Winter 1978), p. 53.

intensive. As a result, such employment cannot be utilized to hire the un-skilled. But for a variety of reasons public sector wages and employment conditions in many cities appear to be superior to those available in the private sector. As a result, queues for such jobs are long, and jobs are fre-quently allocated on the basis of educational attainment or performance on written examinations likely to be biased in favor of better educated persons. The fact that these processes produce a well-educated labor force does not mean that the jobs necessarily require one. Possibilities for substitution of low- for high-skilled labor definitely exist; the problem is to break down institutional restrictions that artificially bias hiring in local government toward the middle class and to provide the incentives neces-sary to force the adoption of management techniques that allow produc-tive use of disadvantaged workers for providing public services.

Third, Johnson points out that incentives exist for local government officials not to hire unskilled persons even if they are supposed to. This problem can be addressed by having an independent agency certify eli-gible persons. If jobs in the public sector become part of welfare reform, this change will have to occur.

Fourth, displacement through the substitution of subsidized workers for workers who would have been hired if no public employment program existed obviously occurs. Unless one adopts on-the-job training as the objective for subsidized public employment, this will continue to be a serious issue. I believe that the better targeted jobs programs are, the fewer are the possibilities for displacement. It simply takes more manage-ment and more workers to do things with unskilled labor, and this should show up as an increase in the number of public sector jobs. The effect on overall employment depends on one's view of labor markets, but that problem has already been discussed.

Care must be exercised in developing remedies for the displacement problem. Paradoxically, the recent revisions of CETA have two features designed to reduce displacement that may have adverse effects on the pro-ductivity of the program as an antipoverty device. The first is the empha-sis on jobs of short (one year) duration. This is an excellent policy for a countercyclical program, but we are presently in the advanced stages of the recovery. I know of no evidence that, whatever are the favorable things a public service job does for previously underemployed workers, such things necessarily can be accomplished in twelve months. The sec-ond is the increased emphasis placed on subsidizing jobs in the nonprofit, nongovernment sector. My prejudice tells me that however "unreal" jobs are in local government, they are likely to be much more like regular employment than those generally provided by community service organizations. Here again, for countercyclical purposes, it might not make much difference. But as unemployment falls, attempts to assure productive use of the resources in public employment programs become increasingly important on both economic and political grounds.

Johnson proposes two tests for congruence of the new CETA title 6 program with the desired low-skilled wage subsidy scheme. The first is that the funds must be fully utilized; the second is that participants look like people receiving training through other CETA-funded programs. I understand neither criterion. Indeed, I think the targets for job-filling rates proposed by the 1976 legislation are based on a gross misconception of how difficult it is to locate people who meet the requirements of the program and how difficult it is to fit them, once found, into productive activities in local government. Slow takeup of the money by local government could indicate, as Johnson would have us believe, that it takes time to engineer displacement and to get regular workers reclassified as unskilled. On the other hand, slow takeup could also indicate that the program is working, but the task is difficult. As a result of this ambiguity, full utilization does not provide a test of anything.

As for the second test, I am at a loss to imagine a model of poverty policy that suggests that all instruments should have the same targets. In a well-run coordinated program it might be reasonable to expect training resources to be devoted to people who are younger than workers who are targets for subsidized employment. Subsidized public employment might be the reserve policy used to boost people who, after four or five years in the labor market, appear to be "losers." The important questions here concern the identifiability of such persons and the productivity of such a policy in dealing with their problems.

The remarkable thing about the 1976 CETA expansion is that Congress proved so willing to adjust requirements for admission to public employment programs in ways that directly conform to recommendations made from the outside. The problem is that while suggestions for running a countercyclical program abound, policy analysts have yet to develop a model of low-income labor markets that really gives clues about what the content and target of antipoverty programs should be. George Johnson has shown that such policies have the potential for grand failure. I wish someone would devote time to development of feasible policy recommendations to enhance the likelihood of success.

Comments by Irwin Garfinkel

George Johnson is quite pessimistic about the ability of wage bill subsidies or public employment programs to reduce the unemployment rate of unskilled labor in the long run. This conclusion is based on a cleverly pieced together equilibrium model of the labor market. Unfortunately, because the model is not carried far enough, Johnson's conclusion is suspect. I will first discuss the shortcomings of his model and the more optimistic evaluation of wage bill subsidies and public employment programs that might emerge from a richer model. Then I will examine two specific issues involved in public employment programs—displacement and targeting.

The primary problem that wage bill subsidies and public employment programs for unskilled labor are supposed to address is the abnormally high rate of unemployment of unskilled labor. As Johnson indicates in the beginning of his paper, the two conventional explanations for this abnormally high rate of unemployment are the existence of minimum wage laws, and high turnover rates that are perhaps exacerbated by government transfer programs. Having duly noted these explanations, Johnson ignores them in his model. He postulates an abnormally high equilibrium level of unemployment among unskilled workers—about 20 percent—which is exogenous in his model. If one begins by assuming that nothing can affect the unemployment rate of unskilled labor, it is not surprising to conclude that neither wage bill subsidies nor public employment programs can reduce unemployment rates. Indeed, if Johnson had derived any other conclusions, he would obviously have made a logical error.

To be fair to Johnson, he does note in his concluding section that there are conditions under which these programs might be effective—for example, "if there is no tendency for the unskilled wage to adjust to an increase in unskilled employment (because, say, it is legally fixed at a certain fraction of the skilled wage)." That is, if one of the conventional explanations for abnormally high unemployment rates among the unskilled—the existence of minimum wage laws—is right, his conclusions about the inefficacy of these programs may be wrong.

If the alternative conventional explanation for high unemployment rates—high turnover—is right, Johnson's conclusions may also be wrong. Wage bill subsidies or public jobs programs for unskilled labor might reduce turnover and, thereby, the natural rate of unemployment by raising net wage rates of unskilled jobs. In both the type of models that emphasize labor supply and that which emphasizes job search, such an outcome is likely. Moreover, Johnson does not allow for the possibility that wage bill subsidies or public employment programs will increase on-the-job human capital investments of unskilled workers and indirectly reduce the equilibrium rate of unemployment. Finally, although Johnson notes that income maintenance programs might be partly responsible for the high turnover rates among the unskilled, once again in his model he does not allow changes in the generosity or availability of programs with income guarantees to affect the equilibrium level of unemployment. Since many advocates of public employment programs view them primarily as substitutes for and not as additions to income guarantee programs for those expected to work, Johnson's model can hardly be considered capable of providing either a fair or an accurate measure of the benefits of such a policy.

In the second part of his paper, Johnson notes two problems that have been encountered by public employment programs: a lack of targeting on the unskilled, and fiscal displacement. Before 1976, our public employment programs provided only a small proportion of their jobs to the unskilled and therefore were not successful in appreciably increasing the demand for low-skilled labor. Johnson argues persuasively that a simple wage bill subsidy to state and local governments would not change this result because they are a skill intensive industry. Moreover, he argues that because state and local governments will want to continue hiring skilled labor, they will undermine federal attempts to focus any subsidy on unskilled labor by calling skilled labor unskilled labor. This conclusion is in my judgment unduly pessimistic. If the federal government pays part or all of the salary for low-salary jobs *only,* the problem should largely take care of itself. For the most part, skilled workers will not work for wages paid the unskilled.

Displacement is a much tougher problem. It takes place when the creation of a special public job leads to the demise of a normal public or private job. The importance of this issue is attested to by the attention devoted to it in the papers prepared for this conference. Johnson has estimated elsewhere that for up to six months the displacement of normal public jobs by CETA jobs is not too pronounced, but thereafter it quickly approaches 100 percent.[34] If the primary policy objective is counter-cyclical, such an outcome does not distress me. In fact, a short-run stimulus with no lasting effect on the size of the public sector is quite attractive. An explicit countercyclical revenue-sharing program would be a more straightforward method of achieving this objective, however.

On the other hand, if the policy objective is a longer term, structural one—what Baily and Tobin refer to as cheating the Phillips curve—then displacement is of crucial concern. For, to the extent that displacement occurs, potential structural benefits of public employment will be vitiated. Johnson, along with Kesselman and Kemper and Moss, makes a great deal of the conflict between doing something useful and avoiding displacement. In my judgment, the displacement issue is the most important part of this paper.

Finally, I want to address an aspect of targeting not raised in the paper, to wit: should jobs in all public employment programs be targeted on the unskilled? Clearly, if the objective of the program is to increase the demand for low-skilled labor, the answer is yes. But what if the objective is countercyclical? An argument can be made that a program with a counter-cyclical objective should not be targeted on the low skilled. Why try to change the employment mix of state and local governments as a by-product of macroeconomic policy? But in this case, the appeal of public employment vis-à-vis other macroeconomic stimulus policies is unclear to me. On the other hand, if the objective is to improve the trade-off between unemployment and inflation, then targeting jobs on the unskilled is crucial to the success of the program. From this I conclude that, to the extent that there are good rationales for public employment programs, they should be targeted on the low skilled.

In summary then, the model developed in the first part of the Johnson paper has convinced me of only one thing—that it should be extended before any conclusion about the efficacy of wage bill subsidies or public employment programs is drawn from it. On the other hand, the possibility of displacement in public employment programs suggests to me that we ought to devote a great deal more analysis to the design of public employment programs.

34. Johnson and Tomola, "The Fiscal Substitution Effect."

Jonathan R. Kesselman

Work Relief Programs
in the Great Depression

If the Federal Government wishes to continue its work program on any large scale it must frankly admit it is invading the domain of local-government responsibility, or, avoiding that, it must admit it is competing in the field normally reserved for private enterprise, and launch on projects such as a housing program and the production of goods, including consumers' goods. . . . Why try to cover the fact that anything but useless work does involve in one form or another such competition? . . . The choice seems to me to be this: either drastically limit the scope of work relief or go ahead in full defiance of the consequences in assuming local-improvement obligations or without regard to opposition from private interests.[1]

Work relief programs of the 1930s afforded a unique opportunity for observing the operation and problems of large-scale special public employment. A conflict between achieving productivity on the relief projects and avoiding the displacement of other activities in the public and private sectors became apparent. The economic, administrative, and political linkages between productivity and displacement were all perceived as part of the unemployment problem in the Great Depression. Today's concern with displacement by public employment focuses on the relatively narrow aspect of intergovernmental displacement—just one of a host of mechanisms suspected or documented in the 1930s.[2] Recent think-

The author is indebted to N. E. Savin, who shared fully in the initial conceptualization of this study, and to Sheila Kesselman for extensive advice and editorial assistance. The helpful comments of Robert C. Allen, Robert H. Haveman, David E. Rose, William E. Schworm, and Arnold R. Weber are gratefully acknowledged. A bibliography of the works most heavily relied on appears at the end of this paper.

1. E. Wight Bakke, *The Unemployed Worker: A Study of the Task of Making a Living Without a Job* (Yale University Press, 1940), p. 401n.

2. Displacement is taken to mean an induced reduction of employment elsewhere in the economy, which partially offsets the relief employment. This may arise through the reduction of a demand component or an input supply affecting

153

ing about public employment has centered on the macroeconomic goal of attaining full employment with minimal inflationary pressures.[3] The equally vital microeconomic choices of what, how, and for whom public production is undertaken have thus been overshadowed. Yet policy choices in this realm can have major repercussions on both displacement and productivity. While some of the macro issues were only sketchily understood during the Great Depression, contemporary analyses of the micro issues were astonishingly prescient. Many of these commentaries can aid in assessing analytical and policy issues common to the 1930s and the 1970s.

Three distinct yet interrelated goals of policies to combat unemployment are the creation of employment, income support, and useful output. All of these goals are desirable, but economic and political realities may force a works program to emphasize one goal over the others.[4] Assisting the unemployed purely by income support is a policy of income maintenance, direct relief, or in the 1930s jargon, the "dole." The policy of requiring work as a condition for income support, but with no special interest in the value of output, came to be known as "made work" or "leaf raking."[5] Work relief in both its traditional and modern-day forms

---

nonrelief employment. A taxonomy of displacement mechanisms appears in Willem H. Buiter, " 'Crowding Out' and the Effectiveness of Fiscal Policy," *Journal of Public Economics,* vol. 7 (June 1977), pp. 309–28.

3. Formal modeling of the macro problem has been undertaken by Baily and Tobin in this volume and by George E. Johnson, "Evaluating the Macroeconomic Effects of Public Employment Programs," in Orley Ashenfelter and James Blum, eds., *Evaluating the Labor-Market Effects of Social Programs* (Princeton University, Industrial Relations Section, 1976), pp. 90–123. I choose not to examine the issues of wage-rate adjustment, which are an important part of any macro theory of displacement. Some of these issues for the 1930s are analyzed in Jonathan R. Kesselman and N. E. Savin, "Three-and-a-Half Million Workers Never Were Lost," *Economic Inquiry,* vol. 16 (April 1978), pp. 205–25.

4. "When the WPA program has been attacked as inefficient, it has been defended on the ground that it was a relief program. When critics from the opposite camp have urged that wages be graduated in accordance with workers' needs, that tests of need be more strictly applied, or that other devices be adopted to make it more strictly a relief measure, these have frequently been opposed as being incompatible with a work program. This basic duality . . . is epitomized within the WPA's own organization by frequent clashes at the district, state, and federal levels between those units which are responsible for placing needy workers on jobs and those which are responsible for project operations." Donald S. Howard, *The WPA and Federal Relief Policy* (Russell Sage Foundation, 1943), pp. 246–47.

5. The made-work approach, characteristic of early municipal programs, is described in Joanna C. Colcord, *Emergency Work Relief as Carried Out in Twenty-Six American Communities, 1930–1931, with Suggestions for Setting up a Program*

reflects society's desire to cope with unemployment in productive ways. In contrast with conventional public spending and regular government employment, work relief activities would not be undertaken for their output alone.[6] Still, obtaining useful output from the relief workers helps to lighten society's burdens of income support. But the productivity goal must be evaluated more broadly in social terms—the goods and services produced on projects, along with the training and nonpecuniary benefits reaped by relief workers. When the federal government undertakes a work program, it may displace the employment, income, and output-generating activities of other public bodies and private actors. The possibility of displacement requires that the objectives of unemployment policy be restated as the creation of *net* employment, *net* income support, and *net* useful output.

In this paper, I shall organize the insights of 1930s work relief observers within a modern macroeconomic framework. The early views will be critically examined and extended using later developments in economic analysis. Administrative and political factors affecting the work relief production process, material and capital inputs, worker eligibility, compensation, and program financing have logical places in the structure of a macro model. I shall postulate structural relations with greater disaggregation and richness than has proven feasible in empirically implemented models.[7] Even the "micro" problems are best explored within such a framework, as it facilitates thinking about reactions in interrelated mar-

---

(Russell Sage Foundation, 1932). Such projects "were invented as an excuse for work, obviously made for the purpose of creating means whereby the recipients of relief could make some payment for what they received. The projects were usually of questionable value." Josephine C. Brown, *Public Relief, 1929–1939* (Holt, 1940), pp. 239–40.

6. In his 1935 message to Congress advocating a major new works program, Franklin Roosevelt conceded, "if it were not for the necessity of giving useful work to the unemployed now on relief, these projects in most instances would not now be undertaken." *The Public Papers and Addresses of Franklin D. Roosevelt*, vol. 4: *The Court Disapproves, 1935* (Random House, 1938), p. 22. "Had the money spent through W.P.A. been spent through established agencies of government using efficient practices and where applicable making use of efficient private contractors, the people would have got more products from the expenditures in structures and in services. And . . . they would have secured things which stood higher on their priority lists. The major justification for W.P.A. must be found in its relief aspects." Lewis Meriam, *Relief and Social Security* (Brookings Institution, 1946), pp. 415–16.

7. For a detailed econometric model of this period, see Bert G. Hickman and Robert M. Coen, *An Annual Growth Model of the U.S. Economy* (Amsterdam: North-Holland, 1976).

kets. The overall assessment of displacement and the mirror-image problem of productivity hinges on this analytical framework and pertinent historical evidence. In some cases, however, the lack of certain evidence and the counterfactual nature of the questions will obscure conclusive answers. Though changed conditions and institutions mean that care is essential in drawing lessons from the historical experience, I shall apply the insights from 1930s work relief to the design of modern-day employment policies.[8]

Scale and Financing of Expenditures

The evolution of work relief programs during the 1930s reflects several important currents of social and economic thought. The need to cope with severe stresses in the economic system clashed with traditional beliefs about the role of government. In particular, the federal government intervened in the finance and operation of activities that were the accustomed preserve of lower jurisdictions and the private sector. As the economy failed to respond to early measures, the federal involvement became progressively deeper. Large federal outlays for relief were tolerated for long only when associated with employment and at least a semblance of useful output. Nevertheless, work relief programs strongly emphasized the provision of income support for the needy, even at the expense of useful work and economic recovery. Concern over continuing deficits held work relief expenditures below the levels necessary to support all of the needy unemployed. The availability of work relief positions fell so far short of the demand that numerous provisions had to be instituted to ration entry. Still, the urgent need for these expenditures stretched the government's willingness to accept deficits as well as the very meaning of budgetary balance. As will be shown, the scale and financing of work relief expenditures affected the value of output and the extent of displacement.

8. Michael C. Barth and Frank H. Easterbrook argue that differences in depression conditions, personal characteristics of the unemployed, size of program relative to the unemployed pool, and type of goods produced "are so large that what we learn may be of little import today." *Work Relief in the Depression, Europe, and the "Manpower Decade": Some Implications for Programs of Public Employment,* pamphlet 3250-2 (Office of Economic Opportunity, 1970), p. 5. For contrast, see Richard E. Hegner, "The WPA: Public Employment Experience in the New Deal," in *Studies in Public Welfare,* paper 19, prepared for the Subcommittee on Fiscal Policy of the Joint Economic Committee, 93:2 (GPO, 1974), pp. 124–37.

Chronology of Proposals and Programs

The economic downturn that began in 1929 brought unprecedented burdens to localities providing direct relief. In 1930 and 1931 most large cities instituted rudimentary programs of "work-for-relief," which were poorly organized for producing useful output. Pressure soon mounted for federal action to augment local public works. At this time no clear distinction was drawn between public works and work relief. In June 1930 the National Unemployment League advocated a $3 billion public works program. President Hoover rejected this proposal but appointed a committee to consider a program for the winter of 1930–31. The Woods Committee proposed a program to spend $840 million; Hoover also rejected this recommendation.[9] Public works expenditures in 1930 amounted to $2.86 billion, of which the federal portion was only $209 million. On this base, large increases in federal spending might have been difficult to implement quickly. A variety of public works proposals advanced by public interest groups and politicians in 1931 suggested spending from $2 billion to $8.5 billion over one or two years. As the depression worsened, the administration in 1932 instituted the Reconstruction Finance Corporation. One of the diverse purposes of the RFC was to rehabilitate the financial system through loans. Congressional Democrats' failure to obtain federal grants for states to expand public works caused them to seek loans for this end. The Emergency Relief and Construction Act of 1932, reluctantly approved by the President, authorized the RFC to loan $300 million to states and localities for relief and work relief (see table 1). The major disbursements occurred in 1933 during the closing months of the Hoover administration and in its successor's inaugural month of March.[10]

Franklin Roosevelt entered office with formative thoughts about emergency employment policies in conservation and public works. In his acceptance speech at the Democratic convention in 1932 he had urged

9. Herbert Stein, *The Fiscal Revolution in America* (University of Chicago Press, 1969), p. 21; and Harry L. Hopkins, *Spending to Save: The Complete Story of Relief* (Norton, 1936; University of Washington Press, Americana Library Ed., 1972), pp. 22–25. Unreferenced material in this section draws on Howard, *WPA*, and particularly Stein, *Fiscal Revolution*.

10. Lester V. Chandler, *America's Greatest Depression, 1929–1941* (Harper and Row, 1970), pp. 50–51; and U.S. National Resources Planning Board, *Security, Work, and Relief Policies* (GPO, 1942), p. 34 and apps. 2 and 4.

Jonathan R. Kesselman

Table 1. Work Relief and Public Works Programs, 1932–43

Program	Dates of operation[a]	Peak enrollment (*thousands*)	Aggregate expenditures (*millions of dollars*)
State and local work relief under loans of Reconstruction Finance Corporation (RFC)	July 1932–April 1933	1,970 (March 1933)	300
Civilian Conservation Corps (CCC)	April 1933–August 1942	505 (August 1935)	2,986
Early work projects of Federal Emergency Relief Administration (FERA)	May 1933–November 1933	1,718 (August 1933)	147
Civil Works Administration (CWA)	November 1933–May 1934	4,264 (January 1934)	952
Emergency Work Relief Program of the FERA (EWRP)	April 1934–December 1935	2,446 (January 1935)	1,195
Works Progress Administration (WPA; renamed Work Projects Administration, July 1939)	August 1935–June 1943	3,330 (November 1938)	13,407[b]
National Youth Administration (NYA; Student Work Program and Out-of-School Work Program)	September 1935–June 1942	808 (March 1940)	534[c]
Public Works Administration (PWA; federal and non-federal projects)	September 1933–June 1942	541 (July 1934)	4,500[d]

Sources: Arthur E. Burns and Edward A. Williams, *Federal Work, Security, and Relief Programs*, U.S. Federal Works Agency, Work Projects Administration, Division of Research, research monograph 24 (GPO, 1941), pp. 27–28; Theodore E. Whiting and T. J. Woofter, Jr., *Summary of Relief and Federal Work Program Statistics, 1933–1940*, U.S. Federal Works Agency, Work Projects Administration, Division of Statistics, and Division of Research (GPO, 1941), pp. 46–48; *Second Annual Report, Federal Works Agency, 1941* (GPO, 1942), p. 313; U.S. Federal Works Agency, Work Projects Administration, *Final Statistical Report of the Federal Emergency Relief Administration* (GPO, 1942), p. 46; U.S. Federal Works Agency, *Final Report on the WPA Program, 1935–43* (GPO, 1946), pp. 99 and 101; U.S. National Resources Planning Board, *Security, Work, and Relief Policies* (GPO, 1942), pp. 30 and 598 and Lewis Meriam, *Relief and Social Security* (Brookings Institution, 1946), p. 440; and *Annual Report of the Secretary of the Treasury on the State of the Finances for the Fiscal Year Ended June 30, 1942* and apps. 2, 3, and 5; 1943 and 1944 issues.

a. Excludes periods of minor activity (enrollment less than 20,000) and liquidation phases.

b. Federal funds, $10,153 million for project operations and $416 million for administration; sponsor funds, $2,838 million.

c. Excludes state and local outlays after fiscal 1940; excludes most administrative costs, which before fiscal 1940 were allocated to WPA.

d. Approximate; includes only federal outlays for administration, grants, and loans from general expenditures and from revolving fund (net outlay).

reforestation projects to employ a million men. The Civilian Conservation Corps was quickly implemented in April 1933, and after only two months its enrollment surpassed a quarter million. The main branch of the CCC, the Juniors, was restricted to single men, eighteen to twenty-five years old, from needy unemployed families. Allotments of up to $25 were made to the enrollee's family from his monthly wage of $30, and he was given food and lodging.[11] While these allotments helped to lighten direct relief burdens, the scale and restrictive eligibility of the CCC prevented it from filling the larger need for emergency employment.

Roosevelt was described as "frankly leery" of the arguments for public works in 1932 and early 1933. He doubted the availability of sufficient "useful" projects and disbelieved the theory of pump-priming expenditures.[12] Nevertheless, his cabinet and associates convinced him of the need to create the Public Works Administration in 1933.[13] The PWA was empowered to stimulate construction under its own auspices and through other federal, state, or public bodies. Loans and grants were both used, and projects were executed primarily through private contractors. Because of these methods the jobs created could not be channeled to the needy unemployed. PWA administrator "Honest" Harold Ickes's deter-

11. Charles Price Harper, *The Administration of the Civilian Conservation Corps* (Clarksburg Publishing, 1939), pp. 7 and 32–35. The restrictions on age and marital status, which were not part of the original proposal, followed the strong reactions of organized labor against the dollar-a-day pay provision. Congress gave the President authority to set wages and enrollment criteria. John A. Salmond, *The Civilian Conservation Corps, 1933–1942: A New Deal Case Study* (Duke University Press, 1967), pp. 13–23 and 30. Until 1937, enrollees were required to be members of families actually on relief. Meriam, *Relief,* p. 437.

12. As described by an associate, "Again and again, when we were formulating the plans for the campaign in 1932, Roosevelt had been urged by Tugwell and others to come out for a $5,000,000,000 public-works program. He repeatedly shied away from the proposal. This seems to have been partly because, as Roosevelt explained, Hoover, despite all his preparations, had not been able to find over $900,000,000 worth of 'good' and 'useful' projects." Stein, *Fiscal Revolution,* p. 50.

13. "If to Hugh Johnson [head of the National Recovery Administration] the object of public works was to stimulate the heavy industries, and if to Harry Hopkins its object was to provide relief and re-employment, to Ickes its object was to beautify the national estate through the honest building of durable public monuments. To Lewis Douglas [director of the budget], it had no object at all." Arthur M. Schlesinger, Jr., *The Age of Roosevelt,* vol. 2: *The Coming of the New Deal* (Houghton Mifflin, 1958), p. 284; see pp. 282–88 for the early development of the PWA. For an assessment of the PWA, see J. K. Galbraith, assisted by G. G. Johnson, Jr., *The Economic Effects of the Federal Public Works Expenditures, 1933–1938,* U.S. National Resources Planning Board (GPO, 1940).

mination to execute projects of permanent value and with complete integrity delayed the program's expenditures. His approach was criticized by groups advocating large, fast spending to stimulate recovery. In time the CCC and part of the public works program gained reputations for performing useful work and attained an air of permanence. This was reflected in the transfer of their expenditures from the "recovery and relief" category to the "regular" category in the 1936 budget.[14]

State and local relief funds had become strained by early 1933. In May the Federal Emergency Relief Administration was instituted to provide grants to states for "unemployment relief." These funds were available for both direct relief and work relief but could not be spent on categorical public assistance.[15] The emphasis on work-oriented relief was pressed by the FERA's energetic administrator, Harry Hopkins.[16] The early state and local work relief projects supported by the FERA operated on relief principles. Workers' eligibility was based on need, and payments were based on the family's "budgetary deficiency"—the gap between its budget needs and its financial resources. The projects were primarily in light construction, though limited cooperative and self-help projects and part-time work for college students provided some diversification.[17]

14. Stein, *Fiscal Revolution*, p. 66; and Meriam, *Relief*, p. 440.

15. Unlike the RFC, the FERA made outright grants partially based on matching with state relief funding. Schlesinger, *Coming of the New Deal*, pp. 263 and 267. "By definition, emergency relief . . . did not include institutional care, hospitalization, burials, old-age assistance, aid to the blind, aid to dependent children, or relief to unemployable cases under provisions of statutory poor laws, all of which were considered regular functions of state and local governments." U.S. Federal Works Agency, Work Projects Administration, *Final Statistical Report of the Federal Emergency Relief Administration* (GPO, 1942), p. 11. In 1932–33 RFC funds had been used for many of the forms prohibited to the FERA. Brown, *Public Relief*, p. 237.

16. "Basically . . . Hopkins objected to direct relief in any form. Keeping able-bodied men in idleness, he believed, could not help but corrode morale. . . . Work relief, Hopkins said, 'preserves a man's morale. It saves his skill. It gives him a chance to do something socially useful.' . . . Although FERA, thrown so suddenly into the breach, could not escape direct relief as its main instrument, a wide variety of work relief projects were devised under Hopkins's relentless prodding." Schlesinger, *Coming of the New Deal*, p. 268.

17. "When the Federal relief agency assumed its task in 1933, it took the position that every encouragement should be given to the continuation and expansion of good local work programs but that Federal funds should not be supplied for the continuation of programs whose value to the workers and their communities appeared to be slight." Arthur E. Burns and Edward A. Williams, *Federal Work, Security, and Relief Programs*, U.S. Federal Works Agency, Work Projects Admin-

The slow start-up of the PWA and fear of the impending 1933–34 winter led to the creation of the Civil Works Administration. This federally run works program was avowedly a pump-priming measure which combined recovery and relief objectives.[18] Although the CWA drew much of its administration, including its administrator, from the FERA, it was a distinct entity. During this time the FERA continued its direct relief grants but drastically curtailed its support of state and local work relief projects. Many of these projects were taken over by the CWA. Within a few months the CWA became the largest work relief program of the Great Depression with enrollment exceeding 4 million. But the CWA was short-lived. It was phased out the following spring—in line with the original intentions, and in response to charges of waste and corruption, but most essentially for budgetary reasons.[19] Despite its short existence, the CWA set the pattern for later work relief. It was federally operated with state and local project sponsors sharing costs, and it paid regular "prevailing" wages. Although only half of its enrollees were drawn from the relief rolls, considerations of family need became paramount in project dismissals as the CWA wound down.[20] Thereafter the FERA resumed support of state work relief activities under the Emergency Work Relief Program. This program reinstituted relief-oriented principles of eligibility and payment. Its activities were similar to those of the earlier FERA projects but were better organized and more diversified.[21]

With economic recovery lagging, in the fall of 1934 the administration began plans for a large-scale works program that would be longer lasting than the CWA.[22] This move reflected Roosevelt and Hopkins's distaste

---

istration, Division of Research, research monograph 24 (GPO, 1941), p. 28. Also see National Resources Planning Board, *Security*, p. 43.

18. Schlesinger, *Coming of the New Deal*, p. 269; Burns and Williams, *Federal Work*, p. 29; and John Maurice Clark, *Economics of Planning Public Works*, a study made for the National Planning Board of the Federal Emergency Administration of Public Works (GPO, 1935), pp. 23–26.

19. Schlesinger, *Coming of the New Deal*, pp. 270 and 277.

20. National Resources Planning Board, *Security*, p. 43; and Burns and Williams, *Federal Work*, pp. 33–34 and 37. Federal funds provided 90 percent of CWA cost, local funds 9 percent, and state funds the balance.

21. The EWRP took over many uncompleted CWA projects. See Burns and Williams, *Federal Work*, pp. 37–39; Brown, *Public Relief*, p. 160; Schlesinger, *Coming of the New Deal*, p. 277; and National Resources Planning Board, *Security*, p. 44.

22. See Arthur W. Macmahon, John D. Millett, and Gladys Ogden, *The Administration of Federal Work Relief* (Public Administration Service, 1941), pp. 28–43; and Stein, *Fiscal Revolution*, p. 62.

for providing a dole to persons able to work. They justified the higher cost of work relief by the increased worker morale and the additional useful output.[23] A major change of policies was undertaken in 1935. The federal government terminated its grants to states for direct and work relief. Four billion dollars was requested from the Congress for federal work relief for 3.5 million workers. Social work and public interest groups attacked the new plan for supplanting badly needed direct relief funds.[24] The proposed works program was of insufficient scale to take on all of the unemployed on relief—much less the unemployed as a whole. From the outset the division of responsibilities and the relative importance of the PWA and the new Works Progress Administration were clouded. Rivalries between Hopkins, chosen to head the WPA, and Ickes at the PWA colored these developments.[25] It was finally resolved that the WPA would resume the light construction and service activities of earlier work relief, whereas the PWA would continue heavy construction under contracts. The WPA quickly outgrew the PWA to become the dominant work program of the 1930s.

In formulating the WPA, the administration had rejected proposals for spending $6 billion to $10 billion, some of which did not require workers to come from the relief rolls. Budgetary factors determined the decision to request only $4 billion.[26] The administration offered two divergent explanations for the proposed scale. First, when eligibility was

23. The WPA estimated that work relief was 37 percent "more costly" than direct relief. Elizabeth W. Gilboy, *Applicants for Work Relief: A Study of Massachusetts Families under the FERA and WPA* (Harvard University Press, 1940), p. 123. "There were also conflicts between the desire to get work done efficiently and the desire to give a maximum of relief to the greatest possible number of people. Direct relief was undesirable, but it was the least expensive method of aiding the destitute." Brown, *Public Relief,* p. 158.

24. Ibid., pp. 169–70.

25. "Beyond the alphabetical confusion, the line between PWA and WPA was far from clear. The effort to make cost the criterion—all construction projects over $25,000 to be automatically assigned to PWA—was frustrated by Hopkins's skill in subdividing his larger projects." Arthur M. Schlesinger, Jr., *The Age of Roosevelt,* vol. 3: *The Politics of Upheaval* (Houghton Mifflin, 1960), p. 346.

26. "If there had been any possibility of securing enough funds to put all of the unemployed to work, the Administration would gladly have set up a huge program of public works without a means test or any form of relief certification." Brown, *Public Relief,* pp. 166–67. "The decision to confine the new work opportunities to relief recipients . . . came as the reflex of two other pending limitations: the proposed withdrawal of the national government from direct relief and the shrinkage of the contemplated financing from nine billion dollars originally hoped for to four billion dollars." Macmahon, Millett, and Ogden, *Administration,* p. 37.

restricted to one worker per relief family and certain age and employability restrictions were imposed, only 3.5 million persons were eligible. The CWA experience had indicated $1,200 to be a reasonable annual cost per worker including all overhead; hence, the $4 billion figure. Alternatively, Roosevelt argued that expenditures on project materials and equipment would indirectly yield another 3.5 million jobs. This was an unusual argument for the President, who did not seriously accept indirect employment effects until three years later.[27] The 3.5 million enrollment goal was further diluted by its inclusion of the nearly half-million CCC enrollees and National Youth Administration participants.

The WPA's expenditures and enrollments varied widely over the life of the program. After its initial 1935 request for funds, the administration offered no clear statement of program goals or of the criteria used to determine the program's size. The President sometimes referred to "useful work for the needy unemployed," but experience showed this to be an elastic concept. Vagueness about the WPA's goals meant that its scale was determined by a loose and changing array of factors. Appropriations requests for the program were affected by: actual or anticipated changes in normal private employment; changes in government-stimulated private and public employment; natural catastrophes such as widespread drought; and, in later years, the number of men entering the armed forces. The WPA appropriation could be translated into yearly employment by subtracting the cost of materials, equipment, and administration and then dividing the remainder by the projected annual wage cost per worker. Of course, these estimates varied with the types of projects undertaken and the volume of sponsor funds.[28]

The critical determinant of annual WPA appropriations was what significant political forces felt the budget could support. The principal contenders in the administration were the Treasury Department, the Bureau of the Budget, and the WPA. The Bureau of the Budget stood most firmly for budgetary stringency and was frequently supported by the

27. Note that this does not include the employment generated by respending of relief wages. Accordingly, and as argued by Stein, *Fiscal Revolution,* it is hard to see how the 20 percent of program nonlabor expenditures could generate an equivalent volume of employment off-site. Howard, *WPA,* p. 562; Macmahon, Millett, and Ogden, *Administration,* pp. 41–42; and Stein, *Fiscal Revolution,* p. 61.

28. Howard, *WPA,* pp. 560–61 and 570–76. For a more systematic method by which program scale might have been determined, see Macmahon, Millett, and Ogden, *Administration,* p. 173. The requirement of sponsors is described in Howard, *WPA,* pp. 140 and 145–50.

Treasury. The President would consider carefully what Congress might find acceptable and thereby usually obtained his requested appropriation. However, political pressure reduced the WPA to a scale below that desired by many advisers to the President.[29] Over eight years, more than $10.6 billion of federal funds were appropriated for projects operated by the WPA. Nevertheless, congressional support for work relief under the WPA was less than unanimous and weakened with economic recovery. It is notable that the WPA appropriations acts up to mid-1939 specified that funds could be used for direct relief as well as for work relief. Moreover, the Taber amendment to the 1942 appropriations act—which aimed to replace the WPA with direct relief—was just narrowly defeated.[30]

Financing of Expenditures

The dividing line between darkness and enlightenment in American fiscal policy was not the transition from Hoover to Roosevelt. Utilizing public works as a countercyclical measure was part of the conventional wisdom of the 1920s. The short-run expansionary effects of public expenditures were not believed to depend on whether they were financed by taxes or bonds. Thus, it is not surprising that the public works proposals of 1930 and 1931 specified little about financing.[31] Nevertheless, some displacement was believed to arise from the financing mechanisms. Hoover remarked, "To increase taxation for purposes of construction works defeats its own purpose, as such taxes directly diminish employment in private industry." The Committee on Public Works of the President's Organization on Unemployment Relief in 1931 argued that massive bond issuance would force up interest rates and crowd out private and local government spending.[32] The expansionary effects of monetary

29. The administration's success "may have meant, rather, that the administration was successful only in guessing how much Congress could be induced to provide for the WPA. Furthermore, various officials have sometimes admitted that they have not even asked, formally, for funds enough to provide as many jobs as they thought should be provided. Instead, they have limited requests to what they thought . . . they could ask for without casting too many reflections upon efforts of the administration to bring about economic recovery." Howard, *WPA*, p. 578; see pp. 576–83.

30. Ibid., p. 809.

31. Stein, *Fiscal Revolution*, pp. 10–11, provides an insightful account of fiscal developments in this period.

32. Hopkins, *Spending*, pp. 25 and 61.

financing of public works expenditures were also recognized in this period.[33] Still, canons of budgetary balance were powerful in the public arena—perhaps decisive with Hoover, and weakening only slowly with Roosevelt.

The sacrosanctity of budgetary balance led to efforts to redefine the concept to allow for borrowing.[34] In 1931 and 1932 it was often suggested that the budget be considered in balance so long as any borrowing were to finance capital expenditures and repayment were provided from the projects' revenues. Members of Congress and the financial community supported the idea of "self-liquidating" public works or "capital reimbursement," but the notion did not win acceptance in the White House until the Roosevelt administration.[35] The major reforestation project that Roosevelt proposed in his 1932 nomination acceptance speech was to be self-liquidating.[36] In late 1934, administration planners argued that public works should be self-liquidating so that problems of finance would not hinder large undertakings. At this time, preliminary surveys indicated the availability of $49 billion of potentially useful construction, $9 billion of which could be implemented immediately. As the plans were elaborated, capital reimbursement assumed a more diffuse meaning. It was argued that public works, by increasing the national wealth, would broaden the tax base and facilitate self-liquidation. Although capital reimbursement was never implemented, its aura influenced many people's willingness to contemplate large undertakings.[37] By the end of the decade, more enlightened views about financing public works had gained a foot-

33. Paul H. Douglas and Aaron Director wrote in 1931: "It is possible for government to increase the demand for labor without a corresponding contraction of private demand, and . . . this is particularly the case when fresh monetary purchasing power is created to finance the construction work." Stein, *Fiscal Revolution*, p. 11.

34. In January 1933 Rexford Tugwell, later a confidant of the President, urged public works spending with "a balanced budget, to be achieved through drastic increase of income taxes and through borrowing." Ibid., p. 44.

35. Hopkins and Ickes prepared a memorandum stating, "The program of work should be undertaken . . . where the returns will be such that the bonds outstanding against them can be retired at regular intervals over a proper period of amortization." Capital reimbursement was estimated to be feasible for 80 percent of outlays for eliminating grade crossings, 90 percent of resource projects, and fully for other project types. Macmahon, Millett, and Ogden, *Administration*, pp. 30–34.

36. The President argued, "That is the kind of public work that is self-sustaining, and therefore capable of being financed by the issuance of bonds which are made secure by the fact that, the growth of tremendous crops will provide adequate security for the investment." Harper, *Administration*, p. 7.

37. Macmahon, Millett, and Ogden, *Administration*, pp. 34 and 41.

hold. The role of macroeconomic considerations in public finance, rather than analogies drawn from private finance, came to be appreciated.[38]

Roosevelt had campaigned on Hoover's failure to balance the budget. One of his administration's first acts was to obtain emergency powers to cut expenditures under the Economy Act of 1933. The President and many of his top officials believed excessive deficit finance to be dangerous. The President repeatedly promised budgetary balance and a reduction in federal spending. Yet in his twelve years in office, Roosevelt never had a balanced budget. His concern for budgetary balance appeared genuine, and the trappings of "sound finance" were useful in getting the programs that he felt the country needed. His 1933 spending program of $3.3 billion proposed that an additional $220 million in taxes be raised to pay the interest and amortization of the newly created debt. As he approached reelection in 1936, Roosevelt tried to reduce the deficit by curtailing CCC expenditures. The Congress recognized the CCC's broad popularity and refused to cut its appropriations.[39]

Roosevelt thought in terms of desired expenditures for specific purposes, not in terms of desired expenditures or deficits for fiscal stimulus. For several years he eschewed arguments about the pump-priming, multiplier, and secondary-employment effects of work relief and public works. The desired scale of work relief was set mainly by urgent relief requirements and then modified by budgetary factors.[40] The recession of 1937–

38. "So far as the Government of the United States is concerned, there are few criteria for borrowing which resemble the justification for borrowing by a private business. . . . In the case of non-self-liquidating projects, it can be argued, of course, that the national productive plant is enhanced and the loan is made against the increased national income which results in the future, but this is largely without meaning. . . . So far as the Federal Government is concerned, very little more can be made out of nonrecurrence or durability as a criterion for borrowing. . . . While . . . public works, by their nature, do not justify or require any particular form of financing, a broad policy of public expenditure to counteract unemployment does have a special fiscal significance." Galbraith, *Economic Effects,* pp. 6–7.

39. Salmond, *Civilian Conservation Corps,* pp. 63–69.

40. "What Ickes noted in his diary on September 13, 1935, seems to be the basic Rooseveltian attitude during the first term. 'No one has been able to mention indirect employment to the President for a long time. He simply has no patience with the thought.' . . . Roosevelt's unwillingness to count the indirect results made Ickes the usual loser in his unending competition with Harry Hopkins. Ickes' public-works program had the advantage, in the President's opinion, that its projects were of greater long-range value, per dollar of expenditure, than the work performed by Hopkins' WPA. The WPA projects were the object of much criticism as wasteful, if not useless. . . . But the President could not get over the fact that, per dollar, the WPA program put about four times as many men to work *directly* as did the public-works program." Stein, *Fiscal Revolution,* p. 57; also see pp. 50–51 and 88.

38, induced by fiscal and monetary restraint, came as a shock to most people including the President. This event impelled Roosevelt to accept a more active role for spending and deficits to promote recovery.

Roosevelt's early devotion to sound finance was partially attributable to concern about business confidence. Revival of private investment was recognized to be an essential part of economic recovery. Jacob Viner, John Maurice Clark, and Keynes had each recognized the importance of business confidence. It is notable that business groups did not strongly oppose public works, work relief, or even deficit spending. However, opposition arose in 1935 over recommendations for social security, a public utilities holding company act, a banking act, extension of the National Recovery Administration, and above all, tax increases that would strike the wealthy. The following year, businessmen's wrath redoubled with the enactment of a tax on undistributed corporate profits. Although Roosevelt had earlier tread lightly on business interests, he chose these policies for reform rather than recovery. He argued that higher taxes for those who were well off would not disturb consumption expenditures. Ironically, the President could argue that tax increases would reduce the deficit, a goal that business groups also supported. Thereafter, business opposition to the WPA grew because of the program's association with budget deficits and their association with higher taxation.[41] By the time of the President's 1938 decision to use fiscal policy overtly for expansion, the idea that budgetary balance would promote private investment was moribund. Despite massive federal borrowing between 1932 and 1937, bond yields had fallen, so there was little basis for fearing that investment would be crowded out.[42]

For most of the 1930s the net fiscal stimulus to aggregate demand from all levels of government was small. The federal government's modest stimulus was offset by the contractionary moves of state and local governments.[43] However, the growing role of the federal govern-

41. "[One] explanation for growing hostility to the WPA was the association between work relief and the increasing federal debt. The expenditures on the work relief program were, until the beginning of the gigantic rearmament program in 1940, the principal channel for execution of the federal spending program. Opposition to the theory and practice of deficit financing associated the WPA in particular with the continued unbalanced budget." Macmahon, Millett, and Ogden, *Administration*, pp. 298–99.

42. Stein, *Fiscal Revolution*, pp. 105–06. As inflation accompanied the recovery, real rates of interest became substantially negative.

43. See E. Cary Brown, "Fiscal Policy in the 'Thirties: A Reappraisal," *American Economic Review*, vol. 46 (December 1956), pp. 857–79.

ment in total expenditures for public aid, including work relief, was expansionary. Federal public aid expenditures for 1933 to 1939 were estimated to be 57.4 percent debt-financed, with the remainder tax-financed. The corresponding state and local figure was only 24.0 percent debt-financed.[44] Financing public expenditures through bonds was clearly more expansionary than through additional taxes. Hence even a dollar-for-dollar displacement of state-local spending by federal spending would have been expansionary. The steadily declining role of debt finance for states and localities reflected a serious deterioration in their ability to support debt. After 1932 their net borrowing was negative, and an unprecedented number of municipal bonds fell into default.[45] The absence of constitutional debt limitations at the federal level allowed extensive deficit financing, subject to periodic congressional revisions of debt limitations. The evidence suggests that little of the federal debt was directly monetized in this period.[46]

Scale, Displacement, and Productivity

Popular pressure to minimize both budget deficits and tax increases constrained the acceptable level of work relief expenditures. Though affected by the financing methods, the resultant fiscal stimulus was subject to similar constraints. To translate the fiscal stimulus into changes in real national income or output, it is necessary to know the numerical value of the expenditures multiplier. Up to 1938, work relief activities were scaled to the relief objective without counting indirect employment generated through project materials purchases or secondary employment from respending of wages. In theory, from the standpoint of recovery, ignoring any multiplier effects could have led to inadequate *or* excessive spending.[47] In practice, the expenditures fell below the levels needed to

44. Work relief accounted for well over half of the public aid category. The methodology of these estimates is necessarily rough. National Resources Planning Board, *Security,* pp. 293–94 and 327.

45. Ibid., pp. 295–99; and James A. Maxwell and J. Richard Aronson, *Financing State and Local Governments,* 3d ed. (Brookings Institution, 1977), pp. 191–92.

46. See Milton Friedman and Anna J. Schwartz, *A Monetary History of the United States, 1867–1960* (Princeton University Press for the National Bureau of Economic Research, 1963); and Lester V. Chandler, *American Monetary Policy, 1928–1941* (Harper and Row, 1971). For a possible channel of indirect monetization, see Kesselman and Savin, "Three-and-a-Half Million Workers," p. 215.

47. "It is sometimes implied that [the relief view of government spending's] function necessarily results in a rate of expenditure that is inadequate or in any

spur the recovery. The inadequacy of spending persisted even after the 1938 decision to use fiscal policy for expansion. Indeed, the ideology and politics of the 1930s foreclosed any possibility of spending enough to restore full employment—short of wartime mobilization.

An econometric model recently estimated for the period 1926–40 yields a value of the multiplier applicable to the Great Depression. The multiplier for bond-financed government spending is 3.77 in the first year of impact and rises to 7.40 in the third year.[48] These figures suggest that 1930s public expenditures substantially influenced output and employment in the private sector. However, conventional multiplier analysis is subject to a number of serious limitations. The multiplier is based on shifts in the aggregate demand for output; conventionally, it ignores shifts in the aggregate supply schedule that may accompany policies. Macroeconomic policy analysts have recently become aware of the aggregate supply shifts resulting from wage-rate responses to higher income taxes. Similarly, a work relief program may affect the aggregate supply schedule through mechanisms such as the sectoral composition of output. Accounting fully for the displacement of a work relief program necessitates a general equilibrium approach. For example, the modeling should include workers' choices between public and private jobs and private firms' production decisions in competition with public output. These mechanisms are likely to reduce the "true" multipliers for specified work relief programs.

Another problem arises because work relief expenditures in any year were an endogenous choice for policymakers.[49] They altered the program scale countercyclically, even if only for relief purposes. Since the volume of relief work tended to move inversely to private work, measures of dis-

case less than if the broader objective were recognized. . . . However, the effects of the spending depend much more on its scale than on how the spending is regarded, and regarding the objective as relief does not prevent the scale from being very large. In fact, a government intending to provide work relief with prevailing wage standards for all the existing unemployed might plan to spend much more than a government calculating that its expenditures would have large indirect, multiplier, effects upon employment." Stein, *Fiscal Revolution*, pp. 60–61.

48. Hickman and Coen, *Annual Growth Model*, p. 188. These current-price multipliers assume that no accommodating monetary policy is undertaken and that the change in the level of government spending occurred in 1926. Still larger cumulative multipliers might be expected for policy actions initiated in the 1930s.

49. An analogous problem besets all efforts to assess the efficacy of fiscal and monetary policy tools. See Alan S. Blinder and Robert M. Solow, "Analytical Foundations of Fiscal Policy," in Alan S. Blinder and others, *The Economics of Public Finance* (Brookings Institution, 1974), pp. 3–115, especially p. 71.

placement are likely to be exaggerated. This difficulty can be eliminated only with a knowledge of policymakers' "reaction function." Lacking this, it is not possible to "prove" the existence of displacement using macro data, although there is a possibility of "disproving" it. Further, hazards are introduced by the counterfactual nature of asking whether work relief displaced private employment. These stem from unknown relationships of the political-economic system, particularly business's response to a changed level of work relief or alternative policies.[50]

The extent to which debt issue to finance public spending crowds out private investment lies at the heart of the contemporary dispute between fiscalists and monetarists. In comparison with estimates for the postwar period, the estimated multipliers for the 1930s are relatively high. However, they are plausible given the differing economic conditions. Some of the channels through which macro displacement are hypothesized to occur would have been weaker during the 1930s.[51] For example, the low interest rates, depressed expectations about sales, and rapid exogenous monetary growth suggest minimal crowding out of private investment. Still, it is possible that deficit finance per se was sufficiently damaging to business confidence that displacement was greater during the 1930s. In the household sector, liquidity constraints from depressed incomes might have caused relatively high marginal propensities to consume. Even if households anticipated the future taxation that would be needed to service the additional public debt, this was unlikely to reduce their near-term consumption. The impact of work relief programs on consumption and investment behavior during the 1930s is examined explicitly in the next section.

The productivity of work relief programs is assessed by their contributions to socially valued output, after netting out any displaced private product. One way to perform this calculation is through the displacement of private workers. For example, assume that one extra man-year

50. "Both the initial and eventual volume of secondary employment will vary considerably under different conditions, in particular with the stage of the cycle. ... The volume of secondary employment will vary with the volume of unemployment, the atmosphere of security or insecurity, and the volume of excess capacity in the economy. . . . The factors making for this variation seem to have been far too heavily discounted by those who have sought for the value of the employment or investment multiplier." Galbraith, *Economic Effects,* p. 117.

51. Hickman and Coen's estimates of nominal expenditures multipliers for 1951–65 are 2.73 after one year and 2.93 after three years. These estimates fall within the normal range found in many studies of the postwar period reviewed by Blinder and Solow, "Analytical Foundations," p. 77. They also review several displacement mechanisms.

in relief work will displace half a man-year of private employment. Then the additional relief worker must be at least half as productive as the displaced private worker in order to achieve a net gain. Of course, the relief aspects must also be considered in any social evaluation. Because the scale of a work relief program affects its displacement—through financing and other mechanisms to be explored in this paper—it is a prime determinant of productivity. The scale of relief work also affects its productivity directly through a number of channels. With a larger program, projects of successively lower social utility will be executed.[52] In general, the larger the program, the greater will be its mix of relief vis-à-vis work in project operations.

Product Market Demand

Like any public expenditures policy, 1930s work relief added to the demand for final output of the economy. The net stimulus hinged on the extent to which other expenditures were augmented or displaced. Nonfederal expenditures included consumption by households, investment by businesses, and direct relief, public works, and services by state and local governments. Federal work relief expenditures directly affected the spending behavior of these agents through conventional channels. In addition, the very output of work relief may have affected the levels and composition of nonfederal expenditures. No "product" effects would have arisen if work relief output had been completely valueless. These effects will be analyzed by examining the program-induced changes in incomes, expectations, and relative prices of particular goods. An overall assessment of displacement via aggregate demand turns out to be quite complex. And the historical record yields no firm conclusions about the stimulus of work relief vis-à-vis other public expenditures. My principal goal is to identify structural elements that are useful in thinking about the problem. These elements may prove useful in future quantitative analysis, although they will be construed by some as evidence of the problem's hopeless difficulty.

52. "These difficulties and disadvantages all tend to become greater as the work is continued for a longer time and as it is done on a larger scale. It is obviously harder to find worth-while jobs for 4,000,000 workers than for 1,000,000, and harder to find them for 2 years than for 2 months. For example, the Civil Works Administration art project seems to have been justifiable as far as it went, but the painting of murals in school buildings could not go on indefinitely." Clark, *Economics*, p. 25.

Consumption Expenditures

As the largest component of aggregate demand, consumption expenditures play a central role in determining the level of economic activity. In respending a fraction of their incomes, households augment the stimulus of government spending. The size of the marginal propensity to consume (mpc) depends on the economic circumstances of the households receiving any additional income.[53] Ordinarily, most households receive incomes consistent with their expected lifetime path of income. They also possess liquid assets and are able to borrow against their less liquid assets. Their spending behavior is determined by long-run considerations denoted as their "wealth." Assets and credit permit these households to maintain their consumption levels despite temporary fluctuations in their income. Such "wealth constrained" households will exhibit a relatively small mpc.

A household whose primary worker has been unemployed for an extended period may behave differently. Attempting to maintain a living standard consistent with its expected lifetime income, the household exhausts its liquid assets and draws upon its credit as far as possible. Since it cannot borrow against the security of prospective earnings, the household is unable to tap its lifetime wealth for current consumption. Such a "liquidity constrained" household will have a large mpc, perhaps spending all additional income for a period. Ordinarily, many unemployed and young households behave in this manner. A chronically poor household that expects to remain poor is not necessarily liquidity constrained. A prolonged depression may so increase the number of liquidity constrained households that it raises the aggregate mpc.[54]

Consumption behavior of the 1930s can be understood in terms of the preceding analysis. A study of 1954–58 data on the spending and financial adjustments of the unemployed found that the longer persons were unem-

---

53. James Tobin and Walter Dolde present the analytics behind the approach taken here, which draws on widely accepted consumption theory. The mpc concept used here pertains solely to short-run responses. "Wealth, Liquidity and Consumption," in *Consumer Spending and Monetary Policy: The Linkages,* Conference Series no. 5 (Federal Reserve Bank of Boston, 1971), pp. 99–146.

54. This position is supported by an estimated short-run mpc of 0.59 for the interwar period as against 0.46 after World War II. Hickman and Coen, *Annual Growth Model,* p. 196.

ployed, the higher were their mpc's.[55] Also, persons who had no assets at the time of becoming unemployed had higher mpc's than the unemployed with assets. Extrapolating from this study to the 1930s setting of frequent lengthy jobless spells, mpc's of the unemployed may have approached unity. A local survey of unemployment insurance recipients in 1938 found that three-fourths had no savings when they became unemployed.[56] Thus, payments to the unemployed—whether unemployment benefits or work relief—would have been largely respent.[57] Some 1930s policies appealed to early Keynesian arguments that the poor, irrespective of employment status, had a high mpc.[58] However, recent studies have found the mpc's of the poor and out of transfer income to be no higher than those of the general population and out of aggregate personal income. These studies focused on groups whose poverty was not necessarily a temporary condition.[59] Consequently, their conclusions do not weaken the assertion that the liquidity-constrained long-term unemployed of the 1930s had high mpc's.

Although relief objectives dominated the design of the federal work programs, the distributional aspects of consumption expenditures were

55. Philip A. Klein, *Financial Adjustments to Unemployment,* occasional paper 93 (Columbia University Press for National Bureau of Economic Research, 1965), pp. 22–24 and 42–45. Bakke, *Unemployed Worker,* pp. 254, 258, and 263, provides tables showing the financial resources and pattern of expenditure adjustments of a sample of unemployed families in 1933, but there is no cross-tabulation of this information by duration of unemployment.

56. Some of them undoubtedly had depleted their assets in previous spells of unemployment. Bakke, *Unemployed Worker,* p. 312.

57. This argument applies for the initial payment to the unemployed person. A long-term WPA worker, however, may partially restore his asset position and sufficiently alter his lifetime earnings expectations that he becomes wealth constrained again. See Galbraith, *Economic Effects,* p. 116, and for an opposing argument based on Keynes see Clark, *Economics,* pp. 93–95.

58. "The major purposes of the wages and hours provisions of the [National Industrial Recovery Act] codes were commonly stated as . . . the enlargement of the purchasing power of the lowest paid workers, who could be counted upon to spend a large proportion of their incomes for consumers goods and hence to stimulate the revival of business activity." Leverett S. Lyon, Victor Abramson, and associates, *Government and Economic Life: Development and Current Issues of American Public Policy,* vol. 2 (Brookings Institution, 1940), p. 1050.

59. Alan S. Blinder, "Distribution Effects and the Aggregate Consumption Function," *Journal of Political Economy,* vol. 83 (June 1975), pp. 447–75; and Lester D. Taylor, "Saving out of Different Types of Income," *Brookings Papers on Economic Activity, 2:1971,* pp. 383–407. Both authors express serious reservations about their findings.

also considered. The anticipated stimulus to spending was cited as a reason to restrict WPA eligibility to the needy unemployed.[60] Cognizant of the inefficiencies of manual labor, policymakers still chose to concentrate program expenditures on labor to obtain maximal respending.[61] Observers recognized that tax finance of work relief could reduce consumer spending and thereby vitiate the net stimulus. There was awareness that the distributional incidence of taxes could affect the extent of consumption displacement. In 1932 it was argued that the relatively progressive federal tax system would displace consumer spending less than the property- and consumption-based state and local tax systems.[62] A study undertaken for fiscal 1939 confirmed that the federal income taxes were more progressive than state and local taxes. The conclusion held when isolating the taxes used to finance public aid programs.[63] One further distributional aspect of work relief may have exerted unanticipated effects. A recent study found the consumption expenditures of lower-income households in 1935–36 biased toward goods and services produced intensively by unskilled labor.[64] Thus, both the primary and secondary employment effects of work relief favored unskilled labor.

60. A 1934 memorandum from FERA officials to the President argued, "Recovery through governmental expenditures requires that Government money automatically goes to the lowest economic strata. It is there that occurs automatically the greatest number of respendings." Macmahon, Millett, and Ogden, *Administration,* p. 30. Also see p. 37.

61. "From the point of view of efficiency it would undoubtedly be more effective to use machines. The point of view of those behind the work relief program, however, has been that the first concern of the FERA and WPA should be to get money directly into the hands of those who need it. . . [in part to] increase consumption expenditures and stimulate business recovery." Gilboy, *Applicants,* pp. 211–12.

62. Testifying before a U.S. Senate committee in 1932, Governor Gifford Pinchot of Pennsylvania "urged that even if it were possible to meet existing needs through state and local taxes, these should not be relied on since they took money primarily from 'the little fellows,' thus cutting down consumption, whereas through federal taxes 'the people who ought to meet this problem can be made to meet it.' " Howard, *WPA,* p. 663n.

63. See National Resources Planning Board, *Security,* pp. 331–34; and Howard, *WPA,* pp. 661–63. State and local taxes were found to be nearly proportional to income for classes with annual income of $500 and higher. More than half of the state sales taxes were enacted during the 1930s, many during the depths of the depression. Also, the progressivity of federal taxes declined with the introduction of payroll taxes in 1936 and their steep growth in the following two years.

64. The study also calculates the total impact on unskilled labor per dollar purchase of output for thirty-eight industries in 1939. Since construction ranked second only to agriculture for intensiveness of unskilled labor, even nonrestrictive public contracts for construction would have substantially aided unskilled workers.

Households' expectations of future earnings determine their perceived "wealth," which in turn affects their current consumption. These expectations are usually based on each household's recent history. Yet, at times many households alter their expectations of economic conditions and abruptly revise their savings rates. These shifts are not well explained by economic analysis; it is simply said that the economic climate has changed. Consumers sharply altered their expectations in 1930, according to Peter Temin. His consumption relation estimated with wealth and liquidity variables is unable to predict fully the decline in expenditures.[65] It is possible that large-scale work relief later in the decade signaled another shift in households' expectations. Such programs may have confirmed fears that private employment would never return to predepression levels. This expectation would have caused consumption spending to rise less than other public expenditures might have. This hypothesis, like most involving the "black box" of expectations, is speculative.

The degree of uncertainty about future earnings may influence current consumption behavior. Economic theory implies that greater uncertainty reduces the household's consumption spending.[66] This relationship suggests a possible explanation of the sharp fall of consumption in 1930 and subsequent years. By the same token, workers' uncertainty about their tenure on emergency relief projects may have depressed their spending.[67] Relief work nevertheless proved for many workers to be more regular than private employment. Thus, relief wages may have induced more consumer spending per dollar than wages in the private sector.

The output as well as the expenditures of work relief projects had the potential to affect consumer spending. Consider the case where relief output was distributed in addition to relief payments or was made available without charge to the general public.[68] While the possibility of con-

---

Jeffrey G. Williamson, "Who Pays for the Services of America's Working Poor?" discussion paper 334-76 (University of Wisconsin—Madison, Institute for Research on Poverty, 1976; processed), pp. 26 and 32.

65. Temin discusses methodological problems in analyzing shifts in expectations. *Did Monetary Forces Cause the Great Depression?* (Norton, 1976), pp. 69–83.

66. See the "income risk" case of A. Sandmo, "The Effect of Uncertainty on Saving Decisions," *Review of Economic Studies,* vol. 37 (July 1970), pp. 353–60.

67. "Neither PWA nor WPA employment has at any time been secure employment. Although sheer subsistence needs make it impossible for workers to reduce their expenditures very much, this uncertainty has doubtless operated to reduce the volume of secondary employment during this period." Galbraith, *Economic Effects,* p. 117.

68. This does not include distribution in lieu of relief wages or of the dole.

sumption effects was greatest when output assumed the form of private consumption goods, it also existed for public works and public services. The real income and the perceived consumption of households were raised to the extent that they valued relief output. Yet with less than unitary mpc's, households desired to raise their consumption by less than any income increase. Hence, their consumption spending out of money incomes would have been reduced. The availability of relief output may also have altered the composition of private demand for particular goods and services.[69] Moreover, if relief output were complementary to private goods and services to be consumed in the future, household savings rates would have risen. This substitution effect reinforces the income effect in reducing consumption demand. Conversely, if relief output were substitutable for future private consumption, contemporaneous demand for consumption goods would have tended to rise. Unfortunately, no empirical or anecdotal evidence on this issue has been uncovered.

Investment Expenditures

Capital goods were the most depressed area of demand in the 1930s. Reduced sales and extensive idle industrial capacity explained the low levels of investment spending.[70] As long as existing plant and equipment exceeded immediate needs, firms would not replace depreciating capital or undertake new investment. For investment to resume, the economy's "desired" capital stock had to rise above the existing capital stock. Barring a recovery of sales, this entailed waiting for the capital stock to depreciate to the point where investment would be undertaken. Low production meant that the rate of depreciation was retarded. Attempting to minimize their outlay of cash for material inputs, firms idled their older, less productive machines and further slowed the depreciation process.[71]

69. An analogous problem became of paramount concern in the surplus commodities program, which was intended to purchase and distribute surplus foods without diverting family food expenditures to nonfood items. See Meriam, *Relief*, pp. 335–39.

70. Hickman and Coen, *Annual Growth Model*, p. 242, present estimates of annual capacity utilization rates for 1924–40.

71. An incentive toward greater capital input in private production, based on risk-minimizing behavior, is discussed in the next section.

In normal times consumers' shifting to new products spurs demand for capital designed to produce the new goods and causes other capital to obsolesce prematurely. This stimulus to autonomous investment was minimized in the 1930s because strained household budgets had no allowance for new goods. One might have expected work relief activities to demand new capital goods and to hasten the depreciation of existing capital. However, as elaborated in the next section, the input mix of work relief was biased toward labor and against machinery. The heavy equipment used by the WPA was rented from private firms whenever feasible.[72] This orientation minimized work relief's contribution to an investment revival. As Keynes astutely observed, "there is nothing President Hoover can do that an earthquake could not do better."[73]

A speedier path to recovery would have been to raise the desired capital stock by lifting sales expectations.[74] Yet that approach would have proved ineffectual if actual sales had not risen. Given their excess capacity, producers would not have created new capacity until the anticipated demands materialized. Similarly, business inventories would not have been replenished until they had fallen below the desired levels.[75] A relation between government policies and "business confidence" was widely recognized during the 1930s, though subject to varying interpretations. A 1931 survey of businessmen by the U.S. Chamber of Commerce suggested that the government might best aid recovery by ceasing to publicize high unemployment.[76] Keynes and others noted that large-scale public works might exert precarious or negative effects on business confidence.[77] Concern about confidence limited Roosevelt's work relief expenditures. Indeed, almost any element of the government's budgetary

72. U.S. Federal Works Agency, *Final Report on the WPA Program, 1935–43* (GPO, 1946), p. 77.

73. Stein, *Fiscal Revolution,* p. 146.

74. "The evidence suggests that expectations as to the extent of demand play as great a role in determining the degree of business activity as the level of costs. Indeed, during the last 10 years the influence of demand expectations appears to have been predominant." National Resources Planning Board, *Security,* p. 323.

75. See Galbraith, *Economic Effects,* p. 33.

76. Hopkins, *Spending,* p. 37.

77. "With the confused psychology which often prevails, the Government [public works] programme may, through its effect on 'confidence,' increase liquidity-preference or diminish the marginal efficiency of capital, which, again, may retard other investment unless measures are taken to offset it." John Maynard Keynes, *The General Theory of Employment, Interest and Money* (Harcourt, Brace, 1936), p. 120.

policy could potentially upset business confidence.[78] The nature of these relationships was elusive in the 1930s and remains so to this day.

A firm's decision to purchase capital goods depends on its calculation of their profitability. The factors to be considered include the cost of inputs, the price of output, sales expectations, and the cost of funds to finance the investment. At higher interest rates, fewer investment projects are profitable. Debt finance of public works may crowd out private investment by pushing up market interest rates, a possibility recognized in 1931. Public works output, whether executed by work relief or contract methods, may affect private investment incentives. For example, new highways may raise the profitability of industries needing access to particular markets. They may also stimulate construction of fuel and lodging facilities along the roadside. At the same time, the highways may depress the profitability of firms exposed to additional competition. The net effects on private investment have not been studied, but they may be large, given the scale of 1930s public works activity.[79]

Government Expenditures

Displacement of state and local spending for public works, services, and direct relief became a major concern for the conduct of federal work relief. This problem was anticipated in 1932 by the head of the President's Organization on Unemployment Relief.[80] As federal work relief programs grew, charges of intergovernmental displacement became more frequent. Because the depression had forced the lower jurisdictions to curtail their spending, it proved difficult to determine whether federal work relief had caused any particular cutback.[81] Communities were inclined to spon-

78. "How much, if at all, private investment during 1933–1940 was held back by lack of confidence resulting from the New Deal, and how much responsibility should be assigned to budget policy as compared with other New Deal measures, is impossible to say." Stein, *Fiscal Revolution*, p. 89.

79. These observations are drawn from Galbraith, *Economic Effects*, p. 10; also see Clark, *Economics*, p. 110.

80. Walter S. Gifford testified to a Senate committee: "Communities, counties, and States undoubtedly would appropriate less public moneys. The net result might well be that the unemployed who are in need would be worse instead of better off." Howard, *WPA*, p. 753.

81. "It was a matter of opinion whether specific public improvements and services would have been undertaken had no work relief existed. In prolonged depressions, communities were often unable to maintain their regular level of expenditures, and it was not always valid to assume that work relief projects which

sor WPA projects of greatest local utility—hence, those they might have undertaken in the absence of WPA. To forestall such displacement the WPA at times approved less useful projects.[82] Moreover, the Bureau of the Budget screened federal-agency sponsored WPA proposals to eliminate work normally financed from regular appropriations.[83]

The extent of intergovernmental displacement of spending on goods and services can be assessed along several lines. On purely theoretical grounds, substantial displacement might be predicted. So far as relief projects perform activities similar to regular governmental functions, the availability of federal funds for work relief raises the income of lower jurisdictions. In fact, 1930s federal work relief was concentrated in types of construction that had been the traditional preserve of state and local governments.[84] It is natural for the lower governments to allocate only a portion of any increase in community resources to public activities; the remainder would be translated into lower taxation and debt burden. Estimates of the effects of *nonmatched* federal grants for public employment in the last decade have found intergovernmental displacement as high as 90 percent.[85] But *matched* federal grants will alter the relative prices of the subsidized public activities vis-à-vis other public and private consumption. The sponsor contributions by state and local governments under the WPA, detailed in the section on the political economy of productivity and displacement, are similar to a matching feature. Matching

---

appeared to be direct substitutions were so in fact." John Charnow, *Work Relief Experience in the United States,* pamphlet series 8 (Washington: Social Science Research Council, Committee on Social Security, 1943), p. 104; also see pp. 103–06.

82. Macmahon, Millett, and Ogden, *Administration,* p. 307. "The objective was to do things which the state and local governments would in all probability not do themselves in the near future and perhaps might never do. . . . [These considerations] thus substituted the criterion of additional employment for the criterion of relative desirability. . . . Like individuals, communities are under pressure to put essentials ahead of luxuries. To insure additional employment the W.P.A. had to tend toward projects that were not essential." Meriam, *Relief,* p. 366.

83. Macmahon, Millett, and Ogden, *Administration,* p. 104.

84. "The amount of duplication may be inferred from . . . the common-sense knowledge that a program to be acceptable in a local area must not be so far out of line with ordinary public works as to get the reputation of useless expenditure; and from the fact that [FERA and WPA] projects have tended to concentrate largely on those types of effort normally carried on as municipal public works." Bakke, *Unemployed Worker,* p. 400n. Also see Meriam, *Relief,* p. 373.

85. See Alan E. Fechter, "Public Employment Programs: An Evaluative Study," in *Studies in Public Welfare,* pp. 93–123; and Michael Wiseman, "Public Employment as Fiscal Policy," *Brookings Papers on Economic Activity, 1:1976,* pp. 61–104.

induces the lower jurisdiction to spend more on the subsidized activity, thus tending to offset the income effect of the federal grant. Unfortunately, this framework cannot be quantitatively implemented for the 1930s to reach firm answers on the net impact.

Other evidence as to the extent of intergovernmental displacement for goods and services is available. It was observed that the materials, supplies, and equipment provided as sponsor contributions to WPA projects would have been purchased by the lower jurisdictions even in the absence of WPA.[86] Hence, sponsor funds may have fully displaced ordinary state and local spending, so that they exerted no net spending stimulus. The pattern of public spending on goods and services does not support the hypothesis of extensive displacement beyond that of sponsor funds. Consider the timing and volume of public construction financed by the various jurisdictions, including work relief projects. State and local expenditures fell precipitously from 1931 to 1933, years of only modest rise in federal spending. Sharp rises in federal outlays from 1933 to 1934 and 1935 to 1936 were accompanied by modest rises in state and local spending.[87]

Because federal relief spending filled the same income support objective as state and local relief, intergovernmental displacement was also an issue with respect to relief expenditures. A portion of FERA grants was disbursed to states on a discretionary, nonmatched basis. The FERA had to press the states to maintain their level of spending on direct relief.[88] After 1935 the WPA was the only federal aid scheme providing matched funds to lower jurisdictions. Thus, larger amounts of state and local funds were diverted from direct relief to sponsor contributions.[89] Direct relief cases displayed a clear, inverse relation to federal works program enroll-

86. Howard, *WPA*, p. 823. Furthermore, part of the equipment contributed by sponsors had earlier been given to them by the federal government under the FERA! Federal Works Agency, *Final Report*, p. 77.

87. Public construction outlays, in millions of dollars, for 1925–29 averaged 188 from federal sources and 2,104 from state and local; for 1930, 307 and 2,469; for 1931, 422 and 2,156; for 1932, 460 and 1,334; for 1933, 647 and 707; for 1934, 1,380 and 794; for 1935, 1,234 and 616; for 1936, 2,335 and 881; for 1937, 2,043 and 845; for 1938, 2,085 and 1,103; for 1939, 2,206 and 1,314. National Resources Planning Board, *Security*, p. 343.

88. Hopkins, *Spending*, pp. 97–98.

89. Brown, *Public Relief*, p. 343; and National Resources Planning Board, *Security*, pp. 308–09. "To the extent that WPA employment was provided in any locality, there were fewer persons in need of direct relief. This was one of the incentives for the sponsoring of WPA projects by State and local governments." Federal Works Agency, *Final Report*, p. 9.

ments. For example, the expected seasonal rise in the relief rolls of October–November 1933 was arrested with the start of the CWA. The shutdown of CWA activities the following spring brought a surge in relief rolls. A falling trend of direct relief beginning in 1935 was explained partially by the initiation of the WPA. Because both programs responded to economic conditions as well as to each other, the inverse relation was not exact. The improving economy of 1936 permitted a simultaneous curtailment of both programs.[90] Intergovernmental displacement of relief spending appears to have been substantial. Yet even if federal work relief had displaced local direct relief dollar-for-dollar, the net effect would still have been expansionary. Direct relief payments are like a reduction in taxes, and these are less expansionary than work relief spending for goods and services.[91]

Input Choice and Labor Demand

The level and composition of aggregate output affect demands for the various productive factors, including capital and labor services. Input choices may differ between private and public production activities. In the 1930s, marketplace factors and public policy goals modified input choices from their cost-minimizing solutions. These matters are germane to the relative productive efficiency of work relief and public works undertaken through contracts. While productive efficiency is examined in this section as it relates to labor demand, all aspects of productivity are explored thoroughly in the section on the political economy of productivity and displacement.[92] The private-sector input choices also provide a background to the labor market strategies of the unemployed analyzed in the next section.

Input Choice in the Private Sector

Uncertainty over sales made firms unwilling to hire workers even at wages below their marginal contribution to the value of output. Unem-

---

90. Federal Works Agency, *Final Statistical Report*, pp. 24–28.

91. This follows from the balanced-budget theorem of macroeconomics. If the mpc of direct relief recipients were unity, the net expansionary effect would disappear. The result is reinforced by the differential degree of debt-financing between jurisdictions. If work relief is merely camouflaged direct relief, the result is an artifact of national-accounting conventions.

92. In their paper in this volume, Kemper and Moss distinguish productive efficiency from allocative efficiency, the social valuation of all project outputs.

ployment, it has been argued, would have vanished if workers had been willing to accept real output in exchange for their labor services.[93] This was not a feasible form of remuneration, since each firm's production was specialized and unlikely to satisfy the needs of any household. The difficulty is inherent in an economy where labor services are exchanged for money, and the money is then spent for consumer goods. As a result of the money economy's partial breakdown in the 1930s, a limited number of self-help cooperatives were formed. Assuming a variety of forms, the cooperatives usually involved the production and barter of goods and services among members. Some units were subsidized by the FERA, which restrained them from competing with private producers in their external sales.[94]

Many firms were strained to the verge of bankruptcy by their large fixed costs in the face of low revenues. Firms arranged their production and finances so as to minimize the risk of failure even at the cost of larger accounting losses—a policy of "safety first."[95] This behavior affected their choice of inputs. By utilizing its machinery more fully, a firm could depreciate it more quickly and avoid additional cash outlays in the current period. Hiring more labor, however, did require current cash outlays on wages. In minimizing the chance of bankruptcy by reducing current outlays, a firm would as far as possible substitute capital for labor. "Safety first" implied a stop-go employment policy by the firm and less labor demand than under simple profit maximization. To minimize cash outlays for holding inventories, the firm would produce only when orders were received and lay off workers in the interim. The high frequency of layoffs in the 1930s was facilitated by employers' assurance that their workers would respond readily to recall.[96]

Given widespread unemployment, employers could be highly selective

93. Axel Leijonhufvud, *Keynes and the Classics,* occasional paper 30 (London: Institute of Economic Affairs, 1969), p. 35.

94. National Resources Planning Board, *Security,* pp. 255–58; and P. A. Kerr, "Production-for-Use and Distribution in Work Relief Activities," *Monthly Report of the Federal Emergency Relief Administration, September 1 Through September 30, 1935* (GPO, 1936), pp. 1–16.

95. For the general theory, see Richard H. Day, Dennis J. Aigner, and Kenneth R. Smith, "Safety Margins and Profit Maximization in the Theory of the Firm," *Journal of Political Economy,* vol. 79 (November–December 1971), pp. 1293–1301.

96. Bakke describes a firm that "does not keep men on steadily but hires them and fires them for the duration of the job only" (*Unemployed Worker,* p. 205) and employers' strong preference for rehiring previous workers (ibid., pp. 167–72).

in their hiring choices. Firms preferred younger experienced workers and their previous employees. Teenagers, inexperienced workers, and older workers faced the greatest difficulties in finding jobs. Attitudes toward hiring former WPA workers varied widely, but graduates of the youth programs (CCC and NYA) were generally well received.[97] Employers tightened up job qualifications, sometimes combining job duties or requiring very specialized experience.[98] In some cases, the effective wage was decreased by replacing hourly rates with piece rates.[99] Despite high unemployment, temporary shortages of workers with specific skills occasionally appeared; their relation to work relief is examined in the next section.

Input Choice in Work Relief Programs

The overriding objective of the federal work relief program was to create maximal employment for needy persons.[100] For example, the WPA's ceiling on hiring of nonneedy workers, initially limited to 10 percent of project employment, was reduced to 5 percent in 1937.[101] The employment goal shaped every facet of the input choices of the work relief program. Such a policy implies the virtual neglect of employment generated off-site, through purchases from the private economy. To conserve funds for more on-site employment, materials and capital inputs were minimized on projects. Limited nonlabor inputs had also character-

97. For employer views on WPA workers, see Howard, *WPA,* pp. 258–59; and Bakke, *Unemployed Worker,* pp. 419–20. For the youth programs see Salmond, *Civilian Conservation Corps,* p. 111; and U.S. Federal Security Agency, War Manpower Commission, *Final Report of the National Youth Administration, Fiscal Years 1936–1943* (GPO, 1944), pp. 107–08.

98. In one case "a large furrier in the city listed an opening with the bureau for an experienced girl to act as a double-entry bookkeeper to take entire charge of an office. One of the major requirements for the job, however, was that the girl be a blonde and be able to model size 16 garments." Gladys L. Palmer, *The Search for Work in Philadelphia, 1932–36,* U.S. Works Progress Administration, National Research Project, report P-7 (University of Pennsylvania, Industrial Research Department, 1939), p. 34.

99. Bakke, *Unemployed Worker,* p. 205.

100. "In the course of the meetings of the [Advisory Committee on Allotments of the works program] the President emphasized . . . the goal of all work undertakings was to take men and women from the relief rolls, not to provide general employment." Macmahon, Millett, and Ogden, *Administration,* pp. 109–10.

101. WPA workers certified as in need never fell below 94 percent of the total and stood at 97 percent in fiscal 1940. Howard, *WPA,* p. 356.

ized early municipal work relief and the FERA production projects.[102] The WPA instituted a dollar limit on federal funds to be spent on non-labor costs per worker per month, thus placing a major burden for those costs on sponsors.[103] Limited materials and inadequate machinery seriously affected the efficiency of WPA workers on certain kinds of projects. To save funds for employment of the needy unemployed, the use of skilled workers and foremen was also curtailed.[104] Often, supervision of relief workers' performance was intentionally slack to facilitate the employment of marginal workers.[105] Moreover, the selection of effective project foremen was compromised by political pressure and the difficulty of securing qualified persons from the private sector.[106]

The private enterprise setting of relief work and its relief function conditioned the types of workers available to projects. Relief workers included some of the most marginal workers, with a higher mean age, a greater incidence of disabilities, and greater loss of confidence and morale than private workers.[107] Minimal notions of employability were utilized in certifying relief persons as eligible for relief work.[108] Those from

102. Colcord, *Emergency Work Relief*, p. 199. "The general policy . . . was that labor-displacing machinery was not to be used when satisfactory articles could be produced with hand labor. Although this policy had the effect of imposing a low man-hour productivity, it resulted in more widespread employment for those on relief." Kerr, "Production-for-Use," p. 10.

103. Over 60 percent of WPA nonlabor costs were met from sponsor funds. Howard, *WPA*, p. 256.

104. "The employment of skilled workers and experienced foremen undoubtedly improves the quality of the product and permits the agency to undertake more difficult and perhaps more permanently useful projects, but it tends to increase the cost per man-year. . . . There is an inherent conflict between using labor taken from the relief rolls and achieving utility, economy, and quality in production." Meriam, *Relief*, p. 406.

105. "There was a general tendency to reduce the work pace of an entire project to that of the less capable workers and to dismiss only those who were hopelessly or deliberately inefficient." Charnow, *Work Relief Experience*, p. 110. Complaints that the WPA was "too efficient" were sometimes raised by "relief officials, who, with every increase in the WPA's effort to emphasize the work rather than the relief aspect of its program, have seen older or less skillful workers dropped by the wayside as 'unemployment.'" Howard, *WPA*, p. 259.

106. Bakke, *Unemployed Worker*, pp. 404–08 and 419; and Howard, *WPA*, pp. 250–52.

107. The program employed some persons who were unlikely to find private jobs, "save in the tightest of labor markets. To utilize the labor of such persons was in itself a sheer social gain." Macmahon, Millett, and Ogden, *Administration*, p. 1. Also see Howard, *WPA*, p. 248.

108. "W.P.A. could not have fulfilled its relief objectives if it had disregarded need and had selected its workers through open competitive examinations. . . . Many

clerical and manufacturing occupations were unaccustomed to the manual, outdoor nature of their work assignments. The most able workers were among the first to be released or to leave relief projects voluntarily, when job opportunities appeared in the private economy.[109] Seeking special skills to operate their projects efficiently, managers would occasionally recruit their own workers and induce the welfare agency to certify them as in need of relief.[110] Even when persons with substantial skills were assigned through the normal procedure, their skills often could not be used effectively because of the limited capital inputs and range of projects.[111]

Scheduling of labor inputs in relief work was distorted in two important ways by the relief objective. First, the desire to relieve higher unemployment during winters caused seasonal variations in the works program. The sudden start-ups and shutdowns seriously diminished the efficiency of public works projects in cold-winter regions.[112] Second, some systems for compensating workers of different skill levels led to diverse work schedules and project inefficiencies. The FERA work programs of 1933 generally paid workers a daily or hourly wage and employed them only long enough for them to earn their relief budgetary deficiency. Departures from this method, with "prevailing wages" subject to scheduled minimums by skill class and region, were tried under the CWA and EWRP.[113] The WPA initially adopted a "security wage" policy, which offered a monthly salary contingent on skill and location for 120 to 140 hours of work. The minimum hours requirement was quickly

were employed who would have been rejected as unqualified by civil service commissions." Meriam, *Relief*, p. 415. Also see Charnow, *Work Relief Experience*, pp. 28–31.

109. Howard, *WPA*, pp. 247–48. "Relief jobs are considered to be a pool for labor, and as soon as the men can be transferred to private employment that is done. It would be logical to suppose that the most efficient men would be taken off first, leaving constantly, therefore, by process of adverse selection, those who are least efficient to do the work-relief job." Bakke, *Unemployed Worker*, p. 402.

110. Meriam, *Relief*, p. 378.

111. National Resources Planning Board, *Security*, pp. 243–46.

112. "Since these men whom private contractors periodically have no use for . . . continue to have the needs of human beings over the cold months, it becomes necessary for the government to undertake its projects during just those times when on the whole private enterprise finds it difficult to continue efficiently and profitably." Bakke, *Unemployed Worker*, pp. 402–03.

113. Payment methods of the various programs are surveyed in Arthur E. Burns and Peyton Kerr, "Survey of Work-Relief Wage Policies," *American Economic Review*, vol. 27 (December 1937), pp. 711–24. For the WPA experience, see Howard, *WPA*, pp. 159–78.

abandoned in favor of a "prevailing wage" policy which became official the following year. Wages were paid at rates similar to those prevailing in the worker's community for his assigned skill, up to the monthly amount of his security wage. This practice yielded discrepant work schedules for the workers on any project.[114] The resulting inefficiency led the WPA in 1939 to mandate a return to the security wage method with more uniform hours of work.[115]

Relief Work versus Contract Work

Federal operation of relief projects was by "force account," meaning direct hiring of workers; this method can be contrasted with contracts to private firms which typify public works undertakings. While the WPA was authorized to contract out work, it rarely did so because of the difficulty of getting contractors to use workers certified as in need.[116] Contractors operating on the cost-minimizing principles of private enterprise had no inherent preference for a high input of labor in production. Early in the depression, the substantial materials orders from Reconstruction Finance Corporation projects were viewed as a means of spurring recovery in the heavy goods industries. These hopes were not fulfilled, and thereafter little attempt was made even in PWA contract work to select projects on the basis of their materials composition.[117]

The exclusive concern for direct employment on relief projects was

114. "In New York City alone there were over 125 different working schedules. Throughout the nation as a whole hours varied from 50 to 140 a month, depending on workers' monthly and hourly rates. The result was said to have been a complex tangle of some 4,000 different working schedules." Howard, *WPA*, p. 214. "In the case of the professional projects, and in research or survey tasks where the most skilled workers were needed to supervise the work, their departure before the end of the week frequently left the unskilled workers without any supervision whatever." Bakke, *Unemployed Worker*, p. 404.

115. Efficiency rose with the return to uniform work hours. Macmahon, Millett, and Ogden, *Administration*, p. 158.

116. "In conjunction with Works Program projects operated under contract, it has been found necessary repeatedly to waive established policies (such as those requiring that at least a given proportion of project employees be taken from among workers found to be in need) because contractors wanted to use their own crews and to be free to select any workers they chose." Howard, *WPA*, p. 151. Also see the White House statement in *Public Papers*, pp. 280–81.

117. Macmahon, Millett, and Ogden, *Administration*, pp. 29–30. "It is doubtful if public works could, in practice, be selected for their expansive effect on existing plant; it is equally doubtful, on the other hand, if any attempt should be made to select projects merely to accord with higher degrees of idleness in plant capacity." Galbraith, *Economic Effects*, p. 9.

exercised at the expense of potential employment in the industries supplying materials and machinery. Ratios of off-site to on-site man-hours varied across programs: FERA, 0.16; CWA, 0.12; EWRP, 0.61; WPA, 0.16; RFC, 1.48; regular federal projects, 1.04; federal PWA, 1.02; and nonfederal PWA, 2.04.[118] Work relief projects also had a higher proportion of unskilled workers in their direct plus indirect labor requirements than that of contracted public works. This is evident in the average costs per man-hour for all projects: nonfederal PWA, $1.12; federal PWA, $0.88; regular federal, $1.03; and WPA, $0.55.[119] Thus, the use of force account facilitated the maximal employment of workers on relief, particularly of unskilled workers.

Work Relief Provisions and Labor Supply

A favorite pastime of economists since Keynes has been to debate the existence and meaning of involuntary unemployment. This controversy has assumed many forms; most recently, it has revolved around the "anticipations-search" model of unemployment.[120] With little theoretical basis, observers of the Great Depression also debated the nature of unemployment. At one pole was the argument that unemployment must be voluntary, since most persons could find some form of paid work.[121] This position highlighted both the role of choice in workers' behavior

118. Ibid., p. 45. The ratios are averages for 1933–38. These estimates include in "off-site" employment those employees engaged in project administration; more conventionally, this group along with "on-site" employees constitutes "direct" employment. "Indirect" employment is that arising in the private firms supplying materials, machinery, and services contracted to the project.

119. Ibid., p. 53. The ranking of these programs is unchanged when their on-site labor costs are adjusted to the nonfederal PWA on-site wage rates.

120. For an application to the Great Depression, see Albert Rees, "On Equilibrium in Labor Markets," *Journal of Political Economy,* vol. 78 (March–April 1970), pp. 306–10; Robert E. Lucas, Jr., and Leonard A. Rapping, "Unemployment in the Great Depression: Is There a Full Explanation?" *Journal of Political Economy,* vol. 80 (January–February 1972), pp. 186–91; and Michael R. Darby, "Three-and-a-Half Million U.S. Employees Have Been Mislaid: Or, an Explanation of Unemployment, 1934–1941," *Journal of Political Economy,* vol. 84 (February 1976), pp. 1–16; and Kesselman and Savin, "Three-and-a-Half Million Workers."

121. In 1931 the chairman of the finance committee of the United States Steel Corporation said in a radio address: "The first step for the individual is to accept that employment which lies at hand, no matter what it may be, and by his efforts and diligence and ambition to raise himself, as has been possible for others, to a better and more remunerative position. Man's field of occupation is like an ever-flowing stream; it is always moving; it can accommodate in one way or another all who are willing to work." Hopkins, *Spending,* p. 38.

and the public relief which enabled workers to reject undesirable jobs. Of course, the available jobs were often low-paying, irregular, and occupationally unsuited for the unemployed. Pushed to an extreme, the position implied a work-or-starve policy as a solution to unemployment. At the other pole was the argument that jobs in most occupations and in the aggregate were simply in short supply. If job opportunities were unavailable, unemployment might be called involuntary.

Evidence from the 1930s labor markets could be cited at great length in support of either side of the debate. Uncontestably, there were persons who could not find any kind of work at any wage, given their skills, experience, and locale.[122] Yet in some localities there were labor shortages in certain occupations. On balance, there is no objective way to assess whether unemployment of the 1930s was voluntary or involuntary. The very terminology of the debate conveys the polemic ends of the contenders.

A more appealing approach draws elements from both positions. Clearly, participants in the labor force make choices, including the decision to pass up a job in order to continue searching for a better job. While possessing the ability to choose, most job seekers in the 1930s faced a severely constricted *set* of choices. Some persons' choices included no form of gainful employment for extended periods. Most of the unemployed were unable to obtain work in their accustomed occupations at the prevailing wages—one standard definition of involuntary unemployment. It would be rational for such persons to continue searching rather that settling on drastically worse jobs that utilized little of their experience or skills.[123] Many persons would have suffered real hardship even if they had obtained one of the few marginal private jobs that were available.

122. Since job vacancy surveys were not undertaken, it is necessary to rely on anecdotal evidence and long unemployment durations reported. See Gladys L. Palmer and Janet H. Lewis, *The Long-Term Unemployed in Philadelphia in 1936,* U.S. Work Projects Administration, National Research Project, report P-8 (University of Pennsylvania, Industrial Research Department, 1939), pp. 43–44 and 56.

123. The Job Refusal Committee of the Philadelphia County Relief Board stated in April 1935: "An offer of employment will be considered 'bona fide' when both the wage offered and the number of working hours requested are the going wages and hours in that industry. . . . Reasons for refusing work or leaving employment will be considered 'justifiable' whenever work offered or required cannot be classed as 'bona fide' employment; the physical ability, previous training, or experience of the employee are not in line with the position offered; the performance of duties will impair the health of the employee or *his possibility of returning to his lifetime vocation.*" Brown, *Public Relief,* p. 269; emphasis added.

A central question about work relief is its impact on the supply of labor to the private sector.[124] In the face of depressed demand, induced changes in labor supply would not necessarily have displaced private employment. Consequently, relief work may have bid workers away from unemployment rather than from private jobs. The worker's choice problem is a complex one; the attractiveness of a private or public job cannot be summarized in a single index such as the rate of remuneration for each activity. As Alfred Marshall observed, "when the earnings in any occupation are . . . spoken of as being its supply price, we must always understand that the term earnings is only used as a short expression for its 'net advantages.' "[125] The considerations of pay, work hours, eligibility requirements, security of work, ability to supplement income, working conditions, opportunities for advancement, and other factors would surely have entered the calculation of "net advantages" for a prospective relief worker of the 1930s.[126]

The general requirements of a formal economic model of the worker's behavior can be outlined briefly. To begin, net advantage has to be recast in a utility formulation. The maximization of net advantage needs to be set in a multiperiod framework with adjustment costs and uncertainty.[127] The activities include job search, private employment, work relief, direct relief, home production, retraining, and their permutations. Private employment choices may include a variety of occupations, differing degrees of on-job training, and part-time or full-time work. Furthermore, the job choices may exclude the worker's accustomed occupation for an uncer-

124. "Regardless of their effect upon the *total* labor supply available for public or private employment, public-aid programs may yet have the effect of restricting the labor supply available for *private* employment." National Resources Planning Board, *Security*, p. 348.

125. *Principles of Economics*, 8th ed. (Macmillan, 1920), pp. 556–57; also see Lyon and Abramson, *Government*, p. 1189.

126. "Men are actually trying to add up the advantages and the disadvantages of leaving relief work and going back to private employment. This is a most natural thing for them to do, and, incidentally, it indicates that they still possess some of the qualities of judgment and self-reliance they are supposed to have lost. . . . Rationally a man must ask, 'Can this source of maintenance supply me with the best possible security and standard of living for my family and satisfaction of my own major desires?' To some, the best possible choice of jobs on this basis falls to W.P.A." Bakke, *Unemployed Worker*, pp. 424–25.

127. See the "pure income uncertainty" case of M. K. Block and J. M. Heineke, "The Allocation of Effort under Uncertainty: The Case of Risk-averse Behavior," *Journal of Political Economy*, vol. 81 (March–April 1973), pt. 1, pp. 376–85. Their model implies that increased uncertainty raises the supply of labor in the current period.

tain period. A formal economic model would also have to account for the sequential aspects of the choice problem which render it dynamic. For private or public work, this sequence may include skill acquisition, employment qualifications, job ladders, access to job information, and other human-capital phenomena. The sequential aspects of public programs involve eligibility criteria, asset position, unemployment duration, length of benefits, reentry to private work, and relations between direct relief and work relief programs. For the institutions of the 1930s as much as for those of today, the development of such a model is a formidable problem.[128] We shall have to rely on economic intuition for exploration of its likely properties.

WPA Provisions, Rationing, and Labor Supply

Program features and administrative practices affected the net advantages of participating in relief work. The "rent" of a work relief program for a particular worker can be defined as the difference between its net advantages for him and those of his next best alternative. The magnitude of the rent for any program was specific to each individual's skills, tastes, and private job opportunities. Clearly, if the rent were negative, the worker would voluntarily quit a work relief job or choose not to apply for one. The size of rents faced by individuals determined the total number desiring relief work. Under the WPA, the volume of relief work supplied was always less than the number of positions demanded. Thus rationing rather than rents must explain the scale of relief work that was undertaken. The extent of job rationing under the WPA is evident in the numbers of employable needy persons who were not eligible for the program, some of whom were granted general relief; persons who were eligible but nevertheless were not certified for WPA jobs; and persons who were certified but were not assigned because of a shortage of projects in their locality. By all measures, persistent and large excess demands existed.[129]

128. For example, see the Greenberg paper in this volume. Such simulation studies of demand for entry to public employment use a wage-rate or income-dominance criterion and generally ignore security, queuing, and nonpecuniary considerations.

129. Numerous studies indicating the excess demand for WPA positions are reviewed in Howard, *WPA*, pp. 610–25. Relief agencies often failed to certify eligible applicants to be in need of WPA jobs because of their shortage and the likely consequence that direct relief would have to be granted.

Rationing the limited number of positions was a paramount factor in the design of work relief provisions. Incentives discouraged all but the needy from applying for work relief and favored the earliest return of project workers to private jobs. My conceptual model of labor supply and the notion of rents are helpful in understanding the provisions. For example, changing the waiting times for certification or assignment to jobs affected the rents for prospective relief workers.[130] Changes in waiting times could alter the length of the queue as well as the intensity of a worker's search for a private sector job. Voluntary separations of relief workers could also be affected by variations in specific provisions to lower their rents. A winding down of the work relief program would induce persons with the highest rents to leave last.[131] These residual persons were the ones with the poorest prospects in the private market relative to their work relief status.[132] This phenomenon was reflected in the rising median age of project workers as the WPA was phased out.[133] Relying heavily on Donald Howard's monumental study, I shall next apply the labor supply model to the major provisions of the WPA.

NEED AND ELIGIBILITY. Job rationing and the relief objective made it essential to restrict certification for WPA employment to those most in need. One WPA definition was: "Need shall be said to exist where the resources of a family or unattached individual are insufficient to provide a reasonable subsistence compatible with decency and health."[134] In practice the criteria for certification of need by local relief agencies varied widely. Frequent strains arose between the WPA administration and relief agencies over the operational assessment of need. The simplest measure of need was whether a family's income fell below the local WPA

130. "Long waiting lists for WPA assignment may in themselves discourage applications for jobs. Thus inadequacy again often masks still more the full extent of the inadequacy!" Ibid., p. 611.

131. "It is likely that as re-employment progresses the work relief rolls will accumulate a residuum of less and less competent and desirable workers, for whom the 'prevailing wage,' if it were to be restored, would be well above what private employers would be able or willing to pay them." Lyon and Abramson, *Government*, p. 1190.

132. Groups having the highest rents from WPA work included: "(1) persons who were rarely employable under a normal competitive system . . . (2) persons whose normal employment had been seasonal or sporadic . . . (3) persons whose compensation had been at least in part in allowances including quarters, whose hours had been long." Meriam, *Relief*, p. 379.

133. Howard, *WPA*, pp. 273–74.

134. Ibid., p. 380.

security wage for the lowest paid unskilled workers. Another common measure was a comparison of the family's income with its estimated budget requirements; unlike the security wage, this measure varied with family size. Regardless of which measure was used, the income threshold for WPA employment was usually much higher than that for direct relief. However, in some areas workers had to qualify for, if not actually receive, direct relief before they would be given WPA employment. And in some localities this practice was retained even after 1936 legislation prohibited discrimination against applicants who had not been granted direct relief. The stigma of applying for work relief was perceived to be higher where certification was linked more closely with the criteria and the administrative machinery of direct relief.[135]

Several other factors were considered in the assessment of need. Property income was sometimes counted along with earned income in evaluating a family's need. Ownership of a home and small savings account balances were not ordinarily a bar to WPA certification. However, families were frequently compelled to dispose of any other real estate before becoming eligible. Although an early executive order proscribed the reassessment of need for workers on WPA jobs, most states instituted tests of continued need. Semiannual reassessment of need of WPA workers was federally mandated in 1939; in 1940 the frequency was reduced to annual. Relatively few workers were terminated on the basis of these periodic reassessments. WPA workers were often permitted to have more assets than new applicants were allowed. Still, it was unlikely that families could save much from WPA earnings alone. The criteria for assessment of need endowed WPA jobs with substantial rents relative to direct relief for large numbers of the unemployed.[136] Consequently, additional provisions had to be instituted to reduce demand for the positions and to induce the timely return of workers to private jobs.

RELATION TO OTHER PROGRAMS. Recipients of social security payments and unemployment benefits were usually barred or removed from

135. Some relief officials argued "that if workers are to be brought to the realization that WPA employment is a form of relief rather than 'just another job,' it is necessary to require them to accept relief as an antecedent to a job." Ibid., pp. 409–10. The undertone of this position is that worker rents will fall as participation stigma rises. Also see ibid., pp. 412–13; and National Resources Planning Board, *Security,* p. 220.

136. Need assessments were typically much harsher in direct relief, as were asset limitations. For colorful examples of attempts to conceal income sources and assets from the welfare administrators, see Bakke, *Unemployed Worker,* pp. 370–76.

WPA work.[137] These policies evolved midstream for the WPA., as unemployment insurance was implemented by the states in 1938–39. At times the restrictions were applied to persons eligible for but not receiving such benefits. Thus, persons waiting for unemployment benefits to begin or living in a state that had not implemented public assistance for the aged and single mothers under social security might be refused WPA work. Until 1939, persons were denied certification even when their public assistance benefits fell below need thresholds and WPA wages. These provisions excluded groups of persons whose prospective rents from WPA employment were among the highest.

Although the practice varied by locale, direct relief payments often supplemented WPA earnings. Similar supplements had been allowed for CWA and FERA earnings under the budgetary deficiency method.[138] As the WPA program gained momentum, the portion of its workers who received relief supplements fell from 61.8 percent in October 1935 to 3.8 percent in June and July of 1936. Supplementary payments were most common among workers with large families, on average ranging from six to eight members.[139] This pattern resulted from the WPA policy of not differentiating wages by family size. In this respect the program emphasized its work rather than its relief function. For most families the WPA wage, originally targeted at twice the average relief payment, far surpassed direct relief levels.[140] For large families, the reverse was often true.[141] Where relief supplementation was prohibited, large families sometimes opted out of WPA assignments. Nevertheless, the average family size for relief workers was higher than that for families on direct relief.[142]

137. Provisions of the early unemployment insurance programs are described in Burns and Williams, *Federal Work,* pp. 77–83 and 141; for an account of an application for benefits, see Bakke, *Unemployed Worker,* pp. 282–95.

138. In March 1935 over 39 percent of relief workers were supplemented by direct relief. Burns and Williams, *Federal Work,* pp. 40–41. General relief under the FERA is described in Federal Works Agency, *Final Statistical Report,* pp. 15–21.

139. Howard, *WPA,* pp. 200–06. Frequencies of various sources of support for families in thirteen cities in 1935–36 are reported in Joseph C. Bevis and Stanley L. Payne, *Former Relief Cases in Private Employment,* U.S. Works Progress Administration, Division of Research (GPO, 1939), p. 18.

140. Macmahon, Millett, and Ogden, *Administration,* p. 149.

141. U.S. Works Progress Administration, Division of Social Research, *Survey of Workers Separated from WPA Employment in Eight Areas During the Second Quarter of 1936* (GPO, 1937), p. 4; and Howard, *WPA,* pp. 189–95.

142. Howard, *WPA,* pp. 347–48 and 419–20; and Federal Works Agency, *Final Statistical Report,* pp. 34–35.

This stemmed from relief officials' attempts to lighten local tax burdens by giving preference for WPA work to persons with larger families. Hence, workers having lower rents from WPA relative to direct relief were most likely to be certified as in need of a WPA job.

EMPLOYABILITY AND UNEMPLOYMENT DURATION. In addition to need, the primary requirements for WPA eligibility were that the applicant be employable and unemployed. Employability hinged on the nature of authorized or available project work as well as the worker's characteristics. For example, a competent white-collar worker unable to do manual labor might be deemed unemployable if service projects were not locally available. Skill matching difficulties in WPA and the program's emphasis on unskilled and manual labor are examined further in the next section. To be considered unemployed, a person had to have previous paid work experience and show promise of performing private work in the future. These restrictions were imposed to reduce the number of secondary workers—particularly inexperienced youth and women—attracted into the labor market. Waivers were granted to persons who had been prevented by the depression from gaining work experience.

A more direct means of avoiding an inflow of secondary labor was to limit WPA employment to one worker per family.[143] Designated the family's "first priority worker," this person was ordinarily the economic head or usual wage earner. Another member of the family might be employed on WPA if the first priority worker became sick, injured, or unavailable. The rule of one worker per family carried other consequences, such as favoring family disintegration. Problems of defining the family group added to administrative difficulties, especially with single adults.[144]

Employment in WPA programs was not restricted to persons who had been unemployed for a specified period. Still, several factors increased the likelihood of a worker's certification after a longer duration of unemployment. First, before becoming eligible for WPA, a worker had to exhaust any unemployment benefits. Second, a period of dissaving might be necessary to deplete his assets to the critical level under the need criterion. Third, it would take time for an unemployed person's perceived net advantages from WPA work to rise above those of his private job prospects. Most of the unemployed prefer reemployment at their accus-

143. Meriam, *Relief,* p. 376.

144. A social worker observed: "Because of the WPA set-up, families are breaking up. Sit in an . . . application office and you will surely hear with astounding frequency the statement, 'I want my own case number so I can get a job.' " Howard, *WPA,* p. 346; also see pp. 341–45.

tomed occupation. As their search for work lengthens, their expectations about acceptable wages and types of work decline.[145] The rents of a WPA job therefore rose with the length of unemployment. These factors made the average length of unemployment for successful WPA applicants exceed the average for other unemployed workers. The requirement of an explicit unemployed waiting period would emphasize the relief aspect of a works program.[146] It would also induce attenuated job search and voluntary resignation among workers with unsatisfactory jobs.[147]

OUTSIDE PRIVATE EARNINGS. The monthly wages of WPA workers were generally lower than their accustomed occupational earnings and below the WPA's standard for an "emergency budget."[148] As a result WPA workers felt strong pressure to supplement their wages. Recognizing the low levels of the security wage, the WPA at first encouraged such outside earnings supplementation.[149] A 1936 survey reported that

145. "The belief that the layoff was merely temporary survived as a rule the first month of idleness. At the end of three months only one third of the workers retained this faith. Confidence that work could eventually be had in one's own trade or industry began to wane for all but 37 percent at about six months after the layoff. . . . After the passage of twelve months eighty-five of every one hundred of the workers unemployed this long had decided they would have to 'take anything.'" Bakke, *Unemployed Worker*, p. 239. For the relation between reservation wages and previous job tenure, see Gladys L. Palmer and Constance Williams, *Reemployment of Philadelphia Hosiery Workers after Shut-downs in 1933–34*, U.S. Works Progress Administration, National Research Project, report P-6 (University of Pennsylvania, Industrial Research Department, 1939), pp. 38–39.

146. "The length of time a worker should be required to go without a job before becoming eligible for one provided under governmental auspices might well depend upon what other provisions are available to mitigate the seriousness of his economic plight and the desirability of the proffered job." Howard, *WPA*, p. 480; also see pp. 478–81.

147. For a model consistent with these effects, see B. Curtis Eaton and Philip A. Neher, "Unemployment, Underemployment, and Optimal Job Search," *Journal of Political Economy*, vol. 83 (April 1975), pp. 355–75. WPA must be viewed as the high-wage industry, in terms of expected wage per hour of work and search. Also, the probability of gaining WPA eligibility is higher for the unemployed.

148. Average monthly WPA earnings ranged across states from $22 to $65, with a U.S. average of $46, in winter 1936; and from $48 to $84, with a U.S. average of $62, in winter 1942. Howard, *WPA*, pp. 182–83. Monthly wages for most WPA workers in every city fell substantially below the emergency budget for a family of four even as late as 1940. National Resources Planning Board, *Security*, p. 177.

149. It was anticipated that workers' keeping contact with private employers would hasten their return to full-time private jobs. Howard, *WPA*, pp. 207–08. Bakke cites the example of a CWA worker unable to retain an outside job because of the hours conflict (*Unemployed Worker*, p. 215) and the FERA practice of deducting outside earnings in accord with the budgetary deficiency method (ibid., p. 221).

12 percent of WPA and other works program participants or members of their families had outside earnings. The incidence of "two-timing" in the WPA was by far the highest among skilled workers under the prevailing wage policy. A late 1937 survey found 63 percent of skilled workers to have outside earnings. Public opposition to two-timing was influential in ending the prevailing wage policy. Two-timing was widely viewed as a threat to the established wage structure. It was argued that WPA workers could undercut unemployed workers, since they did not have to live on part-time earnings alone.[150]

In 1938 a quarterly statement of WPA workers' outside earnings became mandatory. This practice was replaced the following year by periodic eligibility reassessments. With abolition of the prevailing wage policy, the longer work month reduced skilled workers' opportunities to hold outside jobs. Two-timing was further moderated by the gradual rise in the WPA wage scale and by the increased emphasis on need in the initial certification. At one time, families with any outside earnings were placed in a "deferred" category for WPA certification. This may have induced some workers to quit their jobs temporarily and resume part-time outside work once on WPA. Two-timing WPA workers created competition with the unemployed for the scarce jobs in the private market. Since these actions augmented the labor supplied to the private sector, they were the opposite of displacement.[151]

SECURITY OF EMPLOYMENT. Regularity of work ranked high, perhaps second only to wage rates, in workers' calculation of the net advantages of jobs.[152] During the 1930s private firms frequently offered sporadic

---

150. A Senate committee in 1938 noted that the policy of part-time WPA work for skilled workers "tends to defeat the evident intent of Congress, which was the protection of the going rate of pay in private industry, by making it possible for workers with a guaranteed monthly income to underbid other unemployed workers for available jobs." Macmahon, Millett, and Ogden, *Administration,* pp. 156–57.

151. "These objections, said WPA officials, showed how very difficult it was for WPA workers to please everybody. First they were criticized because they would not work enough. Now they were attacked because they worked too much." Howard, *WPA,* p. 208.

152. Bakke describes unemployed workers' "response to our question as to whether on the whole they would prefer high but irregular wages or lower but regular wages. Out of every hundred, ninety voted unhesitatingly for the latter, three . . . preferred the high but irregular wages, and seven couldn't make up their minds" (*Unemployed Worker,* p. 67). He cites the examples of a worker who chose regularity over higher pay (ibid., pp. 205–06) and of a job seeker who "registered for city work . . . not because he wanted it, but just as a precaution—a thing that an intelligent man should do" (ibid., p. 192).

short-term employment.[153] Indeed, the WPA justified its relatively low security wages by the greater regularity of relief work, which afforded it rents for many workers relative to the prospect of private employment.[154] A worker's total earnings over a specified period were usually higher under work relief despite its lower daily rate of pay. The greater regularity and higher mean of WPA earnings was observed following the reductions in WPA rolls of 750,000 in spring 1936 and 550,000 in April through July 1937. After leaving or being forced off the WPA, workers faced greater chances of having very low incomes and also of incomes above WPA earnings. Their mean private earnings were roughly equal to or substantially lower than their previous mean WPA earnings.[155]

In actuality WPA employment was less than fully secure. The vulnerability of relief workers' jobs increased as the program matured. Initially the security wage was intended to be "in the nature of a salary"—paid even if work were halted for weather or other adverse conditions. Instead, WPA developed the practice of paying workers only for time worked, up to the security wage. Some opportunities were given for workers to make up lost time. Over the year, workers' lost time averaged around 5 percent. Still, severe hardship often resulted since lost time was concentrated in the winter months for cold regions.

Various rotation methods were introduced to spread the limited WPA positions among the unemployed. One common method was to dismiss all workers upon a project's completion. This forced the dismissed workers to join newly certified persons in waiting for assignment to other

153. The instability of private work, the frequency of job changes, and the common multiple reliance on private work, direct relief, and work relief are documented in Bevis and Payne, *Former Relief Cases*, pp. 3–5, 8–11, and 18–20.

154. "Labor, it was said, had been misled by the fetich of hourly rates. The true desideratum was an adequate total wage received in the course of a year." Macmahon, Millett, and Ogden, *Administration*, p. 39. An editorial in *Nation* argued, prior to the establishment of security wages, "that although there was something to be said for 'an insured income' there was danger that the reduction in wages on work relief would be more than what could properly be justified as an 'insurance premium.'" Howard, *WPA*, pp. 170–71n.

155. The two episodes are reported in Works Progress Administration, *Survey;* and Verl E. Roberts, *Survey of Workers Separated from WPA Employment in Nine Areas, 1937,* U.S. Works Progress Administration, Division of Social Research (GPO, 1938). Both periods yielded greater earnings variance for workers after leaving the WPA. The 1936 reduction left their mean earnings unaffected, but the 1937 reduction substantially reduced their post-WPA earnings because of the greater proportion of mandatory separations and the worsening economy. For a comparable Massachusetts study, see Gilboy, *Applicants*, p. 132.

projects. Some localities automatically dismissed WPA workers after specified periods of continuous employment. Rotation practices of this kind varied greatly. In one instance, low-income farmers were allowed only two months' work between their growing seasons. Beginning in 1939 a national policy required automatic dismissal of workers after eighteen months' continuous WPA employment and prohibited their reinstatement for thirty days. Introduction of the rule yielded massive dismissals— 612,000 in August of 1939. In addition to rotation, WPA workers were released when funding constraints forced quotas to be pared. A worker could be dismissed at any time for "inefficiency" or inability to perform on a project.[156] As these provisions eroded the security of WPA work, the rents of WPA jobs declined.[157]

PRESSURE TO TAKE PRIVATE WORK. The WPA pressed its workers to accept private employment as soon as suitable openings became available. Workers were at first encouraged and in 1939 required to register with public employment offices. Because the U.S. Employment Service often treated relief workers as less employable than other unemployed registrants, the WPA on occasion undertook its own job placement.[158]

156. Howard, *WPA,* pp. 514–15. "Official reports do not yield information about numbers of workers removed from the WPA program because of inefficiency. It is probable, however, that discharges for this reason are an almost negligible proportion of the total employed." Ibid., p. 245. Other evidence suggests they may not be a negligible proportion of separations. For a sample of workers separated April–July 1937, the following reasons for separation were reported (weighted urban and rural responses): quota reduction, 25 percent; discontinued project, 6 percent; alien status, 10 percent; private employment, 27 percent; incapacity, 11 percent; inefficiency and discipline, 6 percent; adequate resources, 7 percent; and all other, 7 percent. Roberts, *Survey,* pp. x and 14. Also see Gilboy, *Applicants,* p. 125; and Burns and Williams, *Federal Work,* p. 65.

157. Rotation "has a disciplinary undercurrent. Workers are to be deterred from settling down to making WPA work a lifetime career; or else they are to be induced to seek and enter private employment." Howard, *WPA,* p. 516. "As one after another of the elements of security employment was thrown overboard, the defense of low monthly wage rates on the ground that, over a period of time, such rates assured workers 'more than they ever had in their lives' was, of course, vitiated." Ibid., p. 167.

158. Personnel of the exchanges commonly felt "that WPA workers had been the best cared for of any of the unemployed . . . [and had] a tendency to pass over relief workers automatically when referring persons to openings in industry. . . . At a time when nearly 40 per cent of employment service registrants were works program employees, placement of them in private jobs through the exchanges was barely 5 per cent of the total placements." Macmahon, Millett, and Ogden, *Administration,* pp. 353–54. "It has sometimes been urged that instead of transferring WPA workers to possible openings in private employment it is more economical to

Upon threat of discharge, WPA workers were required to accept private work. The initial form of this provision required acceptance even if the private job paid less than the worker's WPA job, so long as it paid the community's "accustomed" wages. From 1937 to 1939, workers were compelled to take private jobs only if they paid as much or more than WPA paid for the same work hours. In 1939 the policy reverted to its earlier form, under which workers could be forced to leave WPA jobs for lower wages and less suitable work in private industry.

Several conditions tempered the administrative demand for WPA workers to accept any available private work. The worker could be required only to take a full-time job, though there did not have to be any assurance about its permanence. The worker could not be forced to take private work contrary to established union relationships. At times, though, labor groups accused the WPA of discharging workers who refused jobs at scabbing. To facilitate workers' acceptance of private jobs, the WPA promised to reinstate any WPA worker who had lost a private job through no fault of his own. The limit on how long reinstatement would be available varied but frequently was six months after separation from WPA work. Uncertainties about reinstatement still hindered many workers from accepting unstable private jobs.[159]

Concerned about accusations that it was creating local labor shortages, the WPA acted forcefully when it saw the need. Entire projects would be halted in areas that were likely to experience general increases in their labor demand. Groups of workers thought to be needed by private employers were sometimes dismissed in wholesale fashion. Selective dismissals were applied to workers having experience in lines of work believed to be in demand. These actions could be undertaken on the basis of WPA administrators' anticipations of emerging private needs. Hence, it was possible for WPA workers to be released with no assurance of having private jobs to fill.

fill these jobs with workers waiting for WPA assignments. By thus reducing both turnover and, consequently, the need for breaking in new workers, it has been claimed that the efficiency of WPA operations is increased." Howard, *WPA*, p. 499; also see pp. 481–82.

159. A worker is quoted: "Why do we want to hold onto these jobs? Well, you know, we know all the time about persons who are on direct relief. We know how they are just managing to scrape along, and we can't help comparing our good luck having $12 to $15 a week to spend as we please. . . . And suppose you go off to a job that blows up in a couple of weeks. You're not so sure you can get back on W.P.A. My advice, Buddy, is better not take too much of a chance. Know a good thing when you got it." Bakke, *Unemployed Worker*, pp. 421–22.

Assessment of Displacement

Any displacement of private employment by work relief is the net outcome of induced shifts in both demand and supply schedules for many types of labor. A number of demand-side factors have been considered in earlier sections; this section focuses on the supply-side effects. The proposition that relief projects bid workers away from private employment is intriguing for the underlying macro model. It suggests that the multiplier for government expenditures on relief workers is less than that implied by conventional analysis. This result also holds for expenditures on regular public employees or civil servants. Thus, the conventional static analysis of government spending is applicable only to purchases of goods and of services *other than labor*. It might be objected that wage rigidities do not allow a diminished supply of labor to the private sector to influence wage rates. But if the rate of wage adjustment were influenced by the excess supply of labor, work relief might still have obstructed wage and employment adjustment in the private market.[160]

Because a direct test of the existence and extent of displacement cannot be implemented, an indirect approach must be followed.[161] I shall investigate a set of circumstances that is likely to accompany displacement: (1) widespread job refusals and labor shortages; (2) a scarcity of unemployed persons without work relief and inferior employability of the unemployed vis-à-vis relief workers; and (3) speedy private employment of workers "involuntarily" terminated from work relief. As was argued in a broader macro context in the section on scale and financing of expenditures, it is easier to "disprove" displacement than to "prove" it. Displacement would be most unlikely to arise in the absence of any labor shortages. The existence of many long-term unemployed also tends to deny displacement, although segmentation of the labor market makes this a loose relation. Conversely, the existence of labor shortages or of little long-term unemployment would not "prove" that work relief had caused displacement.

160. For an early study of wage-rate flexibility and adjustment in the 1930s, see Albert Rees, "Wage Determination and Involuntary Unemployment," *Journal of Political Economy,* vol. 59 (April 1951), pp. 143–53. For a more general treatment, see Robert J. Gordon, "Recent Developments in the Theory of Inflation and Unemployment," *Journal of Monetary Economics,* vol. 2 (April 1976), pp. 185–219.

161. A proper formulation would require fully specifying and estimating an appropriate model. See the more limited test in Kesselman and Savin, "Three-and-a-Half Million Workers."

Charges that work relief was creating labor shortages and job refusals were not uncommon in the 1930s. Exactly what constitutes a labor shortage or a nonjustifiable refusal is open to debate. Does an employer's inability to fill vacancies at grossly substandard wages signify a labor shortage?[162] Most often labor shortages were reported for domestic servants and for seasonal agricultural labor primarily in the South. The record does not suggest that the WPA caused significant labor shortages in other fields·except occasionally in skilled trades.[163] Although the WPA usually acted to avoid complicity in labor shortages, it openly justified the unskilled security wage against the extremely low wages paid in Southern agriculture.[164] Evidence on job refusals is scant; this may also reflect their infrequency. The great majority of allegations of job refusals studied under the FERA in 1935 and the WPA in 1936–37 were found to be unwarranted or the refusals to be justified.[165]

The early CWA projects on occasion attracted workers directly from private employment.[166] While such behavior was rare for the WPA,

162. "The fact that private employers have on occasion complained of labor shortages does not necessarily mean that there is an absolute unavailability of persons able to perform the required work. . . . An employer may find a shortage at 30 cents an hour but have a surplus available at 35 cents an hour." National Resources Planning Board, *Security*, p. 349.

163. Palmer, *Search for Work*, pp. 34–35; National Resources Planning Board, *Security*, pp. 350–52; Howard, *WPA*, pp. 487–90; Gilboy, *Applicants*, p. 26; and Meriam, *Relief*, pp. 390–91. Some examples of urban labor shortages were taxi drivers in New York City in 1935 and specialized welders in Philadelphia in 1934–35.

164. Howard, *WPA*, p. 166. In 1936 Hopkins announced that WPA officials were "instructed that nobody is to have a Works Progress Administration job who has refused private employment at a fair wage. . . . You can be equally sure that we are not going to kick anybody out of these low-paid jobs just so some bird can get a lot of cheap labor. And that goes not only for the farmer, but for any private employer." Ibid., pp. 487–88. "The attempt to employ work relief wages as a means of creating an artificial scarcity in the private labor market, in order to force up private wage rates, must be regarded in any circumstances as a doubtful proceeding." Lyon and Abramson, *Government*, p. 1190; also see p. 1188.

165. Out of 603 alleged cases of job refusals investigated by FERA, "only 20 were discovered which could be clearly adjudged instances of unjustified refusal of jobs. The facts revealed . . . that, contrary to popular assertion, most relief persons are extremely anxious to 'get off relief' and will take any acceptable job." Henry B. Arthur, "Summary Study of Alleged Job Refusals by Relief Persons," *Monthly Report of the Federal Emergency Relief Administration, November 1 Through November 30, 1935* (GPO, 1936), p. 6. Gilboy's examination of unpublished WPA investigations of 100 cases of alleged job refusals found 58 complaints to be unsubstantiated and at least 8 to 20 cases to be justifiable refusals. *Applicants*, pp. 155–56.

166. For two examples, see Bakke, *Unemployed Worker*, pp. 208 and 215. The CWA was required to draw only 50 percent of its project workers from the relief rolls. Hopkins, *Spending*, p. 167.

workers sometimes avoided leaving relief projects for what they perceived to be temporary private employment. What are the implications for the displacement hypothesis? The fact that numerous unemployed persons did not have relief work is important to the assessment. Unemployed persons were qualified to enter most of the same occupations and industries as relief workers.[167] Moreover, the two groups were found in the same regions, since state employment quotas tended to be allocated proportionately to the number of unemployed. WPA provisions and workers' choices favored the certification of older workers and those least able to compete in the labor market. Some relief workers were deemed to be only marginally employable in the private sector.[168] Although the unemployed were often more employable than the relief workers, few could find stable private work.

The existence of wide-scale unemployment undermines the plausibility of displacement for the 1930s.[169] Some economists might argue that the degree of excess labor supply affects the rate of wage adjustment in the face of market rigidities. Still, it does not appear likely that unemployment beyond certain levels would appreciably hasten the adjustment of wages. The labor-force entrants of the 1930s, primarily youth and women, posed a further offsetting force against displacement. Yet, it is

167. See *Census of Partial Employment, Unemployment and Occupations: 1937—Final Report on Total and Partial Unemployment*, vol. 4, *The Enumerative Check Census* (GPO, 1938); Philip M. Hauser, *Workers on Relief in the United States in March 1935*, vol. 1: *A Census of Usual Occupations*, U.S. Works Progress Administration, Division of Social Research (GPO, 1938); Philip M. Hauser and Bruce L. Jenkinson, *Workers on Relief in the United States in March 1935*, vol. 2: *A Study of Industrial and Educational Backgrounds*, U.S. Works Progress Administration, Division of Research (GPO, 1939).

168. "Just how many WPA jobs, from time to time, have gone to those who might be regarded as 'unemployable' because their age, skills, or some other consideration made their employment in private industry and under circumstances currently prevailing unlikely, is not known. However, estimates . . . have run high, amounting in some areas and at stated times to as much as 50, 65, and even 75 percent. These opinions, unfortunately, are of but little value." Howard, *WPA*, p. 468.

169. "It is obvious that . . . the effects of public-aid policies [on private employment] must have been relatively unimportant, or at most confined to specific areas or occupations. For at no time have the various work programs given employment to as much as 50 percent of the estimated unemployed. Hence there were always at least half of the unemployed who could have been drawn upon with an expansion in private industry's demand for labor." National Resources Planning Board, *Security*, p. 348. Also see Arthur E. Burns and Peyton Kerr, "Recent Changes in Work-Relief Wage Policy," *American Economic Review*, vol. 31 (March 1941), pp. 56–66.

hard to assess the extent to which work relief or the severely depressed conditions induced the additional participation.[170]

The employment experience of workers after leaving WPA projects illuminates the role of displacement. Drawing from a series of WPA studies of local project and nationwide administrative curtailments, I shall report two of the more important studies.[171] A 1939 study surveyed 138,000 workers rotated off WPA under the newly instituted eighteen-month rule. Two to three months after discharge, 12.7 percent of the workers had private work, 26.7 percent were reassigned to WPA work, 28.4 percent were receiving direct relief, and 32.2 percent were unemployed and not receiving any relief.[172] The 1937 survey of nine areas, mentioned above, distinguished between "administrative" and "voluntary" terminations.[173] The workers were followed one to four months after leaving the WPA. Only 46 percent of urban workers and 55 percent of rural workers terminated for administrative reasons had any private earnings; the median private earnings for those employed were $25.20 and $24.29 per month, respectively. Among those who left voluntarily, 76 percent of urban workers and 61 percent of rural workers found private jobs at median wages of $71.33 and $51.24 a month, respectively. These contrasts show that workers with good private job opportunities voluntarily departed the WPA, whereas those forced off for administrative reasons had dismal prospects in private employment. Both implications suggest the absence of displacement.

170. "Long-run influences . . . had led to an increase in the proportion of gainfully employed women prior to 1930. The depression accentuated this development. Against this background the influence of a specific program, such as the WPA, must have been relatively insignificant." National Resources Planning Board, *Security,* p. 348. For an early analysis, see W. S. Woytinsky, *Additional Workers and the Volume of Unemployment in the Depression,* Committee on Social Security, pamphlet series no. 1 (Washington: Social Science Research Council, 1940).

171. See Works Progress Administration, *Survey;* and the surveys reported in Howard, *WPA,* pp. 628–33; and Gilboy, *Applicants,* pp. 123 ff. and 143–45.

172. "Even if they had not been forced to leave, most of those who found private employment, it was estimated, would undoubtedly have left WPA rolls voluntarily, as thousands of workers do each month, to accept other jobs. . . . Workers among that large number of persons—nearly one-third of the whole—who had no kind of employment and received no relief (except possibly federal surplus commodities) had no recourse but to borrow, dispose of personal belongings, or beg—sometimes for unsalable or left-over food." Howard, *WPA,* p. 631.

173. In fact, 34 percent of the urban and 20 percent of the rural workers who "voluntarily" left the WPA did so for reasons of incapacity or inefficiency and disciplinary actions. Because such workers would have fared poorly in private employment, this reinforces the study's implication of no displacement. Roberts, *Survey,* p. 14.

Political Economy of Productivity and Displacement

My analysis now turns from the income support and employment objectives of work relief to the productivity objective. Productivity was commonly judged by two kinds of criteria—the tangible goods and services produced on projects and the nonpecuniary benefits for workers. Undoubtedly, much of the early popular support for shifting from direct relief to work relief stemmed from the expectation that useful output would arise.[174] Taxpayers hoped to capture these benefits in the form of reduced burdens of providing relief and obtaining government services. Strong elements of the work ethic also underlay the preference for work relief.[175] In public pronouncements on the emerging works programs, Roosevelt and Hopkins repeatedly emphasized the nonpecuniary advantages for relief workers vis-à-vis direct relief.[176] The preservation of skills, working habits, health, and above all morale of the unemployed were important goals of work relief. Conflicts between work relief productivity and displacement of private-sector activities created the thorniest problems in the choice and design of projects. These problems are examined in detail in the following review of the nonpecuniary benefits and the tangible output of work relief.

Nonpecuniary Benefits

Work relief was popularly believed to raise the morale, or self-esteem, of the unemployed. Its dignifying properties were typically contrasted

174. "Work-relief projects, unlike the old work tests, are not conceived of merely as a means of frightening off applicants for relief. True work-relief . . . [stresses] securing projects which when completed will be of value to the community." Burns and Williams, *Federal Work*, pp. 27–28. In advancing the early FERA work programs, Roosevelt stated "there is no intention of using the public-works funds simply to build a lot of useless projects disguised as relief. It is the purpose to encourage real public works." Brown, *Public Relief*, p. 152.

175. "If maintenance were provided without the requirement of service, no one would want to work. So ran the general opinion of middle-class individuals, an opinion which favored the early adoption of work-relief policies." Bakke, *Unemployed Worker*, p. 388.

176. In his 1935 message to Congress, Roosevelt argued for the establishment of a federal works program: "I am not willing that the vitality of our people be further sapped by the giving of cash, of market baskets, of a few hours of weekly work cutting grass, raking leaves or picking up papers in the public parks. We must preserve not only the bodies of the unemployed from destitution but also their self-respect, their self-reliance and courage and determination." *Public Papers*, p. 20.

with the demeaning aspects of direct relief. Morale was believed to stem from the perception that relief workers were performing useful services for their society, similar in some respects to private employment. It was further contended that work relief promoted mental health, at least when the projects were useful.[177] Thus, the value of the work relief output was a precondition for salutary effects on morale.[178] One study found that the morale and social participation of WPA workers were significantly higher than those of persons on direct relief.[179] A fundamental difficulty arose because morale requires useful output, which in turn tends to displace private employment.[180] Yet as private jobs grew more abundant, the morale-building effects of relief work waned independently of the objective value of the projects' output.[181] The restricted capital inputs to work relief projects, with resulting heavy manual requirements, also served to undermine the morale of relief workers.[182]

177. The U.S. surgeon general pled, "Whatever the cost, I would urge that from the standpoint of public health, in its larger concept, of mental health, economic factors are subordinate to the vital necessity of providing for our destitute citizens an opportunity of a livelihood earned by individual effort. I emphasize useful work; no other type fills the mental needs." Howard, *WPA*, p. 779.

178. The NYA school work projects standard stated: "The student must feel that he is performing a real job; 'made work' must be avoided. . . . The giving of an honest dollar's worth of work for a dollar received is one of the chief bases of the integrity of the student work program." Federal Security Agency, *Final Report*, p. 65. "The fact that the work being done is returning to the community some object or service of real usefulness is a factor in making the role played more socially respectable than the role of one who is merely receiving the community's money without returning something for it. This value, it must be emphasized, exists only when the job being done is an obviously useful and desirable one from the point of view of the community." Bakke, *Unemployed Worker*, pp. 395–96.

179. The study, cited in Howard, *WPA*, pp. 813–15, did not control for income differences between the two types of households.

180. "The demands of morale-producing work are such that the jobs must be made to approximate [private employment] in income and in working conditions, in general usefulness and in the value of the project. . . . The dilemma consists of the fact that in order to make work relief do the best possible job from the point of view of morale building we have to make the job sufficiently attractive so that there is a reduced chance that private employment of a marginal sort will rate comparatively high in the estimation of relief workers." Bakke, *Unemployed Worker*, p. 425.

181. As jobs in private industry increased, "the realization increased among the unemployed that what they were doing was, after all, relief work. . . . Citizens began to renew their opinion that any competent man could find a job if he really wanted it." Ibid., pp. 323–24.

182. "A priori, it would not seem that a worker could find much dignity in a job that could be done better by a donkey, or very much more effectively by a donkey-engine." Howard, *WPA*, p. 781.

Other putative benefits were the maintenance of health, skills, and work habits of relief workers.[183] The programs were observed to promote the general health, physique, and—for the younger CCC workers—physical development of participants, except in the severest weather.[184] Maintenance of workers' skills was impeded by the high proportion of unskilled work, the restricted range of skilled jobs, and the frequent mismatching of workers to job skills.[185] It has been suggested that manual relief work caused some specialized skills to deteriorate more than they would have through idleness. While views were mixed as to the positive effects on skill maintenance, the deleterious effects appear not to have been widespread. Much greater diversity of opinion attaches to the maintenance of work habits of relief workers.[186] Charges of loafing or "soldiering" on projects were common and often had substance. These were attributable to the hard manual nature of most relief work, the depleted physical condition of the long-term unemployed, the inadequacy of machine inputs, the lack of promotion incentives, workers' desire to stretch out a project lest they be out of a job, and the political preference in selection of foremen.[187] Yet, whatever the adverse effects on work

183. "Preservation of work skills and habits is obviously of benefit not only to workers, but also . . . to the public, because workers prepared to re-enter private employment as occasion presents are less likely to need continued employment at public expense, and to industry because the labor reserve is kept intact, ready for re-employment as production resumes." Ibid., p. 782.

184. Bakke, *Unemployed Worker*, p. 413; and Salmond, *Civilian Conservation Corps*, p. 129.

185. See Howard, *WPA*, pp. 228–36; Federal Works Agency, *Final Report*, pp. 39–40; and National Resources Planning Board, *Security*, pp. 243–45. "It is difficult to see how project work can either maintain accustomed skills or fit workers for subsequent absorption by private industry unless a greater measure of diversification of projects is permitted." National Resources Planning Board, *Security*, p. 469. Typically workers' "semiskill consisted in the capacity to operate a particular machine or piece of equipment. . . . With respect to many of those in manufacturing and industries other than building and construction the machines operated or the processes performed were those used in private enterprise. Such semiskills could not be preserved by use unless W.P.A. itself invaded the field of private enterprise." Meriam, *Relief*, p. 419.

186. See National Resources Planning Board, *Security*, pp. 246–48. "To the extent that relief-work projects permit slipshod and careless work habits they may actually be ingraining in the workers habits which will have to be undone. It is quite possible that complete idleness would produce a less difficult reconditioning and retraining problem when the worker went back to work." Bakke, *Unemployed Worker*, p. 414; also see p. 413.

187. "The classic illustration which is used to prove the matter is the illustration of road workers whom one sees leaning on their shovels while the observer is

habits, they were not deep-seated if judged by the generally satisfactory experience of private employers with former WPA and CCC workers.[188]

Upgrading of skills and general education were other more limited nonpecuniary returns of the work relief programs. They figured most prominently in the NYA programs, both for in-school and out-of-school youths. Training and education played a modest role in the CCC, but they have been unfavorably assessed.[189] Within the WPA training was highly restricted, largely because of organized labor's opposition to any competition with its own skilled members. Before 1940, training courses were provided almost solely for domestic workers; thereafter training was expanded to manual occupations needed in the defense program. Arguing that the WPA was jeopardizing the apprenticeship system, labor groups sought unsuccessfully to create boards to review the qualifications of skilled mechanics before they were hired by the WPA.[190] Following early strains, the NYA training activities came to be well regarded by labor officials and management—so long as they did not appear to threaten the established apprenticeship systems.[191]

Value of Output

The output of work relief projects placed heavy emphasis on public works as against public services. Production of commodities for distribution to households, the so-called goods projects, was a negligible part

---

leaning on the cushions of an automobile." Ibid., p. 414. For examples of workers prolonging projects because of the insecurity of their positions at the completion of a project, see Macmahon, Millett, and Ogden, *Administration,* p. 299; and Bakke, *Unemployed Worker,* p. 418.

188. Bakke, *Unemployed Worker,* pp. 245 and 415–20. For examples of employers antagonistic toward hiring former WPA workers, see Howard, *WPA,* p. 258.

189. "Academic courses, while doubtless interesting in themselves, were of limited practical value to youths who would almost certainly lead non-academic lives, while one can legitimately question whether instruction in digging ditches and building dams was fitting the enrollees for life in an increasingly urbanized society." Salmond, *Civilian Conservation Corps,* p. 168.

190. National Resources Planning Board, *Security,* p. 245; and Howard, *WPA,* pp. 237–38 and 241–43.

191. Federal Security Agency, *Final Report,* pp. 104–08. "The building trades were fearful that NYA by constructing buildings at the low wages paid NYA youth would flood the labor market with youth claiming skills as a result of NYA work project employment . . . thus aggravating unemployment among skilled workers and contributing to lower wage scales." Ibid., p. 106.

of the overall program.[192] The only major exceptions were sewing projects developed for the employment of women. The tangible accomplishments of the works programs are featured prominently in their final reports.[193] The general pattern is reflected in the WPA's spending 78.0 percent of its funds on construction and public improvements, including highways, roads, and streets (38.9 percent), public buildings (10.4 percent), water and sewage facilities (10.2 percent), and recreational facilities (8.3 percent). Most of the remaining 22.0 percent of WPA funds was spent on a wide range of community services, the largest of which were the sewing projects (6.4 percent).[194]

Several factors explain the preoccupation of work relief undertakings with public works. Planners' initial, ill-fated hopes for financially self-liquidating projects favored the choice of public works over services or goods. Through their very scale, visibility, and durability, public works may have reflected well upon the governments that undertook them. It is interesting that in 1940 John Kenneth Galbraith warned of public works fetishism—the danger of overrating the value of public works relative to services or goods.[195] Another reason for stressing public works was the desire, expressed both in public policy and in private lobbying, to avoid displacement of private employment. Clearly, a legitimate policy objective was to achieve maximal net expansion of employment.[196] Short

192. "Projects, said the law, must be useful but not competitive. This stipulation meant that with exceptions important in themselves but relatively minor the works program was barred from participation in the production of prime necessities. It does not detract from the value of what it wrought to say that there was sometimes tragic irony in the preoccupation of the works program with embellishments while elementary human needs for useful goods were insufficiently satisfied." Macmahon, Millett, and Ogden, *Administration*, pp. 2–3.

193. For FERA, see Federal Works Agency, *Final Statistical Report*, pp. 53–58; for NYA, Federal Security Agency, *Final Report*, pp. 59–62 and 92; for WPA, Federal Works Agency, *Final Report*, pp. 47–93; and for CCC, Salmond, *Civilian Conservation Corps*, pp. 128–29.

194. For July 1935 to June 1941; Howard, *WPA*, p. 130.

195. "There is, perhaps, some danger of overestimating the special usefulness of public works. For, so far as any individual or group can presume to judge, public works must stand on a parity in terms of usefulness with the other things which the Government provides." Galbraith, *Economic Effects*, p. 2. Roosevelt had emphasized in his 1935 message to Congress: "All work undertaken should be useful— not just for a day, or a year, but useful in the sense that it affords permanent improvement in living conditions or that it creates future new wealth for the Nation." *Public Papers*, p. 21.

196. A key criterion in choice of projects was stated as: "No work-relief project must be allowed to reduce by a dollar the money available for real wages." Colcord, *Emergency Work Relief*, p. 238. "Little has been done in . . . putting relief clients

of "boondoggling" projects, public works were best suited to minimizing the displacement of private sector employment during the same period. Public works concentrate their expenditures in the period of construction, whereas the flow of project services extends far into the future. The value of output was correspondingly reduced during the period of work relief activity.

Business and labor groups, which felt threatened by the competition of work relief, pressed to restrict the range of its activities. While such pressure could readily arise anywhere in the market economy, it would be most effective for industries producing goods for sale to the private sector. For example, private construction firms could complain only that work relief projects replaced public contracts they would like to have had. They could not argue persuasively that these were sales they would ordinarily have obtained. In a market economy, this behavior lies at the heart of the bias toward public works and against goods-producing projects.[197] Thus a conflict arises between the nondisruption of private employment and the value of work relief output.[198] Similar apprehensions about competitive activities in regular governmental agencies were conveyed to Congress by private groups in 1932, before the inception of the federal works program.[199] The CCC experience was very different, having

---

to work to produce the products needed for relief clients . . . partly because of opposition of private enterprises to such competition, partly because of the fear of administrative officials that it might cause loss of employment in private occupations and so create a widening circle of dependence upon public sources of livelihood." Lyon and Abramson, *Government,* pp. 1138–39n.

197. "Given the existence of a large-scale work relief program, no question is more critical than its relation to the range of activities commonly carried on for profit by private enterprises. . . . The extension of [goods projects] has been urged on the ground that more adequate relief could be achieved at lower cost. The basic contention is that it is socially wasteful to use relief labor so largely on projects of a public character when the pressing need is for more and better provisions, clothing, supplies, and housing for the unemployed. This idea is naturally opposed by private enterprises engaged in producing the things which relief labor could be turned to producing." Ibid., pp. 1182–83. Also see Clark, *Economics,* p. 143.

198. "If emergency employment is limited by the general rule of minimizing competition with private enterprise, work projects must obviously consist, in the main, of improvements on public property or the expansion of that broad range of services which are typically produced by public agencies. . . . The longer large-scale work relief is maintained, the more difficult it will become to find non-competitive projects of high grade from the standpoint of need and utility, and the greater will be the temptation to encroach upon the traditional preserves of private production." Lyon and Abramson, *Government,* p. 1184.

199. See *Government Competition with Private Enterprise,* H. Rept. 1985, 72:2 (GPO, 1933).

involved noncompeting activities such as reforestation and improvements to land and waterways. As a consequence, the CCC gained widespread support from the general public and the business community.[200] The popularity of its activities might also be explained by their lesser visibility to the public than the primarily urban work relief programs. The main branch of the federal works program—the CWA, FERA, and WPA—did not enjoy such a congenial relation with the private sector.[201]

The actions of private interests to restrict the types of work relief activity were critical in determining the value of output. Goods projects approved under the Emergency Work Relief Program of the FERA in 1934 encompassed the production of clothing, mattresses, and shoes, the processing and distribution of surplus commodities, and the manufacture of some materials used in work relief construction.[202] Even in their peak months, though, these "production-for-use and distribution" projects accounted for only 15 percent of total program employment.[203] Still, they aroused stormy opposition by the National Association of Manufacturers and by representatives of the affected industries. With this experience close at hand, the WPA was instituted with limited goods production projects. Nevertheless, many of the WPA goods projects paralleled the activities developed under the FERA.

200. "The very presence of a CCC camp was an economic stimulant to local business." Congress refused to go along with the President's plan to curtail the CCC in 1936. According to the Baltimore *Sun,* "local businessmen find it profitable to expand in one way or another to cater for the relief trade. Thus, something in the nature of a vested interest develops . . . [and] curtailment endangers vested interests." Salmond, *Civilian Conservation Corps,* pp. 110–11.

201. As early as December 1934 a report to Hopkins "summed up business opinion as one of opposition to work relief, not only because of its cost but because all work projects—even ditch digging—were deemed competitive with private industry." Schlesinger, *Coming of the New Deal,* p. 274. Favorable attitudes emerged toward the NYA, as "industry, like organized labor, came to understand that the production carried on in the NYA shops in most instances was . . . too small . . . to compete with industry." Federal Security Agency, *Final Report,* pp. 107–08.

202. See Charnow, *Work Relief Experience,* pp. 99–102. "Federal relief officials were not unaware of the competitive nature of these projects, but they believed that on the whole the advantages of the program outweighed its disadvantages. . . . The decrease in the cost of relief—and hence taxes—by having the relief workers produce for themselves would counterbalance whatever competition the projects offered to certain types of private industry." Ibid., p. 100.

203. Kerr, "Production-for-Use." Clark regarded the FERA proposals for "including in relief work the production of goods to be consumed by the otherwise unemployed workers themselves . . . [as] the only obvious method by which a volume of work can be found of whose usefulness there can be not the slightest doubt, and which automatically increases with the increase in the numbers of those who need it." *Economics,* p. 26.

In the initial WPA legislation of 1935, organized labor and private contractors secured a clause that "Wherever practicable in the carrying out of the provisions of this joint resolution, full advantage shall be taken of the facilities of private enterprise." A variety of attempts to obtain more detailed guarantees against competition were unsuccessful.[204] Only in 1940 did the legislation stipulate that no funds be used "to purchase, establish, relocate, or expand mills, factories, stores, or plants which would manufacture, handle, process, or produce for sale articles, commodities, or products . . . in competition with existing industries." This provision did not apply to existing WPA goods projects, since these products were given to the needy rather than sold.[205] Succumbing to business pressure, several states occasionally used a combination of force account and contracts on street and highway work. In 1940 the WPA issued uniform procedures by which sponsors could let contracts for their share of project costs.[206]

Private industry succeeded in restricting WPA activities in several other areas. From the outset the program was prohibited from producing war matériel, although it became heavily involved with the construction of defense facilities in 1941. Construction or repair of prison facilities was prohibited unless it would "not cause or promote competition of the products of convict labor with the products of free labor." Intensive pressure was exerted by contractors' groups to restrict the construction activities of work relief.[207] Beginning in 1939, any building to be constructed with WPA funds was limited to $50,000, a limit later raised to $100,000. A number of WPA service activities also fell under private

204. Macmahon, Millett, and Ogden, *Administration,* pp. 53–55 and 60–62. The chairman of the House Committee on Appropriations argued that further restriction would doom the WPA program "because nearly every useful work you can find in the United States, or at least most of it, comes into competition at least in some degree with private enterprise, because private enterprise has explored and undertaken to engage in activity of practically every describable character." Ibid., p. 60.

205. Howard, *WPA,* pp. 133–34.

206. A cited advantage was that contractors "obtain new opportunities to put idle equipment to work and are able to provide employment under normal conditions for equipment operators and other types of skilled labor." Charnow, *Work Relief Experience,* p. 108n. The use of contracts had been prohibited under the EWRP. Ibid., p. 107n.

207. Howard, *WPA,* pp. 131–40 (text quotation, p. 133). "When a member of a House Committee asked H. B. Zachry, president of Associated General Contractors of America, what he thought might happen to WPA workers who would be thrown out of jobs if the WPA were prohibited from doing construction work, he replied that he would 'put them in the Army and give them military training so they would be of service to the country.' " Ibid., p. 137.

attack. Slum clearance and rat extermination projects were frequently closed after opposition from building wreckers and commercial exterminators. Theater projects were banned in 1939, following outcries from competing private productions and attacks on the "subversive" affiliations of some workers. Even WPA book rebinding services to school boards and public libraries aroused private opposition.[208]

Administrative Factors

State and local sponsorship of federally financed EWRP, CWA, and WPA projects might have helped to ensure the value of the work undertaken. Until 1940 there was no rigid requirement about the share of sponsor contributions in total project costs, except that they were expected to cover a large part of nonlabor costs. To promote projects with a relatively high outlay for labor, the WPA pressed sponsors to meet a larger share of nonlabor costs. Federal expenditures on nonlabor costs for any state were limited to a specified amount per man per month, initially $7 in 1938.[209] This provision led to the overmanning of some projects in order to obtain sufficient federal funds for material and tool costs.[210] Sponsors' shares of costs varied widely by type of project. For example, in its first five years the WPA reported sponsors' shares as 25 percent for airport projects and only 7.3 percent for sewing projects.[211] Heavy burdens of direct relief impelled lower jurisdictions to maximize the federal funding per dollar of sponsor funds.[212] The choice by many

208. The head of the Book Manufacturers' Institute testified to the Congress that the WPA was "shutting off sources of livelihood of established business and throwing people out of work. . . . They are destroying the capital invested in that business." Macmahon, Millett, and Ogden, *Administration,* p. 320.

209. Ibid., pp. 313–17; and Howard, *WPA,* pp. 145–50.

210. "When sponsors were unable or unwilling to make the necessary outlays the limitations on federal expenditures have contributed to inefficiency due either to performing jobs the hard way or to the overloading of projects through assignment of more men than were really needed except for the express purpose of building up a larger allowance for non-labor costs." Howard, *WPA,* pp. 253–54.

211. Macmahon, Millett, and Ogden, *Administration,* p. 314. Similar variations in sponsors' shares had been found under the FERA work programs. Federal Works Agency, *Final Statistical Report,* pp. 53–56.

212. It was not uncommon for the WPA to seek out useful activities and to encourage their sponsorship. Even unreceptive city officials were pressed to sponsor relief work by mayors and governors eager to reduce the burdens of direct relief. Macmahon, Millett, and Ogden, *Administration,* pp. 309–10.

communities of public works projects, despite the higher sponsor cost, might be construed as evidence of their perceived value. Beginning in 1940 the minimum share of project costs to be borne by any state was set at 25 percent. Consequently, some communities were too poor to sponsor WPA projects for urgently needed facilities or services. Others found it difficult to support the maintenance costs of completed work-relief construction projects.[213] Thus, sponsorship could not guarantee the usefulness of projects undertaken even within the restricted range of politically feasible activities.[214]

Federal appropriations for the WPA and their distribution across states were always short term and fraught with uncertainty. Beginning in 1936 the WPA required that "no federal project shall be undertaken or prosecuted under the foregoing appropriation unless and until an amount sufficient for its completion has been allocated and irrevocably set aside for its completion."[215] These factors not only complicated project planning but also ruled out a number of worthwhile projects.[216] Further, the need for flexibility in the timing of public works unrelated to work relief was held to justify some loss of project value.[217] The month-to-month uncertainty about state allocations of WPA funds was reduced somewhat in 1937. Given the duration of large-scale work relief programs of the 1930s, however, the sacrifice of useful output might appear to be irrational. It was the result of the era's political contingencies. If work relief were billed as long-term or indefinite, it was feared, business confidence would be shaken and the recovery hindered.[218]

---

213. Howard, *WPA,* p. 797; and Brown, *Public Relief,* p. 379.

214. "At least, when projects were attacked, the WPA had the defense that the proposals had come from state and local governments, the officials of which were the judges in the first instance of the usefulness of work relief efforts." Macmahon, Millett, and Ogden, *Administration,* p. 304.

215. Ibid., pp. 148–49; also see pp. 40 and 132–33.

216. "This situation has severely inhibited planning by all levels of government for the development of appropriate and worthwhile projects. It is indeed surprising that in these circumstances the quality of the projects developed has so steadily improved." National Resources Planning Board, *Security,* p. 468. Also see Federal Security Agency, *Final Report,* p. 25.

217. Galbraith, *Economic Effects,* p. 5.

218. "Dedicated as it was to the promotion of economic recovery, which public imagination pictured as a condition without joblessness, the Administration hesitated to announce in advance that its efforts were not expected to be successful. The declaration that the work relief policy and its concomitant expenditures were to be fairly permanent would scarcely have fitted a strategy of reassurance." Macmahon, Millett, and Ogden, *Administration,* pp. 390–91.

Assessment of Productivity

An important question was how the efficiency of work relief projects compared with similar work by contractors. Most types of public works construction under the WPA were also undertaken by private builders under contract, administered largely by the PWA. One study of FERA work relief construction projects in New York state for the winter of 1934–35 found them to average 75 percent of the efficiency achieved under private contract. A sample study of WPA construction projects in late 1939 found their total costs about 13 percent greater than the estimated costs under contract. WPA authorities reported instances where the use of machinery could have reduced the costs of performing tasks by as much as two-thirds.[219]

When resources are unemployed, the assessment of productive efficiency may differ from the ranking of production costs. A cost-minimizing private firm hires labor on the basis of its market wage rate rather than its social scarcity value. Because of this factor and "safety first" behavior, private firms may be more capital-intensive than is efficient. Thus, labor-intensive relief projects could be more efficient despite their higher costs. Still, there are good reasons to conclude tentatively that private producers were more efficient. The market prices of capital services probably did not decline fully to reflect their reduced social scarcity value.[220] The labor bias of relief projects was quite extreme, as shown by estimates in the section on input choice and labor demand. Finally, private firms' greater experience, supervision, incentive, and work discipline yielded more output from a given set of inputs, so-called x-efficiency.

219. National Resources Planning Board, *Security,* p. 247; and Howard, *WPA,* p. 252. Of the New York projects it was reported that the "lowest efficiency ratings commonly were associated with projects upon which efficiency had obviously been sacrificed in order to provide work opportunity for a maximum number of persons." National Resources Planning Board, *Security,* p. 247n. For estimates of the value of CCC output, see Salmond, *Civilian Conservation Corps,* p. 129. One study of the productive efficiency of WPA skilled workers found their performance on par with private standards. Gilboy, *Applicants,* pp. 208–09. Also see Macmahon, Millett, and Ogden, *Administration,* pp. 290–91.

220. The scarcity value of capital services in an economy with excess capital stock is approximately the discounted value of depreciation that is "borrowed" from the time when capital next becomes fully utilized. The corresponding scarcity value for labor services of a worker who would otherwise be unemployed is the higher of his valuation on leisure time and his home production services.

The lower productive efficiency of work relief was commonly justified by the relief function of the programs.[221] Work relief was handicapped by a number of features: its workers' characteristics, their higher mean age and turnover rates, and adverse selection as better workers opted for private jobs; wage policies that led to inefficient shifts and difficulty in obtaining skilled workers; slack supervision motivated in part by political considerations; limited equipment and materials, with associated over-manning of projects; weak or perverse incentives for workers to exert themselves or to complete projects; the decision to continue projects even in bad weather when contractors would have stopped operations; and uncertainties over program funding.[222] Some of these handicaps were the consequence of specific regulations adopted, while others were inherent in the relief objective of the programs.[223]

The political economy of work relief placed a web of constraints on the productive factors, the technology, the organization, and the type of products. These constraints affected the social value of the outputs. Not only was the efficiency of work relief operations forced below that of comparable contract projects, but the political forces of a private enterprise economy restricted projects to being noncompetitive. The restriction of project types was probably the more serious factor in reducing the value of output. The nonpecuniary benefits to be derived from work relief—maintenance of morale, skills, and work habits—themselves hinged critically on the value of output. Some of these constraints would have been considerably relaxed if not eliminated had the activities been performed on a contract basis. Yet moving to a contract arrangement would have cost most of the relief objectives of the program.[224] Only with

221. "The cost of several of the large buildings constructed by W.P.A. was reported by independent investigators acting for the House Committee as materially in excess of the cost of construction by private enterprise. The explanation was that relief labor was not as efficient as normal labor and the extra cost really represented relief." Meriam, *Relief*, p. 372.

222. See Howard, *WPA*, pp. 136, 246–55, and 257–62; and Meriam, *Relief*, pp. 413–16. And as Colonel F. C. Harrington, WPA head in 1940, observed: "Our organization has been in existence less than five years. It takes much longer than that for an organization of the size and complexity of the WPA to settle down to work at maximum efficiency. Any industrialist or engineer will corroborate this." Howard, *WPA*, p. 246.

223. The security wage policy brought complexities in work shifts depending on skill level, and the dollars-per-worker-per-month limit on federal financing of nonlabor costs induced the overmanning of projects.

224. "Contractors with their own crews awaiting work disliked being limited to relief labor, and when they operated in strongly unionized areas they were

a much larger program than was undertaken could the relief and employment objectives have been achieved through contract work.

Critical questions must be asked about the restriction of work projects to public works and a narrow range of other noncompeting activities.[225] While threatened private interests would be expected to oppose any competing public activities, this does not confirm the charge of net displacement of private employment in the aggregate. As discussed in the section on product market demand, for the displacement of private expenditures to follow from the public provision of goods and services, the latter must be complementary with private savings. Otherwise, the work relief output will merely shift the composition, not the level of aggregate private demand. Nevertheless, the realism of this condition is irrelevant to behavior, which appears to be dominated by political-economic forces. Potential gainers from the changing composition of private demand do not perceive or pursue their gains as vigorously as the threatened losers will perceive and fight their losses. Even if aggregate displacement had been a realistic prospect, the creation of substantial *net* useful output might still have been a desirable goal for work relief.[226]

Lessons for Today

My analysis leads to the characterization of 1930s work relief programs as primarily a camouflaged form of direct relief; the value of output

---

usually obligated to hire union labor." Charnow, *Work Relief Experience,* p. 106. "The P.W.A. provision reads that the contractor must take men from the State Employment Bureau where they are able to do the work. Well, the Bureau sends its men out. They work for a day, and then they are let go as not fit for the job; then the contractor has fulfilled the specifications and hires his own men." Bakke, *Unemployed Worker,* p. 168.

225. "If the profit interest of private enterprisers were the only objection to what its proponents like to call 'production for use,' the positive case for such a plan would be very strong." Lyon and Abramson, *Government,* p. 1183. They proceed to list a number of circumstances which point toward low efficiency of goods projects, though these would appear to apply equally to public works projects performed by relief workers.

226. William H. Stead, acting director of the U.S. Employment Service in 1939, put the thought as follows: "Perhaps we should begin to think of government work as an essential supplement to private enterprise in rounding out the production of goods and services needed for the 'fuller life.' It may be that we have reached the point where the main question is not whether public work competes with private enterprise, but whether it adds to total over-all needed production—private and public combined." Howard, *WPA,* p. 135.

produced was of secondary importance. Work programs furnished wide-spread income support to unemployed needy households. However, payments were unrelated to the need of participating households and were more costly than direct relief. Because organized business and labor groups restrained work relief from competing activities, the projects yielded relatively few private consumption goods, the form of output having the most urgent value. Most output was in the enduring form of public works that have benefited generations less needy than the one that built them. The decision to maximize on-site employment undermined the efficiency of even the limited range of work relief projects. Relief employment provided substantial rents to workers with erratic or no employment in the private sector. Rationing the limited positions by certification and administrative devices imposed real resource and equity costs on the programs. Numerous precautionary procedures were instituted to minimize the competition with private labor markets. These restrictions and the high-unemployment setting minimized the displacement of private-sector employment. Still, displacement of public spending by lower jurisdictions, mainly on direct relief, may have been extensive. The expansionary effects of work relief expenditures exceeded any displacement operating through labor supply or other channels. In summary, many of the fears and actions relating to displacement were exaggerated in the 1930s. These factors and the heavy relief orientation of the programs accounted for an unjustifiable neglect of productivity objectives.

Some General Lessons

Policies dealing with unemployment must make compromises among three objectives—creation of net useful output, net expansion of employment, and provision of income support. If the net output attainable through work relief is limited, direct relief may be an attractive alternative. Under an "income maintenance" format that does not restrict private work, direct relief could yield more net output than certain forms of work relief.[227] Direct relief requires less public outlay than work relief,

227. An analogy can be drawn from the WPA experience. Under the prevailing wage policy, skilled workers put in as little as thirty hours per month to earn their WPA security wage and simultaneously undertook substantial private work. The frequent supplementation of direct relief with private earnings is documented in F. L. Carmichael and Stanley L. Payne, *The 1935 Relief Population in 13 Cities: A Cross-Section,* U.S. Works Progress Administration, Division of Social Research, research bulletin, series 1, no. 23 (GPO, 1937).

as it does not have the materials and supervisory overhead of work relief. Furthermore, direct relief does not have to compensate beneficiaries for their leisure time, as no work is demanded. Balanced against the advantages of direct relief are the enhanced morale and other nonpecuniary returns of work relief. When unemployment is high, warding off the social disintegration of prolonged joblessness may be a valuable return. This return may be as important for a depressed ghetto area today as it was for the general population in the 1930s. Additionally, taxpayers who bear the burden of financing unemployment relief may prefer work-oriented programs.

If work relief is chosen partially to increase net output, the 1930s experience conveys an unequivocal lesson about how to proceed. Relief work should strive for efficiency in project operations. The input choices may depart somewhat from conventional cost-minimizing combinations in order to augment employment of the skills possessed by the unemployed. Still, project budgeting should allow for sufficient materials, equipment, skilled labor, and supervision to avoid grossly inefficient production. Maximizing on-site employment to the total neglect of other objectives can hardly be justified in the modern context. Indeed, it was justifiable in the 1930s only because of constraints on program budgets and the primacy of the relief objective.

Lowering the rents of work relief can facilitate several important ends.[228] Consider the effects of reducing the compensation for relief work below that for comparable private work. This alleviates the need for complex program provisions designed to lower the rents of relief work. With lower rents the self-selection process induces less displacement of private-sector output. Workers with skills valued by the private sector face stronger incentives to choose private work over relief work. Administrators of work relief, having to ration a limited number of positions, cannot readily discern these productivity differences. Lowering relief wages also allows greater equity in a work relief program, since it enables more positions to be created for a given level of program funding. More important, lower rents allow work relief positions to be opened to more of the unemployed without imposing arbitrary eligibility restrictions. Thus, workers most in need—based on their personal circumstances, preferences, and job opportunities—have greater access to relief employment.

---

228. The Haveman paper in this volume illustrates the problems of high relief wages in a contemporary Dutch public employment program.

Holding relief wages below the rates paid on comparable private work may not allow adequate support for many workers with dependents. If relief wages are uniformly raised to meet the needs of large families, payments to smaller families pose an unnecessary drain on the program budget.[229] One solution is to link a relief worker's wages to his number of dependents. Of course, this approach highlights the relief aspect of work relief.[230] Its major drawback is that it renders relief work most attractive to workers with large families, thus causing administrative difficulties in inducing them to depart for private jobs. A more satisfactory solution is to provide family allowances or other transfers contingent on family size.[231] These would be available to the poor irrespective of their work-relief status. Under this arrangement, work relief could pay relatively low wages without sacrificing the adequacy of income support.

This study found the output of 1930s relief work concentrated in public works and services not competing with private industry. However, relief workers desire to spend most of their wages on private consumption goods rather than public works or public services. Of course, to the extent that their incomes and purchases are taxed, they are compelled to contribute to the financing of additional public output. In an economy with extensive unutilized resources, their demands for consumption goods can also be met by an expanding private sector. But in an economy near full employment, the additional demands for consumption goods cannot be readily met. Since the government's construction and service activities preempt the resources needed for business expansion, the outcome is inflationary. Hence, public policy should increasingly aim at job expansion in the private sector as the economy approaches full employment.

229. "The obvious dilemma . . . is . . . whether a work program can afford to restrict its wages to a level incompatible with acceptable minimum living standards in order not to compete in a private labor market in which wages are extremely low." National Resources Planning Board, *Security,* p. 352. Also see Clark, *Economics,* p. 26.

230. Relief wages were graded by the budgetary deficiency method in some programs before the WPA. "The question arises whether there is any compelling reason why the compensation of relief labor should not likewise be determined by need. It is not easy to see why on a work relief project, the primary purpose of which is to take the place of direct relief for those unemployed, a skilled artisan with one dependent should get two or three times the wage of an unskilled worker with six." Lyon and Abramson, *Government,* p. 1193.

231. This strategy has been proposed for combining wage subsidies, income subsidies, and public employment. See Jonathan R. Kesselman, "A Comprehensive Approach to Income Maintenance: SWIFT," *Journal of Public Economics,* vol. 2 (February 1973), pp. 59–88.

Additionally, as the economy moves closer to full employment, the potential gains from work relief are progressively overcome by the likely losses. As the pool of the unemployed shrinks, its average work efficiency will decline, and the prospective relief output per worker will fall. Simultaneously, the likelihood of displacing employed workers and other resources grows as the economy approaches its capacity. This pattern suggests that reliance be shifted to direct relief from work relief as the economy expands.

Putting the unemployed to work in private production is a viable alternative to employing them on relief projects. The main attraction of utilizing the private sector is its presumably greater productivity. If production were undertaken within private firms, there would be less constraint by private enterprise on what is produced. The efficient input choices and work discipline of cost-minimizing private producers would determine how output is produced. The wider applications of experiences and skills gained in private production, along with the greater morale of a genuine production setting, would constitute valuable nonpecuniary benefits. Thus all the components of productivity as defined for work relief in this study might be enhanced by creating jobs in the private sector.

The Modern Setting

Modern-day policies toward unemployment retain the three basic goals of 1930s work relief. However, the emphases of today's policies are significantly affected by the changed cultural, institutional, and macroeconomic environment. During the 1930s much was made of the morale benefits of relief work. The waning of the work ethic and of the stigma of direct relief demand that work relief be justified by its output value more than in the past. Fear of excessive governmental deficits constrained the work relief programs of the 1930s. While budgetary balance remains a popular goal, it is a lesser consideration in contemporary policy. Relief programs' inflationary impact was not a primary concern of the 1930s, a time when the National Recovery Administration intentionally boosted wage rates and product prices. In the 1970s the fear of inflation restrains popular willingness to increase public expenditures. Critics of expanded public spending now argue that the ability to reduce unemployment without exacerbating inflation through conventional policy tools has been exhausted.

It is hazardous to predict the scope of displacement that might follow the initiation of a large contemporary work relief program. The majority of displacement mechanisms examined for the 1930s would carry greater disruption under fuller employment.[232] Undoubtedly the private sector will continue to resist the entry of relief projects into competitive activities, although the resistance may be less vigorous when private sales are strong.[233] This behavior helped to minimize displacement during the 1930s, but it is unclear whether it would be effective in a more fully employed economy. Even public works and "noncompetitive" public services draw real resources that would be at least partially utilized in the absence of work relief. Individual recipients' benefits under 1930s transfer programs were so far below their accustomed living standards that little displacement resulted. In contrast, today's unemployment insurance and welfare benefits in many cases compete with low-wage employment. Hence, shifting employable persons from cash transfer programs to work relief provides an offsetting potential for less displacement in a contemporary policy. But it is unrealistic to believe that this potential could be exploited fully.

Unlike the widespread unemployment of the 1930s, recent unemployment is concentrated in particular occupations, skill levels, and regions.[234] This lesser dispersion of unemployment has important implications. Ad-

232. The effect on private investment plans is probably an exception. In the 1930s the announcement of large-scale work relief may have disturbed some businessmen's expectations of economic recovery, thus reducing private demand for labor. In recent years the business community has accepted the expansionary effects of public spending, at least in the short run. The relation between economic slack and displacement was early recognized. "Whether the employment and business activity resulting from a given public works expenditure will be a net addition to, or merely a substitute for, the employment and activity which would exist anyway depends . . . upon the level of employment." Galbraith, *Economic Effects,* p. 7.

233. Kemper and Moss, in this volume, argue that contemporary resistance will be weakest in competitive industries with easy entry for firms and loosely attached workers. These are precisely the industries that employ most of the low-skilled, chronically unemployed.

234. Unemployment of both eras has nevertheless fallen disproportionately on nonwhites and youth. The 1937 census reported the rates as a percentage of the labor force: all persons, 16.4 percent totally unemployed and 20.0 percent totally unemployed plus emergency workers; whites, 15.7 percent and 19.1 percent; nonwhites, 23.2 percent and 28.2 percent; ages 15–19, 36.5 percent and 41.1 percent; ages 20–24, 21.3 percent and 24.3 percent; ages 25–64, 13.3 percent and 16.9 percent; ages 65 and over, 16.2 percent and 18.8 percent. *Census of Partial Employment, Unemployment and Occupations,* vol. 4, pp. 22 and 39.

ministering a general economic stimulus under current conditions would create shortages in some labor markets and intensify shortages in others. A less inflationary approach would be to alter the composition of labor demand across occupations, skill levels, and regions. Although not totally neglected in the 1930s, this approach was not a central feature of work relief.[235] Today displacement must be channeled so as to reduce demand for workers who are in excess demand. Displacement of employed workers with traits similar to the assisted unemployed workers would thwart any unemployment policy.

Policy Alternatives

My analysis points to the desirability of policies that target their employment stimulus on the unemployed. One such policy is public service employment of low-skilled, chronically unemployed workers. A counterpart to the 1930s work relief projects, this might offer minimal displacement of private employment. And to the extent that it displaces regular public employment, it might still change the skill mix of public workers. There is no question that *some* useful output can be generated by public service employment. Yet, before implementing this policy on a large scale or as a complete strategy, four questions must be answered. Is there enough highly valued public service work to be undertaken? Would most chronically unemployed persons be productive in these service roles?[236] Would relief wages swell the demand for private consumption goods without augmenting their supply? And would the workers displaced in the process tend to have low skills and chronic unemployment similar to those of relief workers? On all grounds, further study and much caution appear to be in order before implementing a large program. Where the nonpecuniary benefits of experience, acquisition of basic skills, and per-

235. Recall the continual attempts of the WPA to avoid creating local labor shortages for any occupation and the periodic difficulty of projects in securing certain skilled workers and supervisors without disrupting local supply. "Although a town may need a school badly, WPA will not build it unless the local labor reserve contains enough skilled construction workers." Hopkins, *Spending,* p. 167.

236. These issues have been assessed for San Francisco and Oakland. Based on relatively rigid criteria for the feasible expansion of "useful" public services, the amount of labor such activities could absorb is estimated to be far less than the pool of unemployed persons. Accordingly, restrictions on eligibility—unemployment duration, head of household, and presence of dependent children—are proposed to ration the prospective supply of useful jobs. Frank Levy and Michael Wiseman, "An Expanded Public-Service Employment Program: Some Demand and Supply Considerations," *Public Policy,* vol. 23 (Winter 1975), pp. 105–34.

sonal development are primary goals, public employment remains an attractive policy. This applies to a sizable portion of the unemployed— ex-offenders, persons with severe physical and social handicaps, and part of the youth population.

Generally targeted policies are the simplest method of stimulating demand for the unemployed. Government expenditures could be re- aligned toward products utilizing low-skilled labor intensively and toward regions suffering high unemployment. These methods are not costless, as they may necessitate shifts in public spending away from preferred cate- gories or lowest-bid contractors. Another generally targeted policy is the provision of employment tax credits or wage subsidies to private firms. These incentives could be specified so as to encourage the private employ- ment of low-skilled or low-wage labor or the labor of particular regions or industries.[237] Generally targeted policies operate to shift the occupa- tional, skill, and regional composition of labor demand.[238] They cannot channel their increased demand with great precision, but they have the compensating benefit of no need to certify the eligibility of individual workers.

In order to channel demand stimulus more precisely, several selec- tively targeted policies could be considered.[239] Like work relief, these policies require the designation of eligible unemployed persons and a certification machinery. Two of these policies are selective variants of the generally targeted expenditure and taxation methods. Government con- tracts could stipulate that private employers hire quotas of certified per- sons. To minimize their efficiency costs, quotas might be concentrated in industries that can apply the services of the certified workers most productively. Another approach would be to furnish wage subsidies or employment tax credits to firms for hiring certified persons.[240] Alterna- tively, mandatory quotas for hiring certified persons might be imposed

237. The Hamermesh paper in this volume reviews and analyzes several existing programs, including generally targeted and selectively targeted types.

238. Note that the expenditure policy still requires public choices about what is to be produced, mainly by rearranging existing purchases. The policy of tax reduction leaves the choice of what is to be produced to demand in the private sector.

239. Even if additional labor demands are precisely targeted, this does not insure that labor will be displaced from those occupations, skills, and regions in greatest excess demand, or that displacement will not create excess supply in other groups. In an operational program, trial-and-error methods would have to be used.

240. I uncovered a single reference to this policy approach for the 1930s: "Early proposals within the FERA for subsidizing reemployment by private enter- prise were never matured." Macmahon, Millett, and Ogden, *Administration,* p. 62.

on private firms independently of public contracts. The quota could be specified as a proportion of the firm's work force and could be applied to all firms above a critical size. To eliminate the least efficient uses of certified labor, firms could hire less than their quotas upon payment of a penalty tax.[241]

The proposal for employment quotas in public contracts illustrates the use of market mechanisms to improve program efficacy. Private firms have the know-how, capital, supervisors, and incentive to produce goods and services at minimum cost. Business would prefer to obtain government contracts, even with quotas, than to see goods publicly produced.[242] Quotas would raise the minimum bid prices on public contracts; an implicit public subsidy would reflect the differential compensation and productivity of quota labor relative to the displaced inputs. The invisibility of the subsidy would obviate the stigma of public support for quota workers. Wages paid to quota workers could be determined by the market as long as they met an established minimum. Employers would seek to obtain the best available quota workers and the most productive work from them. Unions in these firms might resist the quotas since their members might be displaced.[243] Consequently, it would be prudent to institute the quotas in new public contracts, particularly where firm or industry employment is expanding.[244] Unions might then perceive a convergence

241. European quota employment policies are reviewed by Beatrice G. Reubens, *The Hard-to-Employ: European Programs* (Columbia University Press, 1970), pp. 119–61. West Germany imposes a quota with penalty tax to promote the employment of war invalids and other disabled persons. Ibid., pp. 144–52. The penalty tax affects the relative price of the certified labor similarly to a wage subsidy; it collects revenue, whereas a subsidy disburses revenue.

242. Business actively sought contracts under the PWA even with its pressure to hire workers on relief. "Contractors must, however, give preference in hiring to any union members on relief rolls. Of those at work on the PWA program early in 1940, about one-tenth had relief status." Burns and Williams, *Federal Work*, p. 71. The strains might be aggravated today on account of the lower skills of most quota workers.

243. Under the PWA an "administrative order . . . provided that a preponderance of labor employed on a project should be taken from the bona fide residents of any political subdivision that partly financed the construction of the project. Contractors, on their side, objected to this later order because they claimed that it required them to violate existing union agreements." Macmahon, Millett, and Ogden, *Administration*, p. 160.

244. Unions could claim only that quota workers were taking jobs the unions would like to have for their own members, not jobs that were theirs by any natural right. In practice, the majority of jobs under contract would fall to union members if the contracting firm were unionized.

of interests with management in obtaining contracts. Because they would have to yield the quota positions, unions would be disinclined to enroll quota workers. Employers could maintain work discipline if more persons were certified for quota work than the aggregate of contract quotas.

Careful, innovative thought about combinations of the unemployment policies may be a fruitful exercise. The selectively targeted policies appear to be especially suited for simultaneous implementation. For example, a number of "target" persons could be certified as eligible for any of the operative programs. Public service employment slots and quotas in public contracts could be created concurrently. Certified persons would be free to apply for positions in either sector subject to the limited allocations of each. The relative emphasis and worker rents on the two programs could be geared to local needs. Clearly, many other aspects of program specification require close analysis.

Eligibility Issues

My analysis has considered *what* output might be produced in expanding work for the unemployed and *how* it might be produced. Selectively targeted programs also raise the slippery question of *who* shall be certified. For present purposes, general operating principles rather than specific regulations are needed. Many pertinent lessons can be drawn from the analysis of WPA eligibility criteria in the section on work relief provisions and labor supply. Here the discussion will focus on a couple of the major eligibility issues for contemporary policy. Positions in public employment and subsidized or quota employment in private firms will be called "certified" jobs.

From society's perspective, who shall be certified hinges on both the productivity and income support objectives. I have little useful to say about the appropriate criteria of need, except that they depend upon the accompanying maintenance programs. As proposed earlier, "low rent" certified jobs are assumed to be accompanied by general transfers to dependents in poor households. I shall now focus on some productivity considerations. Persons with scant productivity might best be provided with direct relief. Still, for inexperienced persons with little initial productivity, the acquisition of skills, experience, and work habits is an estimable social gain. A key principle in certification is to reject persons who would be relatively productive off the program. As the 1930s program administrators discovered, this is exceedingly difficult to achieve through eligibility provisions if the rents of certified work are high. If the compensation and nonpecuniary benefits of certified work lie below those of regular private work, only persons having poor prospects off the program would enjoy positive rents from participating.

Should certification be contingent on the worker's unemployment for a specified duration? No such requirement was imposed by the WPA, which relied heavily on assessment of the worker's needs to restrict entry. Nevertheless, arguments for requiring a minimum unemployed spell surfaced in the 1930s, as they have in recent discussions about public employment.[245] Recent subsidized employment experience indicates that imposing such a provision would certify lower quality workers.[246] This finding does not necessarily undermine the appeal of the proposal. Support for the proposal stems from its value as a cheaply administered test of need and as a measure of the applicant's inability to find regular work. Yet, if the rents from obtaining certified work were high, even a long duration rule would not serve its intended purpose. Workers would be induced to quit regular work or to stop searching for work in order to fulfill the spell of unemployment.[247] Lowering compensation rates for certified workers is preferable to requiring long unemployed spells and offering higher compensation. Reduced compensation does not cause workers to quit working and searching.

Once he is certified, how long should a worker remain eligible for public or subsidized private work? The answer depends partially on the size of rents and the pressure to separate from certified work. A segment of the unemployed would find little or sporadic work under the best of economic conditions. Without automatic rotation, many of these persons would remain on the programs indefinitely. Other workers may be unemployable in times of recession but have work opportunities in a buoyant economy. The program needs to distinguish between these two groups—a very difficult task without putting everyone to the market test by releasing all

245. "This issue is inextricably bound up with a variety of questions which go to the very heart of one's philosophy regarding public employment programs. The greater the emphasis upon the relief aspects of a work program, the greater will be the emphasis upon restricting employment to those who have been unemployed a relatively long time." Howard, *WPA*, p. 480.

246. See Otto A. Davis and others, "An Empirical Study of the NAB-JOBS Program," *Public Policy*, vol. 21 (Spring 1973), p. 255.

247. For anecdotal evidence of this kind of intentional unemployment caused by the public employment program authorized by the Emergency Employment Act, see Levy and Wiseman, "An Expanded Public-Service Employment Program," p. 125.

of them. Keeping the rents of certified work low appears to be a preferable method for inducing the desired rate of reentry to regular employment. Still, periodic rotation of all certified workers may be useful, if applied when local labor demands are expansive. Reinstatement of rotated workers after a period of exposure to the market should be guaranteed. This practice would provide an inducement for return to regular work without lowering relief wages excessively.

A Word for the Future

Work relief policies raise a complex set of questions about the what, how, and for whom of production as well as the related issues of macroeconomic displacement. Similar problems arise in the formulation of any unemployment policy. The attainment of productivity is central to the choice and design of policies. Unless work-oriented programs can produce net additions to socially valued output, pure income maintenance would be a preferable course. Glowing talk about the limitless public service work that would be useful seems like misplaced concern so long as the unemployed have urgent needs for private consumption goods. Considerations of productivity and displacement argue for moderate use of work relief and greater reliance on the creation of jobs in the private sector.

Several policies to channel demand stimulus toward low-skilled, low-wage, or certified unemployed workers have been proposed. With selectively targeted policies—including relief work and quota or subsidized private work—the attractiveness of such positions could be held below that of regular private work. There would still be positive rents for workers with the poorest job opportunities, who would have ready access to program positions. Low rents would eliminate the need for myriad eligibility conditions to ration the positions. This approach enhances the net productivity of the program while simultaneously minimizing its displacement effects. As public support for work-oriented unemployment programs allows more generous funding, the rents to participants could be progressively raised.

Bibliography

Bakke, E. Wight. *The Unemployed Worker: A Study of the Task of Making a Living Without a Job.* New Haven: Yale University Press, 1940.

Bevis, Joseph C., and Stanley L. Payne. *Former Relief Cases in Private Employment.* U.S. Works Progress Administration, Division of Research. Washington: Government Printing Office, 1939.

Blinder, Alan S., and Robert M. Solow. "Analytical Foundations of Fiscal Policy," in Alan S. Blinder and others, *The Economics of Public Finance.* Washington: Brookings Institution, 1974.

Brown, Josephine C. *Public Relief, 1929–1939.* New York: Holt, 1940.

Burns, Arthur E., and Edward A. Williams. *Federal Work, Security, and Relief Programs.* U.S. Federal Works Agency, Work Projects Administration, Division of Research, Research Monograph 24. Washington: Government Printing Office, 1941.

Charnow, John. *Work Relief Experience in the United States.* Pamphlet series 8. Washington: Social Science Research Council, Committee on Social Security, 1943.

Clark, John Maurice. *Economics of Planning Public Works.* A study made for the National Planning Board of the Federal Emergency Administration of Public Works. Washington: Government Printing Office, 1935.

Colcord, Joanna C. *Emergency Work Relief as Carried Out in Twenty-Six American Communities, 1930–1931, with Suggestions for Setting Up a Program.* New York: Russell Sage Foundation, 1932.

Galbraith, J. K., assisted by G. G. Johnson, Jr. *The Economic Effects of the Federal Public Works Expenditures, 1933–1938.* U.S. National Resources Planning Board. Washington: Government Printing Office, 1940.

Gilboy, Elizabeth W. *Applicants for Work Relief: A Study of Massachusetts Families under the FERA and WPA.* Cambridge: Harvard University Press, 1940.

Harper, Charles Price. *The Administration of the Civilian Conservation Corps.* Clarksburg, W. Va.: Clarksburg Publishing Company, 1939.

Hickman, Bert G., and Robert M. Coen. *An Annual Growth Model of the U.S. Economy.* Amsterdam: North-Holland, 1976.

Hopkins, Harry L. *Spending to Save: The Complete Story of Relief.* New York: Norton, 1936; Seattle: University of Washington Press, American Library Ed., 1972.

Howard, Donald S. *The WPA and Federal Relief Policy.* New York: Russell Sage Foundation, 1943.

Kerr, P. A. "Production-for-Use and Distribution in Work Relief Activities," *Monthly Report of the Federal Emergency Relief Admin-*

istration, September 1 Through September 30, 1935. Washington: Government Printing Office, 1936.

Kesselman, Jonathan R., and N. E. Savin. "Three-and-a-Half Million Workers Never Were Lost," *Economic Inquiry,* vol. 16 (April 1978).

Lyon, Leverett S., Victor Abramson, and associates. *Government and Economic Life: Development and Current Issues of American Public Policy.* Vol. 2. Washington: Brookings Institution, 1940.

Macmahon, Arthur W., John D. Millett, and Gladys Ogden. *The Administration of Federal Work Relief.* Chicago: Public Administration Service, 1941.

Meriam, Lewis. *Relief and Social Security.* Washington: Brookings Institution, 1946.

Roberts, Verl E. *Survey of Workers Separated from WPA Employment in Nine Areas, 1937.* U.S. Works Progress Administration, Division of Social Research. Washington: Government Printing Office, 1938.

[Roosevelt, Franklin D.] *The Public Papers and Addresses of Franklin D. Roosevelt.* Vol. 4: *The Court Disapproves, 1935.* New York: Random House, 1938.

Salmond, John A. *The Civilian Conservation Corps, 1933–1942: A New Deal Case Study.* Durham: Duke University Press, 1967.

Schlesinger, Arthur M., Jr. *The Age of Roosevelt.* Vol. 2: *The Coming of the New Deal.* Boston: Houghton Mifflin, 1958.

Stein, Herbert. *The Fiscal Revolution in America.* Chicago: University of Chicago Press, 1969.

U.S. Federal Security Agency. War Manpower Commission. *Final Report of the National Youth Administration, Fiscal Years 1936–1943.* Washington: Government Printing Office, 1944.

U.S. Federal Works Agency. Work Projects Administration. *Final Statistical Report of the Federal Emergency Relief Administration.* Washington: Government Printing Office, 1942.

U.S. Federal Works Agency. *Final Report on the WPA Program, 1935–43.* Washington: Government Printing Office, 1946.

U.S. National Resources Planning Board. *Security, Work, and Relief Policies.* Washington: Government Printing Office, 1942.

U.S. Works Progress Administration. Division of Social Research. *Survey of Workers Separated from WPA Employment in Eight Areas During the Second Quarter of 1936.* Washington: Government Printing Office, 1937.

Comments by Robert H. Haveman

Jon Kesselman's paper on public employment–depression style is "old wine in new bottles." However, contrary to most applications of this phrase, its use here is meant to convey a highly favorable judgment. The paper contains the most careful and comprehensive distillation of assertions, evidence of various forms and reliability, and speculation regarding the economics of public employment in the 1930s that is available. The gist of literally thousands of pages of comment and analysis (reflected in a most interesting and lengthy set of footnotes) is captured in his paper. This is the old wine. The new bottles are represented by the contemporary macroeconomic theoretical framework into which the discussion of the 1930s experience is placed.

I found the paper to be both sobering and humbling. It is sobering to learn that the economic issues of the "new" topic of work relief (which I will call special public employment) were confronted, in much the same terms, over forty years ago. And it is humbling to realize that the knowledge possessed today on these issues is not much more reliable than that possessed forty years ago. In addition to encouraging sobriety and humility, Kesselman's paper highlights the unfortunate moratorium on research on the economics of special public employment that persisted from 1940 to 1970.

In these comments, I will first summarize the key points raised by Kesselman. Then I will present a few critical comments. Finally, I will offer some thoughts on a few fundamental issues in the economics of special public employment—thoughts that were triggered by Kesselman's paper.

Kesselman's paper isolates two of the components of a full benefit-cost study of a special public employment program and seeks to determine the value of these two components in the program of the 1930s. These two components are the reductions in wages and salaries elsewhere in the economy induced by the program, and the value of the social output yielded by the program. The first component he terms *displacement* and the second *productivity*.

After defining these two components, Kesselman introduces his analysis by discussing the level and financing of the work programs of the 1930s, once again recalling the enormity of these programs relative to the size of the economy at the time. Following this, Kesselman distinguishes the two primary channels by which displacement can occur—the policy-induced alteration of other demands placed on the economy and the induced effect on worker choices in supplying labor to regular employment (or, for all practical purposes in this case, the private sector).

The discussion of the demand side channel consists of a rather complete catalog of economic phenomena that determine the effect of special public employment on the composition of other public and private expenditures. I count about twenty of these phenomena, including intergovernmental substitution, consumption by special public employees, investment decisions by affected businesses, and program demands for materials, equipment, and supplies. All of these concern potential changes in the bill of final demands in the economy that are attributable to special public employment. In addition to these are the induced indirect effects, only alluded to in the paper. Because the extent of displacement from these demand-side effects is so complex that only a fully specified general equilibrium model could yield a reliable estimate, Kesselman gives no judgment on the extent of such displacement in the 1930s.

The second channel through which displacement can occur is worker choices in supplying labor to the private sector. Kesselman devotes a good deal of attention to this issue and outlines a *net advantages* or rent model to explain such worker choices. The model outlined is a more complete version of that empirically implemented by Greenberg in his paper in this volume. This model can be summarized briefly: Displacement of labor supply is a positive function of the net advantages or rent that a special public employment program provides to a worker.[248] Rent, in turn, is a positive function of the wage rate offered by the program, the steadiness, pleasantness, and meaningfulness of the work that it provides, the advancement and income supplementation possibilities that are afforded, and the ease of gaining eligibility to program rolls. Clearly, the value of the rent of the program is specific to each worker and is determined by his or her skills, tastes, and opportunities.

To form a judgment on the extent of 1930s displacement through this channel, Kesselman applies the net advantages model to the provisions of the WPA and the experience of its participants. Citing evidence of various sorts—from detailed administrative provisions of the act, to waiting times before certification, to the extent of "two-timing"—he concludes

---

248. *Rent* and *net advantages* are analogous if the program does not alter the value of the worker's employment opportunity that most closely relates to employment in the program.

that little if any displacement from this supply-side channel occurred in the 1930s. This conclusion is supported by indirect evidence concerning the scarcity of unjustifiable job refusals and induced labor shortages, the presence of a pool of unemployed workers without work relief opportunities, and the long lags before private sector employment of those released from special public employment.

The other benefit-cost component analyzed by Kesselman is the productivity of special public employment. He notes the relationship of this component to the displacement component (operating primarily through the reduction of demand in the private sector due to the public output), but spends most of his efforts delineating the effect of the 1930s program in biasing production decisions in the economy away from cost-minimizing solutions. Because of safety-first considerations, production decisions in the private sector were biased toward excess capital intensity. Decisions regarding special public employment he finds to be biased toward on-site relative to off-site employment, toward the employment of the most marginal workers, and toward employment of labor rather than increased use of materials, equipment, and supplies. Kesselman presumes that, by and large, these decisions represent serious deviations from the norm of social efficiency.

Finally, Kesselman documents the nonpecuniary outputs of the 1930s program—worker morale and self-esteem and the maintenance of health, skills, and work habits (he is not impressed by them), the bias toward public works rather than production of goods and services that might compete with production of the private sector (he sees this as a powerful constraint on the value of program output), and the inefficiencies caused by the administrative and cost-sharing structure of the program (he finds this to be a rather serious problem).

Kesselman concludes his paper with some lessons for today. These can be summarized as follows: Because of the numerous biases against efficiency in the work relief program and the low value of its output, direct income support may be a more efficient means of aid, especially for low-productivity workers. Special public employment with low rents has several important administrative, efficiency, and equity advantages over a high-rent program. Putting the unemployed to work in the private sector through mandating or subsidizing such employment is likely to be more efficient (and to have other advantages). And, finally, demand for employment in the public sector, from whatever source, should be targeted on high unemployment industries, occupations, and regions to minimize displacement and inflationary pressures.

Kesselman's paper, then, is a systematic look at the economics of the 1930s work relief experience, and its lessons are important. Moreover, his analysis—especially the detailed discussion of the channels of displacement and his application of the net advantages or rent model of labor supply—is important and revealing. Yet it would be unfair not to quibble with him.

My first concern pertains to the conclusion, reiterated at several points, that the special public employment efforts of the 1930s showed an "unjustifiable neglect of productivity objectives" and that they were, in fact, inefficient compared to private sector operations. This lack of productivity is attributed to several factors, including efforts to minimize the displacement of private and normal public sector employment, decisions to emphasize on-site relative to off-site employment and labor rather than capital, the concentration of hiring on the lowest productivity, most needy workers, the offering of higher than necessary rents necessitating job rationing by certification and other administrative devices, and the displacement of state and local relief expenditures. While in no sense wishing to offer a brief for the efficiency of the 1930s policies, I do believe that the basis for this conclusion is not as clear as Kesselman implies.

While Kesselman acknowledges the divergence of private from social-opportunity costs of resource use in a period of less than full employment, his conclusions give this factor little weight. When such divergence exists, input choices should reflect the social-opportunity cost of the alternative use of resources and not the market prices of the resources. If it is reasonable to believe that the value of enforced leisure during a depression as deep as the 1930s is not positive, public policy that is seeking social efficiency should not look to private sector choices as a norm.[249] Choices in the private sector are based on relative market prices and hence deviate

249. An analysis of the divergence of the social cost of labor and its market value when the unemployment rate is about 6 percent concluded that the ratio of social cost to market value was about 85 percent for the skill mix of labor demanded by large-scale public works projects. See Robert H. Haveman and John V. Krutilla, *Unemployment, Idle Capacity, and the Evaluation of Public Expenditures: National and Regional Analyses* (Johns Hopkins Press for Resources for the Future, 1968), pp. 76–77. If one considers the unemployment rate in the 1930s of about four times the 6 percent rate and the concentration of special public employment on workers with the lowest valued alternative use of labor, it does not seem unreasonable to presume that the ratio for this program was very low.

from socially efficient choices. As a result, the labor-skill and labor-capital composition reflected in such choices can hardly be considered an efficiency norm.

Viewed in this light, the concentration of 1930s policy on the lowest productivity workers, on direct on-site employment and intensive use of labor, and on the avoidance of displacement of employment in the private and normal public sectors seems quite consistent with a desire to achieve social efficiency. The divergence of market wages from social opportunity costs is likely to be greater for lower than for higher productivity workers, hence justifying some concentration on them. Similarly, on-site work relief employment can be targeted on workers with few alternatives, and hence low opportunity costs, while untargeted off-site employment demand is likely to fall on higher skill sectors with both greater employment opportunities and higher opportunity costs. Finally, there is no inconsistency between the goal of allocative efficiency and the minimization of displacement in the private and normal public sector. While the inefficiencies of higher than optimal rents, administrative job rationing, and the displacement of state and local relief expenditures in the 1930s programs seem indisputable, the alleged inefficiency in other areas seems far less clear. Indeed, it may well be that, because of the divergence of social from market prices, decisions regarding the allocation of resources in the private sector in the 1930s lay further from the efficiency norm than did those of the special public employment programs.

My second quibble concerns Kesselman's favorable appraisal of subsidized jobs for certified employees in the private sector, or employment quotas in public contracts, relative to special public employment. To be sure, job credit and employment quota proposals appear to have considerable merit. However, serious questions of efficiency and equity also plague them. These questions involve the reliability of estimated parameters on which assertions of effectiveness are based, the pricing response of affected private businesses and the concomitant opportunity for undesired windfalls, administrative costs and the opportunity for fraud (especially in the quota proposals), potential procyclical effects (especially in the job subsidy proposals), and the regional and sectoral biases that such subsidies and quotas create. The important warning that Kesselman raises regarding special public employment—"further study and much caution"—would seem to apply equally to these proposals.

In addition to these quibbles, Kesselman's paper stimulated a number of thoughts regarding special public employment and its evaluation. My first point concerns the role of displacement and its evaluation in the context of large-scale special public employment. Evaluation of this effect requires that some counterfactual be specified. Clearly, the specification depends on the nature of the employment program to be undertaken, the workers on which it is to be targeted, and the output that is to be produced. However, it also depends on the aggregate demand situation with and without the program. For example, if the work program is part of a general reflation program that includes an expansion in aggregate demand apart from the program as well as, perhaps, welfare reform, the static framework that is conventionally used in evaluating displacement would not seem appropriate. In this case (which currently appears to be the most relevant), the appropriate approach would seem to be evaluation of the costs and benefits of the entire package—of which the net increase in employment is surely a relevant consideration. These cost and benefit estimates would then have to be compared with those of other packages of policies that might or might not include special public employment. In any case a good deal of care must be exercised in defining the counterfactual before any conclusion regarding the displacement effects of work programs is accepted.

Second, the net advantages model spelled out by Kesselman leads to what, in my view, should be tantamount to a fundamental principle in the design of special public employment programs. The principle is this: The wage rate offered by the program should be less than the private sector wage rate for unskilled labor (the minimum wage) and greater than the implicit wage rate in the most generous income transfer program available to the eligible worker. Only in this way can the program give incentives for welfare recipients to work and for special public workers to leave the program. Stipulating such a wage rate is increasingly difficult in a world in which the rate of increase in transfer benefits exceeds that of the minimum wage, reducing the gap between them.

Third, is it not possible to convince private sector interests that a special public employment program that would produce marketable goods and services is not so harmful to their interests in a period of high unemployment as they apparently believed in the 1930s and believe now? Such a case could be built on several of the channels of impact indicated by Kesselman, including the demand for materials, inputs, and supplies from a program not designed to minimize contract employment, the increased consumption demands of the workers on which the program is targeted, the increased investment demands stimulated by both of these incremental demands, and the second-, third-, and nth-round interindustry demands that are created. While it is unlikely that the benefits of such a program to the private business community would ever appear to exceed the costs, it does seem that further analysis might demonstrate that the gap is not as large as conventionally thought. Such analysis would appear to require the application of micro-data simulation models—of which a growing number are now operational—to a variety of program designs so as to evaluate the full impact on regional and industrial output.[250] Defusing this source of opposition is necessary if special public employment is to lose the narrow orientation emphasizing the avoidance of competition with the private sector that now constrains the planning and design of programs.

Comments by Arnold R. Weber

My comment will parallel Bob Haveman's in the sense that I do not wish to deal so much with the macroeconomic effects or the economic model implicit in Kesselman's paper. Rather, I want to review his analysis within the framework of a set of programmatic responses to the problems of unemployment and underemployment among the labor force.

My overall view is that Kesselman has done a skillful and detailed job of reviewing the Depression experience with direct creation of jobs. His analysis offers several parallels to more recent experience in the sixties and seventies.

First, I think he clearly indicates the great difficulty of separating job creation from income transfer systems. Indeed there is an analogue to Gresham's law that seems to be at work whereby concern about transfers of income almost always drives out the work aspects of a program to create jobs. This law was applicable to the Neighborhood Youth Corps, Operation Mainstream, and all of those good acronyms that we had during the sixties and the seventies, and it certainly worked in the WPA and the PWA. As the New Deal program evolved, there was a retreat from more noble objectives of socially useful work, a training component, and enhanced positioning in the labor market. Instead, the whole program

250. See, for example, Stephen P. Dresch and Robert D. Goldberg, "IDIOM: An Inter-Industry, National-Regional Policy Evaluation Model," *Annals of Economic and Social Measurement,* vol. 2 (July 1973), pp. 323–41; and Frederick L. Golladay and Robert H. Haveman, *The Economic Impacts of Tax-Transfer Policy: Regional and Distributional Effects* (Academic Press, 1977).

seemed to be increasingly geared to notions of income transfer, and indeed the pay system was organized on that basis.

Second, Kesselman's paper illustrates the difficulty of developing a wage policy in a program of direct wage relief. His concept of rents is very useful, and while it does not point the way to an optimal policy, it certainly underscores the dilemma. To the extent that the program is designed to minimize net rents—paying a person what is necessary to attract him to a job without creating a disincentive for his pursuing jobs elsewhere in the labor market—it undermines, or certainly moves away from, what is perceived as a minimum standard of decency regarding income for the people who are the recipients of direct relief. Kesselman describes how the program administrators squirmed around this issue in their efforts to deal with what they called two-timers (which I always thought had a more romantic connotation). On the other hand, paying a high enough wage to meet family income standards obviously creates both political and individual incentives for workers to stay on the job and undercuts the supposedly transitional nature of direct work relief.

So Kesselman's paper clearly indicates that this was a major issue in the thirties as it is today, when the debate is primarily over whether to pay the minimum wage or one more akin to the "prevailing rate." Arthur Burns, on the other hand, undoubtedly out of concern over potential disincentives for relief recipients to seek regular employment, has suggested that public work-relief programs should pay a subminimum wage.

Third, Kesselman demonstrates that during the thirties direct work relief included very little training, although the WPA did help poets and painters of murals, and at one stage the halls of the Department of Labor were lined with Depression art. That is not to disparage this social output, but there clearly was very little effort to train people and move them up job ladders, however they were identified then.

As a matter of fact, the program might have fostered a deterioration of skills in some cases because it took skilled workers and put them on relatively menial jobs. And if they tried to become two-timers, they ran the risk of being dropped from the program. In this sense, the job-creating program moved the clients down the skill ladder, rather than up.

So Kesselman's study shows that the problem of wage policy, the dilemma between transferring income and providing meaningful work, and the difficulties of skill development were all present in the 1930s as well as today. Although Senator Humphrey waxed eloquent about the CCC, our experience with the Job Corps indicates that the eloquence should be tinged with realism—that taking kids from Bedford-Stuyvesant and teaching them to top trees in Kicking Horse, Montana, is not the route to good life in Brooklyn when they return.

Fourth, Kesselman's review also reveals in an early form the difficulty of deciding who should get the jobs. That has always been a problem in administering manpower programs. We began with the notion that all prospects should be unemployed but employable. That turned out to be a very difficult criterion to administer. To the extent that need for income is used as a guiding concept, we generally end up with a lot of unemployable people. This is particularly true within the context of the thirties. On the other hand, to the extent that economic efficiency is the goal—and it is clearly Kesselman's—we end up with pressure toward "creaming." One of the more interesting asides in his paper is evidence that there were administrative efforts to select the best applicants, and that there was a little informal labor market developing within the WPA program.

The last insight that I got from Kesselman's paper is a reminder of the truism that a work relief program is not a black box that can just be inserted in the economic and social system. It always intrudes on given interests that establish constraints and pose inefficiencies. Unions are always concerned that they will have to compete with nonunion labor. Employers are concerned that the program will provide goods and services that undercut their private markets. Thus, you end up with tree-topping and license-plate manufacture, or mural painting. It seems to me it is reasonable to accept these factors as givens, rather than to think that the system could be designed to overcome them.

Those are all useful points, and they do show us that the problems that we have to deal with today have historical antecedents, even though such programs were developed in a different institutional and economic environment. However, I believe that Kesselman also overstates, or fails to demonstrate, three or four points on which hangs a significant part of his recommendations and conclusions.

First, I think he probably exaggerates the lack of productive output. He makes a flat statement at the end that is reminiscent of the statement in the first veto message by President Nixon attacking public service employment as "leaf-raking." I do not think he has shown this to be the case to the extent he argues for the Depression programs.

Second, even if you could prove that the WPA had a zero net social product, I am not sure that it would have been better to have people on the dole (that is, receiving income-transfer payments) than to continue to reaffirm the connection between compensation and work. Obviously, a simple income-transfer program will influence the recipients' reservation wage for jobs in the private sector. I think this is especially true in the seventies now that we have unemployment insurance, supplemental security income, welfare payments, and food stamps. It is easy to say that what was done in the thirties was not productive, but it is tougher to demonstrate and argue that the same judgment is applicable in the midseventies.

Third, Kesselman does not tell us anything about one of the more critical issues raised in the debate over public work or direct work relief; that is the question of timing. In part this omission reflects the fact that the WPA was not intended to carry us over a short-term blip in the business cycle; rather, it was considered a basic program to ameliorate the consequences of an unemployment rate that ranged between 14 percent and 24 percent for eight years. A current argument is that direct creation of jobs should not be used as a countercyclical policy because it takes a long time to implement and may finally have its biggest impact when inflationary pressures are once again building. It would be useful in this regard if Kesselman had looked at the 1936–37 period when there was a recovery and then a recession.

Kesselman also calls for a lowering of the work relief wage to reduce rents. The economics of this proposal is impeccable, but the administrative difficulties are formidable. In recent efforts at welfare program revision, this was called the "notch" problem. If you reduce wages, people stay on welfare. On the other hand, if you want the recipients to gain economic independence, their total income has to be improved from added work. Therefore, it is misleading to talk about manipulating the wage independent of these elaborate systems of income transfer and income support that have developed in the intervening thirty years.

Fourth, Kesselman emphasizes the superiority of private sector jobs and states that the programs should be oriented in that direction. I think everybody in this room would agree with this, in vacuo, but that really states the problem. You would not have the problem of providing employment for these people if, in fact, the private sector would create the necessary jobs. Kesselman proposes quotas, and hints at other naughty program elements like subsidies. It is not clear that these proposals are better than direct work relief. We have had a lot of experience with this approach in the JOBS program. By and large the jobs created are in taco shops and dry cleaning stores, but not in IBM. It is all right to say the private secto should do its share, but I suspect that in the context in which such programs are most useful, they are less likely to take hold.

Kesselman has done an excellent job in bringing these ghosts out of the closet. His overall conclusion is reminiscent of one that was reached at a conference to which I went twenty years ago on the Scanlon plan. The Scanlon plan was a form of union-management cooperation, and the conference was attended by practitioners from the plants. One of them got up at the end and said, "I want you fellows to know that this plan is no pancreas." Indeed, that's probably true. But even if it is no panacea, direct creation of jobs certainly warrants intensive attention as part of our general array of policies.

No program of public sector employment or public works will completely carry the burden of dealing with a situation such as we have had over the last three years. Kesselman clearly shows the limitations of such programs. I would have been a little happier if he had looked at those specific limitations and told us how direct work relief—or job creation, in current jargon—could have been improved, rather than saying that ergo, it does not work and we should turn to other global solutions whose deficiencies might not be as obvious, but are equally profound.

Robert H. Haveman

The Dutch Social Employment Program

The number of people in the United States who desire to earn income through working, whose productivity is very low, is substantial. This population includes a high proportion of persons classified as disabled or handicapped. It also includes persons with serious social or cultural disadvantages—a language barrier, low educational attainment, a background of alcoholism or drug use, a criminal record, or a lack of job skills. Irrespective of the source of their problems, all of these people can be described by the term *less productive workers*.[1]

Public policy has focused an enormous volume of resources on these workers during the last decade. Education, training, and rehabilitation programs have been instituted and have grown to substantial size. Public transfer programs have assisted them and their families, while simultaneously reducing the incentive for them to seek work. As skepticism

Helpful comments on a draft of this paper were received from Edward M. Gramlich, Victor Halberstadt, Peter Kemper, Jonathan R. Kesselman, J. M. Kwant, Stanley H. Masters, Philip Moss, and Ernst W. Stromsdorfer. Research support from the Netherlands Ministry of Social Affairs, the Institute for Research on Poverty, the Brookings Institution, and the Netherlands Institute for Advanced Study is gratefully acknowledged.

1. The terms *handicapped, disabled,* and *disadvantaged* are separable in concept but overlap significantly in practice. Handicaps and disabilities typically refer to physical or mental conditions that limit either the extent or the type of activity in which a person can engage. They are often categorized as total, partial, or vocational. Persons with partial disabilities are often restricted in the extent or duration of the activities in which they can engage; vocationally disabled persons are unable to carry on effectively in the occupation in which they were employed before becoming disabled. Persons in both categories often work. Disadvantaged workers are those whose activity is also limited by some personal characteristic (or some set of characteristics) other than a physical or mental problem—the combination of older age, illiteracy, and a low skill level would indicate a disadvantaged worker. In most cases, programs defined for the handicapped and disabled also provide benefits to some disadvantaged workers. In all three cases, low economic productivity is the primary characteristic.

regarding the effectiveness of these policies has grown, so has interest in publicly provided or subsidized employment programs for less productive workers. Discussions of such programs focus on guaranteed public jobs for low productivity workers as a complement to a reformed income support system, the extension of federal grants for state and local public employment as a countercyclical policy instrument, and greater public support for sheltered workshops or supported work.

Social policy toward handicapped, disabled, and disadvantaged workers varies widely among countries. Those adopting full employment policies—the Eastern European countries, for example—expect all individuals, including the handicapped and disabled, to contribute to the social product, and these countries make provision for such contribution via public enterprises, state-supported cooperatives, or home work. The social welfare states of Western Europe—for example, Sweden and the Netherlands—generally take the "right to work" concept as a fundamental principle and seek to provide employment for anyone who wishes to work. In the United States, many handicapped and disadvantaged persons are guaranteed some income support, but not employment. Yet through both the nonpublic, nonprofit sector (in efforts such as Goodwill Industries) and regular private or public employment many such persons do find employment.

In this paper, the structure and performance of the Social Employment program of the Netherlands is described and evaluated.[2] While such an analysis is important in its own right, it has special relevance to current policy discussions in the United States. In the first section of the paper, the organization and financial structure of the Dutch Social Employment program are described and major patterns of employment and cost growth are summarized. Analysis of the financial structure and growth patterns reveals adverse incentives and a lack of economic control. This discussion sets the stage for an analysis of the economic efficiency of the program. Using a benefit-cost framework, the industrial centers component of the Dutch program is analyzed in the second section. Both the methodological procedures and the empirical results of the study are described there. In the final section, some lessons of the Dutch experience in providing income support and employment for less productive workers are drawn and related to current U.S. policy discussions.

2. Most of the information and statistics on the Dutch Social Employment program are from Robert H. Haveman, "A Benefit-Cost and Policy Analysis of the Netherlands' Social Employment Program" (Leiden, Netherlands: University of Leiden, Mar. 1, 1977; processed).

The Social Employment Program

The Dutch Social Employment program is a large public undertaking; in 1976, 64,000 workers accounting for 1.5 percent of total employment in Holland worked in the program. Although public responsibility for providing employment for handicapped workers dates back to the 1800s in Holland, the present law dates only from 1969; it combines a program for manual workers and another for administrative workers that were begun as part of the reconstruction after World War II.

While the program that existed before the war was motivated by charity, the postwar program was seen as an integral part of national full employment policy. The Dutch took seriously the right-to-work mandate of the United Nations Universal Declaration of Human Rights.[3] In the postwar program, the employees of the program were given normal public employee status, brought under the provisions of the social insurance laws, and paid a wage that approximated that of regular private or public sector workers performing similar functions (though at substantially greater productivity levels).[4] Moreover, it was stipulated that the output they produced was to be sold at a market price, not less because of available government subsidies nor greater because of appeals to charity.

Management and Financial Structure

The Social Employment program is a complex undertaking by the national government and municipal governments that is defined by numerous complicated regulations. Since 1969 the program has had two primary components—an industrial centers program and an open-air and administrative activities program. The former is revenue-yielding, while the latter seldom produces a salable product or service. The output of the latter activities is typically a part of normal public service provi-

3. This declaration, put forth by the General Assembly in 1948, stated: "Everyone has the right to work, to free choice of employment, to just and favourable conditions of work, and to protection against unemployment" (art. 23), *Yearbook of the United Nations, 1948–49,* p. 536.

4. From 1950 to 1969 the wage was tied to unemployment compensation benefits and ranged from 105 percent to 140 percent of such benefits. In 1976 the entry-level wage ranged from two-thirds to 110 percent of the wage income of the worker in the modal family, depending on the skill level of the worker. In addition, within each of the ten skill levels, wages rose above the entry level by number of years in the program.

sion—the maintenance of sports fields, parks, and highway grounds, and maintenance and clerical work in libraries, museums, and public offices. In 1976, 60–65 percent of total program employment was concentrated in the one hundred and sixty factories that make up the industrial centers program.[5]

In the Social Employment Act of 1969 the national government accepted responsibility for providing employment for handicapped and other workers who cannot find work in the private or regular public sectors.[6] Responsibility for organizing, administering, and financing the program was assigned to the Ministry of Social Affairs. The task of actually providing employment was delegated to municipal governments, which must both recruit a work force from the eligible population and insure that an adequate volume of work is available. Municipalities may function alone or in concert with other municipalities, and they may operate their programs directly or assign responsibility to a special organization with its own quasi-legal status. The organizational unit for administering the program is called a *werkverband* in either case.[7] The municipality is subject to a comprehensive set of regulations regarding management and administrative procedures, accounting and reporting standards, control and oversight structures, the nature of the work provided and of the work place, the admission of employees, the assignment of workers to activities and to wage classes, and the procedures for marketing the product.

The law requires that each municipality or group establish a social employment commission to give advice on which proposed workers should be admitted to the program and on the structure and operation of the *werkverband*. The commission is composed of a member of the municipal council (chairman), three people proposed by the trade unions, and a representative of the national Ministry of Social Affairs. Other members can be added, including representatives of employer groups.[8]

5. In 1976 the average factory employed 225 workers, compared with 35 in 1955 and 108 in 1965.

6. The preamble of the act (Wet Sociale Werkvoorziening) states: "We have considered it desirable to provide regulations concerning the provision of adapted employment, aimed at conservation, restoration or stimulation of the working capacity, on behalf of persons, who are capable to work, but for whom, mainly due to factors connected to their person, employment under normal circumstances is not or not yet available."

7. *Werkverbanden* are responsible to the municipal council, the ruling body of the municipality.

8. As is emphasized later, the composition of this commission is important, given the structure of financial incentives in the program.

While the commission is defined as "advisory," it has substantial de facto influence on the operation of the program.

The actual management of a municipality's *werkverband* is assigned to a manager, who is responsible for all aspects of the program and is assisted by foremen, instructors, and administrative personnel. The government has issued a set of operating guidelines that must be followed by the *werkverband* manager. One important guideline is that the work activities must rehabilitate and improve the participants' working capacity. Another guideline is that the work must meet an economic or social need—it must not be "make work." Finally, the marketing of the output must be done in a professional, businesslike way, not based on appeals for charity, and must not interfere with other employment "in an irresponsible way." No mention is made of the desirability of covering operating costs with sales revenue.

To be eligible for the program, a nonaged person must be able to work but unable to find work under normal conditions because of personal circumstances.[9] This rather vague criterion is interpreted and applied by each municipality through the procedures adopted for the selection and admission of workers. While the municipality ultimately offers the employment contract to a worker, substantial control over admission is exercised by a permanent placement subcommittee of the social employment commission. The subcommittee's recommendation is made only after obtaining full education and employment records on a candidate, a rather complete set of medical and psychological tests, and the recommendation of medical and social work personnel who have examined the candidate.

Once admitted, a worker is placed in a work rehabilitation or a test and training center where, during a few weeks or months, an adapted work function is developed. After this time the worker is assigned a job and a wage group that depend on his skill and the responsibilities that he is judged to be capable of handling.[10]

Because workers are paid a wage that is approximately equivalent to that of their counterparts in the private sector despite the latter's higher productivity, and because many of the activities in the program do not

9. A worker must be judged capable of attaining a minimum of one-third of normal productivity in the adapted circumstances of the program (a limited number of persons not capable of attaining this minimum are admitted into the program).

10. Detailed guidelines and job descriptions for the ten wage groups to which assignments can be made have been issued by the Ministry of Social Affairs.

Table 1. Subsidy Categories in the Dutch Social Employment Program

Subsidy percentage	Subsidy
100	Presence, travel, and lodging expenses for members and invited experts of program committees and subcommittees
	Wages and social costs of workers engaged in projects carried out on behalf of the national government
	Wages and social costs of workers eligible for "Subsidy for Special Groups in Social Employment Decree" of September 30, 1968
90	Wages and social costs of workers in nonrevenue-yielding activities
75 or 90	Wages and social costs of workers in revenue-yielding activities
	Medical care costs
50	Salaries, honorariums, and social costs of persons preparing reports on candidates for placement and selection
	Salaries and other costs of managing personnel
	Necessary costs of schooling and educational activities for younger and older workers
	Expenses for compensation to workers and savings schemes of workers
80	*Werkverband* deficit accruing to the account of the municipality after accounting for other subsidies, sales revenue, and miscellaneous income

Source: Wet Sociale Werkvoorziening (Social Employment Act) of 1967, as amended.

yield revenue, public subsidization is necessary. The subsidy arrangement is complex. The public grant is not based on the total costs or deficit of a *werkverband*. Rather, rates of subsidization vary by both the category of cost and the nature of the activity (see table 1). While the worker wage costs in the revenue-yielding activities (primarily the industrial centers) are subsidized at a 75 percent rate, those in the nonrevenue-yielding activities have a subsidy rate of 90 percent. However, a supplemental subsidy can raise the rate for revenue-yielding activities to 90 percent.[11] The major categories of cost on which a subsidy is not paid are materials, equipment, supplies, and facilities. One final subsidy arrangement allows the Ministry of Interior Affairs to cover 80 percent of any remaining costs out of the municipal fund. This insures that a municipality will be liable for only a very small share of the total costs of the program.

11. The supplemental subsidy is paid by the minister of social affairs upon request of the municipality.

Finally, because workers who have exhausted unemployment benefits shift rather automatically into the disability benefits program, it and the Social Employment program are closely related. The disability transfer program provides benefits up to about 80 percent of normal earnings to workers (including the self-employed) who, for physical or psychological reasons, are declared to be eligible. Recently it has grown at a rate of about 20 percent a year and now supports a recipient population of 530,000—nearly 13 percent of the Dutch labor force.[12] It is generally conceded that the eligibility criteria for the program are not rigorously applied and that medical and psychological personnel do not have the capability to monitor the health status of recipients (as is required by law). Social Employment workers generally can transfer out of the employment program and into the cash disability program. Alternatively, if their wage income before disablement exceeded about 125 percent of their Social Employment wage, they can receive cash benefits from the disability program to supplement their wage.[13]

Growth in Employment and Costs

From 1955 to 1976 the number of workers employed in the Social Employment program grew from 8,800 to over 64,000, with major spurts of growth occurring from 1965 to 1969 (due largely to the admission of severely handicapped workers into the program in 1965) and from 1971

12. The incidence of personal characteristics defined as handicaps or disabilities is substantially greater in the Netherlands than in the United States. For disorders provable by a clinical test, the disability rates are comparable. However, Dutch rates for mental and musculoskeletal disorders are more than five times those of U.S. rates. John H. Miller, "Preliminary Report on Disability Insurance," attributes this to the generosity of the Dutch social security benefits. See *Reports of Consultants on Actuarial and Definitional Aspects of Social Security Disability Insurance,* Subcommittee on Social Security of the House Committee on Ways and Means, 94:2 (GPO, 1976), app. A, pp. 42–45.

13. Social Employment workers with relatively high predisability earnings are entitled to supplemental income (in addition to the program wage) under the disability program to assure them 90 percent of their previous income. In practice, however, workers have often received over 100 percent and up to 125 percent of their predisability earnings. Before August 1976 the supplementation was based on a "standard" Social Employment wage which was very low, and even workers whose wages were above the standard received supplemental benefits as if their wages were at the standard. A new standard wage arrangement, in effect since August 1976, reduces, but does not eliminate, the chance of a worker receiving more income (from the Social Employment and disability benefit programs) after than before his disablement.

to 1976 (due primarily to the recession and high unemployment rates).[14] In the latter period, employment grew from nearly 44,000 in 1970, to 50,000 in 1973, to more than 64,000 in 1976. In 1976, the program accounted for 1.5 percent of total Dutch employment, varying from 0.8 percent to 3.0 percent among the eleven provinces. The open-air and administrative components of the program, which employed less than 13,000 workers, or about 30 percent of the total, in 1970, accounted for 35 percent by 1973 and 42 percent, or nearly 24,000 workers, by 1975.

Total program revenues, which approximate total costs, grew from 660 million guilders ($264 million, at 2.50 guilders per dollar) in 1970 to over 1,700 million guilders ($680 million) in 1975. Meantime the subsidy provided by the national government grew from 460 million guilders ($184 million) to 1,270 million guilders ($508 million). Sales revenue grew from 168 million guilders ($66.4 million) to 362 million guilders ($144.8 million) in the 1970–75 period.

In 1970, revenue from the sale of output accounted for about one-third of the total revenue of the industrial centers; 65 percent came from the national government subsidies and 2 percent from municipal subsidies. Sales revenue as a proportion of the total fell continuously during the six years, and by 1975 it accounted for only 27 percent of total revenue. With the relative share of the municipal subsidy constant, the national share rose to nearly 70 percent in 1975. The net result, then, was a significant shift in the burden of costs to the national government.

In the open-air and administrative projects component of the program, sales revenue rose from 4 percent in 1970 to 8 percent in 1972, remaining at 8 percent through 1975. During this period, however, the contribution of municipalities to program costs fell from 8 percent to 5 percent. The share of the budget covered by the national government subsidy fell from a high of 89 percent in 1971 to 84 percent in 1972, but by 1975 had risen to 87 percent.

Because the growth of the costs of the programs has exceeded the growth of employment in the industrial centers, the total cost per worker has risen rapidly over the period: in 1970 it stood at 16,000 guilders ($6,400); by 1975 it had more than doubled, totaling 36,000 guilders ($14,400). The change in the sources of revenue caused an even more radical shift in the public subsidy per worker. Whereas in 1970 taxpayers were contributing about 10,000 guilders ($4,000) in subsidy for each

14. Much of the material in this section is from Haveman, "Benefit-Cost and Policy Analysis," table 2, p. 53.

worker employed, by 1975 the contribution was nearly 26,000 guilders ($10,400). This per worker figure is about one-third more than the national minimum wage and about 110 percent of the wage income of the modal worker.

While costs per worker have also increased in the open-air and administrative centers, both the absolute level and the growth have been less than in the industrial centers. Total costs per worker stood at about 13,000 guilders in 1970 and had risen to nearly 21,000 guilders in 1975. This 1975 figure is only about 60 percent of per worker costs in the industrial centers. Clearly, this is to be expected as the costs for raw materials and supervision in the industrial centers are greater.

What is not expected, however, is the contrast in pattern of growth in the subsidy per worker in the two kinds of centers. This subsidy stood at 11,000 guilders in 1970 for the open-air and administrative projects, or 107 percent of that in the industrial centers. By 1975, the subsidy in the open-air and administrative projects had risen to over 19,000 guilders. While this growth is, in itself, significant, it is nothing like the more than doubling in the per worker subsidy in the industrial center segment of the program. By 1975, the subsidy for the administrative projects stood at only 75 percent of that in the industrial centers.

These substantial increases in the taxpayer subsidy per worker stand as the most striking aspect of the data on employment and revenue. While the causes of this increase cannot be identified with precision, the most important ones probably are: the significant increase in the minimum wage over the period; the rapid increase in social security taxes for employed workers that have had to be covered by the program; the failure of sales revenue to grow as rapidly as program costs; and the increase in raw material and supervisory personnel costs due to the general inflation. The patterns of real program growth can be observed in the comparison of program financial indicators and relevant variables in the economy as a whole in table 2. As the table indicates, the growth in the program was substantially greater than the growth in the Dutch economy over the 1970–75 period. As a result, the economic burden of the program increased—by 1976 the program's budget was over 1 percent of net national product. Indeed, by 1975 it took all of the gross wage income in a modal family plus 10 percent of such wage income in a second family to support the subsidy for one industrial center worker. This increasing burden is attributable primarily to the rapid growth in per worker costs and subsidies in the industrial centers component of the program.

Table 2. Growth in Indicators of Dutch Social Employment Program Relative to Growth in Selected Dutch Aggregate Economic Indicators, 1970–75

| Year | Cost as a percentage of net national product | | Subsidy as a percentage of labor cost per private-sector worker | | Subsidy as a percentage of modal family wage income | |
	Total program	Total governmental subsidy	Industrial center worker	Administrative and open-air center worker	Industrial center worker	Administrative and open-air center worker
1970	0.62	0.46	67.2	72.0	83.1	89.0
1971	0.65	0.48	74.2	63.9	90.0	77.6
1972	0.68	0.50	78.1	71.2	96.5	88.1
1973	0.73	0.55	77.8	80.1	99.4	102.2
1974	0.83	0.62	82.0	70.1	108.6	93.5
1975	0.92	0.71	86.3	65.1	109.1	82.4

Source: Robert H. Haveman, "A Benefit-Cost and Policy Analysis of the Netherlands' Social Employment Program" (Leiden, Netherlands: University of Leiden, Mar. 1, 1977; processed), table 5, p. 62.

Program Structure and Performance

It is clear that a complex set of organizations and individuals interact within an equally complex set of regulations and subsidy provisions to determine the performance of the Social Employment program. The following conclusions regarding the effect of the program's structure on its performance are based on analysis of the provisions of the law, data regarding program operation, and discussions with individuals involved with the program at all levels.

1. The managers of the *werkverbanden,* municipal officials, and members of the social employment commissions see the provision of work to people admitted to the program to be the overriding objective. The coverage of costs by sales revenue is not considered an important objective. Hence, the structure of the program provides only weak incentives either to increase sales or to economize on costs.

From the manager's point of view, any operating deficit is passed on to the municipality, which in turn passes on the vast bulk of the deficit to the national government. Indeed, except under unique circumstances, no municipality has to cover more than 2 percent of worker wage costs out of its own budget. For this reason, neither *werkverband* managers nor other officials perceive a penalty if the program deficit increases, or reward if the deficit is reduced. Similarly, there is no reward for reducing costs or increasing sales revenue and no penalty if costs drift up or sales revenue falls off.

The lack of incentives for cost reduction or sales increase is reinforced by the composition of the social employment commissions. Representatives of industry organizations and trade unions typically hold positions on these committees. Both groups tend to see Social Employment program sales as a threat to their own interests and are not likely to be strong proponents of efforts to increase them.[15]

2. Because of the large subsidy to administrative and open-air workers, the open-ended and undefined nature of the tasks that can be performed, and the lack of effective control of the growth of these components of the program, municipal governments are able to transfer the budget costs of activities serving the municipality from the municipal budget to the national budget.

Through the Social Employment program and the municipal fund of the Ministry of Interior Affairs, the national government covers 98 percent of the costs of administrative and open-air Social Employment workers. These workers can be assigned to numerous jobs that have traditionally been the responsibility of municipal governments (the operation of swimming pools, museums, and municipal offices, and open-air activities in maintaining parks, sports fields, or municipal grounds). As a result, municipal officials often find it in their interest to expand these components of the program, thus shifting costs onto the national budget. The national government has very limited control over this.

3. The relaxation of eligibility criteria, the rapidly rising benefit levels, and the rapid growth of the disability program have diminished both the referrals of people in the disability program to the Social Employment program and the financial incentive for people in the disability program to accept work. They have also led to a relaxation of eligibility criteria in the Social Employment program.

There is evidence that the program is increasingly serving workers who have difficulty in securing regular employment because of low skill,

15. One aspect of the incentive structure should be noted, however. While the average burden of costs borne by the municipality is very low, the marginal burden of increases in the deficit (whether due to cost increases or sales revenue decreases) rises from zero to 20 percent once the center's deficit (defined as total costs less the sum of the basic subsidy, the special subsidy, sales revenue, and miscellaneous income) goes above zero. The marginal burden of increases in costs varies among the types of costs.

age, or some other personal characteristic, rather than a readily distinguishable handicap. For example, while the program maintains a comprehensive, fifteen-category classification of the types of handicap of workers in the program, "not elsewhere classified" is a large and rapidly growing category. In 1971, 10 percent of Social Employment workers were in this category; by 1975, nearly 15 percent were. From 1971 to 1975 the number of individuals in the category grew from 4,600 to 8,200; over 30 percent of the workers in the administrative component of the program are so classified. Using reasonable assumptions regarding the composition of the workers leaving this program component, it appears that about 50 percent of all workers entering the administrative component of the program in recent years have been placed in the "not elsewhere classified" category.

4. The provision of income (wages plus disability benefits) to Social Employment workers equal to at least 90 percent of previous income levels and the rapid growth in this income in recent years have reduced the flow of workers from the Social Employment program to open industry or regular public sector employment.

A Social Employment worker views his potential salary in open industry as little, if any, above the minimum wage. This wage would typically be below—and in some cases, substantially below—his combined income from the Social Employment and disability programs. There is little incentive for such a worker to attempt a transition since there is strain involved and little economic reward. Similarly, because of rapidly rising disability benefits, a worker not inclined to work may experience little penalty in moving from the Social Employment program to the disability program. No work is required in the latter program and little financial sacrifice may be involved, especially for workers whose Social Employment wage is not already supplemented by disability benefits. The decrease in the flow of Social Employment workers to alternative employment is one of the most notable trends in the program. While 3,400 workers (8 percent of the total) made the transition in 1969, only 1,000 (1.6 percent of the total) did so in 1975. In addition to the small financial incentive for workers to seek normal private or public employment, the slack economy during this period explains some of the trend.

5. While the national government has responsibility for providing financial subsidies to the Social Employment program and for setting standards and organizational requirements, it is able to exercise little financial and economic control over either the growth of employment in the program, or the financial costs of the program.

In a very real sense, the national government is simply in the position of paying bills submitted by organizations (municipalities, and through them, *werkverbanden*) irrespective of social costs or taxpayer burden. The instruments of national government control consist of policy statements and advice by the minister of social affairs, examination and evaluation reports on *werkverband* operation submitted by government evaluation teams (whose reports can lead to denial of the supplemental subsidy), stipulation of budget goals and the communication of them to municipalities, revision of operation and admission criteria so as to constrain decisions of municipalities and *werkverbanden,* presence of government representatives on some of the municipality governing bodies, and annual statistical reports required of *werkverbanden* on costs, revenues, employment, and structure. Although the effectiveness of these instruments is difficult to assess, both the nature of the instruments and conversation with those subject to and administering them suggest a serious lack of program control by the national government.

In sum, the existing program structure is not designed to encourage effective economic performance in the operation of the program. The national government (and, through it, taxpayers) pays the bill, while municipal governments and *werkverbanden* make operating decisions. Program managers or municipal officials have little incentive to control costs or to increase revenues. There is little effective accountability of municipal officials and program managers to the national government. And program managers, through the manipulation of the program, can shift the burden of traditional municipal costs onto the national government. Moreover, there is little incentive for Social Employment workers to move from the program to employment in open industry.

A Benefit-Cost Analysis of the Program

Public employment programs have characteristics similar to those of many other public activities. They use real resources of society—labor, materials, facilities, machines—and they produce outputs that are presumably of benefit to society. These benefits are wide-ranging and include the products produced in the program, the increase in productivity of the participants in the program, and the increase in the psychological well-being of the participants and their families. As a consequence, the standard techniques for evaluating the worth of public programs in general are also applicable to public employment programs.

The analytical framework of benefit-cost analysis measures all of the benefits produced by a public undertaking and all of the costs the program creates. If the benefits exceed the costs, the project is judged a worthwhile social undertaking (although it may have to compete with alternatives for scarce public funds); if there are net costs that cannot be eliminated either by increasing the benefits or decreasing the costs, the continuation of the program should be questioned.

However, some programs that fail to yield net benefits may be direct substitutes for activities that also have net costs. It may well be that if the Social Employment program did not exist, participants in that program would be eligible for full disability program benefits. While this latter program is an income transfer program, its structure and high benefit levels suggest that it may lead to reductions in work effort and, as a result, it may generate net economic costs. If this program and its structure are assumed not to be subject to change, society might gain if the participant remained in the Social Employment program, even though it was evaluated to have net costs. Only if the net cost of participating in the Social Employment program exceeded that for which it substitutes should continuation of the Social Employment program be questioned. (Unfortunately, no estimates of reductions in labor supply or other efficiency effects of the disability benefits program are available to enable a comparison.)

This discussion neglects the equity or distributional effects of the program. For most social programs, income redistribution is an important objective. Since the Social Employment program and its fixed substitute, the disability benefits program, assist individuals with similar types of problems and of labor-market opportunities, it is unnecessary to include the income redistribution effects of Social Employment in the analysis.

In estimating the economic costs of a program for the purpose of a benefit-cost evaluation, only those effects that actually displace or preclude society's resources from other uses are included in the calculations. Hence, the cost of supervisory personnel is taken to be their productivity if they were employed elsewhere in the economy; it is measured by the wage they are paid. However, the forgone output from employing program participants who would otherwise be unemployed is zero—and the wages paid to them are treated as a transfer of income and not as a real cost. Similarly, outputs are valued by the willingness of buyers to pay for them. This is reflected in the price of the outputs if they are sold in a competitive and well-functioning market. (If willingness to pay prices is accepted, it should be noted, the underlying distribution of income that determines these prices is accepted; economic efficiency is again emphasized.) Within this framework, an employment program like the Social Employment program will have net social benefits only if it can use productive resources valued at a given amount and produce various outcomes whose value exceeds that amount.[16]

Calculating Benefits and Costs

The categories of benefits and costs for the Social Employment program, the nature of welfare gains and losses in each category, and the procedures for estimating each gain or loss in an ideal benefit-cost analysis are presented below.[17] Estimates of partial net benefits are calculated for 1973.

SOCIAL BENEFITS. The outputs produced by the Social Employment program are many and varied. Some are material in nature—the production of furniture, for example—while others are services, such as the keeping of financial records.

If the economy is an effectively competitive economy, and if the outputs of the centers are sold on the open market or arranged by competitive bids, the price at which the outputs are sold is an accurate reflection of

16. This discussion presumes that the project should be evaluated from society's point of view. However, benefits and costs could be calculated from the point of view of taxpayers. Interest would center on direct expenditures and receipts in the public sector rather than on full economic benefits and costs. That this is different from the perspective of society as a whole can be seen by considering wage payments to otherwise unemployed program participants. From society's point of view, such payments entail no costs at all—income is simply transferred from one member of society to another. From the taxpayers' point of view, however, such payments are a cost—they result in an increase in tax liability.

From the point of view of participants in the program, their benefits must compare favorably with the costs of their involvement in the program, if there is no coercion to participate in the program. There is coercion, however, to participate in many manpower programs.

17. This discussion presumes that reasonably competitive markets prevail and that monopoly, externalities, and other market imperfections are not serious. Modifications to this framework that are required in the presence of these problems are described in the paper by Kemper and Moss in this volume. See also Bent Andersen, *Work or Support: An Economic and Social Analysis of Substitute Permanent Employment* (Paris: Organisation for Economic Co-operation and Development, 1966).

their social value per unit. However, if the economy is not competitive, or if the outputs are sold under special noncompetitive arrangements, a shadow price must be calculated. This price would seek to reflect the willingness of the purchasers of the output to pay for it. In concept, this willingness to pay is an accurate measure of the real social benefit of the output V.

Data on the sales revenue of each of the industrial centers for 1973 are taken as a good estimate of the value of V.[18] Because the output produced by these centers is sold via a contract with a private sector business or a governmental unit or on the open market, it is likely that the output is sold at a competitive price. This is especially true if the contracts are obtained through a competitive bidding process, as is often the case.

The increased productivity of participants, because of both explicit training activities within the Social Employment program and simply the effect of being in a work setting and engaging in work activities, has characteristics of an investment. Once the increase in productivity is attained, it is likely to persist at some level into the future. This future value for any given social employment worker can be reflected, at least in concept, by calculating the increase in a participant's economic productivity in future years attributable to the program, and discounting this stream back to the present, using an appropriate discount rate. This present value of increased productivity is labeled P.

No reliable estimates of the value of the training are available. There is some weak evidence that the gain in productivity from participating in the program is not substantial, however—the very low, and falling, number of participants who make the transition from the program to private or normal public sector employment. Therefore this variable is assigned a lower-bound estimate of zero. On the basis of rough estimates of worker progress through the wage groups of the program and an assumed duration for which this productivity effect persists (see appendix A), a positive, upper-bound estimate is also assigned to this variable.

The well-being or satisfaction that a worker experiences by being a

18. Sales revenue data may be biased upward because buyers of output are willing to pay a premium over the market price in order to aid handicapped workers. They may be biased downward, however, because the subsidized labor cost of the centers allows them to enter bids on contracts that are below the effective market price of the product or service. Since the magnitude of these biases is unknown, sales are assumed to be a reliable estimate of V. It is judged that, if anything, this estimate is biased downward to some extent.

participant in the program and that results in increased productivity is reflected in productivity improvements. There may be additional gains in well-being stemming from the pleasure of contributing to an ongoing productive process or the social interactions with other workers. This category of social-psychological well-being benefit W is assumed to be unmeasurable.

Another unmeasurable category is the reduction in real social costs or increases in social output that might result because of the improved social-psychological well-being of the worker. Reductions in hospital, doctor, or institutional care costs attributable to the improved psychological well-being of the worker could benefit taxpayers, the worker's family, or the worker himself, depending on who would bear the costs of this treatment if it were required. The value of this benefit M would, in concept, be equal to the cost of the care provided to the worker if he were *not* in the program minus the cost of the care provided the worker when he is in the program—for example, the value of the increased work activity of close relatives of the handicapped person who would be able to hold a job if the person were employed.

An even more distant benefit could be called a third-party or external benefit. Citizens generally might experience satisfaction simply by knowing that their community (or nation) was undertaking a program to aid handicapped or low-skilled workers. This benefit T is equal to the willingness of citizens to pay for the satisfaction that they are experiencing, even if they do not have to pay for it. Again, for any given worker, it would persist only as long as the worker was participating in the program. This benefit also is assumed to be unmeasurable.

SOCIAL COSTS. The output O that is forgone by society because a worker is participating in the program, and not doing something else, can be measured by the wage income that would be earned by the worker if he were not participating in the program, presuming he would be paid the market value for his work. For example, if a person might be, say, keeping the books of a local small business if he were not participating in the program, this output would be lost to society.

In the absence of an experimental design, it is impossible to estimate what participants would be doing if they were not in the program. Some of them would undoubtedly be doing nothing in the way of productive work. Others would be engaging in some part-time free-lance productive activities, for which they might or might not receive remuneration. Still others would be employed in private industry. However, the low and falling number of program participants that transfer from the program to private employment suggests that their options are considerably less attractive than the program. In this analysis the lower bound of the true value of output forgone is assumed to be zero. For the upper bound, workers are assumed to have engaged in activities that would have yielded them income equal to 30 percent of their wage costs in the program.[19]

The operation of the program uses other scarce resources that could be employed in alternative ways. These program operating costs R include the remuneration (including fringe benefits) of supervisory, administrative, and medical workers, materials and sales costs, machinery, building, and other facilities costs, worker transportation costs, the medical and physical training costs incurred on behalf of participants (to the extent that such costs are over and above the costs that would be incurred for participants if they were not working in the program), and other program costs to the extent that they represent the use of real resources in the program.[20] (The wages of program participants, including social insurance taxes, are treated as transfer payments.)

Data for 1973 on the total costs of each of the industrial centers, and the composition of these costs by sixteen categories, collected by the Ministry of Social Affairs are used as an estimate of operating costs R. Presuming that the inputs that these costs represent were purchased in competitive markets, these costs should be accurate reflections of the social costs that the use of these inputs implies.[21]

If the output of the Social Employment program displaces some output in the private sector or normal public sector, and if some of the resources

19. This value would be 40–50 percent of the earnings of the lowest paid workers in the private sector in Holland, allowing for spells of unemployment.

20. The costs of municipal officials, employment office officials, members of advisory committees, and employees of the ministry concerned with the program (whether or not these costs are reimbursed) would be included in this category.

21. If there is a bias present, it would be in the direction of understating costs. This judgment is based on what appear to be excessively low costs for facility rental and equipment depreciation for some of the centers—perhaps because buildings and equipment are owned by the municipalities and provided to the centers for a nominal charge, or because the centers own the buildings without mortgages and hence register no charge for them in their accounts. Because the services of the facilities or the machinery used represent a real economic input, they should be valued at the price they would bring if sold or rented on the open market. The estimates would also be biased downward because *no* costs are included for the time of municipal officials, members of advisory committees to the municipality and the ministry, members of the placement committee, and all of the employees of the ministry who are concerned with administration of the Social Employment program.

(primarily labor) thereby released are idle, the social cost D of the functioning of the Social Employment program equals the lost output due to the increased unemployment in other parts of the economy. Indeed, if the program output displaced an equivalent amount of private sector production and if none of the resources released by the private sector were reemployed, this cost would be equal to the value of program output V. In this case, the net value of the program output would be zero, and any real resources used in producing it would be wasted.[22] This component is extremely difficult to estimate. No direct data on it are available. The lower-bound estimate used here is zero, implying a fully employed economy in which all of the displaced resources are reemployed. The upper-bound estimate presumes that 70 percent of the displaced labor, and all of the other displaced factors of production, are reemployed (see appendix B).[23]

Estimates of Benefits and Costs

The social benefits B from one year's operation of the Social Employment program can be summarized as the value V of program output, plus the present value P of increased productivity of participants, plus the increase W in the social-psychological well-being of participants, plus the reduced medical or psychological care costs M stemming from their increased well-being, plus third-party benefits T stemming from the increased well-being. The social costs C of one year's operation are the value O of forgone participant output, plus the value R of program operating costs, including supervisory salary costs, material costs, machinery and facilities costs, and incremental training costs, plus the value D of forgone output from displacement of private-sector and normal public-sector resources not reemployed. The net social benefit N of the program is the difference between the social benefits B and social costs C.

If only those variables for which some estimate for 1973 is available are used, it is possible to calculate partial net benefits PN:

$$PN = (V + P) - (O + R + D).$$

22. Alternatively, this displacement effect could be treated as an offset to the value of program output and incorporated in the benefit side of the analysis, as Kemper and Moss do in their paper in this volume.

23. The upper-bound estimate was based on judgment. The only empirical support for it is found in Robert H. Haveman and John V. Krutilla, *Unemployment, Idle Capacity, and the Evaluation of Public Expenditures: National and Regional Analyses* (Johns Hopkins Press for Resources for the Future, 1968).

The resulting value of *PN* can be positive or negative; if it is negative, it represents net social costs.

If this calculated value of *PN* for the program or an individual center is, say, $-x$ guilders, the following statement can be made: Neglecting social-psychological well-being benefits, the Social Employment program (or industrial center *z*) imposes a net cost on society of *x* guilders. For the program (or a center) to be judged as contributing to net social welfare, the sum of benefits deriving from the increased social-psychological well-being of workers $(W + M + T)$ must be greater than *x* guilders. If *PN* is positive, then the program (or center) is socially beneficial even if there are no social-psychological benefits. To the extent there are such benefits, the program's justification is that much stronger.

The most favorable evaluation of the program uses upper-bound values of all benefits and lower-bound values of all costs.[24] If a negative value results, it is a lower-bound estimate of the net social costs required to produce the unmeasurable social-psychological well-being benefits. The least favorable evaluation of the program uses lower-bound values of all benefits and upper-bound values of all costs.[25] If a negative value results, it is an upper-bound estimate of the net social costs required to produce the unmeasurable social-psychological well-being benefits. A third estimate uses only accounting values in the calculation and neglects all of those elements of benefit and cost for which no firm estimates are available.[26] It assumes, in effect, that *P, O,* and *D* equal zero—the lower-bound estimate of each.

From these procedures, the following estimates of partial net benefits or costs of the industrial centers component of the Social Employment program in 1973 are obtained:

Values used	Net social cost (millions of guilders)	Cost per worker (guilders)
Most favorable	65.1	2,365
Least favorable	273.7	9,950
Accounting only	107.2	3,896

24. The calculation can be stated as $PN = (V + 1{,}531 \text{ guilders}) - R$; *P* is 1,531 guilders (upper-bound estimate); *O* is zero (lower-bound estimate); *D* is zero (lower-bound estimate). The value of *P* is derived in appendix A.

25. The calculation can be stated as $PN = V - 0.3$ (wage costs per worker) $+ R + 0.1$ (sales revenue per worker); *P* is zero (lower-bound estimate); *O* is 30 percent of wage costs per worker (upper-bound estimate); *D* is 10 percent of sales revenue per worker (upper-bound estimate).

26. The calculation can be stated as $PN = V - R$; *P, O,* and *D* are zero (lower-bound estimates).

Table 3. Distribution of 155 Industrial Centers by Partial Net Social Benefits or Costs per Worker, by Values Assigned to Benefits and Costs, 1973

Net social costs (−) or benefits (+) (guilders[a])	Number of centers		
	Most favorable values	Least favorable values	Accounting values only
−14,000 or less	1	11	2
−14,000 to −12,000	1	17	0
−12,000 to −10,000	0	41	4
−10,000 to −8,000	5	47	5
−8,000 to −6,000	8	31	22
−6,000 to −4,000	21	7	34
−4,000 to −3,000	19	1	22
−3,000 to −2,000	22	0	28
−2,000 to −1,000	29	0	15
−1,000 to 0	22	0	12
0 to +1,000	13	0	5
+1,000 to +2,000	6	0	5
+2,000 to +3,000	4	0	1
+3,000 to +4,000	3	0	0
+4,000 or more	1	0	0
Total	155	155	155

Source: Haveman, "A Benefit-Cost and Policy Analysis," p. 143.
a. Dollar comparisons can be made by using an exchange rate of 2.50 guilders per dollar.

At a minimum, then, the 1973 social costs of providing whatever social-psychological well-being benefits the Social Employment program might have yielded are 65 million guilders and could be as great as 274 million guilders. A reasonable middle estimate of 1973 social costs would be 125–150 million guilders. A medium estimate of partial net social costs per worker would be 5,000–6,000 guilders.

Given the increase in costs since 1973, combined with the lagging sales revenues for the program, partial net social costs per worker in 1977 are likely to be from 8,000 to 11,000 guilders. If this estimate of social costs per worker applied to both industrial center and open-air and administrative workers, the total social cost of the program in 1977 would be approximately 550 million to 700 million guilders.[27]

Because the centers have substantially different results in terms of sales and costs, the partial net social benefits (+) or costs (−) per worker are estimated for each center in table 3. Twenty-seven of the 155 centers yield a positive value for net social benefits when the most favorable values are accepted. This suggests that in those centers, social bene-

27. This is about 125–150 guilders per employed worker in the Netherlands.

fits are being produced over and above the social-psychological well-being benefits. None of the centers display positive values when the least favorable values are used, and the bulk of the centers have net social costs of from 6,000 guilders to 12,000 guilders per worker. The distribution of net social benefits or costs based on only accounting values is intermediate to the other two distributions, with eleven centers estimated to yield net social benefits.

Lessons for the United States

What lessons for public policy toward less productive workers in the United States does this evaluation of the Dutch Social Employment program have? In this section a few tentative suggestions are put forth. First, however, the broad outlines and trends of U.S. policy toward disabled persons are described. Discussion of policy targeted to the disadvantaged—antipoverty policy—is omitted because it has been described often and is generally well understood.[28] It consists of cash welfare (aid to families with dependent children and supplemental security income), in-kind transfers (food stamps and medicaid), and training and education. More recently, public service employment for those disadvantaged workers who are expected to work has been proposed as a component of welfare reform, and experimentation with supported work has been undertaken.[29] There is no program of public subsidization of sheltered workshops or direct employment of disadvantaged workers in effect, however. On the other hand, policy toward the disabled is generally not well understood. Increasingly, the group of persons assisted by disability policy includes workers who are classified as disadvantaged or poor.

Policy toward Disabled Persons

According to 1972 estimates, 15 percent of the adult, nonaged, noninstitutionalized population of the United States is classified as disabled.[30]

28. See Robert H. Haveman, ed., *A Decade of Federal Antipoverty Programs: Achievements, Failures, and Lessons* (Academic Press, 1977).

29. See the paper by Kemper and Moss in this volume for a description and discussion of the Supported Work demonstrations.

30. Much of the descriptive information in this section is from Sar A. Levitan and Robert Taggert, *Jobs for the Disabled* (Johns Hopkins University Press, 1977);

About one-third of these nearly 16 million people are so disabled that they cannot work at all, and another sixth cannot work regularly. These two groups are classified as "severely disabled." About two-thirds of the 10.3 million persons (about 7 million) who can work at least some amount do work either part or full time, usually in very low-paid positions.

Of the 8 million severely disabled persons, about 2 million were receiving income from the disability insurance program in 1972.[31] The median level of these benefits was about $2,100 per year. Since 1972 the number of program recipients has grown rapidly,[32] and by 1976, expenditures had reached more than $9 billion a year. In addition, disabled persons receive cash transfer benefits from about ten other federal programs and five state and local programs whose total benefits are about *four times* the expenditures of the disability insurance program.[33] They also receive medical assistance under medicare and medicaid, both of which target a substantial proportion of their benefits on the disabled,[34] and a number of Veterans Administration programs. In 1976, public expenditures on medical programs that aid the disabled totaled about $30 billion.

A number of programs for disabled persons are designed to improve their work capacity and to assist them in finding jobs. The most important of these is the joint federal-state vocational rehabilitation program. While

---

unless otherwise noted statistics for 1972 related to the disabled are from Mordechai E. Lando and Aaron Krute, "Disability Insurance: Program Issues and Research," *Social Security Bulletin*, vol. 39 (October 1976), pp. 3–17.

31. About 50 percent of the severely disabled men who could not work at all received benefits.

32. From 1969 to 1975, the number of recipients in the disability insurance program rose from 2.5 million to 4.4 million, and expenditures from $2.5 billion to $8.4 billion.

33. These programs include the supplemental security income program, the black lung program, and the Veterans Administration disability compensation and pension programs.

34. In 1973, 85–90 percent of the expenditures in these two programs benefited the disabled; see Bureau of Economic Research, Rutgers University, *An Evaluation of the Structure and Functions of Disability Programs: Year 1 Summary Report* (Rutgers University, 1975). This report estimated that federal expenditures on the disabled were $40.7 billion, including $18.5 billion in cash benefits and $20 billion in medical payments; state and local expenditures $11.6 billion; and private expenditures (primarily insurance benefits) $30.8 billion in 1973, a total of $83 billion (ibid.). A similar tabulation for 1976 would undoubtedly total over $100 billion.

each state administers its own rehabilitation program, the federal government pays 80 percent of the costs, in addition to making grants for facilities and personnel training. In 1976 about 1.4 million persons were served by these agencies and about 450,000 of them were described as rehabilitated. Expenditures in this program exceed $1 billion a year.[35]

About 7 million handicapped people were employed in 1972. About 20 percent of them earned less than $50 a week. Many of these low earnings handicapped people—about 400,000—are employed in sheltered workshops, where the wage rates are, by and large, less than $1 an hour. The workshops are generally a part of the nonprofit-nonpublic sector and receive little in the way of government subsidies.[36]

In recent years the transfer programs—in particular, the disability insurance program—have both relaxed eligibility standards and increased benefit levels to a significant degree. These changes have contributed, in all likelihood, to the rapid growth in the number of recipients and the volume of expenditures. Because of these changes, assistance is now provided to less productive persons more generally, as opposed to those with clear handicaps or physical disabilities. It has been estimated that nearly one-half of eligibility determinations in the disability insurance program are now based on vocational considerations (age, occupation, and educational factors) and not on the medical severity of the disability —and that this proportion is rising.[37]

Work and the Less Productive Worker

The Dutch experience with Social Employment contains a number of warnings pertinent to U.S. discussion regarding publicly provided or subsidized employment programs for less productive workers.[38] The potential size and budget cost of employment programs for less productive work-

35. In addition, payments of up to 1.5 percent of total disability insurance benefits are available annually to provide rehabilitation services for recipients. In fiscal 1975 more than $80 million was so spent.

36. Some of these workshops—for example, some Goodwill Industries enterprises—do receive subsidies from the federal government's vocational rehabilitation program.

37. Lando and Krute, "Disability Insurance."

38. The U.S. policy debate will also bring increased attention to such issues as the statement, interpretation, and application of eligibility criteria, the monitoring of beneficiaries' continued need, the integration of transfer programs for less productive workers (the problem of multiple benefits), and the work incentives implicit in program benefit schedules.

ers in the United States is extremely large. If policies regarding the degree of leniency in applying eligibility criteria in either cash transfer or public employment programs are not carefully monitored and if wage levels established for public employment are not held below prevailing wage levels, program rolls and expenditures could mushroom. The population with some potential claim for benefits or jobs will be very large and could easily expand if vocational, cultural, or social factors, as opposed to medical or psychological considerations, are substantial factors in determining eligibility.

While the objective of providing a job to everyone who wishes to work is laudable, it neglects the serious difficulties in structuring suitable and rewarding work activities, arranging for the sale of products produced at a price that reflects neither charity nor the subsidization of purchaser, and the development of subsidy arrangements that encourage the maximization of the net social benefits of the program. Indeed, even if these obstacles are overcome, the social costs of publicly providing work to less productive workers are large and may remain substantially in excess of the benefits of such an arrangement.

A major component of the social cost is the forgone productivity of the participants in the program. This cost is positively related to the skill level of participating workers—which in turn is positively related to the wage level established for public employment. High-wage programs—by attracting workers with high forgone opportunity costs—are less likely to be efficient in benefit-cost terms than programs designed for those with poor opportunities for employment in the private sector. Moreover, revenue-yielding programs employing participants with high forgone opportunities are likely to displace private employment, which also threatens their benefit-cost efficiency, unless the productivity of participants is equally high in the public employment program.

If an expanded federal program of public employment is to be undertaken, attention should be focused on the arrangements for publicly subsidizing such activities. Program managers should be given incentives to reduce costs (especially staff and supervisory costs), increase worker productivity, and increase sales revenue. Likewise, if the program is to involve grants to state or local governments, the subsidy arrangement should seek to encourage activities that have high social value and that are net marginal additions to public sector output, to constrain staff and supervisory costs, and to maximize worker productivity. Such incentives could tie the size of public grants or increases in managers' salaries to specified performance indicators. They would be particularly difficult to apply, however, in public programs producing nonmarketable outputs.

The transition of less productive workers from public employment programs with adapted work arrangements to regular public or private employment is not likely to be substantial, even when rehabilitation and training are part of the program. The transition is likely to be especially low when there is relatively high unemployment in the economy. The economic success of the program obviously depends in part on macroeconomic policies.

Public employment and income transfer programs for less productive workers should be carefully integrated to enable eligible individuals to increase their income through the employment program. They should also be structured to encourage participating workers to move into regular public or private employment. Thus transfer benefits should lie below the sum of transfer benefits plus earnings from public employment, which should, in turn, lie below potential earnings in regular public or private employment.

Appendix A: Calculation of Training and
Increased Productivity Benefits

The calculation of the benefits from increased worker productivity due to training, familiarity with the work place or work schedules, and accommodation to production procedures is difficult. Ideally, a worker's gain in productivity would be estimated by observing his productivity *with* and *without* participation in the Social Employment program. An alternative method is to observe both a group of program participants and a matched group of similar individuals over a period after which the former group has completed the program. It is the gap in productivity—as reflected in earnings—between the two groups over time that represents the contribution of the program, and that must be counted as a benefit. However, because most participants in the Social Employment program remain in it, this observation method is not possible.

The procedure adopted here is more crude than either of these methods. It is based on the presumption that the movement of a worker from one of the ten wage groups in the Social Employment program to a higher group means that he has attained a higher skill level, a higher competence, and, hence, greater productivity. The observed movement of a worker over time is taken to represent the contribution of the program to his skills and productivity. It is presumed also that the wage level in each group represents the value of the productivity of workers in that group. The correct measure of a worker's productivity would be what he could command in the open labor market, but there is no effective normal demand for Social Employment workers. However, the wage levels attached to the groups are likely to be good proxies of the upper-bound value of the productivity of workers in each group.

The change in a worker's productivity over time is indicated by how he changes wage groups over time. This presumes, of course, that the plant manager is able to evaluate accurately the productivity progress of a worker through time. Because there are no data on the progress of individual Social Employment workers through time, it is further assumed that a center that experiences very little growth or contraction in its size over time has the same group of workers from one period to the next. If that is the case, the change in the distribution of workers among the wage groups from one period to the next can be measured. This yields an estimate of the pattern of progress of workers through the wage groups through time. Observing this change between two years yields an estimate of the contribution of the program in the intervening year to the increased productivity of its work force.

Clearly the same group of workers is not employed in both periods. However, if centers with little growth or reduction in size can be identified, some of the problem caused by the interjection of new workers will be eliminated. The problem that remains is simply the substitution of new workers for those leaving. Such new workers may have higher skill levels than those leaving, or lower skill levels. On balance, however, one would expect the new entrants to have somewhat lower skill levels than those leaving. Hence, observation of the change in the distribution of workers in a center by wage group may yield an estimate of productivity growth that is biased downward to some unknown extent. However, because centers that have little change in size have been chosen, and because entering workers may well be placed in entering wage groups that are about the same as those of workers who leave, the bias is presumed not to be excessive.

To develop an estimate for 1973 a random sample of nineteen centers was chosen, and the distribution of workers by wage groups was obtained for each center for 1973, 1974, and 1975. This yielded thirty-eight observations of year-to-year changes in the distribution of workers by wage groups. The wage levels of each group for December 1973 were presumed to represent the structure of productivity among the workers. All of those that demonstrated an increase or decrease in the number of workers of 10 percent or more were discarded. This left a total of thirty-one observed changes in the distribution.

For each of the thirty-one distributions, the average wage level (using the 1973 structure) was calculated. Then, the difference between the average wage levels of two consecutive years was calculated. This difference is an estimate of the average advancement in wage levels—taken to represent productivity—of the workers in a center. Twenty-six of these had positive values. (The five with negative differences were presumed to reflect an excessive inflow of new, lower productivity workers and they were discarded.) The range of the estimated average differences was from 1 guilder a year to 221 guilders a year. The weighted mean of these annual average increments (using the number of workers in the center as weights) was calculated as 69.96 guilders a year. Hence, a value of 70 guilders per year was accepted as the contribution of one year's operation of the program to the increase in productivity of the average worker.

The question now becomes, how long will this one-year increment persist? Most studies have indicated that there is a rather rapid decay over time in the earnings difference between workers who entered a training program and those who did not—that after ten years, nearly all of the increment to productivity had faded away. Here it is assumed, more optimistically, that the estimated annual increment to productivity—70 guilders a year—persists for each worker for fifteen years, and then falls to zero. That increase in productivity is a stream of benefits through time. It is therefore difficult to use in a benefit-cost analysis because a benefit received in some future year is not worth as much as the same benefit received today. Thus, the present value of the stream of benefits must be calculated by discounting (a compound-interest type calculation). The present value P of a stream of annual benefits R_i is calculated as

$$P = \sum \frac{R_i}{(1 + r)^i},$$

where the interest rate r is 10 percent. The present value of increased productivity benefits based on 1973 wage data is 531 guilders per worker.

Appendix B: Calculation of Costs of Displaced Private Sector Employment

By producing output and selling it in the open market, Social Employment centers are providing competition to private sector business. It seems reasonable to assume that, in the absence of induced price changes, every guilder of Social Employment sales represents equivalent sales that would, in the absence of the program, have been made by private business. Because of this reduction of private sector sales, some workers in the private sector will not have jobs that they otherwise would have had. In a fully employed economy, this is no problem—these workers will, by definition, be employed elsewhere in the economy. When there is general unemployment, these displaced workers may not find an alternative job. In this case, their productivity is lost to the economy. This is a social cost. If none of the displaced workers find alternative employment, the social cost is estimated by the wage income that would have been generated by the displaced workers.

As a first step in estimating this component of costs, the sales of the Social Employment industrial centers are used as an estimate of private sector sales forgone. Then, the number of displaced private sector workers implied by these forgone sales is estimated by calculating the weighted average sales per worker in the industries producing products sold by the Social Employment industrial centers, and then multiplying the inverse of this ratio by the forgone sales. The value of the wages forgone in the private sector because of this displacement was obtained by multiplying the estimated number of displaced workers by the weighted average wage costs per worker in the affected industries. The industry weights used were the following percentages of industrial center sales, by industry, in 1973: textiles and clothing, 7.0 percent; leather, plastic, rubber, and chemicals, 6.3 percent; wood and furniture, 10.7 percent; paper, printing, and editing, 7.8 percent; pottery, glass, and concrete, 0.8 percent; metal and metal products, 32.6 percent; other, 34.8 percent.[39] Sales per worker among the industries ranged from 134,000 guilders in the rubber and plastics industry to 63,000 guilders in the wood and furniture industry. The weighted average sales per worker is estimated at 74,058 guil-

39. The weighted average of the percentages calculated for the identified industries was assigned to the "other" industry category.

ders. The weighted average wage costs per worker in the affected industries—using the same weights—is 24,284 guilders.

In 1973, total sales revenue in the industrial centers program was 240 million guilders, implying that 3,240 private sector workers were displaced because of the Social Employment industrial centers programs.[40] Multiplying the weighted average wage costs per worker by the number of workers displaced (3,240) yields an estimate of the private sector productivity that would be forgone if *none* of the displaced workers finds alternative employment. This value is 78.7 million guilders. If the upper-bound estimate of the proportion of displaced private sector workers who do not find alternative employment is taken to be 0.3, the social costs attributable to the industrial centers program from this displacement effect is 23.6 million guilders, or 728 guilders per worker.

Comments by Victor Halberstadt

Bob Haveman's paper is about the real world. I like that because often discussions on topics like these do not give me the feeling that participants are sufficiently concerned about the realities of today and tomorrow. Too often the topics assigned—and maybe even the selection of participants—for conferences are slightly biased toward theorizing and testing the unreal. If this seems to be an unkind remark, it is in a sense meant to be so: I would like to provoke you to be explicit about some of your own value judgments about the social benefits and costs of direct creation of jobs, and then continue to face the big question for the next few years also on the basis of common sense. That question simply is whether and how to expand the public sector so as to be able to deal with the problem of the structurally unemployed. That can be done by either income transfer programs or by direct creation of jobs.

I am not advocating simply copying some of the programs aimed at solving this question as they have been implemented in the Netherlands, Germany, Sweden, and other countries. But I cannot escape the feeling that a bit more down-to-earth information and discussion about programs in some other countries would have resulted in a more balanced discus-

40. It should be noted that, in 1973, there were 32,714 workers employed in the industrial centers program. Hence, on average, 1 private sector worker is displaced for every 10 disabled workers employed.

sion in this conference. One then might have concluded that it is worth-while to consider experimenting, demonstrating, theorizing, and evaluating a bit less, especially in view of the lack of facts and theory. The intellectual energy saved might be directed toward implementing some—not many—programs.

I believe that direct creation of jobs in or via the public sector is such a pressing issue that a follow-up conference with some cross-national studies is needed. It would be of value to Europe as well as the United States. Many of these concerns have been discussed in the past few years in the Organisation for Economic Co-operation and Development (OECD), in the European Economic Community (EEC), and elsewhere. Unfortunately, there has been little rigorous evaluation of European programs, and the few studies that have been completed are not cited in the footnotes to the elegant and intellectually impressive papers presented here. Greater attention to these international experiences would increase the relevance of conferences of this kind.

The Haveman paper, I think, is a very good one. It is based on a study done while the author was in Holland, and it is the first thorough review of an important social program in Holland. I have very few remarks of a critical nature to make since the crucial points are all there: a discussion of program design, conceptual framework, incentives faced by program operators, and trade-offs that exist among various goals. I would like to make some indirectly related remarks about the paper, raise some larger issues, and give you some background on developments in the Dutch economy relevant to some of the issues raised by Haveman.

I have some difficulty with the concept used by Haveman of *less productive workers,* spelled out in detail in footnote 1. Certainly low economic productivity is a characteristic of the handicapped, disabled, and disadvantaged, but I am dubious for the purpose of policy analysis and program creation that this should be considered the main characteristic. Elsewhere in the economy, low economic productivity is also widespread, sometimes subsidized, and certainly growing. In Holland this goes for many of the "soft" sectors in the economy such as health and education. My question to Haveman really is, why does he need this concept? He knows as well as I do that the Dutch Social Employment program is largely a comfortable shelter for those who are actually disadvantaged but also, and not to a negligible degree, for rather normal workers.

In the introduction to his paper, Haveman states that the social welfare states of Western Europe (for example, Sweden and the Netherlands) generally take the "right to work" as a fundamental principle and "seek to provide employment for anyone who wishes to work." Now, I do not want to judge Sweden, but as far as the Netherlands is concerned, I believe I should be honest with you. Whatever we may say in public, good Calvinists as we all are, we in fact have already given up the goal of providing employment for anyone who wishes to work. Rather we in effect have emphasized increasing income support programs—as have you in the United States.

The most relevant part of the Haveman paper for this conference seems to me to be the discussion of adverse incentives and a lack of economic control. That is a rather harsh conclusion about one of Holland's most cherished social programs, but it is accurate. It is intriguing that it had to be an American economist who did this job in Holland. Interestingly, Dutch economists rather prefer not to analyze social programs. I would guess that the same results are applicable to many other social programs—whether directed at increasing incomes or at job creation—in Holland and elsewhere in Europe. That is, they are plagued by adverse incentives and lack of economic control but, nevertheless, largely supported from the reasonable left to the reasonable right on the political scene. The social benefits therefore seem to be huge, offsetting the direct costs. No wonder that redistribution of income has been very effective in countries such as Holland, Sweden, and Germany.

Tables 4 and 5 provide some basic data on developments in the Dutch economy relating to social policies involving direct creation of jobs and

Table 4. Working Population as a Percentage of Total Population, Selected Countries, 1953, 1963, and 1973

Country	1953	1963	1973
Belgium	41.2	40.1	41.1
France	45.3[a]	42.0	42.1
Italy	39.3[a]	40.8	35.9
Japan	46.0	48.5	48.9
Netherlands	38.4	37.0	35.6
United Kingdom	47.0	47.8	45.7
United States	42.2	39.4	43.3
West Germany	47.0	46.9	43.5

Sources: Organisation for Economic Co-operation and Development, *Manpower Statistics, 1950–1960* (Paris: OECD, 1961), and *1950–62* (1963); and OECD, *Labour Force Statistics, 1962–1973* (Paris: OECD, 1975).
a. Figure for 1954.

Table 5. Rough Estimate of Number of Recipients of Income Transfers in the Working Population of the Netherlands, 1976–77[a]

Type of transfer	Number of recipients
Sickness benefits (10 percent annual average, only employed are covered)	400,000
Unemployment benefits	220,000
Social assistance (as only source of income)	100,000
Public work programs (temporary)	30,000
Social Employment program	65,000
Disability benefits for employed[b]	400,000
Disability benefits for self-employed and handicapped[b]	100,000
Total	1,315,000
Addendum	
Working population 15–65 years old[c]	4,700,000

Source: Author's computations.

a. Figures are averages for 1976 and 1977. Because the law changed on Oct. 1, 1976, data cannot easily be broken down for 1976 and 1977. Figures do not take into account transfers (disability benefits only) to the 600,000 civil servants in the working population.

b. Recipients of disability benefits generally do not work.

c. The working population declined from 60 percent of total population between 15 and 65 years old in 1960, to 57 percent in 1970, to 51 percent in 1976.

other policies targeted on less productive workers. These do not provide a complete picture, but they serve as a useful framework for understanding what is happening in Holland and some other countries.

As table 4 shows, the working population was a low percentage of total population in the Netherlands in 1973; again Calvinism perhaps. Most women, it seems, still stay in the home cooking and raising children full time, though some very recent forecasts suggest a dramatic change toward greater participation of women in the labor force in the next few years, perhaps partly because of the social programs available to workers only.

I find the number of beneficiaries of income transfers in the working age population in Holland (shown in table 5) quite remarkable. The numbers of recipients of disability benefits are astoundingly high—equivalent to more than 10 percent of the actively working population. In general the Dutch—whether economists or not—do not get very excited about them. Why this is so is discussed later.

Estimates over a decade of the number of workers receiving disability benefits are shown in table 6; those are workers no longer contributing to economic production. The growth rate of beneficiaries of disability benefits is slightly astonishing. To a large extent this is nothing more

Table 6. Number of Recipients of Disability Benefits in the Netherlands, 1968–77

Year	Number of recipients
1968	164,000
1969	194,000
1970	215,000
1971	237,000
1972	261,000
1973	287,000
1974	313,000
1975	345,000
1976–77	530,000[a]

Sources: Centraal Bureau voor de Statistiek, *Statistisch Zakboek, 1977*, and preceding issues; and for 1976–77, author's estimates. Figures are rounded.

a. Average for 1976 and 1977. Includes 70,000 self-employed workers and about 30,000 early-handicapped workers who came under the law in October 1976.

than an expensive way of providing unemployment benefits and of retiring people at an early age—over half of all male workers, for instance, become beneficiaries of disability or similar programs after the age of fifty-seven.

Why has all of this happened and what are its consequences? The macroeconomic effects are apparent in tables 7 and 8. In a sense these effects were expected, or put differently, they reflect the social goals set in economic policy over the last ten years. The redistribution of disposable income is huge, as is readily evident. The result is that the profit rate has deteriorated seriously in the ten-year period. I expect this to change only slightly for the better. Therefore the overall conclusion cannot be escaped that there is little incentive for creating jobs in the private sector. That is a fairly serious development, not unknown elsewhere in

Table 7. Percentage Distribution of Disposable Net National Income in the Netherlands, Selected Years, 1969–77

Source	1969	1971	1973	1975	1976	1977
Labor	44.9	44.4	41.5	44.2	41.9	40.9
Transfers	18.7	20.3	21.4	26.0	26.1	26.6
Public sector	22.2	24.2	24.0	23.6	23.2	22.6
Capital[a]	8.9	5.2	7.1	−1.7	1.2	2.5
Life insurance companies and pension funds[b]	5.2	5.8	6.0	7.9	7.6	7.5

Sources: De Nederlandsche Bank n.v., *Report for the Year 1976*, Statistical Annex, table 10.1; and for 1977, data supplied by De Nederlandsche Bank. Figures are rounded.

a. Profits, dividends, rent, etc., received by persons and businesses.

b. Income received by these organizations.

Table 8. Percentage Changes in Disposable Income in the Netherlands, Selected Years, 1967–76

Source	1967	1969	1971	1973	1975	1976
Labor	6.5	14.5	10.5	11.5	12.0	8.5
Transfers	14.0	16.0	19.0	16.5	21.5	15.0
Capital[a]	24.5	14.5	−9.0	42.5	b	b
Life insurance companies and pension funds[c]	13.5	14.5	17.5	16.5	26.5	11.0
Public sector	8.0	9.0	15.5	15.0	4.0	12.5
Net national income	10.0	13.5	12.5	15.5	7.5	14.5

Sources: Same as table 7.
a. Profits, dividends, rent, etc., received by persons and businesses.
b. Not calculable because disposable income from capital in 1975 was a negative amount.
c. Income received by these organizations.

Europe. In effect, only the public sector has shown a net creation of jobs—about 3 percent per year—over the last fifteen years. Private industry has not done so.

Of what relevance is this discussion for the United States? Bob Haveman draws some conclusions for the current U.S. discussion about less productive workers based on the Dutch Social Employment program. I find this the least convincing part of his otherwise excellent paper.

I do not think that creating employment for low productivity workers can be looked at separately from job creation in general for all the structurally unemployed. We have made that mistake in the Netherlands so far, and I hope that you will not do so.

Whatever kinds of programs are designed, there is little doubt that the management arrangements are crucial and that the programs should be controlled at the national level. They are not in the Netherlands and the disastrous results for the economy are partly evident in Haveman's analysis.

Finally, it is highly doubtful whether one is on the right course if one rules out a much shorter working week and early retirement in the future; however, this should be accompanied by a more or less corresponding drop in disposable income. Whether high or low productivity workers are the focus here does not really matter. I think—and there is some European evidence supporting my view—that many problems, such as adverse incentives, can be prevented if this option—with some government subsidy, of course—is not totally ruled out in favor of massive job creation programs or income maintenance.[41]

41. For further comments on the Haveman paper, see comments by Stromsdorfer following the Kemper-Moss paper.

Peter Kemper and Philip Moss

Economic Efficiency
of Public Employment Programs

Public service employment is currently the subject of considerable discussion and debate. This interest arises at least in part because it is hoped that public employment can address simultaneously a number of social goals including the employment of disadvantaged workers. Public employment directed at those with labor market handicaps might reduce aggregate unemployment with less inflationary pressure than alternative means by providing jobs specifically for those groups whose unemployment is high. Public employment might also attack pov-

The authors gratefully acknowledge the support of Mathematica Policy Research, Inc., and the Institute for Research on Poverty at the University of Wisconsin. The research on which this study is based is part of an evaluation of the Supported Work program for the Manpower Demonstration Research Corporation, whose cooperation the authors appreciate. The MDRC work is being carried out under Employment and Training Administration, U.S. Department of Labor Grant No. 33-36-75-01 and Contract Nos. 30-36-75-01 and 30-34-75-02, and Ford Foundation Grant No. 740-0537A. The Employment and Training Administration of the Labor Department is the lead agency in a federal funding consortium that sponsors the Supported Work program. The points of view expressed in this paper are solely those of the authors and do not represent the official position or policies of the sponsoring agencies. The staff of the Supported Work program at Hartford, Jersey City, and Oakland provided information for the case studies on value of output and cost.

The authors are also grateful to Steven F. Dichter, Gary S. Fiske, David A. Long, and Stephen M. Werner, who analyzed program output and costs; to Suzette Swoboda for administrative assistance; to Felicity Skidmore for editorial assistance; and to Katharine L. Bradbury, Joseph Ball, John H. Bishop, Kenneth Burdett, Glen G. Cain, Lee S. Friedman, Judith M. Gueron, Robert H. Haveman, Robert I. Lerman, and David R. Zimmerman, who commented on a draft. They especially thank Irwin Garfinkel, Robinson G. Hollister, Jr., and Stanley H. Masters for encouragement and intellectual guidance.

erty directly, by providing satisfying employment and income to disadvantaged workers. It thus could reduce associated problems of crime, drug use, and welfare dependence. Moreover, because the work experience might create job skills and a work record that make finding and holding a regular job easier, some of its effects may endure for the participant. And society may gain needed social services not otherwise provided.

These goals of public service employment are laudable and would be endorsed by most voters. It is important, however, to have a realistic sense of the extent to which they can be attained. Advocates often argue that there are many needed social services to be provided by such a program, but overlook the practical issues of identifying those activities and mobilizing the resources needed to produce the output. Critics, on the other hand, often reject the idea simply because of its alleged administrative nightmares and inefficiencies. In general neither advocates nor critics have carefully examined the practical aspects of implementing a job creation program—nor have economists done sufficient theoretical or empirical research for the development of a fully appropriate evaluation framework. In short, as with any new social program, there is a wide gap between the general statement of goals and the development of a specific, implementable program to further these goals.

This paper presents a framework for evaluating the efficiency of public employment programs and examining potential trade-offs among their multiple goals. The analysis is based on insights gained from examining the early experience of a public service employment program called Supported Work, which began as a national demonstration in 1975.

Examination of a particular program can provide a realistic sense of the trade-offs likely to exist among multiple program goals. Ultimately, the evaluation of the demonstration will have quite a bit to say about the effect of such a job creation program on later employment opportunities of participants and about their output while in the program. This information is not yet available. Nonetheless, there is sufficient experience to suggest some hypotheses about alternative job creation strategies and their probable effectiveness.

After a brief description of the national Supported Work demonstration, the tasks involved in creating jobs and the criteria used for evaluating the demonstration are discussed. The heart of the analysis of the efficiency trade-offs follows. Finally, there is a summary of implications of the analysis.

The Supported Work Demonstration

Supported Work is a transitional work experience program for workers with serious employment difficulties.[1] It differs from other public employment and manpower programs in the population it serves, its objectives, and its structure.

The program is designed for persons with severe labor market problems: former drug addicts and law offenders, unemployed disadvantaged youth, and women who are long-term recipients of aid to families with dependent children (AFDC). By enforcing strict eligibility criteria and paying low wages, the program ensures that only individuals with the most severe employment problems participate. Participants are far more disadvantaged than those in the more familiar Public Employment Program (PEP) and programs funded under the Comprehensive Employment and Training Act (CETA).[2]

Supported Work is designed both to provide participants with job skills that will increase their earnings after the program and to produce useful social output during their participation in it.[3] The premise of the program is that its participants can be successfully employed if they work in the company of their peers (who provide "peer group support") and under close and supportive supervision, and if job-related stress is introduced gradually. Productivity, attendance, and punctuality demands

1. The Supported Work demonstration is in part an expansion of a program initiated by the Vera Institute of Justice in New York City that sought to rehabilitate former drug addicts by providing them with work experience in low-stress jobs and that later included ex-offenders, unemployed youth, and mothers receiving aid to families with dependent children. The Vera program has become a nonprofit corporation to provide public services to New York City. For information on Supported Work and its evaluation, see Manpower Demonstration Research Corp., *First Annual Report on the National Supported Work Demonstration* (New York: MDRC, 1976).

2. Almost two-thirds of the first year's participant population had not graduated from high school, one-fifth had never had a job; their average job tenure in the six months before joining the program was eight and one-half weeks. Among former addicts and offenders the average number of adult convictions was four. All the groups except those on AFDC had spent a significant amount of time in correctional institutions. Ibid., chap. 2.

3. Depending on the target group, Supported Work has the additional objectives of reducing welfare dependence, drug use, and crime, and of encouraging high school dropouts to return to school.

placed on workers are low initially and are slowly increased until they reach normal labor market standards.

It may be argued from several points of view, depending on different assumptions about the specific problems of the target groups, that creating special jobs is a good way to improve the future employment and earnings of program participants. From one perspective, the skill content of program jobs can be linked to later jobs in such a way that the flow of participants to regular jobs should be greatly facilitated. This is the model used in this paper to discuss the relation between various program strategies and the future employment gains of participants. From another perspective, work experience in and of itself develops habits, skills, and motivation that are not tied to a specific occupation but should enhance participants' general employability; in this case it is simply the provision of a job that is relevant. A third model suggests that, by succeeding at special jobs, participants can develop an employment record that distinguishes them from an overall group that regular employers view as a poor employment risk.

The Supported Work demonstration is operated at fifteen sites by local organizations that are, in most cases, independent agencies whose major or sole function is running the program. Because they must match their national funding by marketing their output or by raising untied grants, they must sell the program's concept as well as its output to the local communities. And because Supported Work is new in most of the cities, with emphasis on designing special jobs, these organizations have had to establish entire production operations in order to provide job experience.

Supported Work, in contrast to countercyclical public employment programs, operates continuously irrespective of overall economic conditions and seeks to increase postprogram earnings. It differs from other permanent programs in that (in most cases) it operates independently of local governments. It is different from sheltered workshops because, although it is an ongoing program, it is transitional for the program participants.[4] It is different from manpower training programs because it is designed to improve employability through direct work experience rather than counseling, classroom education, or formal training in job skills. And unlike the few manpower programs that have con-

4. The length of stay in the program is limited to either one year or eighteen months.

centrated on the same target groups, it does not select the most promising participants and therefore avoid the more difficult to employ.

Because it is a demonstration, the program is small relative to the local labor market. At the end of 1976, the largest program had just under three hundred participants, and over half had fewer than a hundred. The type of work done by the participants has ranged across a great many industries, as shown in table 1. Despite this variety, the jobs tend to be concentrated in relatively low-skill activities, with correspondingly low wages in the private sector. Also, the production processes tend to be fairly labor intensive. The type of work is approximately evenly divided between production of goods and provision of services. Most activities—with the possible exception of construction and certain public-sector activities such as education and social services—are in industries in which barriers to entry are low and the markets are competitive.

As one might expect, most of the work is done for the public and nonprofit sectors, and much of that is done for a nominal charge, if any. Much of it is traditional public employment work, though a portion of the output is sold on a competitive, fee-for-service basis, in which case the projects' production and marketing activities closely resemble those of a private firm.

In the first year and a half, the program's survival and growth clearly demonstrated the feasibility of a program to create jobs for the target groups on this small scale. It also demonstrated the difficulty faced by operators attempting to create jobs, especially during periods of high unemployment. Matching jobs to an extremely disadvantaged group of workers is difficult under any circumstance, but during a recession, lay-offs of local government workers and reduced demand in the private sector make the task all the more problematic. In addition, because it is a demonstration, the program operates under constraints imposed by the experimental research design.[5]

Counteracting these special constraints are some special advantages. The program's small size may have enabled it to avoid some of the problems a large-scale program would confront. Since administering agencies were chosen on the basis of grant applications, they are likely to be among the best qualified to run such programs. The unrestricted funding of the

---

5. An important example is the random assignment of eligible persons as participants or as control-group members. On average a program takes in only half the eligible persons referred to it.

Table 1. Distribution of Hours Worked in Supported Work Program, by Industry, First Five Quarters of Program Operation[a]

Industry[b]	Percent of total hours worked
Agriculture (01-09)	7.79
Construction	38.77
General building contractors (15)	8.93
Painting (1720)	12.69
Wrecking and demolition (1795)	2.19
Deleading (1799)	6.40
Other special trades (all other 17)	8.56
Manufacturing	3.96
Furniture (25)	0.87
Printing (27)	1.80
Other manufacturing (24, 28, 31, 32, 36)	1.29
Transportation, communications, and utilities (42, 47)	3.52
Wholesale trade (50)	0.93
Retail trade	3.73
Gasoline service stations (5540)	1.36
Eating and drinking places (58)	2.20
Other retail trade (52, 59)	0.17
Services	40.22
Clerical (7330, 7339)	8.71
Cleaning and maintenance (7349)	12.48
Guard (7393)	2.05
Microfilming (7399)	3.33
Other business (all other 73)	3.24
Auto repair (75)	3.70
Reupholstery and furniture repair (7640)	1.74
Health (80)	0.86
Educational (82)	1.88
Social (83)	2.01
Other (79, 7620, 89)	0.22
Not classified	1.07
Total	100.00

Source: Compiled from data in Supported Work Management Information System.
a. Programs began at different times in different cities, with most beginning in the spring of 1975.
b. Standard industrial classification numbers are shown in parentheses.

program, while covering less than total expenses, provides a financial base that allows great flexibility in the choice of projects. Finally, a considerable amount of technical and other support is available because the program is a demonstration.

Evaluation Criteria

Innumerable criteria exist for evaluating public service employment programs and the value of output produced on the created jobs. Those generally considered are: budget impact, a program's effect on government receipts and expenditures;[6] equity, its effect on poverty and the distribution of income; structural effect, its ability to reduce unemployment with minimal inflationary pressure; economic efficiency, its ability to increase the total output of society; progressiveness, its capacity to innovate and improve performance over time;[7] and implementation, the conformity of program operations to program design. Because different people attach varying importance to these criteria, an evaluation is most useful if it presents the effects on as many of the criteria as possible. This paper is restricted to economic efficiency. This is not meant to suggest that it is the most important consideration in evaluating public employment. In this kind of program, with its rehabilitative and redistributive objectives, other criteria may ultimately be more important. But efficiency is an important consideration, especially when comparisons are being made among various programs designed to achieve the same objectives. At a minimum, a program should be as efficient as possible for any chosen level of the other program objectives. An efficiency evaluation tells the policymaker what efficiency price must be paid to achieve the other objectives.[8]

The overall efficiency of a public employment program depends primarily on the value of the output produced by the program and the extent

6. Budget impact is especially important when target group members would be receiving transfer payments in the absence of the program.

7. Some analysts would subsume progressiveness under efficiency by labeling it *dynamic efficiency;* however, technological change in social programs is sufficiently important and involves issues sufficiently different from those of static efficiency to merit separate treatment.

8. For a further discussion of the importance of the efficiency criterion see Robert Haveman's paper in this volume.

to which the program increases the postprogram earnings of the participants.[9] The emphasis in this paper is on the first of these. The value of output accounted for almost 80 percent of the total benefits in the evaluation of a pilot demonstration of Supported Work;[10] without this, costs would have exceeded benefits by a large amount. More generally, criticism of public employment as "leaf-raking" and the paucity of existing research on value of output make this aspect of public employment particularly worthy of analysis.

The value of output produced by public employees is determined by the employees' productivity and the usefulness of their output—their *productive efficiency* refers to the productivity of the public employment program compared to that of alternative suppliers of the same output, and their *allocative efficiency* refers to the usefulness of the output, regardless of how efficiently the output is produced. For example, public employees who dig unneeded ditches and fill them up again could be efficient in production, but the output produced would not be useful. In contrast, park maintenance may be a very useful social service, but a maintenance crew that spends its time sleeping would not be efficient. For the value of output to be high relative to costs, a project must be efficient in both senses.

The distinction between allocative and productive efficiency (which are defined more precisely in the appendix) is not essential for program evaluation. Nonetheless, there are good reasons to examine the two separately.

First, policymakers are likely to disagree with each other and with researchers about the allocative efficiency of a project. A study that not only presents estimates of allocative efficiency but also describes both the output produced and who receives it is valuable because policymakers can make their own judgments concerning the usefulness of the output.[11] What they cannot easily judge for themselves, however, is how much

9. There may be additional economic efficiency benefits of a program, depending on the target group. For example, providing jobs for ex-offenders might reduce crime. Drug use might fall among former addicts. Society also appears to attach particular importance to having people working instead of receiving welfare. Analytically, these additional benefits are similar to earnings increases.

10. Lee S. Friedman, "An Interim Evaluation of the Supported Work Experiment," *Policy Analysis,* vol. 3 (Spring 1977), p. 166. See also, Lee S. Friedman, "The Use of Ex-addicts to Deliver Local Services: The Supported Work Experiment," in Joel Bergsman and Howard L. Wiener, eds., *Urban Problems and Public Policy Choices* (Praeger, 1975), chap. 6.

11. This is particularly important for outputs that are not sold in markets.

output is being produced relative to the inputs used; for that, a measure of productive efficiency is needed. Distinguishing between allocative and productive efficiency therefore permits researchers to present the detailed information policymakers need to evaluate the program, rather than burying the controversial value judgments in an overall comparison of value of output to cost.

Second, the separation of the value of output into its two components makes measurement somewhat easier. A practical method exists for measuring productive efficiency, but measuring allocative efficiency is much more difficult. The logical separation may make it somewhat easier to place bounds on the overall ratio of value of output to program cost.

Finally, and most important, to be useful in a policy context an evaluation should go beyond an overall assessment to suggest ways of improving program design. If productive efficiency is high but allocative efficiency is low, then overall social value may be low relative to costs because of poor choice of markets rather than low productivity of workers. It may be possible to redirect this output to other sectors in which the benefits are higher.[12]

Creating jobs in a public employment program like Supported Work is analogous to operating a private firm, in that the production process must be organized and the output marketed. It is more complex, however, because of the many additional objectives and constraints. The task of organizing production differs from that of a private firm because of the special characteristics of target group members and the objective of

___

12. In order to say something systematic about the way in which the design of a public employment program could be improved, the evaluation criteria need to be related to the behavior of program operators. The state of the art provides little foundation on which to build a model for such an examination. Standard microeconomic maximization theory is not obviously suited to analyzing this range of behavior. Program organizations have a large number of objectives and constraints. The environment they face does not necessarily reward behavior in well-defined or predictable ways. Most important, the production function for an untried social program is unknown. Application of constrained maximization tools is therefore difficult and not likely to capture the essence of the problem. Institutional theories are likely to be helpful for analysis of this problem, but existing models are fairly case-specific and not easily used to analyze the relation between behavior and evaluation criteria such as efficiency. The challenge is to model behavior so that the relevant objectives, environmental constraints, and institutions are included, and the relation between policies and normative criteria is apparent. This paper attempts to move in this direction by defining the different strategies for accomplishing the two main tasks of job creation and then analyzing the likely relation between those strategies and efficiency.

providing work experience that creates skills useful in later jobs. The very nature of public service employment, moreover, makes the marketing task different. Low wages and public funding make certain marketing strategies illegal or politically inadvisable. But the special status of a subsidized social program like Supported Work creates a number of possibilities for expanding output that are not available to a private firm.

More generally, the operator of such a program has no one to imitate. The manager of a private firm often enters a market in which existing firms' operating procedures provide models for organizing the production process and marketing output. Their performance provides a ready standard of comparison. Because few such models and standards exist for a public employment program, program managers face greater uncertainty about the effects of their decisions and how to judge their performance.

Implementing an economically efficient program to create jobs for disadvantaged workers is likely to be very difficult, as the following discussions of strategies for organizing production and marketing output indicate. It should come as no surprise that it is hard to increase economic efficiency by producing new outputs. If one starts from the very simple, if extreme, assumption that markets and governments are allocating resources efficiently, then the marginal benefits of additional output will equal marginal production costs in all sectors of the economy and outputs will be produced at minimum social costs. In such a situation, by definition, no program will be able to increase economic efficiency.

No one, however, not even the most intransigent economist, believes that markets and governments allocate resources with perfect efficiency. Although the economy may adjust in such ways as to eliminate large disparities between marginal benefits and costs, there are undoubtedly numerous opportunities to improve the efficiency of resource allocation. A job-creation program, to be successful in terms of the economic efficiency of the output produced, should try to exploit those market discrepancies by discovering innovative management techniques, creating new outputs, expanding output in monopoly markets, identifying unmet public needs—in general by identifying and rectifying market failure.[13]

13. A similar argument can be made concerning attempts to improve postprogram employment opportunities of participants. That no easy solution to the labor market problems of the disadvantaged has been found suggests that an innovative program design or implementation is needed.

Productive Efficiency

Productive efficiency, as defined here, can be measured by comparing the market cost of providing a service to the cost of providing the same service through public service employment. Given the assumption that the alternative private suppliers produce efficiently, the ratio of their price to the program's cost will indicate the productive efficiency of public service employment. By design, program participants must have some labor market problem, so that the productive efficiency of a Supported Work project should not be expected to equal that of alternative suppliers.

Nor is it necessarily desirable to have a high level of productive efficiency in a public employment program, since it may only come at the expense of the other program objectives. It is desirable, however, to design the program so that productive efficiency is as high as possible for any given level of performance with respect to the other program objectives.

Factors Affecting Productive Efficiency

The productive efficiency of a project depends on the type of output produced and the way in which the production process is organized. The type of output produced places broad constraints on the kind of nonlabor inputs, the skill of the labor, and the manner in which the inputs can be combined in the productive process. The program manager then can organize the production process in different ways with different combinations of inputs. For instance, Supported Work has been developed to provide a supportive environment for participants and gradually prepare them for regular jobs. The productive efficiency of specific projects is thus very likely to depend on the intensity of supervision and how much the supportive aspects of the program are stressed relative to the efficient production of output.

Thus, a number of factors associated with the industrial activity and the way in which the production is organized are likely to affect productive efficiency. The skills required to do the work in comparison to the skills of the participants are obviously important. The managerial requirements for the work probably vary with the complexity of the project, and the special supervisory requirements may vary substantially across projects depending, for example, on the extent to which materials and equipment are necessary. In this type of program, projects may have to begin on such a small scale that the ability to maximize productive efficiency is low. Any production activity faces start-up problems and a learning process; when all the workers are new, as in this program, start-up costs are likely to be high. Hence, the age of a project should affect its productive efficiency.

There is also reason to expect the productive efficiency of projects to depend on certain aspects of their external environment. Projects selling output at market prices, for instance, face competitive pressure and may be able to imitate unsubsidized firms that are directly subject to such pressure.

Finally, a great many noneconomic factors may affect productive efficiency. Specifically, the degree to which the output is a tangible one that can be pointed to with pride and the type of peer support provided by the work crew are two variables that program staff have suggested as important determinants of productivity.

From eleven case studies of Supported Work projects,[14] it is possible to compare productive efficiency along some of the dimensions outlined here. The patterns discerned in such a small sample must, of course, be viewed as extremely tentative and should be conceived as a first step in learning about programs of this type. They suggest some hypotheses about the variance in productive efficiency, start-up costs and economies of scale, and differences among industrial activities.

VARIANCE OF ESTIMATES. The variance of productive efficiency across the small sample of projects is quite large. This implies that a large sample must be evaluated if any reliable conclusions are to be drawn about the factors that affect productive efficiency or of the overall productive efficiency of the program. The high variance in efficiency creates an important policy opportunity, for if it can be explained by variables under policy control, then those variables can be manipulated to improve productive efficiency through changes in program design.

START-UP COSTS AND ECONOMIES OF SCALE. For a number of projects, estimates of productive efficiency during more than one time period are available. Most of them show a pattern of improvement in efficiency from the initial start-up period to subsequent periods. This result is not

14. These studies were performed by Steven F. Dichter, Gary S. Fiske, and Stephen M. Werner of Mathematica Policy Research.

surprising. Any job requires the worker to perform tasks specific to the job and the organization. No matter how educated and skilled the worker, an initial period of learning job-specific procedures is unavoidable; the existence of a learning curve is well documented. In job creation programs these learning periods are likely to coincide for all workers. When a new project is begun, everyone, often even the supervisor, must learn job-specific skills. Over time, productivity can be expected to improve as the crew learns the procedures and as incapable workers are transferred to other jobs or leave the program. But there are limits to this improvement in a program whose workers are encouraged to seek a regular job as soon as they have acquired a certain level of skill. Thus, by design, this type of public employment program may incur some of society's costs of screening and training disadvantaged workers—costs that appear in the form of low productive efficiency.

Economies of scale may also exist, at least over a range of low levels of output.[15] Since initial output is often low, unit costs first will be relatively high and then fall with increased output. Furthermore, if programs are not permitted (or their administrators choose not) to produce for inventory, then insufficient demand for output will interact with economies of scale to raise unit costs, thereby reducing productive efficiency. This is a failure not of organizing the production process, but rather of marketing.

The hypothesis is that there may be a significant start-up period associated with public employment projects. This suggests that early evaluation can be misleading. It also raises the question of whether the start-up costs are lower or the start-up period shorter for some projects than others.[16]

INDUSTRY DIFFERENCES. From eleven case studies it is dangerous to do more than speculate about differences in productive efficiency across industries. But the projects do tend to fall into two groups with a number of correlated characteristics. The projects with high productive efficiency tend to be relatively low-skill, labor-intensive projects that probably have few start-up costs, such as painting, park maintenance, and

15. Typically, half a dozen to a dozen workers are assigned to a single project. Evaluation of such a small demonstration risks understating the productive efficiency of a national program of projects operated on a larger scale.

16. Although the concern here is not with the usefulness of this kind of public employment as a countercyclical tool, it is worth noting that the existence of high start-up costs would make such programs unattractive as macroeconomic stabilization policies.

building maintenance. The less productively efficient are ones that tend to be somewhat more high-skill, materials-intensive, or equipment-intensive projects, such as tire recapping, furniture refinishing, furniture manufacturing, operation of gas stations, and Christmas tree sales. This suggests that skill level and labor intensity may be industry characteristics related to productive efficiency for these target groups.

Although they are impossible to separate from the problems of low skill and inexperience, the problems of managing a production process that requires substantial nonlabor inputs may be especially difficult with extremely disadvantaged workers.[17] The supervisory requirements for these types of projects are likely to be high. Intensive and skillful supervision, knowledge of specific production processes, and the capacity to relate to target group members are all needed. In addition, the match of individual workers to jobs is likely to be more difficult in projects having higher skill requirements. The necessity of using low-skilled workers for jobs requiring nonlabor inputs may lead to the destruction or damage of equipment and materials. This would not only increase costs directly, but also indirectly through the necessity of more intensive supervision.[18]

Other problems have surfaced from participants' lack of particular skills. At least one of the business projects had problems with administrative tasks such as keeping records and accounts. Some jobs (such as library work) have been difficult because participants' reading skills are generally quite low. Lack of drivers' licenses among program workers has been a problem for other projects.

The possibility that lower skill, labor-intensive projects are more likely to be productively efficient for public employment programs has its limits, however. Experience on some projects suggests that some work is too unattractive to motivate workers at all. A few projects, some of which were labor contracts to other organizations, were terminated because the workers refused the work. It might have been possible to organize the production in a manner that made the work more attractive if the project had been operated "in house."

Given the variety of factors that may affect productive efficiency, is it possible to anticipate what behavior is likely? There appears to be no

17. One problem directly related to materials inputs is theft. For projects located in low-income areas the risk of crime is high. A gas station project was ended in part because the station had been broken into so many times; some housing rehabilitation projects have had a continuing problem with theft of materials.

18. The case studies include examples of having to redo tire recapping and furniture refinishing work.

simple model that can predict the way managers organize the production process. Program managers have a number of objectives, some in conflict with others. Producing output efficiently or picking activities that can be run most efficiently may not be prominent among them.

Business firms, regardless of their overall objectives, receive a relatively clear signal in terms of profits if they produce efficiently; perhaps even more convincing is the signal received if they do not produce at minimum cost. In addition, private firms can assess their performance against similar firms and imitate effective techniques. The organizations creating special public jobs, in contrast, are financially rewarded for efficient production only slightly, if at all. In the Supported Work demonstration, for instance, sales revenue plays a fairly small role in the financial security of the program. Neither are the organizations penalized for inefficient production as long as the outputs are satisfactory. Moreover, except for projects in which output is sold at competitive market prices, program managers have little information on which to base an assessment of a project's productive efficiency. Thus, productive efficiency may be pursued, but only to the degree that individual program managers conceive it to be an important objective in its own right and not because of the inherent incentive structure.

No single pattern emerges from the variety of behavior exhibited in the program so far. Much appears to depend on the individuals who direct the programs.[19] This is to be expected, in large part because the program was designed not to constrain behavior tightly with respect to the type of projects undertaken or the organization of the work but to allow for natural experimentation.

Inferences to Be Drawn

Early Supported Work experience demonstrates that this kind of program can put members of the target groups to work and produce outputs. It also suggests, however, that matching work and workers is a difficult task and is likely to be even more difficult if productive efficiency is not to be reduced as the program attempts to create relatively skilled jobs. In addition, as people acquire the skills needed to perform the jobs, they

19. This particular subject of program director philosophy is analyzed from an organizational perspective in Joseph Ball, *Implementing Supported Work: Job Creation Strategies During the First Year of the National Demonstration* (MDRC, 1977).

will have the incentive to leave the program and seek higher wages. Thus, the difficulty of attaining high productive efficiency should be expected to persist beyond an initial start-up period.[20]

If management is inherently difficult, if economies of scale combine with insufficient demand to reduce productive efficiency to a low level, or if learning is faster or easier in the presence of other experienced workers, then will locating the production out of house increase productive efficiency? By selling only participant labor services and perhaps some extra program supervision, and by leaving the marketing and management task to an existing firm or agency, productive efficiency may be increased. There will be a resulting loss in peer support and the ability to specially structure jobs, but this may be offset by other gains in productive efficiency. Moreover, the program may be able to teach host supervisors about the special work problems of participants and train them to use effective techniques of supervision.

If pushed to its extreme, this argument implies that job creation by new organizations is likely to be less productively efficient for this population than some form of general labor subsidy, perhaps with support for extra supervisory needs. Such a conclusion, however, must be weighed against the record of programs that have attempted to subsidize labor; the Hamermesh paper in this volume shows that in most cases the programs did not serve as disadvantaged a population as Supported Work's and, even so, were not considered very successful. In addition, independent organizations can make selective use of labor service contracts to serve their own needs. To the degree that their needs can be made consonant with the goals of the program, there is some pressure to make these conditional labor subsidy arrangements work well. This pressure would not exist under a simple labor subsidy.

Nonetheless, it is important to ask to what extent the difficulty of organizing production is inherent in the task and to what extent it results from specific problems of working with the disadvantaged target groups. If it is simply an inherent problem, then the case for setting up new,

---

20. A further indication of the difficulty of creating jobs that match the skills of workers in the target groups is the substantial rates of firings and dropouts that are not a result of transition to another job. No matter how these rates compare with those of nonsupported jobs, they suggest that even with special design and support, created jobs must face problems of labor relations and discipline. This is a particularly important issue when larger programs guaranteeing jobs are considered. The more unconditional the guarantee, the more difficult the objective of maintaining productivity is likely to be.

independent organizations is weakened. If it is the result of problems of creating attractive jobs for the specific target groups, then the case for a separate program using special supervisory and management techniques to organize the production process is much stronger.

Another hypothesis suggested by this analysis is that a trade-off may exist between the productive efficiency of projects and the postprogram earnings gains of workers on those projects. If rehabilitative or training goals are emphasized, this may reduce the effort exerted to increase productive efficiency. The preceding discussion also suggests, however, that the projects that are easiest to run with a high level of productive efficiency may also be the ones requiring the least skill. They consequently are less likely to enable workers to develop specific skills that command a high wage in the regular labor market. Hence, a program of this kind may not be able to rely on work experience or high-productivity projects being linked directly to better paying jobs in the same occupation or industry.

Nonetheless, the productively efficient projects may be valuable in developing general work habits and motivation or in providing the credential of a stable work record. Either may improve postprogram employment opportunities. If so, the hypothesized trade-off between productive efficiency and postprogram earnings gains may not exist, and the total benefits of the program will be high when productively efficient projects are selected. In any event, the effects of job creation strategies on a program's value of output and on later earnings gains must be considered together.

Allocative Efficiency

A crucial issue in the consideration of various marketing strategies is whether the incentives facing local managers result in behavior that is consonant with the national objectives for the program. The discussion here proceeds from the narrow perspective of the individual organizations, for which project survival and growth are the primary task and the clearest signal of success, to the broader perspective of economic efficiency. The analysis is based to some degree on the early experience of the Supported Work demonstration, but primarily on deductive argument. The generalizations drawn from the descriptive record must be viewed as hypotheses for longer term observation, analysis, and testing. The argument involves drawing out reasons that some work projects and not others were undertaken and suggesting plausible links between those reasons and the factors that affect the allocative efficiency of the projects.

Factors Affecting Allocative Efficiency

The task of managers of public employment programs is to create jobs for their employees. They must find some demand for the labor services of program employees in other organizations or some demand for the output of projects run by the program. Identifying these demands is necessary for the survival of the program organizations. The actions taken to secure demand for the output and labor services of program employees and, more generally, demand for the programs are referred to as marketing output.

Three aspects of marketing decisions are particularly relevant to allocative efficiency. The first is the choice of a market. This includes the choice of actual output or activities and the choice of customers for that output, which may involve the selection of a segment of a larger market. Second are the actions taken to disarm or avoid potential opposition by existing producers and unions to the entry of program activities. Third is the extent to which output or labor services sold are subject to a market test. This involves pricing policies and efforts to sell output by selling the program concept—that is, the concept of employing particularly disadvantaged groups or producing goods for the poor.

Judgments concerning the usefulness of project output depend on what would have happened in the absence of the public employment program. With the introduction of a project into a particular sector, total output in that sector can remain constant, increase by the full amount of the program output, or increase by less than the full amount of program output. Since the less than full increase is intermediate to the other two cases, allocative efficiency can be analyzed by considering the two extremes.[21]

Where total output in the sector remains unchanged, the program simply produces output that would have been produced by other suppliers if the program did not exist. Total benefits to the consumers of the output will be the same in the presence of the program as they would

---

21. A more formal analysis of the allocative efficiency of projects is included in the appendix.

have been without it (because the total output consumed in that sector is the same in both cases). The efficiency effects of this displacement of other suppliers depend on what happens to the displaced resources that they would have used to produce the output. At one extreme, the displaced resources may be unemployed. Then the value of the public service output is zero because the job creation has simply idled resources that would have produced the same output. At the other extreme, the displaced resources could be fully employed producing useful output elsewhere in the economy, in which case the allocative efficiency of the program is measured by the value of the additional output produced by the displaced resources.[22] This is customarily referred to as the "opportunity cost" of the resources, although in this context "opportunity benefit" might be a more appropriate phrase.[23]

The Supported Work program is targeted to precisely those individuals whose labor market difficulties are thought to persist even at relatively full employment throughout the economy. Under conditions of full employment, quick reemployment of displaced resources may be a reasonable assumption. However, to the extent that work projects are developed in markets or submarkets that involve other workers with similar employment problems, the opportunity cost of these freed labor resources

22. An alternative and equivalent way to handle the displacement effect is to count it as a cost in the benefit-cost calculation. This approach is taken in Haveman's paper.

23. This partial equilibrium analysis assumes there are no adjustment costs of moving resources from one sector to another. A general equilibrium model that analyzes the increase in adjustment costs is needed to estimate the opportunity cost correctly. Projects that displace resources may become relatively more efficient overall during periods of full employment than during a recession. The value of output increases with the level of economic activity because the opportunity benefit of the displaced resources increases. The social cost of the program also increases with the level of economic activity, however, because the opportunity cost of program participants and other resources required to run the program increases. Thus, allocative efficiency increases, but productive efficiency decreases. The net effect of the level of economic activity on the ratio of value of output to program cost, therefore, could be either positive or negative. Because the opportunity cost of disadvantaged participants is extremely low even in periods of full employment, it is assumed that the overall efficiency of projects that displace resources increases with full employment. If this is so, it is in sharp contrast to public employment projects that expand output and to many other government programs whose efficiency increases during recessions because the benefits remain constant but the opportunity cost of the participant labor decreases. The implication for public employment is that shifting from output-expanding projects to displacing projects as the economy moves from low to high levels of economic activity is an efficient policy, other things being equal.

may be quite low. This issue merits further theoretical analysis; results are surely sensitive to the model of unemployment in the relevant portion of labor and product markets.

If total output of the good is increased by the full amount of the program output, the value of output equals the marginal benefits of this additional output to consumers. The magnitude of these benefits depends on the sector in which the expansion of output occurs and on which consumers in that sector receive the output. Additional output will be more valuable in those sectors in which the market or political process has failed (in the sense of efficiency) to produce enough output relative to consumers' willingness to pay for it. Expanding output in those sectors in which output is undersupplied will increase allocative efficiency. However, regardless of the sector in which output is produced, the total value to consumers depends on whether the output is distributed to those who value it the most. Quite valuable output from society's overall point of view might be distributed to consumers who do not value it highly.

Both the sector entered and the distribution of output to consumers within the sector are related to the pricing policy of the public employment program. In theory, market pricing encourages suppliers to produce output that consumers value (and therefore are willing to pay for), and it insures that *only* those who value the output enough to be willing to pay for it in fact receive it. Thus, the pricing policy of a public employment program is intrinsically related to allocative efficiency.

Charging market prices is not a guarantee that the output of a public employment program will be what consumers value most highly, however. An employment program for the disadvantaged has a special status as a redistributive and training program with hypothesized benefits in addition to the output produced. Buyers may therefore purchase the output of such a program not only because they want it, but also because it helps the poor by paying them wages and increasing their future employment opportunities and has other desirable side effects such as reducing crime. Although both components of the demand for output are important, it is useful to separate that for output per se from the demand for redistribution and the other program benefits. The demand for the output would exist no matter who produced it, but the second component of demand depends on the special characteristics of the program. The separate treatment of the two components permits an evaluation that indicates the efficiency cost of redistributing income through a public employment program.[24] This can then be compared to the efficiency cost of other means of redistributing income.

Separating demand for output from demand for altruism is also helpful in tracing the efficiency implications of strategies taken for marketing program output. As is discussed below, selling the program concept by stressing redistributive and training benefits in addition to output may be an important part of a strategy to avoid opposition and secure demand. This has implications for how strict a market test is applied to the choice of outputs.

Marketing Strategies

What might be the expected behavior of operators of public employment programs in developing work for their employees?[25] That is, what marketing strategies are feasible and likely to survive in the long run? A primary hypothesis is that they are the strategies that do not step on toes (either by lowering prices or by displacing workers), that are not perceived to step on toes (because the incursion is small or its adverse effects diffused among many people), or that step on the toes of people without any power to oppose the job creation. Because Supported Work is relatively small and has been undertaken as a demonstration, generalizing from its experience to a large-scale, national program requires caution.

Distributional effects are often not discussed in program evaluations. Benefit-cost analysis, for example, simply asks to what extent benefits outweigh costs, regardless of how they are allocated. The distribution of benefits and costs is likely to be important for predicting the behavior of program operators, however, because the strategies that do not make identifiable groups perceptibly worse off are more likely to survive even if their benefits are negligible. Adam Smith's well-known argument that what survives in a competitive economy will maximize social welfare does not necessarily follow in the case of public employment programs, because there is no mechanism to ensure that what survives is also efficient when resources are allocated partly through the political system. Thus, an efficient project may not survive if it concentrates costs on a well-defined group that has the power to kill it. Conversely, inefficient projects

24. For an analysis from this perspective, see Haveman's paper.
25. The experience of the operators in the Supported Work program in creating jobs is documented in detail and analyzed in Ball, *Implementing Supported Work*.

may survive if the distribution of costs is such that no one is made perceptibly worse off.

The nature of the markets in which the Supported Work program has been able to sustain its operation is suggestive of feasible operating strategies. The markets typically have had low barriers to entry and existing suppliers who were not able to resist the impact created by a new entrant. The Supported Work projects have frequently been undertaken in subsectors of larger markets, where competing suppliers are relatively small firms that are less likely to use unionized labor and use relatively little capital. In several of these submarkets there is a high turnover of firms.

More than one Supported Work project has been developed in furniture refinishing and reupholstery, operation of gasoline service stations, and food service projects, which are relatively competitive industries.[26] Their entry into these markets appears to be similar to that of an ordinary firm, with the projects charging prevailing market prices.

Supported Work has been able to develop a good deal of work in the construction industry—painting, housing rehabilitation, demolition, deleading, and sealing of abandoned buildings. Larger contractors and skilled craft unions appear not to work in the segments of the markets in which Supported Work has been active. The buildings that the projects work on are usually located in low-income neighborhoods and are often owned by city authorities or the Department of Housing and Urban Development, indicating perhaps that the expected return is low or quite risky.

Building maintenance is another industry where Supported Work projects have survived. The industry seems to contain relatively large firms serving large office buildings and apartment complexes and a subsector of smaller firms serving small customers. The entry and exit rates of these smaller firms is relatively high, and they appear to utilize short-term labor that resembles the Supported Work target groups. These firms in all probability are less likely to notice the entry of a public employment program into the market and are less able to oppose it through the channels that the more powerful large contractors and unions might employ.

In these examples of Supported Work projects the employment program operates basically as a contractor for output. Public employment programs also can operate directly in labor markets by selling labor services to private firms or public and nonprofit organizations. The distinc-

26. Technically the market structure appears to be monopolistic competition.

tion between selling final services and selling labor is difficult to make in many contexts; the actual tasks workers perform are often very similar. There may be some important differences, however, in the efficiency implications of the two arrangements.

In the Supported Work demonstration there are only a few instances of labor service contracts with private firms. They generally are for short-term labor for firms with a variable demand that is difficult for them to meet. In these cases, the program may be providing a service by specializing in the management of their employment in this segment of the labor market.

Most labor services are marketed to the public or nonprofit sector at prices lower than market wage rates. Contracts for labor services seem to have fallen into two groups. In one, the purchasing organizations do not have the budget to take over support of these jobs. In the other there is some assurance that a fraction of the subsidized work crew can eventually be placed in regular unsubsidized jobs.

The jobs in both cases usually involve services—for example, general maintenance, security, and clerical services—and therefore are similar to the services provided under contract. The efficiency implications for contract and direct labor services may differ, however. In the product market, the employment program competes with other contractors and is under pressure to charge prices that do not involve unfair competition. This constraint is absent in the labor market. To the degree that the employment programs have some secure source of financial support, the price charged for the labor services can be lowered as far as is necessary to make the transaction. There may be, however, an analog to unfair competition that affects not the wage rate but the type of work performed, the result of not competing with the existing work force of the host organization. To the degree that there is variation in the attractiveness of work tasks, the subsidized employees are very likely to be encouraged to do those tasks that the other workers prefer not to do. In the extreme it appears to be politically difficult for public agencies to take on subsidized work crews from a program of this kind when, for budget reasons, the regular employees are being laid off, even if the subsidized workers do not compete directly for either funds or work assignments.

The Supported Work program has undertaken a number of projects in partially unionized markets. In almost every case, steps were taken to avoid potential union opposition by encouraging liaisons with local labor union leaders either informally or by having them sit on the boards of the local programs. During the initial period of operation, the position taken by relevant unions as to which types of work would be sanctioned appears to have been an important influence on the course of job development. Some work projects have been explicitly ruled out; others have been limited in size or scope; still others have involved agreements with unions permitting the program to operate, provided union supervisors were hired. In short, the union response has been varied both across cities and industries. It is difficult to assess whether this has been due to differences in the unions' strength or in the program operators' willingness to accommodate to or anticipate union resistance.

Unions appear to have an important indirect impact on the program through their effect on the markets. By restricting supply, unionization creates an opportunity for expanding output that the program can exploit without necessarily confronting union opposition. In some industries— painting and building maintenance, for example—unions customarily do not do certain types of work. This may be either because customers will not purchase the work at union rates, because it is not suited to the more capital-intensive technology used by union suppliers, or because the type of work or the areas in which it is located are simply unattractive. Whatever the reason, the informal segment of the market created by the unions is a niche in the existing market structure that the program can enter with less risk of opposition.

While it is difficult to generalize from early experience about the response of unions, it appears that their very existence may well result in work projects that do not directly displace union labor, that are marketed at a price below the union price, and that are in the informal segment of the market.

Inferences to Be Drawn

Although there is obviously a great deal of variety in the type of market a targeted job creation program such as Supported Work will enter, it appears that the incentives facing such programs will lead them into particular niches of the economy. The program's size and status require that it gain the cooperation of existing institutions and may also require avoidance of established producers' territory.

What can be said about the allocative efficiency of filling these niches and about their relation to later job opportunities of participants? Although there are exceptions, avoiding opposition appears likely to push the program away from activities that are most allocatively efficient and away from activities that generate opportunities for postprogram earnings gains. The incentives and constraints facing operators appear to create a trade-off between allocative efficiency and other program objectives.

Projects that are allocatively efficient either will be profitable for an existing supplier or will be opposed by the supplier or union because they threaten displacement. If linking specific experience in the program to later jobs is the mechanism for improving postprogram employment and earnings, then avoiding opposition may make it impossible to create those links. Neither firms nor agencies nor unions now have the incentive to change the terms on which they will hire individuals from these target groups. This kind of program offers some subsidies of limited duration without necessarily changing incentives beyond the period of that subsidy. Therefore, the gains that individuals may make are more likely to result from the general skills and habits acquired than from direct links of program jobs to later jobs.

These arguments stand up whether the marketing strategy followed is one of entering output markets on a competitive basis, selling labor services at subsidized wages, or entering the nonunion segment of a partially unionized market.

ENTERING COMPETITIVE OUTPUT MARKETS. If projects in competitive output markets try to avoid opposition or legal difficulty by pricing their output at or near the market price, then displacement rather than expansion of output is very likely. If the displaced resources have poor prospects for reemployment, then the allocative efficiency benefits will be low. Moreover, the program will be unlikely to improve employment opportunities by creating jobs in markets in which existing firms use workers resembling program participants. Thus, to the extent that the displaced workers have better employment opportunities than do participants, both the allocative efficiency benefits of displacement and the improvement in postprogram employment opportunities will be greater. To achieve these two goals the program should ensure that participants have serious labor market problems and should create jobs in sectors in which employment opportunities are relatively good. Doing the latter will be difficult.

Although other uses are possible, public service employment programs can use their federal subsidy to charge below-market prices in output markets. If they do charge low prices, they will be more likely to expand output than to displace other producers. But charging a low price reduces the market test for this output, thereby making it difficult to ensure that the value of the output is at all commensurate with the costs of producing it. For example, if output is given away, many customers will demand it, and there is no mechanism to ensure that it will go to those who value it most.

PROVIDING SUBSIDIZED LABOR. By providing labor services to the public or nonprofit sectors at rates below market wages, the program is most likely to be able to expand output, thereby avoiding the opposition caused by displacement. The expansion in output will increase allocative efficiency, if it occurs in areas where services are undersupplied, and if the output is distributed to consumers who value it most.

In the public sector, services may be undersupplied because credentials required for civil service employment are unnecessarily demanding, because of budget pressure caused by recession, and because the local political process fails to register fully constituent demands. This last may well be the case for the poor who, it is argued, cannot exert their rightful influence on local and state governments. In designing projects such as park maintenance and the cleaning and sealing of abandoned houses to fulfill undersupplied social needs, the challenge is to ensure that the services are really undersupplied and that the tasks are not merely makework. Again, marketing these projects to local public agencies at low prices eliminates the discipline ordinarily imposed by markets to choose activities whose output is highly valued and to distribute the output efficiently.

The effect of such jobs on postprogram opportunities is difficult to assess. On the one hand, it can be argued that credential requirements for government employment will remain, that an undersupply of services will remain, and that public organizations without the budget to hire additional workers still will not have the funds. Hence, identical jobs could not be expected to be open to participants after the program. On the other hand, work experience in a public employment program may substitute for formal hiring credentials at some organizations. In any case, if the program can demonstrate that disadvantaged workers can work as productively as employees with credentials and convince governments to drop the credential requirements or make exceptions, postprogram jobs may become available. Moreover, output of previously undersupplied services may be expanded permanently if the program demonstrates the usefulness of the output; the program may even cause a community to discover a latent demand for an output simply by providing it for a short time. Finally, in some instances similar jobs at reasonable wage levels may exist in the private sector, and the program work experience may increase further employment opportunities for participants in these areas.

When host agencies have roll-over (guaranteed placement) arrangements as part of their labor contracts, some measure of displacement is more likely. A plausible hypothesis is that these contracts are accepted for jobs with high turnover rates and they allow for screening (at very low cost to the host agency) of a relatively uncertain population to determine who will be likely to stay at the job. The roll-over arrangements with host organizations are also likely to improve prospects for postprogram employment. There may be no social benefit if the program is absorbing screening costs that the organization would have ordinarily incurred but is happy to pass on. However, to the extent that the program specializes in performing screening and training functions that individual employers would not ordinarily perform, it may create general benefits to society.

ENTERING THE NONUNION SEGMENT OF A UNIONIZED MARKET. Allocative efficiency will be improved if the avoidance of existing territory leads the programs to expand markets that are undersupplied. This applies not only to the public sector but also to monopolies. When market power restricts supply or, equivalently, prices some customers out of the market, then the created jobs can certainly provide valued output by expanding supply. Projects in the partially unionized industry fall in this category.

As in the case of public services, the challenge is to ensure that the expanded output is valued by society. In this case, however, charging below-market prices or appealing to the special program status appears less likely to be an important element of the marketing strategy. Consequently, a market test is more likely to exist and ensure allocative efficiency. Postprogram job opportunities in these sectors are likely to be poor, however, because the formal, unionized segment of the market restricts output by limiting union membership, and because the informal, nonunion segment tends to be a low-wage, high-turnover submarket, in which jobs may not be attractive. Jobs in the program survive as long as they do not threaten organized labor groups, but when individuals leave the program they still will not have access to jobs in the organized segment of the market.[27]

27. This may be less of a problem during periods of high and growing demand in the construction industry.

SUMMARY. Encouraging operators of public employment programs to market output efficiently is a difficult task. Charging low prices or relying on the appeal of the special status of the program weakens the market test of the usefulness of output. Charging a market price and competing with private firms is difficult in any case and may push the program into markets in which postprogram job opportunities are unattractive. Expanding output of undersupplied public services is allocatively efficient, but identifying such services and negotiating their expansion with existing employees is no easy matter. Expanding output in a monopolized market also is allocatively efficient, but is likely to have a limited effect on future job opportunities.

Conclusion

The early experience of the Supported Work program has clearly demonstrated that small-scale job creation is technically feasible. Such a program *can* put workers with severe labor market difficulties to work. The experience has also shown that the form that job creation takes can vary a great deal. Jobs can range from public sector projects providing services to the poor to revenue-producing manufacturing projects similar to private enterprise, from low-skilled maintenance jobs to moderately skilled clerical jobs, from completely in-house production operations to placement of individual workers in public agencies or private firms with minimal program support.

Although direct creation of jobs on this scale has proved feasible, it is too early in the Supported Work demonstration to evaluate its effectiveness.[28] Economic efficiency is neither the only nor necessarily the most important criterion in evaluating the effectiveness of public employment; society may be willing to run an economically inefficient public employment program because it redistributes income to the poor or because it appeals to the nation's work ethic or for other reasons. This paper

28. The formal evaluation of the Supported Work demonstration eventually will provide quantitative evidence on participants' postprogram earnings gains (as well as other out-of-program benefits), quantitative evidence on the productive efficiency of a sample of work projects, and qualitative evidence on the allocative efficiency of those projects.

focuses on economic efficiency because it is an important consideration that has received little systematic attention in analyses of public employment programs. It is an especially relevant consideration when different programs designed to achieve the same objectives are being compared.

It has been argued that job creation that is efficient in the economist's sense is likely to be difficult. This follows from the observation that a job creation program must function within the existing environment. If there are substantial efficiency gains to be made by hiring disadvantaged workers, why have existing institutions not discovered them?

Of course existing institutions have not discovered all efficiency improvements—especially in the area of working with disadvantaged workers and providing useful public services. But creating such an employment program so that its benefits exceed its costs requires innovative design and implementation—discovery of special management and supervision techniques needed for organizing the production process with disadvantaged workers, ferreting out areas where resource allocation is inefficient, discovering new public services for which significant demand exists, and devoting careful thought to the link between the program work experience and future employment opportunities. The process of innovation is extremely hard to routinize, however, and the diffusion of innovations is far from automatic.

The belief that the program is indeed a significant social innovation is what makes it worth spending considerable resources to run the demonstration. But the skepticism concerning the ease of increasing economic efficiency is what makes it also necessary to spend considerable resources on a formal evaluation. The really important policy issue and intellectual challenge is not the evaluation of existing programs but how such evaluation can guide the design of future programs. How should a program be designed and organized so that the incentives and feedback mechanisms attract and reward strategies that achieve society's desired objectives and guide the program in the right direction?

The analysis was begun by comparing the tasks of a program operator to those of a manager of a private firm. Economists have a well-developed theory that argues that, in the private sector, profit incentives and price signals provide a self-correcting mechanism that selects efficient strategies and kills off the others. But a public service employment program operates in a very different world. There is uncertainty concerning the trade-offs between important objectives. Incentives to increase program size, generate local funding, and avoid opposition may push the program toward inefficient job creation strategies. Very few signals and feedback mechanisms exist, and it is not clear whether those that do exist signal movement in the direction desired by society. The environment faced by a public employment program, therefore, will not encourage behavior that is consistent with national objectives unless careful attention is paid to the design of incentives and feedback mechanisms.

Some of the questions that might be addressed in an analysis of design are:

If avoiding opposition is likely to push operators into areas where the output may not be highly valued, what could signal the operator that it is not useful? What incentives would ensure that the operator heeds the signals? Are there standard operating procedures that could routinize the signals and incentives?

If operators give too little attention to the productivity of work crews, what changes in incentives and information would encourage greater effort to improve productivity?

If the link between experience gained in the program and job opportunities later is poorly understood, what follow-up information about that link will be instructive? What incentives can be created to lead operators to adapt their job creation strategies toward those types of work with greater future payoffs? If some participants drop out, are fired, or fail to apply, what wage and other incentives will ensure that those appropriate to the program enter, stay, and leave when they are ready for outside jobs? For example, can an evaluative mechanism or remuneration scheme be designed to incorporate turnover rates or quality of job placements?

More generally, and most important, what mechanisms of communication are required to ensure that successful innovations diffuse to other programs?

The variety of job creation strategies, the variation in expected effectiveness, and the trade-offs among objectives make it likely that any public employment program will have considerable opportunity for improved performance. The variation provides an opportunity to learn what strategies are effective. The challenge is to obtain the information necessary to design signals and incentives so that the effective strategies survive and grow. Only then can public employment be expected to live up to its promise.

Appendix: Conceptual Framework for Efficiency Evaluation

The benefit-cost ratio is a measure of overall economic efficiency and the starting point for an analysis of productive and allocative efficiency.[29] The ratio can be divided into three components:

$$(1) \qquad b/c = e/c + v/c = e/c + (v/c^s)(c^s/c),$$

where b represents combined program benefits; c the social cost of the program; e the change in postprogram earnings;[30] v the value of the output produced by the program; and c^s the cost of having the same output produced by an alternative supplier. Equation 1 is simply an identity that highlights three dimensions of program effectiveness. The first ratio, e/c, can be thought of as the effectiveness of the program in raising postprogram earnings. The second and third ratios separate the effectiveness of the program in producing useful social output during the program, v/c, into two components—allocative efficiency v/c^s, and productive efficiency c^s/c.

These terms can be defined in the context of welfare economics. In order for an allocation of resources to be efficient (that is, Pareto optimal), there must be efficiency in (1) engineering, (2) input mix, (3) output mix, and (4) exchange. Efficiency in engineering and the mix of inputs ensures that the economy is on the production possibilities frontier. The concept of productive efficiency used in this paper encompasses both these aspects of efficiency. The concept of allocative efficiency concerns the other two aspects of efficiency and is independent of the degree of productive efficiency. Allocative efficiency is sometimes used elsewhere to refer to all four conditions for efficiency.[31]

29. To simplify, small changes in output are considered; changes in marginal costs and benefits, and thus welfare loss "triangles" and the distinction between marginal and average quantities, are ignored. Accounting for these complications would not significantly alter the framework.

30. For programs such as Supported Work that are designed to reduce crime, drug dependence, welfare dependence, etc., additional benefits also exist. For purposes of this analysis, e can be thought of as including the change in all of these benefits.

31. Because the concept of efficiency is a general equilibrium concept but a partial equilibrium analysis is performed here, the distinction between productive and allocative efficiency is somewhat artificial, and the concepts do not correspond

Productive Efficiency

Many measures of productivity are used in the economics literature. Here the measure is one of total factor productivity, the ratio of the cost of alternative suppliers to the cost of the public employment program, c^s/c. The higher the ratio, the higher the productive efficiency of the program.

Beginning with the presumption that the price charged in competitive markets equals the social cost of producing the output, the general strategy for measuring productive efficiency is to ask what price alternative suppliers would charge to provide the same service. This supply price, p^s, which is typically the prevailing market price, can then be adjusted if there is reason to believe that the price does not reflect the marginal social cost of the output, as in cases of monopoly or union power. The following identity provides a framework for measuring productive efficiency:

$$(2) \qquad\qquad c^s/c = (c^s/p^s)(p^s/c).$$

The first ratio represents the adjustment factor for the difference between the measured price of alternative supply and the social cost of alternative supply. This adjustment will equal one when they are the same and will incorporate estimates of monopoly waste when they are not. Finally, the cost of alternative supply is intended to be the cost at full employment so that the measure of productivity is not dependent on the level of economic activity.

This index of productive efficiency is relatively straightforward theoretically and contains a clear set of questions for empirical estimation.

---

perfectly to the general equilibrium conditions. For example, if the program simply employs unemployed workers, freeing displaced workers to produce output elsewhere in the economy and thereby shifting out the production possibilities frontier, then overall efficiency is increased. Most economists would think of that as an increase in productive efficiency, whereas it is treated here as an increase in allocative efficiency. In the literature on productivity in the public sector a similar distinction is made using the terms *efficiency* and *effectiveness* where *productive efficiency* and *allocative efficiency* are used here. See John P. Ross and Jesse Burkhead, *Productivity in the Local Government Sector* (Heath, 1974), especially chaps. 3 and 4.

Allocative Efficiency

The index of allocative efficiency, v/c^s, has as its denominator the cost of alternative supply. The numerator, the value of output to society, is extremely difficult to analyze theoretically, to say nothing of empirically measuring it. A simple identity can be developed that shows what factors affect allocative efficiency and what information is most useful to collect in order to quantify it.

THE COMPETITIVE MARKET CASE. While public employment programs will not typically sell output in competitive markets, the simple competitive case serves as the point of departure for the more complicated cases.

The fundamental assumption is that the price consumers are willing to pay, p^d, represents the value of output to society. If the program sells a small amount of additional output at prevailing prices in a perfectly competitive market, then the value of output, v, will equal that demand price and, hence, project revenue, r. Thus, project revenue is a good measure of value of output to society and one that can easily be measured.[32]

If, instead of producing additional output, the program displaces other producers, the value of output is the same as in the expanded output case. If the entire economy is a frictionless competitive economy at full employment, displaced resources will immediately be reemployed, producing useful output elsewhere in the economy. The value of the output they produce is their opportunity cost, c^o. But in a competitive economy, opportunity cost equals supply price, which equals demand price—and the value of output is the same as it was in the output expansion case.

In short, in a perfectly competitive, full employment economy, the value of output to society, consumers' willingness to pay, revenue actually paid, the price charged by alternative suppliers, and the opportunity cost of the resources used by alternative suppliers are all equal. But public employment programs do not typically produce output for sale in com-

---

32. Assuming the market is in equilibrium, revenue will also equal the supply price, so that revenue can be used to measure supply price and hence to calculate productive efficiency. The index of allocative efficiency, v/c^s, will therefore equal one in the competitive case (provided the social cost of alternative supply equals its price) because $v = p^d = r = p^s = c^s$.

petitive markets. If they did there would be little concern about low value of output; advocates would be able to argue that the market test would ensure the usefulness of the output produced. Once the world of a perfectly competitive full employment economy is left, value of output, revenue, supply price, and opportunity cost need no longer be equal, and there is no longer any simple way to assess the value of output.

DEPARTURES FROM THE PERFECTLY COMPETITIVE CASE. Departures from perfect competition can be reflected in several different outcomes: revenue may not represent consumers' willingness to pay;[33] external benefits may exist;[34] opportunity cost may not equal the cost of alternative supply.[35]

Analysis requires consideration of a fair number of cases. Because the value of output to society depends on whether output in a sector is increased by the program or whether the program displaces existing producers, these two extreme cases are considered first. The intermediate case of part output expansion and part displacement is then a simple combination of the two. Because supply price and project revenue are both measurable, they are emphasized in the analysis.

In the case of expanded output, the value of output depends on consumers' willingness to pay for the output, the extent to which that willingness to pay represents altruism, and the extent of external benefits.[36] The price, p^d, on the market demand curve for the output is the amount the consumers of the output would be willing to pay for the service. It need not be equal to the market price before job creation, or to the price paid to the public employment program, because of existing allocative inefficiencies. For example, a failure of the political process might mean that too few public services are provided, so that the benefits of additional services would exceed their cost. By increasing output, public employment would improve the allocative efficiency of such a sector.

Neither does the amount of money paid to the public employment pro-

33. For example, federal subsidies may be used to purchase services for poor individuals.
34. For example, property values in a whole neighborhood may be improved as a result of rehabilitating a few houses on the block.
35. If, for example, resources are not reemployed immediately and without adjustment cost because unemployment is high.
36. By *consumers* is meant the recipients of the output; they may differ from the contracting organization that pays for the services. *External benefits* refers only to the externalities associated with consuming the output, not to the other program benefits such as increased postprogram earnings and reduced welfare payments.

gram for the output necessarily equal the amount the recipients would be willing to pay for the service. A public employment program generally requires a subsidy from the federal government or another organization, and this permits the program to charge a price less than people are willing to pay—or even to give services away.[37] Another reason project revenue may not represent willingness to pay arises from consumers' desire to redistribute income. Altruistic buyers may be willing to pay more for output produced by disadvantaged workers than they would for the same output produced by an ordinary supplier.[38] Thus, the amount they are willing to pay can be thought of as including two components, a part for the output per se and a part to support the overall program and its concept. This latter benefit is different in kind from value of consuming the output per se; it is not included here as part of the value of output.[39]

Another kind of additional benefit of expanding output includes externalities as conventionally defined. For example, when public employees rehabilitate several houses on a block, the whole neighborhood benefits. These neighborhood benefits should be added to those of the residents of the rehabilitated houses. Thus, $v = p^d + x$, where x represents external benefits per unit of output.

Since revenue, r, is easily observed, it can sometimes be used to place bounds on the value of output, using the following identity:

$$(3) \qquad v/c^s = x/c^s + (p^d/\hat{p}^d)(\hat{p}^d/r)(r/c^s),$$

37. The Comprehensive Employment and Training Act restricts payments to particular target groups—presumably expressing a national altruism in support of redistribution to those groups. The local government receiving restricted funds will be willing to pay more for services provided by target group members than it would for the same services provided by other suppliers (provided that the restriction is binding).

38. Altruism may also exist because the recipients of the output are disadvantaged. When the organization paying for the output is different from the recipient, this benefit may be reflected in project revenue. In any case, this additional benefit is also treated separately from v in the analysis.

39. The efficiency benefits of redistribution (that is, citizens' utility increases from having income redistributed to the poor) are often lumped together with other externalities. The separation of this externality from those other externalities is useful because there are other policies, such as welfare payments, that do not require job creation but can achieve the same redistributive benefits. Thus, the assessment of the value of output produced on the created job is better done using the narrower definition of efficiency. The separation of the efficiency benefits of redistribution from the value of output should not be interpreted to mean that these benefits do not exist or are unimportant. In deciding whether to run a public employment program, the benefits should definitely be counted; indeed, for many voters they may be the overriding concern.

where $\hat{p}^d$ is the price consumers are willing to pay for the output, given that it is produced by disadvantaged workers. In this case the desired information is: whether the program is charging the maximum price it can get (does $\hat{p}^d/r = 1$?); whether the consumers are paying for the service and whether their altruism is a significant factor in their decision to buy (does $p^d/\hat{p}^d = 1$?); and whether there are significant external benefits (is $x/c^s > 0$?). Clearly, accurate quantitative estimates of $\hat{p}^d/r$, $p^d/\hat{p}^d$, and x/c^s are unattainable, but qualitative information on each can be obtained and used to place rough bounds on them.[40]

At the other extreme from output expansion is the case in which total sector output remains unchanged, so that the public employment output displaces some existing producers. There are no benefits to consumers in that sector because the quantity of output consumed does not change. The value of output depends on what happens in other sectors of the economy. If the displaced resources are unemployed, then no additional output is produced and the value of output is zero. If the displaced resources are immediately employed producing useful output in some other sector, then the value of output equals the value of their marginal product in that sector. In other words, the value of output is given by the opportunity cost of the displaced resources, c^o, and $v/c^s = c^o/c^s$.

If this ratio looks suspect, it should. Assuming that markets are working well, it is literally the ratio of the opportunity cost to itself. But recall that in order to have measures of productive efficiency that were independent of the business cycle, c^s was defined to be the social cost of producing a unit of output when the economy is at full employment. Thus, c^o/c^s equals one by definition if the economy is at full employment. But below full employment it will be less than one, and it will depend on the probability and duration of unemployment compared to

---

40. An alternative way of placing a bound on the value of output is to assume that the sector was allocatively efficient before the expansion of output. Then the amount consumers would be willing to pay for additional output can be no more than the supply price ($p^d \leq p^s$). Thus, an estimate is given by $v = x + p^s$. For all the reasons discussed in the text, however, this estimate may exceed the actual value of output. When revenue is much lower than supply price, this estimate is especially likely to be too high because of the absence of a market test and because it assumes that the expanded output is distributed among consumers in the most efficient way possible. If output is not competitively priced or is given away free of charge, it need not be given to those who would be most willing to pay for it. Indeed, a program with income redistribution objectives might intentionally not do so.

that at full employment.[41] Thus, the index of allocative efficiency depends on the unemployment rate but the index of productive efficiency does not (except to the extent that the opportunity cost of participants varies with the unemployment rate).

Once the extreme cases have been analyzed it is simple to analyze the general case because the value of output is the sum of the value for the increased output and the value for the displaced output. The index of allocative efficiency is given by the following identity, which is simply a weighted average of the indexes in the two extreme cases, where the weights depend on the fraction of output that causes displacement,

$$(4) \qquad v/c^s = \lambda(c^o/c^s) + (1 - \lambda)(x/c^s + p^d/c^s),$$

where

$$p^d/c^s = (p^d/\hat{p}^d)(\hat{p}^d/r)(r/c^s),$$

and λ is the fraction of output that would have been produced in the absence of the program.

The allocative efficiency of the created jobs, thus, depends on the extent of displacement, λ; the allocative efficiency in the sector before job creation, p^d/c^s; the pricing policy of the program, r/c^s; the probability and duration of unemployment in the sector relative to full employment, c^o/c^s; the extent of altruism, $p^d/\hat{p}^d$; the extent to which revenue represents willingness to pay, $\hat{p}^d/r$; and the extent of externalities, x.

Comments by Robert Taggart

In a recent article on job creation, Labor Secretary Ray Marshall was quoted as saying, "If the alternative is not working, anything you do to put people to work is beneficial. I have that kind of simple-minded view."[42] I do not think anyone will really accuse Dr. Marshall of being simple-minded. My analysis of his thinking is that the pros and cons of public service employment have not been and may never be resolved, and that we have to make judgments based on common sense and the rule of

41. In fact, the issue is more complicated than this simple partial equilibrium model suggests. Analysis of the benefits of displacing resources depends on the model being used and the alternative being compared. The analysis properly requires an economy-wide model, within either a general equilibrium or a macroeconomic framework.

42. *Congressional Quarterly Weekly Report*, vol. 35 (February 19, 1977), p. 307.

thumb, and that these suggest that public service employment is worthwhile. If such a view is simple-minded, I am proud to share it.

When the National Council on Employment Policy reviewed the experience of the Public Employment Program in the early 1970s, we found that mostly unemployed persons were being hired to do what seemed reasonably productive tasks. They appeared to function as well as other employees. Almost all the federal funds went for wages. Substitution was evident, but we reasoned there were slippages in any form of spending. The most disadvantaged persons were not receiving priority; yet experimental projects that gave them emphasis functioned as well as regular programs. We therefore concluded that public service employment was worthwhile as a countercyclical tool and could be used to provide jobs for the hard-to-employ. We also concluded that it would be difficult, if not impossible, to fully resolve the issues that had been debated since the New Deal's employment programs, so we turned our attention to other issues.

As resources expanded for public service employment, so did the number of researchers. Econometricians calculated the cost per created job and the inflationary impact using their mathematical models. Others postulated on the scale of substitution from theoretical simulations. While this work has been technically sophisticated, it is not apparent that we have advanced our real understanding. With attention focused on these analyses, we have almost totally ignored the collection and assessment of basic information on the permanent and temporary public employment programs (titles 2 and 6) of the Comprehensive Employment and Training Act, so that we have very little basis for making even simple-minded judgments, much less for testing and improving theoretical models. It is perhaps time to step back and critically examine the past and potential contributions of our professional skills on this important public issue.

The paper by Peter Kemper and Philip Moss offers a timely opportunity for such stock-taking. The authors have done a good job of analyzing the conceptual issues involved in assessing the output of work programs. They focus on two questions: how effectively do the subsidized workers perform their jobs; and how useful is the output produced? *Productive efficiency* refers to productivity as compared to that of alternate suppliers and *allocative efficiency* to the usefulness of the product relative to other uses of the same resources.

Measuring productive efficiency is not straightforward even where a product is sold in the marketplace or under a competitive bid approach.

The purchase price does not necessarily reflect real value, since altruism may be involved on the part of the purchaser. A private firm, for instance, might offer to paint houses for $250 each while the Supported Work project also bids $250 but does a job worth only $175. Alternatively, union workers may not normally do this type of work because it is uneconomical; if they were willing to do the job at $250, this price might be inflated by their union wage and might not reflect the value of the product. In a broader sense, labor-intensive approaches may not be most efficient. No one might be able to paint single units more cheaply than subsidized workers, but it might cost much less to restore whole buildings at a time. The availability of labor or "do-goodism" might encourage the less efficient approaches.

Kemper and Moss suggest even more uncertainties in measuring allocative efficiency. The degree of allocative efficiency depends on: (1) the degree public employment project outputs substitute for existing similar outputs and the extent the resources that otherwise would have been used to produce the latter are reemployed; and (2) the benefits to consumers of the outputs that are net additions. As an example, suppose that a Supported Work project hiring ex-offenders starts up a tire recapping business. It may compete with a similar operation in the prisons, and one in the private sector operating in the central city and employing many disadvantaged persons, including large numbers of ex-offenders. The success of Supported Work in securing business may have little effect on the net output of recapped tires or on the well-being of the offender population. The utility of a project where there is no substitution is anyone's guess, since there is no test of what the public would pay. As Kemper and Moss note, it is impossible to determine how much the public wants the product or takes into account the additional hiring of the disadvantaged per se in agreeing to purchase it.

What Kemper and Moss have done, then, is to break down the familiar question, "Is it made work, or real work?" into a subset of questions that are just as difficult to answer. Even if guesses could be made about the real value of the output in the Supported Work experiment or in public service employment programs, uncertainties would still exist about the replicability of the experiment, about the extent of the learning curve phenomenon, and about likely success under different economic conditions. Kemper and Moss also suggest that there may be trade-offs between the value of the product and the value of the work experience for participants, so that no one variable can be considered alone.

While the authors hold out the hope that analysis will yield answers about the comparative effectiveness of different strategies, this is as unlikely as answers to the more aggregate questions. For example, these authors (as well as Haveman) conclude that it is most efficient to specialize in labor-intensive service projects. One must doubt whether the results are not skewed by the fact that in manufacturing there is a competitive market standard providing a hard measure of productive efficiency and an indication of the desirability of the product to buyers, whereas in the service sector the Supported Work efforts look comparatively better because the standards of comparison are themselves less efficient.

Judgments on all these issues ultimately rest on the normative issue of how much we are willing to pay to put a person to work. I think we probably should have tried to resolve this before launching the Supported Work experiment, since when it is completed, we will be arguing about what constitutes success or failure. I am not sure we will benefit from refined analyses as much as we would from some ball-park judgments.

For instance, the subsidy cost per person-year under the Supported Work experiment after two years of operation was just below $10,000, and costs seem to be stabilizing at roughly this level. Participant wages account for half of total expenditures, but this means that it is costing about $2 to get $1 paid in wages rather than transfers. Is this reasonable in the sense that benefits to participants or improved efficiency over time will make the program worthwhile? Benefit-cost analyses of past work experience programs have suggested earnings gains less than $200 annually for around five years at best—that is, a current value of less than $1,000. This would mean we are paying several thousand dollars per person net of any long-range impact or immediate output in order to organize work for this group. What are we willing to pay? Are there alternatives?

I would compare, for instance, the Supported Work experience with that of the welfare demonstration program under the Public Employment Program where wages accounted for 95 percent of expenses. Subtracting the value of the output produced from this yields the net cost to taxpayers, which was certainly less than providing transfer payments as high as program wages. Does this make the welfare demonstration approach more effective than Supported Work? Can it serve the same types of clients as Supported Work? Can it be implemented nationally? Even if we get more data on the Supported Work program, there will be incredible difficulty in grappling with such questions. This does not mean that the experiment was not worthwhile. It will certainly help improve our judgments. But I am not sure how much highly sophisticated analysis of the results will add to our understanding, given the inevitable underlying uncertainties.

The Kemper and Moss paper thus suggests to me the difficulties of moving beyond "rough and ready"—or in Secretary Marshall's term "simple-minded"—judgments. I find in reading the papers in this conference, and in assessing other literature on productivity, substitution, and valuation of services, that it is very difficult to move out of the range where untestable assumptions dictate results. I believe this situation is inherent and that we ought to admit it, putting less emphasis on highly sophisticated speculations and more on providing basic and descriptive information that will be useful to pragmatic policymakers. During the two days of this conference, between $30 million and $35 million was spent around the country under work experience and public service employment programs. We know nothing about the jobs being done and next to nothing about the workers who have been hired. One must question the value, then, of arguing here about how many angels can dance on the head of a pin.

Comments by Ernst W. Stromsdorfer

The discussion at this conference reflects the fact that we are far from a clear understanding either in conceptual or in empirical terms of both the equity and efficiency effects of a large-scale program of public service employment. The papers by Haveman and Kemper and Moss are, therefore, helpful, though they emphasize monetary costs and benefits at the expense of programmatic and operational issues that may be less quantifiable at present but contribute to a more fundamental understanding of ultimate program feasibility and performance.

Since so little is understood about the ultimate economic effects of this type of subsidy, we may do well to follow Hamermesh's example and set up a taxonomy of the economic problems that accompany this program. The Haveman and Kemper and Moss studies can then be compared against this taxonomy.

First, as the authors recognize, both efficiency and equity considerations must be discussed. Each equity or efficiency issue must be considered in its long-run and short-run context. Each issue should be discussed from a private, social, and governmental economic perspective. Each issue should be discussed for different economic conditions—cyclical unemployment, structural unemployment, and frictional unemployment, at some defined full-employment rate. Policy weights for the significance of different good and bad outcomes can change over the business cycle. Analytical focus will differ when public service employment is considered as a short-run cyclical program rather than as a program to deal with long-run structural unemployment or labor market disability. Even more demands are made on the analysis when one tries to achieve cyclical and structural objectives simultaneously.

Fiscal displacement, restructuring of the skill mix of the labor force, the skill-specific income distribution, the potential loss in national output, the relative shares of public and private output, the composition of public output relative to private consumption needs, the size of the multiplier for public service employment, the valuation of public sector output, and the structure of incentives to individuals and governments receiving subsidies are just a few of the major issues that should be organized in a broader framework so that this potentially significant program can be properly analyzed.

We should explicitly consider both the complementary and competitive relationships among these issues and how these issues interact within the design of any given program variant. These relationships and interactions are complex and full of paradoxes. For instance, an aim may be to make the program permanent but to provide for transitional tenure of any potential public service employee. To do this, wages have to be kept low or the tenure of employment specified. But, low wages or fixed tenure will conflict with the equity and income distribution objectives of such a program. Similarly, concern over high budget costs may result in arguments for low-wage low-quality supervision, and high labor-intensity jobs—a program structure that can conflict with long-run efficiency and reduce on-the-job training and, consequently, impair the program's ability to deal with frictional or structural unemployment. Or again, at full employment of bookbinders, government production of bookbinding is less of a competitive threat to the private sector than at less than full employment of bookbinders. Yet, at less than full employment it is less costly in a social sense to build more books and the effects of errors in decision making will be less if the wrong kind or amount of books is built. But, even this statement is qualified if bookbinders in the public employment program are paid less than the going wage rate. A distinct competitive edge is then given to these bookbinders even at full employment, and displacement, even if not inevitable, will be enough of a fear to result in strenuous efforts to stop public employment in that area of endeavor.[43]

With these general thoughts in mind, I would like to turn to a set of more specific comments on the papers at hand.

As Haveman points out, if two programs are perfect substitutes for each other in terms of both the clientele they serve and the expected equity effects, then the analysis of the competing programs can concentrate on efficiency concerns. However, this puts a heavy demand on the efficiency analysis—a demand that becomes more severe as the simplifying assumptions stipulated are less well met. Since practical politics are such that it will be the equity concerns, much more than the efficiency concerns, that will dominate the design and operation of such a program, the Haveman paper, for all its excellence and clarity, should have focused more on these former concerns. It could have done so, while still maintaining an efficiency emphasis, through the development of a more complete double-entry cost-benefit taxonomy for the gainers and losers of such a program. Haveman's benefit-cost formula is helpful, but still does not go far enough. Table 2 gives a much more complete accounting of the gainers and losers and the categories of benefits and costs they face. A detailed cost-benefit analysis based on such a taxonomy, even if given variables are not well quantified, can give a much more complete picture of the equity considerations involved, even while focusing on efficiency measures. In fact, these variables provide the building blocks for an equity analysis.

Importantly, but perhaps regrettably, as one develops the estimates in this double-entry system, it becomes increasingly clear that it is the benefits and costs as narrowly viewed from the perspective of the taxpayer and various levels of government, not the more appropriate social costs and benefits, that generally determine public perceptions of the success or failure of government programs.[44] This is an obvious fact, but it bears repeating.

43. If there were a better understanding of these factors and their interrelationships, perhaps the Carter administration would not have itself boxed into a situation where it claimed to be able to develop a welfare reform program in which public service employment or a welfare job simultaneously is able to: be productive; not displace other labor or output; pay a low or minimum wage; help get people out of poverty; be highly labor intensive; give people skills; and be a job people will take willingly but will not want to keep.

44. Most governmental units only imperfectly reflect societal goals in their decision-making behavior and some fail to do so completely on any given issue.

Table 2. Benefits and Costs of a Program of Public Service Employment from the Perspectives of Society, the Program Participant, the Taxpayer, and the Government[a]

Perspective	Benefits	Costs
Society	Value of output and services produced	Value of output and services displaced
	Resources released due to displacement of output and services (such as workers, machinery and facilities, raw materials, supervisory and administrative costs, and training costs)	Resources consumed due to increased output and services (such as workers, machinery and facilities, raw materials, supervisory and administrative costs, and training costs)
	Social and psychological benefits to reemployed workers, their families, and third parties (such as reduced medical or psychological care costs or other nonmonetary or noneconomic benefits)	Social and psychological costs to displaced workers, their families and owners of displaced factors of production other than labor (such as increased medical or psychological care costs or other nonmonetary or noneconomic costs)
	External benefits (such as reduced crime and delinquency or other nonmonetary or noneconomic benefits such as an increase in the perception of justice or equity being served)	External costs (such as increased crime and delinquency or other nonmonetary or noneconomic costs such as a decrease in the perception of justice or equity being served)
Program participant	Value of wages received	Value of wages forgone
	Value of subsidies or transfers received	Value of subsidies or transfers lost
	Social and psychological benefits to reemployed worker (such as reduced medical or psychological costs)	Psychological costs of becoming employed due to governmental coercion
Taxpayer[b]	Reduction in taxes (as welfare roles and transfer payments decrease), resulting in increase in value of goods or services the taxpayer may consume, and resources released due to the displacement of output and services[c]	Increase in taxes (as transfer payments increase because of displacement of labor), resulting in decrease in value of goods or services the taxpayer may consume, and resources consumed due to increased output and services[c]
Government[d]	Reduction in payments due to reduced case load and, hence, reduction of administrative costs, and reduction of transfer payments	Increase in payments due to displaced persons entering welfare roles and resulting in increased case load and, hence, an increase in administrative costs, and increase in transfer payments

Finally, if such an expanded taxonomy had been carried out, perhaps the potentially confusing statement concerning the flow of persons from public to private jobs in Haveman's definition of social costs in the Dutch program could have been avoided. At the high wages being paid, the lack of movement from public service to private employment could just as easily mean that net benefits to participants for staying in the public program are greater than net private employment benefits. This could occur even though the public program might have increased a worker's marginal revenue product over time enough that he could earn a higher wage in the private sector than he had before entering the program. Thus, a variety of components and perspectives develop out of a more detailed accounting framework.

The major benefit of the Kemper and Moss paper is its procedure for measuring the cost of producing a unit of output in public service programs, first in terms of the number of different physical units of input required and then in terms of the sum of the products of the actual or estimated prices of these inputs times the number of inputs of different types used. This simple but useful technique should lend considerable clarity to the discussion concerning the relative costs and efficiency of output in the public service sector versus that in the private sector or other sectors of government. Much confusion and emotionalism can thus be avoided. Since the function of Kemper and Moss was more methodological in nature, they discuss the efficiency considerations of cost-benefit analysis and the conflicts in behavior that are likely to result from pursuing multiple competitive goals somewhat more thoroughly than the

---

Notes to table 2:

a. Omission of the *bureaucrat* from this list of economic actors may be a serious one. The bureaucrat is one of the most critical links in determining whether a social program has a ghost of a chance of succeeding in its stated purposes. Not only do bureaucrats openly as well as covertly thwart programs that are hostile to their personal or institutional goals, they can also change the programs radically either through the writing of that vast body of law known as Federal Regulations or through direct intervention in the field.

b. The set of individual taxpayers is not the same group as "citizens other than program participants," whose costs and benefits are most closely approximated by those of society.

c. These opportunity costs are essentially the same as those for society.

d. The specification of "government" may have to be broken out into two or more levels. With respect to public service employment, a variety of governmental levels gets into the act: the Office of the President ("The White House"), the several federal bureaucracies, the regional offices of the federal bureaucracies, and state offices at the state, regional, and local levels. This complexity leads federal bureaucrats who fund research to stress process analysis and political feasibility heavily rather than "impact" or cost-benefit analysis. Apart from the practical problems of setting up and running a program, the basic Gordian Knot to be cut is an adjudication of the equity losses and gains among such groups. In such a context, it becomes transparently clear that the ability to compensate losers from the efficiency gains of a "socially efficient" program is irrelevant if compensation is not or cannot be made from the net increase in output. The uncompensated losers will block the program if at all possible.

Haveman paper. This is especially true of their section on allocative efficiency.

In contrast, however, the practical lessons highlighted in the Haveman paper are important and serve to balance the picture. Haveman points out in dramatic relief the difficulties in maintaining social control over an entitlement program wherein there is no logical limit to the size of the beneficiary population.[45] Second, he points out the serious inefficiencies that result when the receipt of benefits by one level of government is separated from the tax-cost burden imposed at a higher level. The basic condition for social inefficiency is built into the program and, instead of an underproduction of social goods, which some analysts assert to be the general case, the stage is set for overproduction; moreover, there is a general likelihood of exacerbating the maldistribution of public and private output.

As a final criticism of Kemper and Moss, there is no reason to separate demand into altruistic and nonaltruistic components. Insofar as individuals in the private sector ultimately receive psychological utility or disutility from all economic acts, the benefits they receive from altruistic, but voluntary, purchase of a good or service are no different from any other component of utility. The value of the output of a public service program is not reduced, nor should it be stigmatized in any way thereby. Instead of lending clarity to the discussion of the value of the program's output, this distinction merely confuses the issue with its departure from correct treatment of economic value. Value is ultimately subjective. Unlike the bifurcation in method of estimating the cost of outputs, this division adds nothing. In addition, if it is a government agency that is altruistic in its overgenerous purchase and reward of output from a public service employment program, this altruism component is no different from any other subsidy and should be treated as such.

In conclusion, these two excellent papers, in conjunction with the encyclopedic paper of Kesselman, contain excellent lessons and advice on the development of a program of public service employment or a work-conditioned welfare program in the United States.

---

45. Congress usually puts limits either in money or categorical terms on the population to be served. A more important problem is that there is almost an infinite set of interest groups that seek special favors, and Congress has considerable trouble in resisting their claims of need. The result is that major laws—like the Occupational Safety and Health Act of 1970—are passed in relative ignorance and lack of awareness of their overall social import.

David H. Greenberg

Participation in Public Employment Programs

Over the last thirty years, Congress has considered legislation from time to time that would establish the government as the employer of last resort, guaranteeing a job to all those who are unable to secure employment in the regular labor market. This possibility appears to have been seriously considered during debate over the Employment Act of 1946. More recently, the Humphrey-Hawkins bill would have established "a comprehensive structure for guaranteeing . . . the right for useful and meaningful employment to every adult American able and willing to work."[1] Less ambitiously, the Carter administration has advocated a welfare reform program in which the government would attempt to provide jobs for the heads of low-income families with children, whenever these persons could not obtain conventional employment.

This paper is concerned with an aspect of guaranteed employment programs about which there is very little information: the number and characteristics of persons who would participate in these programs were the opportunity available.[2] Information about the supply of applicants to guaranteed employment programs is required to address important

1. *Equal Opportunity and Full Employment Act of 1976,* Hearing before the Subcommittee on Equal Opportunities of the House Committee on Education and Labor, 93:2 (GPO, 1974), p. 96.
2. Estimates have been made of the "universe of need" for public employment, but there is no reason to believe either that every person within this universe will wish to participate in public employment or that all public employment participants will be drawn from the universe of need. See, for example, Garth L. Mangum, "Government as Employer of Last Resort," in Sar A. Levitan, Wilbur J. Cohen, and Robert J. Lampman, eds., *Towards Freedom From Want* (Madison, Wis.: Industrial Relations Research Association, 1968), pp. 135–61; and "Public Employment: Policy Issues and Data Needs," discussion paper (Office of Economic Opportunity, Office of Planning, Research, and Evaluation, Aug. 10, 1971; processed), p. 13.

questions about the programs and is also useful in assessing less ambitious public employment programs with limited numbers of slots.
Among the questions addressed in this paper are the following: What
would be the cost of guaranteeing employment? How effective and efficient would such a program be in alleviating poverty? How many slots
would be required for a guaranteed employment program? If the supply
of applicants is excessive, should the stipend or wage paid under the program be lowered? If so, by how much? If not, how should the available
slots be rationed? How many persons in major program target groups—
for example, the currently unemployed and persons who have withdrawn
from the labor force after becoming discouraged with job search—will
actually enroll in particular programs? How will these numbers change
as the wage rate offered by the program changes? If the stipend is generous enough to help those who cannot find a job, will the program also
attract persons who are able to secure conventional employment but only
at relatively low wages? If so, how many? How effective are policies
aimed at reducing the number of low-wage workers who quit their jobs
to enroll in public employment programs? (Although information about
the size and composition of the potential supply population for guaranteed employment programs should provide considerable insight into all
these questions, complete answers to several require information on the
demand side of employment programs as well—for example, on the number of jobs that can be created and on the extent to which federal, state,
and local governments will substitute public employment jobholders for
persons they otherwise would hire from regular labor markets. Such
issues are beyond the scope of this paper, but are examined elsewhere in
this volume. Fortunately these demand problems are analytically quite
distinct from the supply issues with which this paper is primarily concerned. Policymakers need both types of information, but estimates of
supply populations are, in themselves, very useful.)

Although the methodology that is used to attempt to answer these
questions is sufficiently flexible to encompass a broad range of assumptions about individual behavior and program design characteristics, relatively few of those characteristics are examined in this paper. Moreover,
the scope of the paper is limited to how a single population group—
husbands and wives in intact households—would have responded to variously defined job creation programs had they been operating during 1973.
It is also obviously important to know how other population groups
would respond to such programs and how the response of various groups

would change under different economic conditions than those that existed in 1973, when the unemployment rate was around 5 percent. Consequently, the estimates reported here are of limited applicability. They do, however, provide an impression of the magnitude of the supply response of a very important population group and how the response varies with important program characteristics such as the program wage rate, hours of work offered, waiting period of unemployment before becoming eligible, and length of stay permitted in the program.

The paper first considers some of the factors that determine whether individuals will decide to participate in a job creation program and suggests a methodological framework for simulating supply responses to public employment programs. After a brief discussion of the primary data source, the required parameters, and important program characteristics to be varied, the methodological framework is used to estimate supply response to several alternative guaranteed employment programs.[3] Finally, the paper summarizes the major results of the simulation, discusses some of the limitations of these results, and describes some aspects of an effort to extend this research.

Determinants of Participation

Governmental agencies that employ participants in public employment programs can be viewed as major purchasers of labor from markets that also serve conventional employers, both in the private sector and in the government sector.[4] Like conventional employers, public employment programs may tap three sources of labor: the employed, the unemployed, and those who are out of the labor force. The relative importance of these three sources depends on the relative magnitudes of wage rates in the program and the conventional sector, the responses of workers and employers in the conventional sector to changes in wage rates, and the state of the overall economy.

When the wage the program pays is above the market wage workers can obtain, they will be attracted toward public employment even if they

3. For a detailed development of the methodological framework, see David H. Greenberg, "The Supply Population for Public Employment Programs," technical analysis paper, U.S. Department of Health, Education, and Welfare, Office of Income Security Policy (December 1977; processed).

4. The characteristics of these markets and the likely effect of public employment programs on them are examined in ibid.

hold jobs in the conventional sector or are outside the labor force. Consequently, in order to retain workers who are eligible to participate in public employment, employers would have to pay them at or near the program wage. As wage rates for these workers are forced up, however, employer demand for the workers will probably decrease. Those whom employers do not want to retain will presumably join the public employment program. Availability of higher wages would probably also draw persons into the labor market who had been unwilling to work because of low wage rates. Thus, the number of employed workers who actually enter public employment ultimately depends on the extent to which employer demand is reduced as market wage levels are forced up, while the supply of nonworkers is contingent on how responsive these persons are to improvements in earnings opportunities.

If program wages fall below the market wages workers usually receive, they will tend to consider public employment only when they are unemployed, preferring a higher paying conventional job whenever one is available. However, some unemployed workers would refuse to accept any public employment job, if it paid substantially less than the wage that they usually command in the conventional sector, and those who do accept would leave the program as soon as they could find a conventional job.

Any attempt to simulate public employment programs must take account of these factors. The simulation methodology outlined below is designed to do this.

Comparison of Alternatives

It seems reasonable to view an individual who is eligible for public employment as engaging in a comparison of the program and his best opportunity within the conventional job sector and as choosing the alternative that makes him best off.[5] In general, one would expect that the chosen alternative offers the highest income level at the hours he prefers to work.[6] The choice is not necessarily confined to picking one sector over

5. The choice is assumed to be made on the basis of perfect information about the alternatives, which probably results in an overstatement of the public employment population. Unless persons are aware of public employment and know something about it, the program is not a viable alternative for them. Knowledge of the program is likely to be positively related to the publicity given the program, the length of time it has been in operation, and its size.

6. In the simulation, it is assumed that a worker will participate in public employment whenever the program is viewed by him as marginally superior to his best alternative in the conventional sector. In practice, however, a substantial differ-

the other, however, since a worker may participate in public employment during weeks of involuntary unemployment and return to the conventional sector when an opportunity becomes available. Such a "mixed-sector" strategy seems, in fact, to be the possibility stressed most by advocates of large-scale public employment programs.[7] Nevertheless, under certain circumstances, the mixed approach may not be a viable alternative to either of the two pure strategies. First, some unemployed persons may be unwilling to participate in public employment if the program wage is substantially below their usual market wage. Second, involuntary unemployment may be in the form of working fewer hours per week rather than fewer weeks in a year than desired. Third, even if involuntary unemployment is in the form of weeks per year, a public employment program may require a waiting period for eligibility that exceeds the length of unemployment. Fourth, it may be more difficult for a person to search for a job in the conventional sector while working in the public sector.

To determine whether various persons would participate in given public employment programs and whether they would select the pure program or the mixed-sector approach if they do participate, it is necessary to estimate the number of hours they would work under each of the three alternatives, and then—given these hours estimates—determine earnings under each strategy.[8] In conducting the simulation, it is assumed that workers will make the choice that maximizes their earnings.[9]

---

ential between public and conventional employment may be necessary, if only to overcome inertia. Nevertheless, over the long run many of the frictions that exist in labor markets would be reduced. For example, many persons may not actively consider voluntarily leaving their present job to participate in public employment; but once they have been fired or laid off they may seriously examine public employment as a possible alternative to the conventional jobs available to them. Thus, the methodology presented in this paper is best viewed as being based on a static model of economic behavior; the adjustments to the introduction of a public employment program would not take place instantaneously, but only over time. The larger the comparative advantage of public employment, the more rapidly the adjustments would be expected to occur.

7. A major premise that appears to underlie most proposals for public employment, particularly guaranteed employment, is that there are too few conventional job slots to absorb all those who are willing and able to work full time. This excess supply could result from minimum wage legislation, union wage setting, or some other source. In any event, the simulation methodology is consistent with the existence of involuntary unemployment.

8. These estimates are developed in ibid., app. A.

9. Although this assumption is probably the best that can be made at the present time, it has a serious shortcoming for workers who are unable to choose freely the number of hours they work in either the conventional sector or the public employ-

Since workers presumably are interested in maximizing not only their immediate income but also their future income, the simulation projects the time profile of their earnings under each of the alternatives facing them. To compare these alternative earnings profiles, the present discounted value of each is computed by summing earnings under each across time, using a discount or interest rate to take account of the fact that earnings to be received in the near future tend to be more highly valued than those that are not to be received until later.[10]

Determinants of Earnings

Computing the value of a worker's earnings in the conventional sector requires that values be obtained for his market wage and working hours. Hours of work, in turn, depend on the hours the worker is willing to supply at his market wage and the hours of unemployment that are experienced. The sources of data on these variables that are used for purposes of the simulation are described later.

The earnings a worker would receive as a public employment participant depend on the program wage rate, the length of the unemployed waiting period before he becomes eligible to participate, the length of search for conventional employment after leaving the program, the hours worked while participating, and the duration of his participation. Each of these variables is influenced directly or indirectly by policy decisions that are made by those who create and manage the public employment program.

---

ment sector. In such cases, earnings might be higher in one sector than the other only because it offered longer work hours. If so, workers must trade off higher earnings against shorter hours (and a higher wage rate), and the outcome is not obvious. This indeterminateness is treated in the simulation by using three definitions—restrictive, unrestrictive, and intermediate—of the public employment supply population that differ in their treatment of those whose participation decisions are uncertain. The restrictive definition, for example, classifies persons as nonparticipants if it is uncertain whether they would participate in public employment at all and classifies those who would definitely participate as mixed-sector participants if it is unclear whether they would take the pure program approach to public employment or would only participate when unemployed. These uncertainties are resolved in exactly the opposite manner under the unrestrictive definition. The estimated public employment supply populations are larger under the intermediate definition than under the restrictive, but smaller than under the unrestrictive. Results based on the intermediate definition might be viewed as a best estimate, with the others suggesting lower and upper bounds. Only those results computed under the intermediate definition appear in the text. Results based on the other two definitions and a fuller description of all three definitions are reported in ibid.

10. See ibid., app. B.

The wage rate for the public employment program is a major policy variable. Probably the simplest assumption that can be made about it, and the one that is used here, is that all participants are paid the same hourly wage. This may also be the most reasonable assumption, at least for programs such as the ones simulated here that are oriented toward low-productivity workers.[11] The assumption implies, however, that the program wage is unaffected by the worker's productive capacity in either the conventional or program sector, by age, by geographic location, or by duration of program participation.[12]

Another potentially important policy variable is the length of the waiting period for public employment. The waiting period presumably is required in order to keep short-term, frictionally unemployed persons out of the program. Thus it would probably be short, perhaps a quarter of a year or less. In addition to keeping the frictionally unemployed out of the program, a waiting period should also discourage employed persons from quitting jobs in the conventional sector to participate in the program, since they would have to forgo earnings during the period.

For purposes of the simulation, it is assumed that unemployed workers would search for a job as effectively while participating in public employment as they would have had they not participated at all. This assumption seems reasonable since a policy goal in most public employment programs would probably be to facilitate reentry into the conventional sector.[13]

The hours that a person would work in public employment are estimated in three steps.[14] First, since the worker would no longer be subject

11. If public employment is directed toward displaced professional workers as well as low-wage workers, and these persons are given jobs that reflect their skills in the conventional sector, program wages probably would vary among participants.

12. The assumption is not meant to suggest that program wages would be insensitive to economy-wide inflationary or productivity trends. It implies rather that these trends would have roughly similar effects on earnings streams in both the public and the conventional sectors and hence can be ignored without substantially biasing the simulation results.

13. An analysis that suggests that public employment simulations are relatively sensitive to this assumption appears in David Betson, David H. Greenberg, and Richard Kasten, "A Microsimulation Model for Analyzing Alternative Welfare Reform Proposals: An Application to the Program for Better Jobs and Income," in Robert H. Haveman and Kevin Hollenbeck, eds., *Microeconomic Simulation Models for the Analysis of Public Policy* (Academic Press, forthcoming).

14. Although the simulation methodology is general enough to allow several alternative assumptions about hours, in this paper it is assumed that persons in both the public employment and the conventional sectors *may* not be able to work as many hours as they are willing to supply, but would not work very much in excess of their supply hours. Operationally, this can be interpreted to mean that

to involuntary unemployment, his reported hours of unemployment are added to the hours actually worked. Second, this hours amount—hours supplied to the conventional sector—is adjusted through the use of estimated labor supply parameters to account for the response to any difference between the appropriate market wage and the program wage. This provides an estimate of the hours the worker would be willing to supply to the program, given the program wage rate. Third, program supply hours are compared to the maximum hours participants in the program are allowed to work—several alternative assumptions for this value are used in the simulation—and the smaller of desired and permitted hours is denoted as program hours worked.

The length of time workers would remain in public employment, if they did join, is needed in computing the present discounted values of the pure and the mixed-approach earnings profiles. Moreover, length of stay is of considerable interest in its own right, since it is an important determinant of the program's ultimate size and cost, and indeed the program's very character. The time a worker leaves the public employment sector may be voluntarily decided on by the worker himself, determined by a rule requiring that participants terminate after some fixed period, or necessitated by the program's going out of existence, as might happen with a program specifically designed as an antirecessionary measure. Most of the simulation results presented in this paper are based on the assumption that no constraints will be imposed on length of time in the program; however, the implications of a limit on time in the program are also examined.

---

public employment participants would not be allowed to work more than some fixed number of hours during a week, and that involuntary unemployment occurs in the conventional sector and is accurately measured by weeks of reported unemployment.

The assumption that reported unemployment accurately reflects the involuntary loss of time to the labor market appears consistent with the premise underlying most proposals for public employment programs. It also appears reasonable to anticipate that some restrictions would be imposed on hours worked by public employment participants, if for no other reason than ease of administration. Even though some persons in both the public employment and the conventional sectors might work fewer hours than they would like, however, one would not expect many to work an appreciably greater number of hours, except possibly for short periods of time. Unpaid vacations, absenteeism, voluntary job termination, and early retirement are but a few examples of potential adjustment to overemployment. Although conventional employers and managers of public employment programs might be able to limit the use of some of these adjustment mechanisms by firing workers with excessive absences and by making it difficult for those who voluntarily leave to find future employment, such measures are probably only partially successful.

If workers are free to choose how long they remain in the program, some will stay until they retire from the labor force. Some persons, however, will find it advantageous to follow a mixed-sector approach toward public employment, participating only during periods of unemployment. In addition, the public employment sector may serve as an "aging vat" for some young people who, as they mature, have considerably brighter employment opportunities in the conventional sector.[15] Moreover, the program itself may also improve a participant's outside opportunities.[16] The simulation methodology is capable of treating all of these possibilities, but at a cost of considerable computational complexity. Hence the "aging vat" and training possibilities are ignored here. Earnings profiles in public employment and the conventional sector are assumed to be flat and program participation to have no effect on the conventional-sector earnings capacity of participants.

There are important interactions between the length of time participants remain in public employment programs and the length of the program waiting period. For example, economic returns from following the mixed approach are reduced by longer waiting periods, since the number of weeks workers do not receive any earnings is increased. Many of those who are discouraged from taking the mixed-sector approach may not

15. These workers may participate in public employment once again, if they find that their opportunities in the conventional sector begin to deteriorate as they age.

16. Public employment programs may influence the earnings of former participants after they have left the program, by their effects on the wage rates these persons obtain in the conventional sector and on the hours they work. Although the size of these effects depends on how long a worker remains in public employment, their direction may be positive or negative. On the one hand, the program may have a substantial training component. If the training is effective, the value of a worker's (potential) wage in the conventional sector should continue to increase while he remains in the program (although probably at a diminishing rate), reflecting the increasing value of his human capital. Potential hours of work may also increase, either because of adjustments in labor supply in response to the investment in human capital or because the worker is less subject to unemployment in the conventional sector. On the other hand, if the program does not emphasize training and the work performed in the program has little transferable value, a worker's stock of human capital could deteriorate.

If a public employment program does have an effective training component, a participant will not leave the program until the marginal benefits of leaving (earnings anticipated in the conventional sector during the next time period) exceed the marginal costs of leaving (earnings the worker would have received in public employment during the next time period *plus* the value of the increment to his human capital that would have occurred during the period). Procedures for determining when this occurs—that is, for finding the optimal length of training for the participant—are developed in Greenberg, "Supply Population."

participate in public employment at all, but others may opt for the pure approach to public employment. In other words, long program waiting periods should reduce the number of persons who participate in public employment. However, those who do participate are likely to remain in the program for considerably longer periods of time. On the other hand, long waiting periods coupled with restrictions on the number of weeks persons may participate in the program will simply discourage participation—at least by those who might otherwise leave jobs in the conventional sector—because there will be less opportunity to recoup earnings that are forgone during the waiting period.

Demand Responses

As the program wage becomes, in effect, a wage floor for those for whom public employment is an option, the accompanying increase in wage rates in the conventional sector will allow employers to retain workers who otherwise would have transferred to the public employment sector. At the same time, however, their demand for those workers will be reduced. Thus, some proportion of those who would have transferred had there been no wage adjustment probably will stay in the conventional sector, while the remainder will be released to the public employment sector because employers will no longer want their services at the higher wage levels they must pay.

In order to estimate the potential supply population for public employment, it is obviously necessary to know what proportion would stay in the conventional sector and what proportion would move. From the worker's perspective, these proportions may be respectively viewed as his probability of staying in the conventional sector and his probability of transferring to the public employment sector.[17] The formula developed to compute these probabilities implies that the probability that an individual

17. See ibid. The probability that a given individual will transfer to the public employment sector, P_i^T, is $P_i^T = [1 - H_i^d (1 - \eta_d \dot{w})]/h_i^s$, where H_i^d is the hours the individual would have worked in the conventional sector in the absence of the public employment program, h_i^s is the hours supplied to the program in the absence of an employer response, $\dot{w}$ is the proportionate increase in the worker's wage rate as a result of implementation of the program, and η_d is the elasticity of demand for the hours of workers eligible for the program whose wages in the conventional sector are forced up by the program. The elasticity of demand is defined as the percentage decrease in the demand for the hours of those workers that would result from a percentage point increase in their wages. The formula for P_i^T is derived in ibid.

will remain in the conventional sector is the number of hours he desires to work at the program wage divided into the number of hours of work he can find in the conventional sector after wages are forced up by the program. The latter number reflects the reduction in demand for the worker's hours after wage increases have been induced by the program. The size of this reduction in demand is determined by the size of the public employment wage relative to the wage rate in the conventional sector before the program and the responsiveness of employers to changes in wage levels.

Data Sources, Key Parameters, and Program Characteristics

Data used in this paper for the simulation of public employment programs are based on the March 1971 Current Population Survey (CPS), a national sample interview survey conducted by the Bureau of the Census.[18] The data in the survey have been "aged" to represent the structure of the population in 1973.[19] Thus, the results of the simulation may be viewed as estimates of what the supply population would have been for the public employment programs had they been in operation in 1973. The estimates are based on the more than 27,000 married couples in the CPS file—both those with and those without children—in which the husband has not reached his sixty-fifth birthday nor the wife her sixty-second. The sample is appropriately weighted so that it is representative of the entire U.S. population with similar characteristics.

Estimates of the behavioral responses of employers and workers to changes in wage rates and of the value of the discount rate of potential public employment participants have been obtained from previous empirical work. Most of the labor market variables required for the simulation—measures of hours, earnings, and unemployment—have been taken directly from the CPS file or constructed by combining data from the CPS file with values for program characteristics and behavioral parameters. Measures of wage rates in the conventional sector and of future

18. For a detailed discussion of the data, see Greenberg, "Supply Population," app. B.

19. The earnings of all workers are treated by the aging procedure as if they increased at the same rate between 1971 and 1973 as *average* earnings did. However, the earnings of some workers increased at less than the average rate and in some cases actually fell. Thus, the aging process probably results in an overstatement of some persons' earnings and an understatement of the number of persons who could improve their earnings by entering public employment.

unemployment experience are predicted by regression equations that
were estimated from cross-sectional data.[20]

Simulation estimates are reported for a number of different sets of
program characteristics so that the effects of alternative policy decisions
on the public employment supply population can be assessed. The supply
population is evaluated at hourly wage rates for the program of $2.00,
$2.50, $3.00, and $3.50. This permits the derivation of the segment of
the public employment supply curve that is just above the federal minimum wage, which was $1.60 in 1973. Similarly, it is alternatively as-
sumed that public employment participants could work a maximum of
20, 30, and 40 hours a week (or 1,040, 1,560, and 2,080 hours a year)
under the program. Three different values—5, 13, and 26—are also used
for the number of weeks in the waiting period. Finally, although most of
the simulation is for public employment programs that have no restrictions on length of stay—allowing persons to remain in the program until
they retire if they wish—programs that limit participation to two years
are also examined.

The simulation estimates also have been computed under three alternative assumptions about employer responses to the effects of public
employment programs on market wages.[21] It is assumed that, in response
to increases in wages expected by workers eligible for public employment,
employers would: (1) reduce their demand for the services of workers
whose wages are forced up by public employment by 0.5 percent for each
percentage-point increase in the wage they had to pay them, (2) reduce
their demand by 1 percent for each percentage-point increase, (3) be
unwilling to employ these persons. These assumptions respectively imply
low, moderate, and very large adjustments in employer demand for these
persons.[22]

A review of previous empirical studies of the demand for low-wage
workers suggests that the low and moderate adjustments provide reasonable alternatives for simulating universal employment programs under
which virtually all persons of working age are eligible, while the moder-

20. Procedures followed in estimating behavioral responses and measuring labor
market characteristics are described in ibid. The sensitivity of the simulation results
to alternative values for some of the behavioral parameters is also reported in ibid.

21. For assumptions about workers' decisions to participate, see note 9 above.

22. The first two assumptions imply demand elasticity values of 0.5 and 1.0,
respectively, for these persons. The third implies a value approaching infinity, since
under the assumption employer demand would be reduced to zero by any increase
in wage rates.

ate and high demand responses probably provide an appropriate range for simulating categorical public employment programs (for example, programs that limit eligibility to heads of households).[23] This second pair of assumptions allows for the possibility that employers would replace at least some workers who are eligible for the program with persons who are ineligible (wives and single persons, for example), rather than pay eligible persons the program wage.

Simulation Results

Table 1 summarizes many of the major results of the simulation. The table compares the person-years of labor, defined as 2,080 hours per year, that would have been demanded in 1973 under several variations of public employment programs paying hourly wages of $2.00 and $3.50. The first pair of programs requires a five-week waiting period, offers a forty-hour workweek, and allows persons to participate in the program until they retire. The second pair varies the waiting period, the third pair the length of the workweek, and the final pair the length of participation in the program.

The estimated numbers of person-years of husbands' and wives' labor that are reported in table 1 can be converted to measures of the size of the simulated programs in terms of slots and wage bills. A slot is simply the maximum number of hours a program participant would be paid for during a year, while the wage bill is the product of the number of slots in the program and the cost of a single slot. For example, a slot would be equivalent to 1,560 hours for a program that allowed participants to work 30 hours a week, 52 weeks a year, and the wage cost of that slot would be $3,120 for a program that paid participants $2 an hour.[24] A single program slot may, of course, be occupied by one worker for the entire year or by several for different parts of the year.

Perhaps the most important implication of the estimates in table 1 is that a guaranteed employment program that places no restrictions on

23. An examination of the existing evidence on the elasticity of demand for low-wage workers appears in ibid.

24. The wage cost of a slot represents only part of its total cost. The remaining costs, which could be rather substantial, depend on the administrative requirements of the program, the need for supervisory personnel, the size of the program's training component, the program's physical capital requirements, and so forth.

Table 1. Estimate of Labor Available for Public Employment Programs in 1973
Thousands of person-years

Program characteristics	Husbands Employer demand response			Wives Employer demand response		
	Low	Moderate	High	Low	Moderate	High
$2.00 wage rate						
5-week waiting period, 40-hour week, unlimited stay	534	539	586	415	459	653
13-week waiting period, 40-hour week, unlimited stay	281	286	340	314	358	560
5-week waiting period, 30-hour week, unlimited stay	444	447	471	353	381	493
5-week waiting period, 40-hour week, 2-year stay*	556	559	600	387	428	576
$3.50 wage rate						
5-week waiting period, 40-hour week, unlimited stay	820	1,054	2,307	2,928	4,172	8,917
13-week waiting period, 40-hour week, unlimited stay	579	817	2,128	2,902	4,153	8,957
5-week waiting period, 30-hour week, unlimited stay	602	728	1,307	2,268	3,069	5,870
5-week waiting period, 40-hour week, 2-year stay*	809	1,010	2,103	2,813	3,983	8,370

a. Estimate based on a 10 percent, randomly selected subsample of the full simulation sample.

who may participate is likely to be quite large,[25] even if the program pays relatively low wages. For example, the estimates imply that in 1973 preretirement-age husbands and wives alone would have offered about one million person-years of labor to a program paying $2.00 an hour and having a five-week waiting period and a forty-hour workweek. The program's wage bill for these persons would have been about $4 billion (see appendix table A-1). Single persons, female heads of families, and persons from other groups no doubt would have also supplied an appreciable number of person-years to such a program if they had been eligible.

25. The size of the simulated programs probably would have increased substantially between 1973 and more recent periods such as 1976. For example, unemployment rates for husbands and wives increased from 2.3 percent and 4.6 percent, respectively, in 1973 to 4.2 percent and 7.1 percent in 1976. And the number of preretirement-age wives in the labor force grew by about 7 percent between 1973 and 1975 (that group of husbands remained almost constant). In addition, wage costs would have increased considerably if adjusted to the consumer price index, which rose by 28 percent between 1973 and 1976.

Program Wage and Employer Demand Response

The size and cost of guaranteed employment increase rapidly as program wage rates rise (table A-1). Wives appear especially responsive to wage rates. When program wages are relatively high, a substantial segment of wives in the labor force would probably be in the public employment sector, while only a relatively small proportion of husbands would be. For example, the person-year and slot estimates may be compared to the approximately thirty-eight million husbands and nineteen million wives of preretirement age who were in the labor force in March 1973. Apparently, public employment programs limited to husbands could afford to offer substantially higher wage rates than ones that also permit wives to participate.

At low program wage rates, estimates of program size do not appear to be strongly influenced by the assumption about employers' demand response that is used to compute them, but at higher rates they become extremely sensitive to the demand assumption that is made.[26] The reason for this is that at lower rates relatively few persons who hold jobs in the conventional sector are willing to participate in public employment, except when they are unemployed; but at higher program wage rates, substantial numbers of workers consider moving into the public employment sector. The number who actually do leave their jobs depends partially on the size of the employer response to the increases in market wage rates induced by the program; the more employers reduce their demand for those with increased wages, the larger will be the movement from the conventional into the public employment sector.

These interrelationships may be seen more clearly in estimates of the percentage distribution of the three sources of labor supply for the public employment sector: (1) labor that would have been employed in the conventional sector in the absence of a public employment program, (2) labor that would have been in the work force but unemployed, (3) labor that was induced into the labor force by the existence of the program.[27]

26. At low program wage rates, there is also relatively little difference between results based on different participation definitions, but at higher wage rates the unrestricted definition implies considerably larger slot and wage bill requirements than do the other two definitions, where differences in results are negligible (see ibid., app. A). The unrestricted definition of course represents an upper bound; actual slot and wage bill requirements are likely to be considerably lower.

27. Induced labor includes persons who would not have participated in the labor force at all in the absence of the program, and those in the labor force who increase

The estimates (table A-2) suggest that a public employment program that paid $2.00 an hour would have drawn relatively little labor away from the conventional sector in 1973 and, consequently, probably would not have had very damaging effects on the low-wage labor market. In fact, it appears that most participants in such a program would have been unemployed workers; relatively few employed workers or persons who were out of the labor force would have been attracted. At higher program wage rates, however, a substantial fraction of the hours supplied to the public employment sector would have been drawn from employed workers; among wives, a considerable proportion of hours supplied would also have been in the form of induced labor.

Estimates of the number of person-years of labor that the conventional sector would have lost to public employment programs in 1973 (out of roughly 50 million person-years actually worked) are extremely sensitive to the assumption made about employer demand response, as table 2 illustrates. If the low to moderate assumptions about demand response are accepted as most appropriate for examining universal guaranteed employment programs, the tabulation suggests that the conventional sector would have lost from about 0.2 million to 0.5 million husband person-years and from 1.3 million to 2.6 million wife person-years in 1973 as a result of a universal program that paid $3.50 an hour. If the moderate to high assumptions about demand response may be accepted as most appropriate to categorical programs, a program that paid $3.50 an hour and only allowed heads of households to participate would have resulted in a loss by the conventional sector of between 0.5 million and 1.7 million husband person-years.

Three additional measures of the effects of public employment on husbands—the number of husbands who would have participated in 1973, the percentage that would have taken the pure approach rather than adopt the mixed and only participate when unemployed, and the average number of weeks they would have participated during 1973—follow a pattern similar to that in table 1, increasing as program wage rates and employer demand response increase (see table A-3). At the highest rate and re-

---

their hours in response to differences between the program wage and their conventional-sector wage rates. The simulation estimates allow for both of these possibilities for wives, but only the latter for husbands (see ibid., app. B, for a discussion of the reasons for this). Thus, the estimates are understated to the extent that husbands who were out of the labor force during all of 1973 might have been induced into a public employment program. Few husbands stay out of the labor force, however, for an entire year and most who do are disabled or attending school full-time.

Table 2. Estimates of Labor Lost by Conventional Sector Employers to Public Employment Programs in 1973[a]

Thousands of person-years

| | Husbands | | | Wives | | |
| | Employer demand response | | | Employer demand response | | |
Wage rate	Low	Moderate	High	Low	Moderate	High
$2.00	6	11	65	42	84	234
$3.50	228	451	1,663	1,326	2,556	7,258

a. Simulated programs have a 5-week waiting period and a 40-hour workweek.

sponse, therefore, more job slots are needed not only because of a larger number of potential participants, but also because they stay in the program longer. This smaller rate of program turnover results from a larger proportion of participants choosing the pure approach, thereby making a permanent commitment to public employment rather than participating only when unemployed.

The measure of the average weeks husbands stay in public employment during the year is important because it indicates whether participants are likely to move back into the conventional sector. In the absence of such mobility, at least on the part of a substantial fraction of participants, the public employment and conventional sectors will tend to become isolated from one another and persons in public employment may become separated from the mainstream of society. On average, participating husbands would have remained in a public employment program that paid $2.00 an hour in 1973 for about one-fifth of the year, and in a program that paid $3.50 an hour for one-quarter to one-half of the year. Thus many public employment slots would be occupied by several different persons during a year.

Program Waiting Period

The major purpose of a program waiting period presumably is to preclude participation by those who are unemployed for relatively short periods. A longer waiting period simply means that the unemployed have fewer weeks available to participate in the program. Waiting periods also have two additional effects, which tend to be offsetting and which perhaps are unintentional. On the one hand, they should discourage employed persons from quitting jobs in the conventional sector in order to participate in public employment, because such persons must sacrifice earnings they could otherwise receive. The longer the waiting period, the greater this sacrifice becomes. On the other hand, a waiting period limits the opportunity for workers to take the mixed approach toward public employment. The longer the waiting period, the more workers are forced to take the pure approach toward public employment, if they are going to participate at all. Thus, long waiting periods would be expected to reduce program turnover.

Estimates of the effects of waiting periods (table A-4) suggest that as the length of the period increases, the program's size usually falls. The rate at which it falls, however, tends to be considerably greater for a $2.00 an hour public employment program than for a more generous $3.50 an hour program. In fact, the estimates indicate that, at a high employer demand response, slot requirements for wives could be slightly higher under a $3.50 an hour program with a thirteen-week waiting period than with a five-week waiting period. The reason for this is that low-wage programs draw a much higher proportion of their work force from among the unemployed than do high-wage programs (table A-5), although this proportion tends to decrease as waiting periods lengthen. Since it is the unemployed who are most directly affected by the number of weeks in the waiting period, programs most dependent on this group as a source of supply are also most sensitive to the length of the waiting period. A longer waiting period probably also discourages some employed persons from participating in the program. This may be more than offset, however, by an increase in the number of workers who become full-time, pure participants, rather than mixed participants.

As expected, the number of husbands who participate in public employment declines as the waiting period increases, but a larger proportion of those who do participate choose the pure approach (table A-6). Length of stay in relatively high-wage programs tends to increase with the length of the waiting period. In lower wage programs, however, the influence of the waiting period on turnover is less clear because of two offsetting effects: the waiting period directly reduces the number of weeks unemployed persons have available to participate in the program, and the percentage of pure-approach participants increases with the length of the waiting period while that of mixed-approach participants declines. The former type of participant tends to remain in the public employment sector considerably longer than the latter.

Program Hours

A shorter program workweek results, of course, in a lower public employment wage bill (table 3). The length of the workweek appears especially important when the program wage is relatively high.

Program costs fall as the public employment workweek is shortened, most obviously because those who are employed by the program are paid for fewer hours of work. Of course as the workweek is shortened, program participants will partially compensate by extending the number of weeks they remain in the program during the year. Also, by reducing the earnings potential of public employment, a relatively short program workweek discourages employed workers from quitting their jobs for public employment. Consistent with this, the simulation estimates of the sources of labor supply to public employment (table A-7) indicate that the importance of the program to employed workers diminishes rapidly as the length of the program workweek falls.

Although reducing the length of the workweek can lower the program's wage bills and mitigate its adverse effects on low-wage labor markets, this approach does not appear to be as effective as reducing the program's wage rates. For example, a public employment program that offers a $2.00 hourly wage and a forty-hour workweek affords

Table 3. Estimated Wage Bill for Public Employment Programs in 1973, by Wage Rate and Weekly Hours[a]

Billions of dollars

Wage rate and workweek	Husbands Employer demand response			Wives Employer demand response		
	Low	Moderate	High	Low	Moderate	High
$2.00						
20 hours	1.3	1.4	1.4	1.1	1.2	1.4
30 hours	1.8	1.9	2.0	1.5	1.6	2.0
40 hours	2.2	2.2	2.4	1.7	1.9	2.7
$3.50						
20 hours	2.8	3.1	4.2	11.1	13.7	22.5
30 hours	4.4	5.3	9.5	16.5	22.3	42.8
40 hours	6.0	7.7	16.8	21.3	30.3	64.9

a. Simulated programs have a 5-week waiting period and no limit on length of stay.

participants a greater earnings opportunity than a program with a $3.50 wage and a twenty-hour week. Nevertheless, the simulation results imply that the former program would be less expensive (table 3) and would attract a smaller proportion of its labor from among employed workers (table A-7) than the latter program.

Length of Stay

The simulation results that have been reported so far are based on the premise that persons who enter the public employment sector may remain there, if they wish, until they reach retirement age. In actual practice, however, they may be required to leave after some fixed period, or the program may have a limited life. Such constraints on length of stay may affect the participation decisions of persons who hold jobs in the conventional sector, at least when the program has a waiting period.

Most employed persons would need some assurance before quitting their jobs to participate in public employment that they could stay in the program at least long enough to receive full compensation for the loss of earnings they forgo during the program waiting period. In other words, employed workers would not only require that their earnings stream under the program be higher than that on their conventional jobs, but that they receive these higher earnings for a sufficiently long time to offset any loss of income resulting from the program waiting period. Unemployed persons or nonworkers, however, would not have to forgo such earnings, and their participation decisions therefore should be unaffected by program restrictions on length of stay.

Estimates of the distribution of program slots by the minimum length of stay in public employment required to offset any loss of earnings resulting from a waiting period (table A-8) suggest how the program's limits on length of participation would reduce its size. Given moderate employer demand response to a program paying $3.50 an hour and having a thirteen-week waiting period, for example, the estimates imply that about 40 percent of the slots required by husbands would be virtually unaffected by restrictions on length of stay, but that husbands demanding nearly one-fourth of the slots would have to remain in the program for a year or more before being fully compensated for earnings losses suffered during the waiting period. Direct comparison of programs that limit participation to two years to those that permit participation until retirement (table A-9) suggests that limits on length of stay become more important as waiting periods lengthen and as program wage rates and employer demand response increase.[28] In no case, however, do limits on length of stay appear to cause more than a modest decrease in program slot requirements.

Characteristics of Participants

It is useful and interesting to know something about the characteristics of persons who would choose to participate in guaranteed employment programs. Thus table 4 provides estimates of how the supply population for selected programs would have been distributed among various income and demographic groups had these programs been in operation during 1973.[29]

Possibly the most interesting is the distribution across income classes. A surprisingly small proportion of public employment slots would go to families with very low annual incomes—say, below $4,000—and a substantial fraction would be taken by persons in families with incomes over $15,000. Wives who participate in public employment appear especially likely to be from relatively high—rather than very low—income families; many of them from higher income families are secondary workers attracted into the program by the opportunity to supplement their husbands' earnings. Higher income husbands, on the other hand, tend to be persons who usually hold conventional jobs, but participate in the program during periods of unemployment.

Table 4 suggests also that the public employment supply population would be largely composed of persons in the middle age range—twenty-five to fifty years old—who live in moderate-sized families of three to six persons.[30] However, husbands and wives with no children constitute about

28. The role of these latter two factors results from their influence on the number of employed workers who consider entering public employment. As noted earlier, it is the participation decisions of the employed that would be affected by restrictions on length of stay.

29. The estimates in table 4 are based on the assumption that employer demand response is moderate. Results based on assumptions of low and high response follow a similar pattern, although there are a few exceptions (see table A-10). Estimates based on the restrictive and unrestrictive definitions of participation are very similar to those reported in table 4, which is based on the intermediate definition.

30. Although the reported estimates exclude single persons, recent additional simulations suggest that young single persons would comprise the majority of the supply population of almost any guaranteed employment programs in which they were eligible to participate.

Table 4. Distribution of Labor Available for Public Employment Programs in 1973, by Income and Demographic Group[a]

Percent

	Husbands						Wives					
	Hourly wage rate / waiting period / weekly hours						Hourly wage rate / waiting period / weekly hours					
Group characteristic	$2.00 5 weeks 40 hours	$3.50 5 weeks 40 hours	$2.00 13 weeks 40 hours	$3.50 13 weeks 40 hours	$2.00 5 weeks 30 hours	$3.50 5 weeks 30 hours	$2.00 5 weeks 40 hours	$3.50 5 weeks 40 hours	$2.00 13 weeks 40 hours	$3.50 13 weeks 40 hours	$2.00 5 weeks 30 hours	$3.50 5 weeks 30 hours
Thousands of person-years	539	1,054	286	817	447	728	459	4,172	358	4,153	381	3,069
Total family income (dollars)												
4,000 and under	14.0	13.4	19.1	15.7	14.9	18.1	6.4	3.6	7.9	3.6	7.3	4.8
4,001–6,000	16.5	20.1	18.1	22.5	16.6	22.0	10.3	5.6	11.5	5.6	10.5	6.9
6,001–8,000	16.5	21.7	15.6	23.0	16.4	17.1	14.9	9.5	17.5	9.6	14.9	11.5
8,001–10,000	13.9	14.9	13.5	15.0	13.9	13.4	14.3	11.8	14.9	11.7	13.7	13.6
10,001–15,000	23.2	19.2	20.2	16.4	22.8	18.3	28.6	34.9	26.2	35.0	29.1	35.5
Over 15,000	15.9	10.7	13.5	7.3	15.4	11.0	25.5	34.6	21.9	34.5	24.6	27.7
Age												
Under 25	11.7	12.2	11.2	12.4	11.9	12.3	15.3	13.6	15.1	13.7	16.0	13.9
25–50	59.3	56.8	57.2	56.0	59.0	55.3	63.8	66.1	62.7	66.1	63.2	65.6
51 and over	29.0	31.0	31.6	31.7	29.1	32.4	21.0	20.3	22.1	20.2	20.8	20.5
Race												
White	86.2	65.2	84.2	56.6	87.0	70.4	62.3	79.9	55.5	79.8	65.7	78.9
Black	12.9	33.4	14.6	41.6	12.1	28.4	35.5	19.1	42.2	19.2	32.1	20.1
Other	0.9	1.3	1.2	1.5	0.8	1.1	2.2	0.9	2.4	1.0	2.2	1.0

Education												
8 years or less	30.4	48.1	29.1	54.2	29.6	45.7	31.4	22.3	33.1	22.3	30.2	23.4
9 to 11 years	24.0	23.6	22.8	23.7	23.9	22.0	28.2	27.9	29.5	27.9	27.4	29.1
12 years or more	45.6	28.3	48.1	22.1	46.5	32.3	40.4	49.8	37.4	49.8	42.4	47.5
Size of family												
2 persons	28.1	24.8	29.2	24.0	28.5	26.7	24.5	29.1	23.2	28.9	24.7	27.4
3 or 4 persons	41.5	40.3	40.5	39.0	41.8	39.7	40.0	42.5	39.8	42.6	40.8	42.7
5 or 6 persons	21.2	22.1	20.8	22.5	20.7	21.9	24.5	20.8	25.2	20.9	23.7	21.6
7 or more persons	9.1	12.8	9.5	14.5	9.1	11.8	10.9	7.6	11.8	7.5	10.8	8.3
Census region												
Northeast	22.6	14.7	23.6	12.3	22.9	15.7	20.0	19.5	17.0	19.5	20.4	18.5
North Central	27.3	18.3	25.2	13.9	27.2	20.1	17.9	21.3	15.6	21.3	19.0	19.8
South	24.7	51.6	24.4	61.5	23.9	46.4	45.8	49.7	52.3	49.7	43.5	51.6
West	25.4	15.4	26.8	12.4	26.0	17.8	16.4	9.5	15.0	9.5	17.2	10.0
Extent of urbanization												
Central city	54.7	39.9	56.8	35.3	55.3	41.9	47.1	43.5	44.4	43.5	49.0	42.2
Suburban	13.1	11.4	11.5	10.3	13.3	12.1	11.7	12.3	11.6	12.3	12.1	12.8
Rural area	32.2	48.7	31.7	54.4	31.4	46.0	41.3	44.2	44.0	44.2	38.9	45.0
Industry												
Agriculture	4.3	13.7	5.7	17.2	3.7	14.5	1.8	1.6	1.7	1.7	1.8	2.0
Manufacturing	31.1	27.2	29.5	25.1	31.1	27.4	34.4	28.1	28.8	27.9	31.8	23.5
Wholesale and retail trade	13.5	18.5	14.6	21.4	13.5	16.6	13.9	17.9	13.3	18.0	14.0	19.0
Private household	0.2	0.3	0.1	0.4	0.2	0.3	7.9	3.8	9.9	3.8	8.7	4.7
Services	10.1	14.2	10.0	15.2	10.0	11.8	21.4	28.6	21.2	28.6	19.6	27.3
Other[b]	40.9	26.1	40.1	20.8	41.5	29.5	20.7	19.9	25.1	20.2	24.2	23.5

a. Assumes that employer demand response is moderate. None of the simulated programs restricts length of stay.

b. Includes those who did not work during the year or could not be classified into an industry, as well as persons who worked in the mining, construction, transportation, public utility, finance, and insurance industries.

one-quarter of the supply population. A majority of those who participate in public employment would have worked previously in various manufacturing, wholesale and retail trade, or service industries. Moreover, programs with relatively high wage rates would attract substantial numbers of agricultural workers.

Not surprisingly, persons with somewhat limited earnings opportunities are especially likely to participate in public employment. Grade school and high school dropouts, for example, would supply more than half the person-years available to public employment. Blacks, southerners, and residents of central cities and rural areas also tend to be drawn disproportionately toward public employment.

Table 4 suggests that increasing the public employment wage rate would have a very different effect on the characteristics of the wives who would participate than it would on the traits of participating husbands. Most husbands in programs with low wage rates would be unemployed, but at higher program wage levels a substantial fraction would leave their jobs in the conventional sector in order to participate. Table 4 implies that the husbands who would leave low-wage jobs for a public employment job with a $3.50 wage rate are more likely to be black, to have relatively few years of formal education, and to live in rural areas and in the South than are the unemployed husbands who would enter a program with a $2.00 wage rate.

Like husbands, most wives who would accept a position in a low-wage public employment program are unemployed. At higher program wage levels, a substantial fraction of the supply of wives to public employment would consist of nonworking women who would be drawn into the labor force, as well as of working women who would leave their conventional jobs to participate in the program. These two groups tend to be secondary workers, with more middle-class characteristics than the unemployed wives who would participate in low-wage public employment programs. Thus, table 4 indicates that wives who would participate in a public employment program with a $3.50 wage rate tend to come from higher income families and have more years of formal education than wives who would enter a program with a $2.00 wage. A disproportionate share of the group also is likely to be white.

Conclusions

The estimates of supply responses to alternative public employment programs presented in this paper have several important implications.

They suggest, for example, that even relatively low-wage programs could be quite large. The simulation estimates indicate that had a public employment program paying a $2.00 hourly wage and requiring a five-week waiting period existed in 1973, a million slots would have been demanded by husbands and wives of preretirement age alone. One way that the size and cost of such a program might be reduced is to limit eligibility to family heads or to the primary earner in each family. Apparently, many of the wives who would participate in the program in the absence of such a limit are secondary workers from moderately well-off households.

At a $2.00 program wage rate (in 1973 terms), most of those who would wish to participate in public employment would probably be unemployed persons who would return to a conventional job as soon as one became available. At higher program wage levels, however, considerable numbers of employed persons would be willing to quit their jobs to participate and the supply population for public employment would be much larger. The extent to which the conventional-sector work force would be reduced depends largely on how categorical the program is and on employers' reactions to program effects on the wages they have to pay workers who are eligible for public employment. The results also imply that wives, including many who would remain outside the labor force in the absence of a program, would be particularly eager to participate in high-wage public employment programs.

The simulation estimates indicate that at low program wage rates, slot requirements for public employment programs fall rapidly as waiting periods increase in length and fewer short-term unemployed persons are able to participate. At higher program wage levels, however, program turnover tends to decrease as waiting periods lengthen, and this partially offsets the reduction in unemployed participants. The estimates also suggest that shortening the program workweek is one means of lowering costs and reducing the number of employed workers who quit their jobs to participate in public employment. Apparently, however, the same results can be accomplished more effectively by reducing the program wage rate. Restrictions on how long persons can remain in public employment also seem to reduce the number of workers who will choose to participate initially. For most program alternatives, however, this effect appears to be relatively modest.

The simulation results that have just been summarized are subject to several limitations. First, although the simulation permits treatment of employer responses to the impact of public employment on the wages of persons who are eligible to participate in the program, it ignores other possible macroeconomic effects. One such issue is how the public employment program might affect the relationship between inflation and unemployment.[31]

Second, the simulation results are limited by the fact that the procedure rests on an assumption that involuntary unemployment is accurately measured by reported unemployment. This implies that a person would always accept public service employment during his weeks of reported unemployment if the job paid at least as much as his market wage. It also implies that persons who do not report unemployment will not take additional work, unless they receive a wage that exceeds their market wage. Both implications are likely to be only partially true.

Third, in addition to differences in money wage and hours opportunities, conventional and public employment may vary in their fringe benefits, working conditions, transportation costs, treatment of day care costs, job security, and social status. If any of these differences are large, they should be taken into account in estimating the potential supply populations for public employment programs. Because of the difficulty of measuring these factors, they have not been incorporated into the simulation methodology.[32] It is possible, however, to obtain some idea of the

31. For discussions of this issue, see the paper by Baily and Tobin in this volume; Michael C. Barth and Edward M. Gramlich, "The Inflation-Unemployment Tradeoff and Public Employment," working paper (Office of Economic Opportunity, Office of Planning, Research, and Evaluation, May 1971; processed); and Joshua E. Greene, "The Economics of Making Government An Employer of Last Resort in the United States: Some Important Issues" (Ph.D. dissertation, University of Michigan, 1977), chaps. 3 and 4.

32. It is difficult to draw conclusions about what sort of biases this omission causes. For example, it seems apparent that jobs in the public employment sector should be more secure than those in the conventional sector and that one will understate the comparative advantages of public employment jobs by not taking this factor into account. The advantage may actually be rather small, however. Funding levels for manpower programs have varied widely over the years and have largely depended on the vagaries of fashion. More important, the very existence of a public employment program reduces the risk of accepting a conventional job, since a person who loses that job has the program to fall back on. It may also seem likely that working conditions in public employment jobs would be superior to those in conventional jobs with similar pay. But many of those who consider public jobs are unemployed persons who usually work at conventional jobs with somewhat higher wage rates than the program. These higher wage jobs may also have superior working conditions. Moreover, public employment jobs may be more stigmatized and less accessible to workers than conventional jobs. (It may also be useful to note that conventional-sector earnings, particularly those that are illicit or illegal, tend to be underreported on the Current Population Survey; this, of course, would also result in overestimating the number of public employment participants.)

sensitivity of simulation estimates to this omission simply by examining how the estimates vary with changes in program wage rates. One could assume, for example, that public employment must pay, say, 50 cents more per hour than conventional jobs to overcome various unfavorable nonwage differences. In this case, the reported estimates for a $2.00 wage program would be viewed as pertaining to a program that paid a nominal wage of $2.50.

Finally, the simulation reported in this paper does not treat potential interactions between public employment and existing and proposed income maintenance programs. Depending on exactly how they were integrated with public employment, income maintenance programs could have substantial effects on public employment supply populations. A comprehensive negative income tax program, for example, would probably reduce labor supplied to both the public employment and the conventional sectors. On the other hand, a wage subsidy or earnings supplement program applied to jobs in the conventional sector would most likely increase their attractiveness relative to those in the public employment sector. Unemployment compensation would also have considerable potential for influencing workers' decisions about participating in public employment—if unemployed workers lost their eligibility for unemployment compensation on taking a public employment job, for example, participation would be discouraged.[33]

33. The simulation described in this paper is being extended to incorporate various interactions between job programs and both income assistance programs and the positive tax system. This additional work is also examining how population groups besides preretirement-age husbands and wives would respond to public employment and testing the sensitivity of public employment supply responses to economic conditions different from those that existed in 1973, when the unemployment rate was around 5 percent. Results from some of this additional work appear in Betson, Greenberg, and Kasten, "A Microsimulation Model."

David H. Greenberg

Appendix: Simulation Results

Table A-1. Estimated Slot and Wage Bill Requirements for Public Employment Programs in 1973, by Wage Rate[a]

	Wage rate			
Employer demand response	$2.00	$2.50	$3.00	$3.50
	Husbands			
Slots (thousands)				
Low response	534	571	653	820
Moderate response	539	597	745	1,054
High response	586	786	1,304	2,307
Wage bill (billions of dollars)				
Low response	2.2	3.0	4.1	6.0
Moderate response	2.2	3.1	4.6	7.7
High response	2.4	4.1	8.1	16.8
	Wives			
Slots (thousands)				
Low response	415	675	1,513	2,928
Moderate response	459	837	2,064	4,172
High response	653	2,024	5,936	8,917
Wage bill (billions of dollars)				
Low response	1.7	3.5	9.4	21.3
Moderate response	1.9	4.4	12.9	30.3
High response	2.7	10.5	37.0	64.9

a. Simulated programs have a 5-week waiting period, 40-hour workweek, and no limit on length of stay.

Table A-2. Distribution of Sources of Supply for Public Employment Programs in 1973, by Wage Rate[a]

Percent

Employer demand response and source of labor	Wage rate			
	$2.00	$2.50	$3.00	$3.50
Husbands				
Low demand response				
Employed	0.6	3.1	10.0	21.9
Unemployed	99.0	96.4	89.5	77.5
Induced	0.4	0.4	0.5	0.6
Moderate demand response				
Employed	1.2	6.1	18.4	35.9
Unemployed	98.4	93.4	81.2	63.6
Induced	0.4	0.4	0.5	0.5
High demand response				
Employed	6.6	22.7	46.7	66.1
Unemployed	93.0	77.0	53.0	33.6
Induced	0.4	0.3	0.3	0.3
Wives				
Low demand response				
Employed	8.8	22.6	37.6	45.8
Unemployed	85.6	61.9	32.5	17.7
Induced	5.6	15.5	29.9	36.5
Moderate demand response				
Employed	16.1	36.2	53.6	61.8
Unemployed	78.8	51.0	24.2	12.5
Induced	5.1	12.8	22.2	25.7
High demand response				
Employed	36.9	70.5	82.8	81.6
Unemployed	59.3	23.6	9.0	6.0
Induced	3.9	5.9	8.2	12.4

a. Simulated programs have a 5-week waiting period, 40-hour workweek, and no limit on length of stay.

Table A-3. Estimated Number and Behavior of Participating Husbands in Public Employment Programs in 1973, by Wage Rate[a]

	Wage rate			
Employer demand response	$2.00	$2.50	$3.00	$3.50
	Number of participants (thousands)			
Low response	2,727	2,796	2,861	2,984
Moderate response	2,734	2,834	2,986	3,294
High response	2,803	3,097	3,731	4,962
	Percent of participants choosing pure approach[b]			
Low response	6.2	8.9	11.3	19.3
Moderate response	6.4	10.1	14.9	26.7
High response	8.7	17.9	32.5	51.4
	Average weeks of stay in program			
Low response	10.2	10.6	11.9	14.3
Moderate response	10.2	11.0	13.0	16.6
High response	10.9	13.2	18.2	24.2

a. Simulated programs have a 5-week waiting period, 40-hour workweek, and no limit on length of stay.
b. Workers transferring to public employment rather than mixing public and conventional employment.

Table A-4. Estimated Number of Slots in Public Employment Programs in 1973, by Wage Rate and Waiting Period[a]

Thousands of slots

Wage rate and waiting period	Employer demand response			Employer demand response		
	Low	Moderate	High	Low	Moderate	High
	Husbands			Wives		
$2.00						
5 weeks	534	539	586	415	459	653
13 weeks	281	286	340	314	358	560
26 weeks	123	127	182	223	267	477
$3.50						
5 weeks	820	1,054	2,307	2,928	4,172	8,917
13 weeks	579	817	2,128	2,902	4,153	8,957
26 weeks	443	664	1,933	2,849	4,081	8,828

a. Simulated programs have a 40-hour workweek and no limit on length of stay.

Table A-5. Distribution of Sources of Supply for Public Employment Programs in 1973, by Wage Rate and Waiting Period[a]

Percent

Employer demand response and source of labor	$2.00 wage rate Waiting period			$3.50 wage rate Waiting period		
	5 weeks	13 weeks	26 weeks	5 weeks	13 weeks	26 weeks
Husbands						
Low demand response						
Employed	0.6	0.9	1.8	21.9	28.9	42.6
Unemployed	99.0	98.5	97.0	77.5	70.3	56.3
Induced	0.4	0.6	1.2	0.6	0.8	1.1
Moderate demand response						
Employed	1.2	1.8	3.6	35.9	44.8	59.6
Unemployed	98.4	97.6	95.3	63.6	54.6	39.6
Induced	0.4	0.6	1.1	0.5	0.6	0.8
High demand response						
Employed	6.6	10.4	19.8	66.1	74.2	83.9
Unemployed	93.0	89.1	79.3	33.6	25.5	15.8
Induced	0.4	0.5	0.9	0.3	0.3	0.3
Wives						
Low demand response						
Employed	8.8	10.2	14.6	45.8	46.6	47.5
Unemployed	85.6	83.4	76.4	17.7	16.9	15.2
Induced	5.6	6.4	9.0	36.5	36.5	37.3
Moderate demand response						
Employed	16.1	18.3	25.3	61.8	62.5	63.4
Unemployed	78.8	75.8	66.8	12.5	11.9	10.6
Induced	5.1	5.8	7.9	25.7	25.6	26.1
High demand response						
Employed	36.9	41.3	52.0	81.6	82.1	82.7
Unemployed	59.3	54.5	42.9	6.0	5.7	5.0
Induced	3.9	4.2	5.1	12.4	12.2	12.3

a. Simulated programs have a 40-hour workweek and no limit on length of stay.

Table A-6. Estimated Number and Behavior of Participating Husbands in Public Employment Programs in 1973, by Wage Rate and Waiting Period[a]

Employer demand response	$2.00 wage rate Waiting period			$3.50 wage rate Waiting period		
	5 weeks	13 weeks	26 weeks	5 weeks	13 weeks	26 weeks
	Number of participants (thousands)					
Low response	2,727	1,546	687	2,984	1,823	1,013
Moderate response	2,734	1,553	695	3,294	2,145	1,330
High response	2,803	1,635	783	4,962	3,944	3,112
	Percent of participants choosing pure approach[b]					
Low response	6.2	11.0	26.6	19.3	29.5	60.3
Moderate response	6.4	11.5	27.2	26.7	38.9	69.6
High response	8.7	15.4	33.0	51.4	65.0	86.9
	Average weeks of stay in program					
Low response	10.2	9.5	9.3	14.3	16.5	22.2
Moderate response	10.2	9.6	9.5	16.6	19.8	25.9
High response	10.9	10.8	12.1	24.2	28.1	32.3

a. Simulated programs have a 40-hour workweek and no limit on length of stay.
b. Workers transferring to public employment rather than mixing public and conventional employment.

Table A-7. Distribution of Sources of Supply for Public Employment Programs in 1973, by Wage Rate and Weekly Hours[a]
Percent

Employer demand response and source of labor	*$2.00 wage rate Workweek*			*$3.50 wage rate Workweek*		
	20 hours	*30 hours*	*40 hours*	*20 hours*	*30 hours*	*40 hours*
			Husbands			
Low demand response						
Employed	0.1	0.6	0.6	4.9	13.8	21.9
Unemployed	99.5	99.3	99.0	94.3	85.5	77.5
Induced	0.4	0.4	0.4	0.8	0.7	0.6
Moderate demand response						
Employed	0.2	0.7	1.2	9.3	24.2	35.9
Unemployed	99.5	98.9	98.4	90.0	75.3	63.6
Induced	0.4	0.4	0.4	0.7	0.6	0.5
High demand response						
Employed	1.2	3.5	6.6	21.7	49.4	66.1
Unemployed	98.4	96.1	93.0	77.7	50.2	33.6
Induced	0.4	0.4	0.4	0.6	0.4	0.3
			Wives			
Low demand response						
Employed	3.2	6.1	8.8	24.6	39.0	45.8
Unemployed	91.8	88.6	85.6	28.1	21.0	17.7
Induced	5.0	5.4	5.6	47.3	40.1	36.5
Moderate demand response						
Employed	6.1	11.2	16.1	37.6	54.5	61.8
Unemployed	89.0	83.7	78.8	23.3	15.6	12.5
Induced	4.9	5.1	5.1	39.2	29.9	25.7
High demand response						
Employed	14.8	26.3	36.9	59.4	75.1	81.6
Unemployed	80.8	69.5	59.3	15.1	8.5	6.0
Induced	4.4	4.2	3.9	25.4	16.3	12.4

a. Simulated programs have a 5-week waiting period and no limit on length of stay.

Table A-8. Distribution of Slots for Public Employment Programs in 1973, by Weeks Required to Compensate for Waiting Period, Wage Rate, and Waiting Period[a]

Percent

Employer demand response and length of compensating period	$2.00 wage rate Waiting period			$3.50 wage rate Waiting period		
	5 weeks	13 weeks	26 weeks	5 weeks	13 weeks	26 weeks
			Husbands			
Low demand response						
1 week	99.0	97.6	93.1	72.6	54.4	34.5
2–52 weeks	0.8	1.4	1.4	23.4	28.5	24.7
Over 52 weeks	0.2	1.0	5.5	4.0	17.1	40.8
Moderate demand response						
1 week	98.3	96.0	89.7	58.4	40.3	24.1
2–52 weeks	1.4	2.2	2.0	35.5	36.4	27.3
Over 52 weeks	0.4	1.8	8.3	6.1	23.3	48.5
High demand response						
1 week	90.7	81.5	63.5	30.8	18.2	9.9
2–52 weeks	6.0	7.3	5.2	48.1	32.1	18.3
Over 52 weeks	3.3	11.2	31.3	21.1	49.7	71.8
			Wives			
Low demand response						
1 week	89.0	83.6	74.6	48.2	43.9	39.8
2–52 weeks	9.4	11.6	14.4	47.7	43.0	33.3
Over 52 weeks	1.6	4.8	10.1	4.0	13.1	26.9
Moderate demand response						
1 week	82.3	75.4	64.6	38.2	34.3	30.9
2–52 weeks	15.0	16.9	19.4	56.7	49.3	36.2
Over 52 weeks	2.7	7.6	16.0	5.1	16.4	32.9
High demand response						
1 week	61.3	51.4	39.5	24.1	21.2	18.7
2–52 weeks	29.6	25.0	22.6	66.9	51.7	32.8
Over 52 weeks	9.0	23.7	37.9	9.0	27.1	48.6

a. Simulated programs have a 40-hour workweek.

Table A-9. Estimated Number of Slots in Public Employment Programs in 1973, by Wage Rate, Waiting Period, and Length of Stay[a]

Thousands

Wage rate and waiting period	Low demand response Length of stay		Moderate demand response Length of stay		High demand response Length of stay	
	2 years	Unlimited	2 years	Unlimited	2 years	Unlimited
Husbands						
$2.00						
5 weeks	556	556	559	559	600	612
13 weeks	322	322	328	328	377	386
26 weeks	130	136	131	140	151	187
$3.50						
5 weeks	809	827	1,010	1,051	2,103	2,263
13 weeks	589	594	778	817	1,791	2,057
26 weeks	376	438	512	657	1,206	1,883
Wives						
$2.00						
5 weeks	387	387	428	429	576	580
13 weeks	274	288	301	330	422	480
26 weeks	194	208	219	250	327	420
$3.50						
5 weeks	2,813	2,880	3,983	4,111	8,370	8,802
13 weeks	2,592	2,844	3,620	4,081	7,356	8,826
26 weeks	2,200	2,773	2,992	3,979	5,732	8,597

a. Simulated programs have a 40-hour workweek. Estimates are based on a 10 percent, randomly selected subsample of the full simulation sample.

Table A-10. Distribution of Labor Available for Public Employment Programs in 1973, by Group Characteristic, Wage Rate, and Employer Demand Response[a]
Percent of person-years

	$2.00 wage rate Employer demand response			$3.50 wage rate Employer demand response		
Group characteristic	Low	Moderate	High	Low	Moderate	High
Husbands						
Family income: $6,000 or less	30.1	30.5	34.8	32.9	33.5	31.7
Education: 8 years or less	29.8	30.4	34.8	41.7	48.1	55.1
Black	12.1	12.9	19.3	26.4	33.4	31.8
South	24.1	24.7	30.8	42.3	51.6	59.2
Rural	31.6	32.2	37.4	42.7	48.7	53.9
Wives						
Family income: $6,000 or less	15.8	16.7	17.1	10.8	9.2	5.9
Education: 8 years or less	28.0	31.4	33.8	22.6	22.3	22.4
Black	29.1	35.5	51.6	19.6	19.1	12.2
South	40.4	45.8	59.8	50.6	49.7	38.2
Rural	38.6	41.3	41.1	44.2	44.2	35.5

a. Simulated programs have a 5-week waiting period, 40-hour workweek, and no limit on length of stay.

Comments by Robinson G. Hollister

David Greenberg has provided a great service to public policy planners by doing the very hard work of developing the framework that will permit simulations of the supply response to various types of guaranteed public employment programs. This paper is a basic description of the development of his model and some first results. It is clear that—as the income maintenance simulation models have shown—this kind of tool leads to a quantum jump in the quality of decisionmaking with regard to the details of design of new programs. The author's detailed descriptions of his model give a concrete picture of the basic mechanics of the simulation and are an indispensable source for understanding the outcomes it yields. They also provide a number of useful results on additional sensitivity tests.[34]

It is difficult to provide a useful critique of this paper. The methodology appears sensible and sound. Beyond this one could question the choice of the appropriate behavioral elasticities here and there, but with the exception of the wage elasticities, Greenberg provides adequate sensi-

34. They are described in Greenberg, "Supply Population," apps. A and B.

tivity tests so that one can judge which parameter selections are likely to prove important.[35] Therefore, it seems to me the best I can do is to give my assessment of what Greenberg's current results appear to tell us about relevant policy questions and to suggest some issues to be addressed in future uses of the model.

It is clear from Greenberg's estimates that the aggregate supply of workers offering themselves for a guaranteed public employment program will be extremely large even at low wage levels if the program has no categorical barriers. Even at a wage of $2.00 per hour in 1973 (when the minimum wage was $1.60), he estimates that about a million husbands and wives will want to participate. A quick look at some labor force numbers leads me to guess that if single workers were also eligible, there would be on the order of two million program participants. (At higher wage levels, addition of single workers would probably lead to much smaller percentage increases over the husband-wife figures.) This figure of two million exceeds the growth in total employment from 1973 to 1974. Thus starting a program of this magnitude would require the creation of more new jobs than the U.S. economy generated in one year. There can be no question but that the process of job creation and related administrative problems would be enormous.

Adding single workers to the total of husbands and wives would increase the total wage bill commensurately. Greenberg's wage bill estimate for the $2.00 per hour program is about $4.1 billion.[36] Experience suggests a conservative estimate for administrative costs of 30–50 percent of the wage bill cost. Thus, if we add a million single workers, the wage bill goes up to $8.2 billion, and administrative costs raise it to $10.7 billion to $12.3 billion total costs in 1973. Clearly a guaranteed jobs program even at a very low wage is a huge and expensive undertaking.

An important question is whether Greenberg's gross supply estimates are likely to be overstatements or understatements of reality. Three factors suggest the former and one the latter.

First, the wage response for switching from conventional-sector to public employment is probably somewhat overestimated because the full marginal tax rates on earnings are not included. Adding the tax would reduce the after-tax differential between the two, and the elasticities multiplied by the difference would yield lower responses.

35. Ibid., app. B.
36. For a moderate employer response to a program with a five-week waiting period, a forty-hour week, and no limit on length of stay, see table A-1.

Second, Greenberg assumes that both conventional and public employment earnings profiles are flat. This may be a reasonable assumption for the public employment program, if it has no, or limited, longevity or merit increases, but it seems unlikely for the conventional sector. Perhaps the employment experience of the types of workers considered here is so irregular that there is little prospect for wage increases; but I doubt it. So this assumption probably biases choices in the simulation toward the guaranteed public sector—though the degree of bias may be small given the discounting of future earnings in the decision model.

Third, I am skeptical about the magnitude, in the simulation, of husbands who will take the mixed approach, that is, use the public employment program when they are unemployed in the conventional sector. (I will detail the source of my concern below.) For the $2.00 per hour program,[37] only 6.4 percent of the 2.7 million husbands in the supply estimate take the pure approach.

On the other hand, the fact that there is no uncertainty about obtaining the guaranteed public job may induce a greater response from the unemployed, and particularly those out of the labor force, than the conventionally derived wage and income elasticity estimates imply. This may be particularly true for secondary workers. This type of consideration is very difficult to take into account in a simulation of this sort. One might try to infer something about the effects of reduced uncertainty from the literature on the discouraged worker, but sensitivity analysis is probably the best solution.

Finally, of course, there are those factors that could go either way which are summed up in the question of the relative attractiveness of guaranteed public employment as opposed to conventional employment (or no employment). Greenberg indicates his awareness of them. Public sector employers in general have been shown to be less discriminating than private employers and this reputation may carry over to guaranteed public employment. The stability of public employment will be attractive, but the lack of any upward career path may be unattractive. As in the 1930s, public employment may develop a negative image in certain quarters so that association with the program may become stigmatizing. These types of considerations may well be the most important determinants of the supply response. Given our very limited success in explaining different rates of participation—both over time and across programs—in public

---

37. See table A-3, moderate employer response.

benefit programs, anyone would be foolhardy to pretend that he can predict the dimensions of these responses. So the simulator should not be taken to task for leaving them out.

In adding up all overestimate and underestimate factors, my guess— a very tentative one—is that Greenberg's estimates of supply response may be somewhat high, particularly for the lowest wage programs.

I think it also would be useful to summarize briefly the results of the sensitivity tests that Greenberg carried out but discussed only in passing in his paper.[38] These are of two general types, the sensitivity of the supply response to estimates of behavioral parameters and to variations in the features of the guaranteed public employment program.

At the risk of some misrepresentation I have reduced his behavioral test results to a simple matrix whose entries rank the sensitivity of the supply response to the differing reasonable values of the parameter in question:

	Income elasticity	Employer demand elasticity	Restrictiveness of participation assumption
Husbands	Medium	Medium to high	Medium to high
Wives	Low	High	Low to medium

Greenberg tried strong income elasticities of supply (-0.15 for husbands and -0.2 for wives) and weak income elasticities (-0.05 for both) and found that the sensitivity of the simulated supply results to this parameter was medium for husbands and low for wives. The elasticity of employers' demand for workers varied from 0.5 to 1.0 to infinity. He found a medium to high level of sensitivity of the aggregate results for husbands to this variation, with the highest sensitivity for the estimates for high-wage programs. The results for wives were highly sensitive for all levels of wages. The assumption for marginal cases of whether workers would participate or not[39] also was varied and the sensitivity of estimated supply to this variation was medium to high for husbands and low to medium for wives. The higher sensitivity is at higher wage rates for both groups.

In light of these sensitivity tests, if one focuses particularly on the low-wage program, the most important behavioral parameter seems to be employers' demand elasticity. For the most likely range of demand elasticities, 0.5 to 1.0, the husbands supply to the $2.00 per hour program

38. The details are in ibid.
39. For discussion of this assumption see note 9 above.

varied by about 2 percent whereas that of wives varied by about 15 percent. Greenberg argues that the estimates for supply at a demand elasticity of infinity are perhaps relevant to the case of a categorical program —say, one limited to family heads—since employers will simply substitute noncategorical workers rather than raise wages. If we ignore this variation (since it is really a program variation rather than behavioral), the magnitude of sensitivity to the assumed behavioral parameters appears small for the low-wage program.

The program variations presented in table 1 can be summarized as follows:

	Wage	Hours per week	Wait before entry	Maximum length of stay
Husbands	High	Medium	Medium	Low
Wives	High	Low to medium	Low to medium	Low

The wages were varied from $2.00 to $3.50. The supply response to the two wage levels is quite high. It ranges from 50 percent to 300 percent for husbands, and for wives it is always over 600 percent. Maximum weekly hours were varied from thirty to forty and showed medium sensitivity for husbands and low to medium for wives. The waiting period before entry was varied between five and thirteen weeks of unemployment, and a medium response for husbands and a low to medium response for wives at the low wage rate was indicated. The maximum length of stay varied from two years to unlimited and had low effects on supply. From this, the wage rate is clearly the key program feature, but manipulation of maximum weekly hours and of the initial waiting period do appear to have noticeable effects on supply.

When one looks at Greenberg's report (in table 4) on the disaggregation of those choosing guaranteed public employment by income, age, and so forth, the immediately striking figures are those on income distribution. Even in the lowest wage program, 53 percent of the husbands and 68 percent of the wives come from families with income over $8,000 and nearly 40 percent of the husbands and 54 percent of the wives from families with income above $10,000. As the wage is increased or the program becomes more restrictive in hours per week or by lengthening the initial wait, the percent of husbands in the high-income brackets declines somewhat; wives show no consistent pattern. However, even in the most restrictive case those with incomes over $10,000 still represent at least 24 percent of participants.

Though it is largely a matter of guesswork, based on looking particularly at Greenberg's tables A-4 and A-5 (in conjunction with table 4), it appears that a substantial portion of these high-family-income participants comes from among those who take the mixed approach of filling in the periods of unemployment from the conventional sector. It is this that leads me to skepticism about Greenberg's estimates of the numbers that will use the mixed approach. The decision logic of the simulation has the participants enter, but it is hard for me to believe that all of these high-income short-term unemployed will do so. Many of these must be persons who are unemployed but expect to be recalled to their normal jobs or have a regular and expected seasonality built into their jobs. I suspect that reluctance to be entangled with low-skilled public employment jobs and just sheer inertia would yield a lower participation rate than the simple discounted income calculation embedded in the simulation indicates. This just reemphasizes the importance and difficulty of understanding what causes eligibles to take up or not take up public programs that yield them net monetary benefits.

If this guess on my part is incorrect and 30–40 percent of the participants do come from families with incomes over $10,000, two interesting possibilities can be speculated about. First, what would be the political acceptability of such a program? Some have argued that poverty programs would achieve greater acceptability if their benefits reached higher into the middle class. Others would argue that this is an unacceptable state subsidy of the well-off. Second, the operational nature of a program that can draw on substantial numbers of higher income workers with some skills and regular work habits may be quite different from one that draws preponderantly on those with only irregular work experience and no skills.

In any case, the major message of Greenberg's results is that an openended, noncategorical program is likely to be simply too big to handle efficiently, at least in the short run. Then the key question is how best to target the program so as to keep it at a reasonable size, but yield benefits to those most in need. Can the simulation model prove helpful in seeking answers to this question?

I think the answer is yes. Greenberg's sensitivity tests yield some first insights. There are several aspects of the question that might be usefully addressed via the simulation model. For example: what happens to supply if there are different wage levels for different regions? What would be the effect on supply of making eligibility conditional on family income?

What happens if rules limit guaranteed public employment to one family member?

The extensions and refinements that David Greenberg indicates are under way are most important and timely. We owe him thanks for both the present work and for these important forthcoming studies.

Comments by Leonard J. Hausman

The gross cost of a guaranteed jobs program depends largely on the supply of persons interested in accepting such employment. In turn, the supply of job seekers depends on the characteristics of the guaranteed jobs program—not only on the wage rate it offers, but also the minimum duration of the spell of unemployment preceding entry, and the limits on hours per week as well as on weeks of participation in the program. Beyond the nature of the program itself, the elasticity of labor demand among employers in the conventional sector with respect to (rising) wage rates contributes to determining the supply of workers seeking specially created jobs. David Greenberg's purpose is to predict the cost of guaranteed jobs programs that vary along the indicated dimensions by estimating the supply of persons seeking special jobs.

The author's central findings are for a program offering a $2.00 hourly wage, containing a requirement that a person be unemployed for five weeks before becoming eligible, and fixing a limit on hours of work per week at forty, but fixing no limit on weeks of participation. Assumed also is a unitary wage elasticity of demand among conventional sector employers. This program would have required the creation of one million full-time jobs costing $4 billion in 1973 if it were restricted to husband-wife families. My estimate is that with rising unemployment and infla-tion—the former freeing more workers for created jobs, the latter as-sumed to result in a proportionate increase in the $2.00 hourly wage—and with rising labor force participation of wives in two-parent families, the cost of such a program in 1976 would have been $9 billion.

To assess the quality of the estimates resulting from Greenberg's simu-lations, my comments divide into a discussion of the author's assumptions which, first, lead to the cost estimates being lower and, second, being higher than they might be in reality.

Costs are underestimated in the simulations to the extent that, at wage rates equal to or less than the (partially effective) social minimum, not only unemployed persons, but also those either with jobs or out of the labor force, would apply for created jobs. According to table 1, the simulations assume, for example, that persons working at the social minimum wage would not leave and ask for created jobs; only unemployed persons, as these are defined conventionally, would take such jobs. That, however, is doubtful. If a program truly guarantees jobs, firings will not be effected easily within the program. Working conditions are likely to be more pleasant than at low-wage jobs in the conventional sector and fringe benefits more attractive. Consequently, contrary to the author's assumption, workers in low-wage jobs in the conventional sector will apply for created jobs—and program costs will rise above estimated levels. (The author acknowledges that as the program wage rises above the minimum, some workers will vacate their conventional jobs to take created jobs.)

In addition to persons switching from conventional to created jobs at wages below the social minimum, people not in the labor force will be interested in participation in the jobs program. With the costs of job search lowered substantially by the jobs program, groups whose participation in the labor force is low are likely to start "coming out of the woodwork." That was the experience in the Canadian local initiatives projects program, where 40–50 percent of those seeking created jobs were not in the labor force just before entering this program. Among certain groups, such as black men between the ages of thirty-five and forty-four, where the labor force participation rate is almost 6 percentage points below that of their white counterparts, this effect will be judged by most observers to be socially desirable. Among others, the net social value of such increases in labor force participation may be more doubtful. In either case, program participation and the budgetary costs will exceed levels estimated in the simulations.

The cost estimates flowing from Greenberg's simulation also may be low because he has underestimated a "stockpiling" phenomenon in a guaranteed employment program. The simulations do allow those whose earnings in the created sector always exceed their earnings potential in the conventional sector to remain permanently in created jobs. Such persons would constitute the permanent minimum stock of occupants of created jobs. Stockpiling of persons in guaranteed jobs would arise also from other sources. Mature adults facing flat earnings profiles in the conventional sector, for example, may be reluctant to incur search costs associated with leaving created jobs for small additional gains. Some persons, being risk averters, may seek to avoid the vagaries of the conventional sector, even when they face the prospect of monetary gains on leaving created jobs. Lastly, created jobs may change people's tastes, heightening their interest in job security while lessening their concern for pecuniary advantage.

In fact, experience under a series of federal public employment programs in Massachusetts, dating back to the Emergency Employment Act of 1971, suggests the difficulty—almost impossibility—of getting people to leave created jobs. As a direct result, recent programs designed to create jobs have instituted the rule that those entering first must leave first—and not become automatically eligible for vacant slots in the newest federal employment program. In sum, many persons who in the simulations are assumed to rotate back to the conventional sector after a stretch of created employment may not do so, forming thereby a stockpile of jobholders in the created-job sector.

The author makes explicit two assumptions that he rightfully contends may result in overestimates of costs. First, no account is taken in the simulations of the impact of the income transfer system on the interest of people in created employment. Second, measured weeks of unemployment is taken as a measure of involuntary idleness and, thus, time available for created employment. One further consideration is added to these two factors in the discussion that follows.

That income transfer programs are several in number and sizable is well known. That they may make people more selective in their choice of jobs and may stretch out periods of nonemployment is a widespread concern. Even for two-parent families, transfer programs are significant and possibly damaging to work effort. Food stamps, medicaid, the unemployed-fathers component of aid to families with dependent children, general assistance, and unemployment insurance are programs for which two-parent families are eligible under certain circumstances in particular locations. It is doubtful that these programs will be rolled back significantly under any welfare reform plan emanating from Congress. Thus, persons in two-parent families having the option to choose between a direct income transfer and a guaranteed job occasionally will choose the former. Such decisions will reduce program costs below their estimated level because the existing simulations assume no impact of existing income transfers. (Along the same lines, opportunities for illegal income also will reduce participation rates below the estimated levels in Greenberg's simulations.)

Greenberg acknowledges that the measure of their weeks of unemployment may exaggerate the number of weeks that persons would want to participate in the jobs programs. Some measured "unemployment" obviously is leisure time taken voluntarily. This may be particularly true among secondary workers within households. In the low-income population, there is substantial movement in and out of employment, the voluntary components of the latter being particularly difficult to identify. To the extent that weeks of unemployment do not translate into weeks of created employment, costs will fall below their estimated levels.

My concluding point injects a dynamic, political consideration into this discussion. Over time, if costs rise via the "woodwork" and "stockpiling" effects, the public will become uncomfortable with the high budgetary cost of the program. Rising costs would be especially apparent if, as I believe is likely, the program wage is forced up by labor unions. Under these circumstances, a guaranteed jobs program will go the way of other income-like commodity subsidies. Costs will be contained by giving some eligible persons high-wage jobs and other eligible persons no jobs. The upshot will be a less costly but highly inequitable program. The public will not tolerate a program of great size that is designed to use labor resources just to create jobs rather than to create demanded outputs.

Conference Participants

with their affiliations at the time of the conference

Bernard E. Anderson *University of Pennsylvania*
Martin Neil Baily *Yale University*
Barbara R. Bergmann *University of Maryland*
Benjamin Chinitz *State University of New York, Binghamton*
Alan E. Fechter *Urban Institute*
Lee S. Friedman *University of California, Berkeley*
Irwin Garfinkel *Institute for Research on Poverty*
Eli Ginzberg *Columbia University*
Edward M. Gramlich *University of Michigan*
David H. Greenberg *U.S. Department of Health, Education, and Welfare*
Judith M. Gueron *Manpower Demonstration Research Corporation*
Victor Halberstadt *University of Leiden, The Netherlands*
Daniel S. Hamermesh *Michigan State University*
Leonard J. Hausman *Brandeis University*
Robert H. Haveman *University of Wisconsin*
Robinson G. Hollister *Swarthmore College*
Charles C. Holt *University of Texas at Austin*
George E. Johnson *University of Michigan*
Peter Kemper *Institute for Research on Poverty*
Jonathan R. Kesselman *University of British Columbia*
Charles C. Killingsworth *Michigan State University*
William H. Kolberg *Kolberg and Associates*
Robert I. Lerman *Institute for Research on Poverty*
Sar A. Levitan *George Washington University*

Index

Institute for Research on Poverty Monograph Series

TITLES PUBLISHED

*The Measurement of Economic Welfare: Its Application
to the Aged Poor*
Marilyn Moon

*The New Jersey Income-Maintenance Experiment,
Volume 2: Labor-Supply Responses*
Harold W. Watts and Albert Rees, Editors

Improving Measures of Economic Well-Being
Marilyn Moon and Eugene Smolensky, Editors

*Political Language: Words That Succeed
and Policies That Fail*
Murray Edelman

*The New Jersey Income-Maintenance Experiment,
Volume 3: Expenditures, Health, and Social Behavior;
and the Quality of the Evidence*
Harold W. Watts and Albert Rees, Editors

Earnings Capacity, Poverty, and Inequality
Irwin Garfinkel and Robert H. Haveman, with
the assistance of David Betson

*Estimating the Labor Supply Effects of
Income-Maintenance Alternatives*
Stanley [H.] Masters and Irwin Garfinkel

An Analysis of the Determinants of Occupational Upgrading
Duane E. Leigh

☞ *Order any book listed above from Academic Press*

*Creating Jobs: Public Employment Programs and
Wage Subsidies*
John L. Palmer, Editor
☞ *Order from the Brookings Institution*

Brookings Institution

Studies in Social Economics

TITLES PUBLISHED

☛ *Order from the Brookings Institution*